OXFORD SHAKESPEARE CONCORDANCES

HOWARD-HILL, Trevor Howard
c.

OXFORD SHAKESPEARE CONCORDANCES

LOVE'S
LABOUR'S LOST

A CONCORDANCE TO THE TEXT OF
THE FIRST QUARTO OF 1598

OXFORD
AT THE CLARENDON PRESS
1970

Oxford University Press, Ely House, London W. 1

GLASGOW   NEW YORK   TORONTO   MELBOURNE   WELLINGTON
CAPE TOWN   SALISBURY   IBADAN   NAIROBI   DAR ES SALAAM   LUSAKA   ADDIS ABABA
BOMBAY   CALCUTTA   MADRAS   KARACHI   LAHORE   DACCA
KUALA LUMPUR   SINGAPORE   HONG KONG   TOKYO

FILMSET BY COMPUTAPRINT LIMITED
AND PRINTED IN GREAT BRITAIN
AT THE UNIVERSITY PRESS, OXFORD
BY VIVIAN RIDLER
PRINTER TO THE UNIVERSITY

GENERAL INTRODUCTION

IN this series of Oxford Shakespeare Concordances, a separate
volume is devoted to each of the plays. The text for each concordance
is the one chosen as copy-text by Dr. Alice Walker for the Oxford
Old Spelling Shakespeare now in preparation.

Each concordance takes account of every word in the text, and re-
presents their occurrence by frequency counts, line numbers, and
reference lines, or a selection of these according to the interest of the
particular word. The number of words which have frequency counts
only has been kept as low as possible. The introduction to each
volume records the facsimile copy of the text from which the concordance was prepared, a table of Folio through line numbers and
Globe edition act and scene numbers, a list of the misprints corrected in the text, and an account of the order of printing, and the
proof-reading, abstracted from Professor Charlton Hinman's *The
Printing and Proof-Reading of the First Folio of Shakespeare* (Oxford,
1963).

The following notes on the main features of the concordances may
be helpful.[1]

A. *The Text*

The most obvious misprints have been corrected, on conservative
principles, and have been listed for each play in the introduction to
the corresponding concordance. Wrong-fount letters have been
silently corrected.

Obvious irregularities on the part of the original compositor—
for example the anomalous absence of full stops after speech prefixes—have been normalized and noted. Colons, semicolons, exclama-
tion and interrogation marks after italicized words have been
modernized to roman fount after current practice, since this aspect of

---

[1] An account of the principles and methods by which the concordances were
edited appears in *Studies in Bibliography*, vol. 22, 1969.

compositorial practice would not normally be studied from a concordance. The spacing of words in the original printed texts, particularly in 'justified' lines, is extremely variable; spacing has been normalized on the basis of the compositor's practice as revealed in the particular column or page.

For ease of reference, the contractions *S.*, *L.*, *M.*, and forms such as *Mist.* and tildes, have been expanded when the compositor's own preferred practice is clear, and the expansion has been noted in the text. For M^r, the superior character has been lowered silently. Superior characters like the circumflex in *baâ* and those in ẙ, ẙ, ẙ, and ẘ, have been ignored. The reader should find little difficulty in distinguishing the original form of the pronominal contractions when they are encountered in the text. They are listed under Y and W respectively.

B. *Arrangement of entries*

The words in the text are arranged alphabetically, with numerals and & and &c listed at the end. Words starting with I and J, and U and V, will be found together under I and V respectively. The reader should note that the use of U for the medial V (and I for J) leads in some cases to an unfamiliar order of entry. For example, ADUISED is listed before ADULTERY. The reader will usually find the word he wants if he starts his inquiry at the modern spelling, for when the old spelling differs considerably from the modern spelling, a reference such as 'ENFORCE *see* inforce' will direct the reader to the entry in the concordance.

In hyphenated compounds where the hyphen is the second or third character of the heading-word (as in A-BOORD), the hyphenated form may be listed some distance from other occurrences of the same word in un-hyphenated form. In significant cases, references are given to alert the user.

Under the heading-word, the line numbers or lines of context are in the order of the text. The heading-word is followed by a frequency count of the words in short and long (that is, marked with an asterisk) lines, and the reference lines. When a word has been treated as one to have a frequency count only, or a list of the line numbers and count, any further count which follows will refer to the reference lines listed under the same heading. Where there are two counts but no reference lines (as with AN), the first count refers to the speech prefix.

C. *Special Forms*

(*a*) The following words have not been given context lines and line references but are dealt with only by the counting of their frequency:

A AM AND ARE AT BE BY HE I IN IS IT OF ON SHE THE THEY TO WAS WE WITH YOU

These forms occur so often in most texts that the reader can locate them more easily by examining the text of the play than he could by referring to an extensive listing in the concordance.

Homographs of these words (for example I = *ay*) have been listed in full and are given separate counts under the same heading-word.

(*b*) A larger number of words, consisting mainly of variant spellings, have been given line references as well as frequency counts.

These words are: ACTUS AN AR ART ATT AU BEE BEEING BEEN BEENE BEING BENE BIN BUT CAN CANST CE COULD COULDST DE DECIMA DES DID DIDD DIDDEST DIDDST DO DOE DOES DOEST DOETH DONE DOO DOOE DOOES DOOEST DOOING DOON DOONE DOOS DOOST DOOTH DOS DOST DOTH DU E EN EST ET ETC FINIS FOR FROM HA HAD HADST HAH HAS HAST HATH HAUE HEE HEEL HEELE HEL HELL HER HIM HIR HIS IE IF IL ILL ILLE INTO LA LE LES MA MAIE MAIEST MAIST MAY ME MEE MIGHT MIGHTEST MIGHTST MINE MOI MOY MY NE NO NOE NON NONA NOR NOT O OCTAUA OFF OH OR OU OUR OUT PRIMA PRIMUS QUARTA QUARTUS QUE QUINTA QUINTUS SCAENA SCENA SCOENA SECUNDA SECUNDUS SEPTIMA SEPTIMUS SEXTA SHAL SHALL SHALT SHEE SHOLD SHOLDE SHOLDST SHOULD SHOULDE SHOULDST SIR SO SOE TE TERTIA TERTIUS THAT THEE THEIR THEIRE THEM THEN THER THERE THESE THEYR THIS THOSE THOU THY TIS TU VN VNE VOS VOSTRE VOUS VS WAST WEE WER WERE WERT WHAT WHEN WHER WHERE WHICH WHO WHOM WHOME WHY WIL WILL WILT WILTE WOLD WOLDE WOLDST WOULD WOULDE WOULDEST WOULDST YE YEE YF YOUE YOUR YT & &C 1 2 3 4.

Homographs of words on this list (e.g. *bee* = n.) have been listed in full, and also have separate counts.

(*c*) All speech prefixes, other than *All.*, *Both.*, and those which represent the names of actors, have been treated as count-only words. In some cases, however, where a speech prefix corresponds to a form already on the count-only list (e.g. *Is.*), a full entry has been given. In some other cases, when two counts are given for the same heading-word for no apparent reason, the count which does not correspond to the following full references or to the list of line references is that of the speech prefix form (for example AN in *The Tempest*).

(*d*) Hyphenated compounds such as *all-building-law* have been listed under the full form, and also under each main constituent after the first. In this example there are entries under ALL-BUILDING-LAW, BUILDING, and LAW. When, however, one of the constituents of the compound is a word on the count- or location-only list (((*a*) or (*b*) above), it is dealt with in whichever of these two lists applies. References such as 'AT *see also* bemock't-at-stabs' are given to assist the reader in such cases.

Simple or non-hyphenated compounds such as *o'th'King* have been listed only under the constituent parts—in this example under OTH and KING.

(*e*) 'Justified' lines where the spellings *may* have been affected by the compositor's need to fit the text to his measure are distinguished by an asterisk at the beginning of the reference line. If only location is being given, the asterisk occurs before the line reference. If only frequency counts are being given, the number *after* the asterisk records the frequency of forms occurring in 'justified' lines. Lines which do not extend to the full width of the compositor's measure have not been distinguished as 'justified' lines, even though in many cases the shorter line may have affected the spelling.

D. *Line Numbers*

The lines in each text have been numbered from the first *Actus Primus* or stage direction and thereafter in normal reading order, including all stage directions and act and scene divisions. Each typographical line has been counted as a unit when it contains matter for inclusion in the concordance. Catchwords are not included in the count. The only general exception is that turn-overs are regarded as belonging to their base-lines; where a turn-over occurs on a line by itself, it has been reckoned as part of the base-line, and the line containing only the turn-over has not been counted as a separate line. Turn-overs may readily be distinguished by vertical stroke and single bracket after the last word of the base-line; for example *brought with* | (*child*,.

When two or more lines have been joined in order to provide a fuller context, the line-endings are indicated by a vertical stroke |, and the line reference applies to that part of the line before the vertical stroke. For the true line-numbers of words in the following part of the context line, the stated line-number should be increased by one each time a vertical stroke occurs, save when the next word is a turn-over.

The numbering of the quarto texts has been fitted to that of the corresponding Folio texts; lines in the Quarto which do not occur in the Folio are prefixed by +. The line references are similarly specified. The line references of these concordances therefore provide a consistent permanent numbering of each typographical line of text, based on the First Folio.

PROGRAM CHANGES

Preparation of concordances to the first few texts, and the especial complexity of *Wiv.*, have enabled some improvements to be made to the main concordance program. For texts other than *Tmp.*, *TGV*, *MM*, and *Err.*, the concordances have been prepared with the improved program.

Speech-prefixes now have separate entries under the appropriate heading-word and follow any other entry under the same heading-word. Entries under AN in *Wiv.*, AND and TO in *TN*, and AD in *AYL* offer examples. This alteration provides a clearer record of the total number of occurrences of words which occur both as speech-prefixes and also as forms on the 'count only' or 'locations only' lists.

Another modification supplies a more precise reference to the location of words such as BEENE for which line numbers but no full lines are given. When a 'location only' word is encountered to the right of the 'end-of-line' bar (which shows that lines of text have been joined together in order to provide a sufficient context), the line number is now adjusted to supply the exact reference. In the concordances to the texts listed above, users will find that in some instances the particular occurrence of a 'location only' word which they wish to consult in the text is to be found in the line after the one specified in the concordance; this depends on whether lines have been joined in the computer-readable version of the text from which the concordance was made. It is not expected that readers will be seriously inconvenienced by this. Should a concordance to the First Folio be published, it will, of course, incorporate all improvements.

LOVE'S LABOUR'S LOST
(QUARTO)

The facsimile of the British Museum's Heber copy (C.34.1.14: Heber—Daniel) edited by Sir Walter Greg for the Clarendon Press, 1957, has provided the copy for the concordance to *LLL*. The table of press variants given by Greg shows that these are not important for the text. The Globe act and scene numbers in the table below follows the numeration of the facsimile, save that for prose lines at the ends of pages, the reference corresponds to the Globe line containing the last word in the line of text.

TABLE OF ACT AND SCENE NUMBERS

Page	Comp.	F line nos.	Globe act/scene nos.
A2		1–34	1.1.1–1.1.30
A2ᵛ		35–73	1.1.68
A3		74–113	1.1.104
A3ᵛ		114–55	1.1.145
A4		156–91	1.1.181
A4ᵛ		192–235	1.1.225
B1		236–74	1.1.280
B1ᵛ		275–317	1.2.6
B2		318–55	1.2.50
B2ᵛ		356–94	1.2.93
B3		395–438	1.2.140
B3ᵛ		439–80	1.2.184
B4		481–519	2.1.28
B4ᵛ		520–57	2.1.65
C1		558–96	2.1.101
C1ᵛ		597–635	2.1.140
C2		636–73	2.1.176
C2ᵛ		674–714	2.1.214
C3		715–52	2.1.248
C3ᵛ		753–95	3.1.27
C4		796–835	3.1.66
C4ᵛ		836–67	3.1.104
D1		868–912	3.1.147
D1ᵛ		912–50	3.1.186
D2		951–87	4.1.13
D2ᵛ		988–1027	4.1.51
D3		1028–67	4.1.89
D3ᵛ		1068–108	4.1.122

Page	Comp.	F line nos.	Globe act/scene nos.
D4		1109–160	4.2.10
D4ᵛ		1161–206	4.2.49
E1		1207–44	4.2.83
E1ᵛ		1245–87	4.2.126
E2		1287–328	4.2.170
E2ᵛ		1329–69	4.3.37
E3		1370–407	4.3.74
E3ᵛ		1408–44	4.3.107
E4		1445–82	4.3.145
E4ᵛ		1483–520	4.3.182
F1		1521–63	4.3.216
F1ᵛ		1564–602	4.3.253
F2		1603–40	4.3.291
F2ᵛ		1641–77	4.3.326
F3		1678–714	4.3.363
F3ᵛ		1715–53	5.1.16
F4		1754–95	5.1.62
F4ᵛ		1796–839	5.1.112
G1		1839–81	5.1.157
G1ᵛ		1882–918	5.2.31
G2		1919–56	5.2.66
G2ᵛ		1957–94	5.2.102
G3		1995–2032	5.2.140
G3ᵛ		2033–70	5.2.173
G4		2071–108	5.2.209
G4ᵛ		2109–48	5.2.239
H1		2149–93	5.2.274
H1ᵛ		2194–233	5.2.309
H2		2234–69	5.2.343
H2ᵛ		2270–307	5.2.381
H3		2308–48	5.2.416
H3ᵛ		2349–87	5.2.449
H4		2388–426	5.2.485
H4ᵛ		2427–68	5.2.524
I1		2468–508	5.2.562
I1ᵛ		2509–48	5.2.599
I2		2549–86	5.2.634
I2ᵛ		2587–623	5.2.672
I3		2624–63	5.2.714
I3ᵛ		2664–700	5.2.752
I4		2701–38	5.2.790
I4ᵛ		2739–76	5.2.826
K1		2777–814	5.2.863
K1ᵛ		2815–50	5.2.897
K2		2851–83	5.2.926
K2ᵛ		2884–2901 (Finis)	5.2.942

Misprints, etc. corrected in the text were:

A2	28	thee		Ee^v	1358	*King,*
A2^v	35	pome,		E3	1393	heanenly
A3^v	140	publibue		E3^v	1408	ydotarie.
A4	178	inchannting			1435	Odo
A4^v	201	Contempls		F1	1539	*Iaqn.*
	228	sinplicitie		F2^v	1663	womas
	231	*welkis*		F3	1693	Subtir
B1	266	G*fficer*		F3^v	1718	standars,
B1^v	277	wost.			1736	forsorne,
	294	*Col.*		F4	1787	*Poda.*
	308	prosperie,			1795	wane
		affliccio		F4^v	1796	vene we
B3	409	Eor			1814	*Peda,*
B4	493	Cosider		G1	1843	secretie,
B4^v	532	l. *Lady.*		G1^v	1894	asheete
	536	peereisse			1917	*Rasaline,*
C1	566	tales.		G2^v	1981	Siccamone,
C1^v	597	*Prin,*			1988	thy
C2	636	faiendship		G3^v	2058	*Berow,*
	638	pemaund			2059	*euen*
	658	spciall		G4	2071	stranges?
C2^v	684	*Bar.*		G4^v	2123	*Rosa,*
	698	*Bo*ᴧ			2125	measue
	707	*Bo*ᴧ			2130	cennot
	711	*Ber,*		H1	2166	Loke
C4	804	Necligent		H1^v	2199	perhapt.
C4^v	846	pline		H2	2267	spaches
D1	901	ouce		H2^v	2302	Wtih
	904	remuration,		H4^v	2444	thy
D1^v	941	Crietick,		I1^v	2527	Conqueronr,
D2	985	*Qnee.*		I2	2559	Flder.
D2^v	1017	*Boyet,*		I2^v	2587	*Eeter*
	1025	Mistrs		I3	2624	*Boyet*ᴧ
D3	1050	couercame,		I3^v	2663	hane
D4	1109	Frannce			2673	interrnpptest
	1110	touchiug		I4^v	2751	rherefore
	1114	*Exit*ᐟ			2772	inriled
E1^v	1265	stauze,			2776	herrite
E2	1308	forgine		K1	2807	wi:

When reading the film before printing, I found that the SP *Iaq.* in 1.1294 is incorrectly printed as *Iag.* Readers should therefore correct their copies of the concordance accordingly.

August, 1969   T.H.H.

LOVE'S LABOUR'S LOST
(QUARTO)

A = 316*162, 19*10
*Ber. The Spring is neare when greene geese are a bree- |(ding.	103
*but a' must fast three dayes a weeke: for this Damsell	433
Ber. What time a day? | Kath. The houre that fooles should aske.	617
*A. No Page, it is an epilogue or discourse to make plaine,	855
*a leuenpence-farthing better: most sweete gardon. I will	936
Still a repairing: euer out of frame,	957
And neuer going a right, being a Watch:	958
Quee. Who ere a was, a showd a mounting minde.	978
One a these Maides girdles for your waste should be fit.	1026
Stand a side good bearer. Boyet you can carue,	1032
*Clo. Indeed a'must shoot nearer, or hele neare hit the clout.	1125
*To see him kisse his hand, & how most sweetly a wil sweare:	1144
Or Pricket-sore, or els Sorell, | the people fall a hooting.	1221
*againe a my side. I will not loue; if I do hang mee: I'fayth	1341
He standes a side. The King entreth.	1353
Enter Longauill. The King steps a side.	1376
God amende vs, God amende, we are much out a th'way.	1409
But are you not a shamed? nay, are you not	1496
Peda. I will repeate them: a e I.	1793
Writ a both sides the leafe, margent and all,	1895
Ros. Youle neare be friendes with him, a kild your sister.	1900
nimble stiring spirit, she might a bin Grandam ere she died.	1903
A can carue to, and lispe: Why this is hee	2248
Quee. A speakes not like a man of God his making.	2471
*and a feard to speake? Run away for shame Ali- | sander.	2532
*are Worthies a comming will speake their minde in some | other	
sort. Exit Curat.	2537
A man so breathed, that certaine he would fight; yea,	2608
*of Iaquenettaes, and that a weares next his hart for a | Fauour.	2669
AB = 1	
is Ab speld backward with the horne on his head?	1786
ABATE see also bate = 1	
Abate throw at Nouum, and the whole world againe,	2487
ABBOMINABLE = *1	
*which he would call abbominable, it insinuateth me of in- | famie:	1763
ABHOMINABLE = *1	
*vocatur nebour; neigh abreuiated ne: this is abhominable,	1762

1

ABHORRE = *1
  *then the staple of his argument. I abhorre such phanatticall   1757
ABHORTIUE = 1
  Why should I ioy in any abhortiue byrth?   113
ABIDE *see* bide
ABOUE = 3
  Aboue their functions and their offices.   1683
  Aboue the sence of sence so sensible,   2175
  Aboue this Worlde: adding thereto more ouer,   2384
ABOUT = 3*3
  A Maide of grace and complet maiestie, | About surrender vp of
  Aquitaine,   146
  *selfe to walke: the time When? about the sixt houre, When
  Beastes*   245
  And where my Liedges? all about the brest. | A Caudle hou!   1510
  *about your Infamie *vnu(m)* *cita* a gigge of a Cuckolds horne.   1805
  *A Ladie walde about with Diamondes: Looke you, what I | haue
  from the louing King.   1890
  Haue brought about the annuall reckoning.   2758
ABREEDING *see* breeding
ABREUIATED = *1
  vocatur nebour; neigh abreuiated ne: this is abhominable,   1762
ABROAD = 1
  Doth noyse abroad *Nauar* hath made a Vow,   513
ABROD = 1
  Ther's villanie abrod, this letter will tell you more.   200
ABROGATE = 1
  Nath. Perge, good M.(aister) *Holofernes perge*, so it shall please |
  you to abrogate squirilitie.   1211
ABSENCE = 1
  Rosa. Your absence onely. | *King.* That can neuer be.   2128
ABSTINENCE = 1
  And abstinence ingenders maladies.   1645
ABUSED = 1
  On *Nauar* and his Bookmen, for heere tis abused.   731
ACCENT = 2
  accent. Let me superuise the cangenet.   1285
  Action and accent did they teach him there.   1991
ACCIDENTALLY = *1
  *of the stranger Queenes: which accidentally, or by the way   1304
ACCOMPLISHT = *1
  2. Lad. The young *Dumaine*, a well accomplisht youth,   548
ACCOMPT = 1
  That we may do it still without accompt.   2099
ACCOUNTED = 1
  And shooting well, is then accounted ill: 1000
ACE = 1
  summe of deus-ace amountes to.   354
ACHADEME = 1
  Our Court shalbe a lytlle Achademe,   17
ACHADEMES = 1
  They are the Bookes, the Artes, the Achademes,   1703
ACHADEMS = 1
  They are the Ground, the Bookes, the Achadems,   1653
ACHILLES = *1
  Ber. Hide thy head *Achilles*, here comes *Hector* in Armes.   2588

2

ACOMMING *see* comming
ACQUAINTED = 1
    acquainted you withall, to the ende to craue your assistance.   1848
ACQUITTANCES = 1
    Boyet you can produce acquittances,   657
ACTION = 2
    As motion and long during action tyres   1657
    Action and accent did they teach him there.   1991
ACTORS = *1
    **Clow.* O Lord sir, the parties themselues, the actors sir   2442
ACUTE = 1*1
    Brag. A most acute Iuuenall, volable and free of grace,   836
    *gyft is good in those whom it is acute, and I am thankfull | for
    it.   1235
AD = *1
    *Go to, thou hast it *ad dungil* at the fingers ends, as they say.   1813
ADAM = 1*1
    * *Holo.* The Moone was a month old when *Adam* was no | (more.   1196
    Had he bin *Adam* he had tempted *Eue.*   2247
ADAY = 1
    King. Come sir, it wants a tweluemonth an'aday, | And then twill
    ende.   2838
ADD = 1
    Now to our periurie, to add more terror,   2409
ADDE = 1
    + *Pag.* I will adde the *lenuoy*, say the morrall againe.   856 +5
ADDED = 1
    Peda. Ba, *puericia* with a horne added.   1787
ADDES = 1
    It addes a precious seeing to the eye: 1684
ADDING = 5
    By adding a tongue which I know will not lie.   757
    +And staied the oddes by adding foure.   856 +9
    Staying the oddes by adding foure.   862
    Of one sore I an hundred make | by adding but one more l.   1225
    Aboue this Worlde: adding thereto more ouer,   2384
ADDREST = 2
    And he and his compettitours in oth, | Were all addrest to meete
    you gentle Lady   576
    Toward that shade I might beholde addrest,   1984
ADEW = 2
    Ber. O you are welcome sir, adew.   713
    Pag. Like the sequell I. Signeur *Costard* adew. *Exit.*   899
ADIEU = 1
    Duma. Please it you, as much in priuat, & ile bid adieu.   2152
ADIEUS = 1
    Quee. Twentie adieus my frozen Muskouits.   2183
ADIUNCT = 1
    Learning is but an adiunct to our selfe,   1664
ADMIRE = 1
    Which is to mee some prayse, that I thy partes admire,   1278
ADMIRED = 1
    Or vainely comes th'admired Princesse hither.   150
ADMITTANCE = 1
    Prin. Now, What admittance Lord?   574
ADORE = 1
    Brag. I do adore thy sweete Graces Slipper.   2623

ADRAMADIO = 2
   King. Where hadst thou it? | *Cost.* Of *Dun Adramadio, Dun
   Adramadio.*   1540
ADRIANA = 1
   Thine in the dearest designe of industri, | Don Adriana de
   Armatho.   1066
ADRIANO = 1*1
   heate of duetie. | Don Adriano de Armado.   273
   *who is intituled, nominated, or called, *Don Adriano de
   Ar-* | matho.*   1746
ADUANCE = 1
   And euery one his Loue-feat will aduance,   2015
ADUAUNCE = 1
   Berow. Aduaunce your standards, and vpon them Lords.   1718
ADUE = 5*1
   Ferd. Well, sit you out: go home *Berowne*: adue.   119
   *men. Adue Valoure, rust Rapier, be still Drum, for your   483
   *concerne much: stay not thy complement, I forgiue thy | dewtie,
   adue.   1307
   Rosa. Then cannot we be bought: and so adue,   2130
   Quee. Seuenth sweete adue, since you can cogg,   2140
   And so adue sweete *Iude.* Nay, Why dost thou stay?   2578
ADUISD = 1
   Pell, mell, downe with them: but be first aduisd,   1719
ADUISDE = 2
   Rosa. Good Madame, if by me youle be aduisde,   2223
   Quee. And were you well aduisde? | *King.* I was faire Madame. 2369
AETHIOP = 1
   Iuno but an *Aethiop* were,   1455
AETHIOPS = 1
   King. And *Aethiops* of their sweete complexion crake.   1617
AFEARD *see* feard
AFFECT = *2
   **Arm.* I do affect the verie ground (which is base) where her   470
   **Holo.* I wil somthing affect the letter, for it argues facilitie. 1213
AFFECTED = 3*1
   reason for it. He surely affected her for her wit.   393
   Prin. With what? | *Bo.* With that which we Louers intitle
   Affected.   735
   note men that most are affected to these.   794
   *& thrasonicall. He is too picked, to spruce, too affected,   1751
AFFECTES = 1
   For euery man with his affectes is borne,   162
AFFECTION = 1*3
   *If drawing my Sword against the humor of affection, would   365
   *wittie without affection, audatious without impudencie,   1743
   **Bra.* Sir, it is the Kings most sweete pleasur & affection,   1821
   Three pilde Hiberboles, spruce affection: 2339
AFFECTIONS = 2
   That warre agaynst your owne affections,   13
   Haue at you then affections men at armes,   1640
AFFLICCION = *1
   *welcome the sower Cup of prosperitie, affliccio(n) may one day   308
AFFOORD = 1
   Rosa. We can affoord no more at such a price.   2126
AFFORD = 1
   Quee. Only for praise, and praise we may afford,   1014

4

AFFORDE = 1
And would afforde my speachles vizard halfe.   2158
AFFRIGHT *see* fright
AFOREHAND = 1
Knowing aforehand of our meriment,   2400
AFORESAYD = *1
apprehended with the aforesayd Swaine, I keepe hir as a vessell of   270
AFTER = 4*5
Ferdinand. | Let Fame, that all hunt after in their lyues,   4
Clow. Such is the simplicitie of man to harken after the flesh   228
Ar. And so farewell. | *Ma.* Faire weather after you.   446
*man after the olde painting, and keepe not too long in one   789
Ber. It must be done this after noone,   927
*after his vndressed, vnpolished, vneducated, vnpruned,   1166
Of his faire Mistres, in the after noone   1727
*congruent, and measurable for the after noone: the worde is   1826
*The wordes of Mercurie, are harsh after the | songes of Apollo.   2897
AFTER-NOONE *see also* noone = 2
Clow. When would you haue it done sir? | *Ber.* O this after-noone. 920
of this day, which the rude multitude call the after-noone.   1823
AGAIN = 1
to insert again my *haud credo* for a Deare.   1168
AGAINE = 11*4
smile againe, and till then sit thee downe sorrow. *Exeunt.*   309
Prin. Faire I giue you backe againe, and welcome I haue   586
And go well satisfied to France againe.   648
To morow shall we visite you againe.   674
+ *Pag.* I will adde the *lenuoy,* say the morrall againe.   856 +5
Quee. What, what? First praise mee, and againe say no.   988
*I will looke againe on the intellect of the letter, for the
no- | mination   1298
*againe a my side. I will not loue; if I do hang mee: I'fayth   1341
Immediatly they will againe be heere,   2208
And vtters it againe when God dooth please.   2241
You gaue me this: but take it sir againe.   2392
What? will you haue me, or your Pearle againe?   2397
We are againe forsworne in will and error.   2410
Abate throw at Nouum, and the whole world againe,   2487
*Ile flash, Ile do it by the Sword: I bepray you let me bor- | row
my Armes againe.   2651
AGAINST *see also* gainst = 5*3
Ferd. How well hees read to reason against reading.   99
A dangerous law against gentletie.   138
*If drawing my Sword against the humor of affection, would   365
*A dangerous rime maister against the reason of white & red.   411
Against the steepe vp rising of the hill?   976
Against your Peace Loue doth approch, disguysd: 1975
That charge their breath against vs? Say scout say.   1980
Long. I must rather giue it the raine: for it runnes against |
Hector.   2614
AGAYNST = 1
That warre agaynst your owne affections,   13
AGE = 1
Beautie doth varnish Age, as if new borne,   1593
AGED = 1
That aged eares play treuant at his tales,   566

5

AGEN = 1
Kath. Yet sweare not, least ye be forsworne agen. 2792
AGES = *1
*three ages since, but I thinke now tis not to be found: or if it 416
AGO = 1
Long. Foure dayes ago. 131
AGONIE = 1
Mirth cannot moue a soule in agonie. 2818
AGOT = 1
His hart like an Agot with your print impressed, 740
AGREE = 1
Prin. Good witts will be iangling, but gentles agree, 729
AH = 3*2
Ah heauens, it is most patheticall nit. 1147
*and so foorth. Ah good olde *Mantuan,* I may speake 1258
Ah neuer fayth could hold, yf not to beautie vowed. 1268
Ah good my Leidge, I pray thee pardon mee. 1489
Berow. Ah you whoreson loggerhead, you were borne to | do me
shame. 1548
AHAUE = *1
Bero. I, if a'haue no more mans blood in his belly then wil |
suppe a Flea. 2647
AHOOTING *see* hooting
AIAX = *2
*as *Aiax,* it kills Sheepe, it kills mee, I a Sheepe well prooued 1340
*will be geuen to *Aiax.* He wilbe the ninth Worthie: a
Con-|querour, 2531
AIRE *see also* ayer, ayre = 2
Playing in the wanton aire: 1441
Blow like sweete Roses, in this sommer aire. 2215
AL = 1*1
Clo. God dig-you-den al, pray you which is the head lady? 1018
Brag. That is al one my faire sweete honie monarch, 2472
ALACKE = 5
Ros. Alacke, let it blood. 683
O short liu'd pride. Not faire? alacke for woe | *For.* Yes Madam
faire. 989
On a day, alacke the day: 1438
But alacke my hand is sworne, 1448
Vow alacke for youth vnmeete, 1450
ALANSOES = 1
I saw him at the Duke *Alansoes* once, 553
ALANSON = 1
Boyet. The heire of *Alanson, Rosalin* her name. 693
ALAS = 1*1
Alisander, alas you see how tis a little oreparted, but there 2536
Quee. Alas poore *Machabeus,* how hath he bin bayted. 2585
ALEXANDER = 1*2
*parish Curate *Alexander, Armadoes* Page *Hercules,* the Pe-|dant 2479
Enter Curate for Alexander. 2511
Qu. The conqueror is dismaid: proceed good *Alexander.* 2520
ALIKE = 1
For none offende, where all alike do dote. 1463
ALISANDER = 2*4
My Scutchion plaine declares that I am Alisander. 2515
Boy. Most true, tis right: you were so *Alisander.* 2524
Bero. Take away the Conquerour, take away *Alisander.* 2527

ALISANDER *cont.*
  *Clow. O sir, you haue ouerthrowne *Alisander* the Conque-|rour: 2528
  *and a feard to speake? Run away for shame *Ali-|sander.*   2532
  *Alisander, alas you see how tis a little oreparted, but there   2536

ALL = 80*7
  Ferdinand. | Let Fame, that all hunt after in their lyues,   4
  And make vs heires of all eternitie.   11
  With all these lyuing in Philosophie.   36
  And not be seene to wincke of all the day.   47
  When I was wont to thinke no harme all nyght,   48
  Bero. Why? all delightes are vaine, but that most vaine   77
  Dum. Proceeded well, to stop all good proceeding.   100
  Ber. Necessitie will make vs all forsworne   160
  A man in all the worldes new fashion planted,   175
  Clow. In manner and forme folowing sir all those three.   216
  *hir to tryall. Thine in all complements of deuoted and hartburning   272
  *Boy. Of all the foure, or the three, or the two, or one of | the
foure.   385
  Of all perfections that a man may owe,   497
  Be now as prodigall of all Deare grace,   500
  And prodigally gaue them all to you.   503
  You are not ignorant all telling fame   512
  Prince. All pride is willing pride, and yours is so: 527
  Of all that Vertue loue, for Vertue loued.   549
  Prin. God blesse my Ladyes, are they all in loue?   569
  And he and his compettitours in oth, | Were all addrest to meete
you gentle Lady   576
  All liberall reason I will yeelde vnto.   665
  Prin. Your reason. | *Bo.* Why all his behauiours did make their
retire,   737
  His tongue all impacient to speake and not see,   742
  All sences to that sence did make their repaire,   744
  Mee thought all his senses were lokt in his eye,   746
  That all eyes saw his eyes inchaunted with gazes.   751
  Ile giue you *Aquitaine,* and all that is his,   752
  *Boy. And out of hart Maister: all those three I will | proue.   806
  Brag. I am all these three.   814
  *Boy. And three times as much more, and yet nothing | at all.   815
  Liedge of all loyterers and malecontents: 949
  Nay to be periurde, which is worst of all: 960
  And among three to loue the worst of all,   961
  *Where all those pleasures liue, that Art would comprehend.   1273
  All ignorant that soule, that sees thee without wonder.   1277
  Your Ladiships in all desired imployment, Berowne.   1301
  Thy grace being gainde, cures all disgrace in mee.   1400
  Berow. All hid, all hid, an olde infant play,   1412
  All vnseene, can passage finde: 1443
  For none offende, where all alike do dote.   1463
  For all the wealth that euer I did see,   1486
  All three of you, to be thus much ore'shot?   1497
  And where my Liedges? all about the brest. | A Caudle hou!   1510
  Therefore of all handes must we be forsworne.   1567
  Of all complexions the culd soueraigntie,   1583
  Lend me the florish of all gentle tongues,   1587
  O tis the Sunne that maketh all thinges shine.   1595
  King. But what of this, are we not all in loue?   1631
  Ber. O nothing so sure, and thereby all forsworne.   1632

ALL *cont.*
But with the motion of all elamentes,   1680
And when Loue speakes, the voyce of all the Goddes,   1695
That shew, containe, and nourish all the worlde.   1704
Els none at all in ought proues excellent.   1705
For Wisedomes sake, a worde that all men loue: 1708
Or for Loues sake, a worde that loues all men.   1709
*let that passe; the very all of all is: but sweet hart, I do implore 1842
* *Peda. Via* good-man *Dull,* thou hast spoken no worde all | this
while.   1880
Writ a both sides the leafe, margent and all,   1895
Quee. A Poxe of that iest, and I beshrow all Shrowes,   1934
Since all the power thereof it doth apply,   1967
With that all laught, and clapt him on the shoulder,   1999
The thirde he caperd and cryed, All goes well.   2005
With that they all did tumble on the ground,   2007
Page. All haile, the richest Beauties on the earth.   2053
Take all and weane it, it may proue an Oxe.   2165
Bero. By heauen, all drie beaten with pure scoffe.   2180
Rosa. They were all in lamentable cases,   2192
Quee. Berowne did sweare him selfe out of all suite.   2194
King. All haile sweete Madame, and faire time of day.   2265
Quee. Faire in all Haile is foule, as I conceaue.   2266
Ber. O, I am yours and all that I possesse. | *Rosa.* All the foole
mine.   2310
King. That more then all the world, I did respect her.   2373
Bero. By Ioue, I all wayes tooke three threes for nine.   2438
Peda. But you haue outfaste them all.   2575
For all your faire endeuours and intreat: 2688
All causes to the purpose of his speede: 2699
All wanton as a childe, skipping and vaine.   2719
Remote from all the pleasurs of the world: 2756
With three folde loue I wish you all these three.   2785
Which you on all estetes will execute,   2806
With all the fierce endeuour of your wit,   2814
Enter all.   2854
And Ladi-smockes all siluer white,   2862
When all aloude the winde doth blow,   2888
ALLUSION = 1 *1
Th'allusion holdes in the Exchange.   1199
* *Holo.* God comfort thy capacitie, I say th'allusion holdes | in the
Exchange.   1202
ALLWAYES *see* all
ALMIGHTIE = 1 *1
Of his almightie dreadfull little might.   969
* *Braggart. The Armipotent* Mars, *of Launces the almightie,* | *gaue*
Hector *a gift.*   2600
ALMIGHTY = *1
* *Brag. Peace. The Armipotent* Mars, *of Launces the almighty,*   2606
ALMOST = 1
Brag. Almost I had. | *Boy.* Negligent student, learne her by hart. 803
ALMSBASKET = *1
* *Clow.* O they haue lyud long on the almsbasket of wordes.   1778
ALONE = 6
As I for praise alone now seeke to spill   1009
Enter Berowne with a paper in his hand, alone.   1333
Liues not alone emured in the braine: 1679

ALONE *cont.*
  Ber. Alone alone sowed Cockell, reapt no Corne,   1734
  Ped. Alone, we will employ thee.   1883
ALONG = 3
  Did poynt you to buy them along as you past.   749
  Rosa. Madame, came nothing els along with that?   1892
  And trauailing along this coast I heere am come by chaunce,   2502
ALOUDE = 2
  You put our Page out: goe, you are aloude.   2417
  When all aloude the winde doth blow,   2888
ALOWDE = *1
  *I must keepe her at the Parke, she is alowde for the Day |
  womand. Fare you well.   434
ALREADY = 2*1
  So much deare Liedge, I haue already sworne,   38
  *Well, she hath one a'my Sonnets already, the Clowne bore   1348
  *wench is cast away: shee's quicke, the childe bragges in her |
  bellie already: tis yours.   2632
ALTHOUGH = 2
  But I beleeue although I seeme so loth,   170
  Although not valued to the monies worth.   632
ALWAYES = 1
  And Iustice alwayes whirles in equall measure: 1735
AM = 41*14
AMAINE = *1
  Kin. The Ship is vnder sayle, and heere she coms amaine.   2489
AMAZDE = *1
  Quee. Amazde my Lord? Why lookes your highnes sad?   2321
AMAZES = 1
  His faces owne margent did coate such amazes,   750
AMBASSADOURE *see* embassadoure
AMBASSADOURS *see* embassadours
AMBER = 3
  Duma. Her Amber heires for foule hath amber coted.   1421
  Ber. An amber colourd Rauen was well noted.   1422
AMBITIOUS = *1
  *discourse peremptorie: his tongue fyled, his eye ambitious,   1749
AMEN = 2
  Ber. And send you manie louers. | *Kath.* Amen, so you be none.   621
  Ber. Amen, so I had mine: Is not that a good word?   1430
AMENDE = 2
  God amende vs, God amende, we are much out a th'way.   1409
AMONG = 2*1
  And among three to loue the worst of all,   961
  *curtesie. I beseech thee apparrell thy head: and among other   1832
  Brag. Dost thou infamonize me among potentates: 2634
AMOUNT = 2*1
  Arm̄. It doth amount to one more then two.   355
  Clow. Vnder correction sir we know where-vntill it doth |
  amouñt.   2436
  *will shew wher-vntill it doth amount: for mine owne part, I   2443
AMOUNTES = 1
  summe of deus-ace amountes to.   354
AMY = *1
  *Well, she hath one a'my Sonnets already, the Clowne bore   1348
AN *see also* and *l.*109 227 304 *327 337 338 339 346 468 *476 551
  556 560 592 626 *703 740 *758 821 *855 1007 *1108 *1116 *1178

AN *cont.*

1187 *1207 1225 1283 1382 1406 1412 1422 1455 1481 *1522 1565
1580 1599 1664 1685 *1798 *1802 1868 *1869 *1871 *1878 1982
1995 1997 2165 2295 2363 2390 2419 *2533 2559 2566 2577 2832
2835 = 44*16, 2

Ber. Nay then two treyes, an if you grow so nice,   2137
King. Come sir, it wants a tweluemonth an'aday, | And then twill
ende.   2838

AND *see also* &. = 424*122, 6*5

Berow. Let me say no my liedge, and yf you please,   54
Boyet. A woman sometimes, and you saw her in the light.   696
And you giue him for my sake but one louing kisse.   753
Sir, your penny-worth is good, and your Goose be fat.   866
Boy. And I cannot, cannot, cannot: and I cannot, an other |
(can,   1116
Boy. And if my hand be out, then belike your hand is in.   1127
Clow. And I had but one peny in the world thou shouldst   1807
*purse of wit, thou Pidgin-egge of discretion. O and the   1810
And if my face were but as faire as yours,   1920
Bero. And thou weart a Lyon, we would do so.   2576

ANGEL = *1

*There is no euill angel but Loue, yet was *Sampson* so temp-|ted,   475

ANGELL = 3

Then for that Angell knowledge you can say,   122
For quoth the King, an Angell shalt thou see: 1995
The Boy replyde, An Angell is not euill: 1997

ANGELS = 1

Are Angels varling cloudes, or Roses blowne.   2220

ANGER = 1

Which not to anger bent, is musique, and sweete fier.   1281

ANIE = 1*1

*Desire prisoner, and ransome him to anie French Courtier   367
Can anie face of brasse hold longer out?   2327

ANNIMALL = *1

*His intellect is not replenished, he is only an annimall, only   1178

ANNOTHANIZE = *1

Veni, vidi, vici: Which to annothanize in the vulgar, O base   1048

ANNOTHER = 1

Here sweete, put vp this, twilbe thine annother day.   1091

ANNOYNTED = 1*1

Th'annoynted soueraigne of sighes and groones: 948
Brag. Annoynted, I implore so much expence of thy royal   2467

ANNUALL = 1

Haue brought about the annuall reckoning.   2758

ANON = 1*1

*of *Celo* the skie, the welken the heauen, & anon falleth like   1155
And euer and anon they made a doubt,   1993

ANOTHER *see also* other = 1

Another with his fynger and his thume,   2003

ANSWERD = 1

Boy. I am answerd sir. | *Arma.* I loue not to be crost.   342

ANSWERE = 2*1

Boy. So I may answere thee with one as olde that was a   1111
Boyet. They will not answere to that Epythat.   2067
What humble suite attendes thy answere there,   2800

10

ANSWERES = *1
*_Arma._ I do say thou art quicke in answeres. Thou heatst | my
blood.   340
ANT = 2*1
Antho. Me ant shall please you? I am _Anthony Dull._   268
I see the tricke ant: here was a consent,   2399
*There ant shall please you a foolish mylde man, an   2533
ANTHO = 1
Antho. Me ant shall please you? I am _Anthony Dull._   268
ANTHONIE = *1
*_by thy sweete Graces Officer_ Anthonie Dull, _a man of_   266
ANTHONY see also Antho. = 1
Antho. Me ant shall please you? I am _Anthony Dull._   268
ANTIQUE = *2
*or pageant, or antique, or fierworke: Now vnderstanding   1845
*_Brag._ We will haue, if this fadge not, an Antique. I be-|seech
you follow.   1878
ANY = 8*2
Before the Birdes haue any cause to sing?   112
Why should I ioy in any abhortiue byrth?   113
*_Item,_ Yf any man be seene to talke with a woman within   139
Bero. Ile lay my Head to any good mans Hat,   303
If vertues glose will staine with any soyle,   540
To any Lady that subdewes a Lord.   1015
For where is any Authour in the worlde,   1662
*_Page._ An excellent deuice: so if any of the audience hisse,   1869
O he hath drawen my picture in his letter. | _Quee._ Any thing like? 1926
me any seruice to her thither,   2237
ANYTHING _see_ any
APACE = 1
And talkt apace: and in that houre (my Lord)   2296
APE = 4*1
 +The Fox, the Ape, and the Humble-Bee,   856 +2
 +_Ar._ The Foxe, the Ape, and the Humble-Bee,   856 +6
The Foxe, the Ape, and the Humble-Bee,   859
*the Ape his keeper, the tyred Horse his rider: But _Damosella_   1291
This is the Ape of Forme, Mounsier the nice,   2250
APETHATON = *1
*_Arm._ I spoke it tender iuuenal, as a congruent apethaton   324
APOLLO = 1
*The wordes of Mercurie, are harsh after the | songes of Apollo. 2897
APOLOGIE = 1
and I will haue an Apologie for that purpose.   1868
APOSTRAPHAS = *1
*_Pedan._ You finde not the apostraphas, and so misse the   1284
APPARILED = 1
Boy. They do, they do; and are appariled thus, | Like _Muscouites,_
or _Russians,_ as I gesse.   2012
APPARRELL = *1
*curtesie. I beseech thee apparrell thy head: and among other   1832
APPEARE = 1
Berow. Now in thy likenesse, one more foole appeare.   1378
APPEARES = 2
There is no certaine Princesse that appeares.   1493
That in this spleene rediculous appeares,   2009

APPERTEINING = *1
    *apperteining to thy young dayes, which we may nominate |
    tender.   325
APPERTINENT = *1
    *Boy. And I tough signeor, as an appertinent title to your   327
APPLE = 1
    And laugh vpon the apple of her eie?   2414
APPLY = 1
    Since all the power thereof it doth apply,   1967
APPOLOGIE = 1
    Ergo, *I come with this Appologie.*   2546
APPOLOS = 1
    As bright *Appolos* Lute, strung with his haire.   1694
APPREHENDED = *1
    *apprehended with the aforesayd Swaine, I keepe hir as a vessell of 270
APPROCH = 4*1
    No Woman may approch his silent Court: 515
    Boyet. Nauar had notice of your faire approch,   575
    Against your Peace Loue doth approch, disguysd: 1975
    King. Berowne, they will shame vs: let them not approch.   2453
    Brag. Holla. Approch.   2853
APREHENTIONS = *1
    *Ideas, aprehentions, motions, reuolutions. These are begot in 1232
APT = 7*1
    olde time, which we may name tough. | *Arma.* Prettie and apt. 328
    Boy. How meane you sir, I prettie, and my saying apt?   330
    or I apt, and my saying prettie?   331
    Boy. Little prettie, because little: wherefore apt.   333
    Arma. And therfore apt, because quicke.   334
    Deliuers in such apt and gracious wordes,   565
    Youth so apt to pluck a sweete.   1451
    *well culd, chose, sweete, & apt I do assure you sir, I do assure. 1827
AQUITAINE = 8
    A Maide of grace and complet maiestie, | About surrender vp of
    Aquitaine,   146
    Then *Aquitaine* a Dowrie for a Queene.   499
    One part of *Aquitaine* is bound to vs,   631
    We will giue vp our right in *Aquitaine,*   635
    To haue his title liue in *Aquitaine.*   641
    Then *Aquitaine,* so guelded as it is.   644
    And if you proue it, Ile repay it backe, | Or yeelde vp *Aquitaine.* 654
    Ile giue you *Aquitaine,* and all that is his,   752
AR = 13*9
ARBITRATE = 1
    That, which long processe could not arbitrate.   2701
ARE = 80*26
AREPAIRING *see* repairing
ARGUES = *1
    Holo. I wil somthing affect the letter, for it argues facilitie. 1213
ARGUMENT = 3*4
    *doth tread. I shall be forsworne (which is a great argument   472
    *Ar. Come hither, come hither: How did this argument | (begin? 869
    Clow. True, and I for a Plantan, thus came your argument | (in, 873
    Gainst whom the world cannot holde argument,   1394
    *then the staple of his argument. I abhorre such phanatticall   1757
    Therefore Ile darkly ende the argument.   1910
    Yet since Loues argument was first on foote,   2705

ARGUMENTES = 1
  Armed in argumentes, you'll be surprisd.   1976
ARGUS = 1
  Though *Argus* were her eunuch and her garde.   965
ARIGHT *see* right
ARM = 9*10
ARMA = 9*2
ARMADO see also Ar.. Arm.. Arma = 6*2
  This childe of Fancie that *Armado* hight,   181
  Bero. Armado is a most illustrious wight,   188
  Fer. A letter from the magnifisent *Armado.*   203
  heate of duetie. | Don Adriano de Armado.   273
  Fer. And *Don Armado* shall be your keeper.   299
  Enter Armado and Moth his page.   311
  Boy. This *Armado* is a *Spaniard* that keepes here in court,   1079
  *special honours it pleaseth his greatnes to impart to *Armado*   1839
ARMADO = *1
ARMADOES = *1
  *parish Curate *Alexander, Armadoes* Page *Hercules,* the Pe- | dant   2479
ARMATHO = 2*2
  Thine in the dearest designe of industri, | Don Adriana de
  Armatho.   1066
  Armatho ath toothen side, o a most daintie man,   1142
  *it was geuen me by *Costard,* and sent me from *Don Armatho*:   1255
  *who is intituled, nominated, or called, *Don Adriano de
  Ar-* | matho.   1746
ARMATHOES = 1
  That put *Armathoes* Page out of his part.   2261
ARMD = 1
  If you are armd to do, as sworne to do,   26
ARME = 4
  Const. Signeour *Arme Arme* commendes you: 199
  Arme Wenches arme, incounters mounted are,   1974
ARMED = 1
  Armed in argumentes, you'll be surprisd.   1976
ARMES = 5*3
  Well fitted in artes, glorious in armes: 537
  *your eyes, with your armes crost on your thinbellies doblet   787
  Regent of Loue-rimes, Lord of folded armes,   947
  Nor neuer lay his wreathed armes athwart   1472
  Haue at you then affections men at armes,   1640
  *And lay my Armes before the Leggs of this sweete Lasse of
  France.*   2503
  Ber. Hide thy head *Achilles,* here comes *Hector* in Armes.   2588
  *Ile flash, Ile do it by the Sword: I bepray you let me bor- | row
  my Armes againe.   2651
ARMIE = 1
  And the hudge armie of the worldes desires.   14
ARMIPOTENT = *2
  Braggart. The Armipotent Mars, *of Launces the almightie,* | gaue
  Hector *a gift.*   2600
  Brag. Peace. The Armipotent Mars, *of Launces the almighty,*   2606
ARREST = 1
  Princ. We arrest your worde.   656
ARROWES = *1
  *Fleeter then Arrowes, bullets wind thought swifter thinges.   2177

ART *l.*340 *758 1042 *1043 1072 1282 1491 *1780 1781 2201 2264
2446 2553 = 9*5, 1*1
   Still and contemplatyue in lyuing art.   18
   *Where all those pleasures liue, that Art would comprehend.   1273
ARTERIES = 1
   Why vniuersall plodding poysons vp | The nimble spirites in the
   arteries,   1655
ARTES = 3
   Well fitted in artes, glorious in armes: 537
   Other slow Artes intirely keepe the braine: 1675
   They are the Bookes, the Artes, the Achademes,   1703
ARTICLE = 2
   Ber. This Article my liedge your selfe must breake,   143
   Therefore this Article is made in vaine,   149
ARTS-MAN = *1
   Brag. Arts-man preambulat, we will be singuled from the   1815
AS = 109*38
   If you are armd to do, as sworne to do,   26
   As not to see a woman in that terme,   41
   As thus, to study where I well may dine,   66
   As paynefully to poare vpon a Booke,   79
   shame as the rest of the Court can possible deuise.   141
   Tis won as townes with fire, so won so lost.   157
   Suggestions are to other as to me: 169
   Haue chose as vmpier of their mutenie.   180
   Clowne. Sir the Contempts thereof are as touching me.   201
   Bero. Well sir, be it as the stile shall giue vs cause to clime | in
   the merrines.   211
   Clow. The matter is to me sir, as concerning *Iaquenetta*:   213
   Clow. As it shall follow in my correction, and God defend | the
   right.   224
   Bero. As we would heare an Oracle.   227
   of thy health-geuing ayre: And as I am a Gentleman, betooke my   244
   that shallow vassall (Clown. Still mee.) which as I remember,   258
   more sweete vnderstanding a Woman: him, I (as my euer esteemed   264
   apprehended with the aforesayd Swaine, I keepe hir as a vessell of   270
   Ber. This is not so well as I looked for, but the best that | euer I
   heard.   275
   Arm. I spoke it tender iuuenal, as a congruent apethaton   324
   Boy. And I tough signeor, as an appertinent title to your   327
   Arm. I will hereupon confesse I am in loue: and as it is   363
   *thee in my rapier, as much as thou didst me in carying gates.   380
   Boy. As I haue read sir, and the best of them too.   390
   *therfore I will say nothing: I thanke God I haue as little
   pa-|tience   467
   as an other man, & therfore I can be quiet. *Exit.*   468
   Be now as prodigall of all Deare grace,   500
   As Nature was in making Graces deare,   501
   As our best mouing faire soliciter: 520
   Prin. Such short liued wits do wither as they grow.   546
   But say that he, or we, as neither haue   628
   Then *Aquitaine*, so guelded as it is.   644
   As honor (without breach of honor) may,   667
   As you shall deeme your selfe lodgd in my hart.   671
   Boy. I was as willing to grapple as he was to boord.   719
   As Iewels in Christall for some Prince to buy.   747
   Did poynt you to buy them along as you past.   749

AS *cont.*

*loue sometime through: nose as if you snufft vp loue by	785
*Boy. And three times as much more, and yet nothing | at all.	815
Brag. The way is but short, away. | Boy. As swift as Lead sir.	824
To sell a bargaine well is as cunning as fast and loose:	867
As thou wilt win my fauour, good my knaue,	918
As I for praise alone now seeke to spill	1009
And your waste Mistres were as slender as my wit,	1025
Gainst thee thou Lambe, that standest as his pray:	1069
*was a man when King *Pippen* of Fraunce was a litle boy, as |	
touching the hit it.	1109
*Boy. So I may answere thee with one as olde that was a	1111
*woman when queene *Guinouer* of Brittaine was a litle wench | as	
toching the hit it.	1112
*When it comes so smoothly off, so obscenly as it were, so fit.	1140
*Ped. The Deare was (as you know) sanguis in blood, ripe	1153
*as the Pomwater, who now hangeth like a Iewel in the eare	1154
*as it were *in via,* in way of explication *facere*: as it were	1164
*replication, or rather *ostentare,* to show as it were his	
inclina-|tion	1165
*He hath not eate paper as it were: he hath not drunke inck.	1176
*For as it would ill become me to be vaine, indiscreet, or a |	
(foole,	1183
*What was a month old at *Cains* birth, that's not fiue weeks | old	
as yet?	1190
*Iaque. Good M.(aister) Parson be so good as read me this letter,	1254
*of thee as the traueiler doth of *Venice, vemchie, vencha, que non*	1259
*Vnder pardon sir, What are the contentes? or rather as *Hor-|race*	1262
Celestiall as thou art, Oh pardon loue this wrong,	1282
and as a certaine Father saith	1313
*foole: Well proued wit. By the Lord this Loue is as madd	1339
*as *Aiax,* it kills Sheepe, it kills mee, I a Sheepe well prooued	1340
As thy eye beames, when their fresh rayse haue smot.	1360
As doth thy face through teares of mine giue light:	1364
No drop but as a Coach doth carrie thee:	1366
Duma. As vpright as the Ceder.	1423
Duma. As faire as day.	1425
Ber. I as some dayes, but then no Sunne must shine.	1426
King. Come sir, you blush: as his, your case is such.	1468
You chide at him, offending twice as much.	1469
As true we are as flesh and blood can be,	1563
Do meete as at a faire in her faire cheeke,	1584
Beautie doth varnish Age, as if new borne,	1593
King. By heauen, thy Loue is blacke as Ebonie.	1596
King. No Diuel will fright thee then so much as shee.	1624
Duma. O vile, then as she goes what vpward lyes?	1629
The streete should see as she walkt ouer head.	1630
As motion and long during action tyres	1657
Teaches such beautie as a womans eye:	1663
Such fierie Numbers as the prompting eyes,	1673
Courses as swift as thought in euery power,	1681
Subtil as *Sphinx,* as sweete and musicall,	1693
As bright *Appolos* Lute, strung with his haire.	1694
Such as the shortnesse of the time can shape,	1729
to od as it were, too peregrinat as I may call it.	1752
*such rackers of ortagriphie, as to speake dout fine, when he	1759
*art not so long by the head as honorificabilitudinitatibus:	1780

15

AS *cont.*
 *Go to, thou hast it *ad dungil* at the fingers ends, as they say. 1813
 *and sodaine breaking out of myrth (as it were) I haue 1847
 *Sir *Holofernes*, as concerning some entertainement of time, 1851
 none so fit as to present the nine Worthies. 1855
 *that worthies thumbe, he is not so big as the end of his Club. 1864
 Quee. Nothing but this: yes as much loue in Rime, 1893
 As would be crambd vp in a sheete of paper 1894
 And if my face were but as faire as yours, 1920
 My Fauour were as great, be witnesse this, 1921
 Quee. Beautious as Incke: a good conclusion. 1929
 Kath. Faire as a text B in a Coppie booke. 1930
 As Wit turnde Foole, follie in Wisedome hatcht: 1960
 As grauities reuolt to wantons be. 1964
 As foolrie in the Wise, when Wit doth dote: 1966
 Boy. They do, they do; and are appariled thus, | Like *Muscouites*,
 or *Russians*, as I gesse. 2012
 Theres no such sport, as sport by sport orethrowne: 2044
 Theres no such sport by sport, as sport orethrowne: 2045
 King. Blessed are cloudes, to do as such cloudes do. 2103
 Duma. Please it you, as much in priuat, & ile bid adieu. 2152
 Boyet. The tongues of mocking Wenches are as keene | As is the
 Rasors edge inuisible: 2172
 Quee. Goe sicknes as thou art. 2201
 Mar. Dumaine is mine as sure as barke on tree. 2206
 Lets mocke them still as well knowne as disguysde: 2224
 Quee. Whip to our Tents as Roes runs ore land. *Exeunt.* 2232
 Berow. This fellow peckes vp Wit as Pidgions Pease, 2240
 The staires as he treades on them kisse his feete. 2255
 To shew his teeth as white as Whales bone, 2257
 Quee. Faire in all Haile is foule, as I conceaue. 2266
 Now by my maiden honour yet as pure, | As the vnsallied Lilly I
 protest, 2277
 Rosa. Nor shall not, if I do as I intende. 2362
 As precious ey-sight, and did value me 2383
 *am (as they say, but to parfect one man in one poore man) |
 Pompion the great sir. 2444
 sweete breath, as will vtter a brace of wordes. 2468
 *Too too vaine, too too vaine: but we will put it (as they say) 2474
 Boyet. Therefore as he is, an Asse, let him go: 2577
 As to reioyce at friendes but newly found. 2709
 As Loue is full of vnbefitting straines, 2718
 All wanton as a childe, skipping and vaine. 2719
 Varying in subiectes as the eye doth roule, 2722
 As bombast and as lyning to the time: 2739
 If for my Loue (as there is no such cause) 2752
ASHAMED *see* shamed
ASIDE *see also* side = 1*1
 **Clow.* Walke aside the true folke, and let the traytors stay. 1561
 Quee. Stand aside good *Pompey.* 2539
ASKE = 6
 Kath. How needles was it then to aske the question? 612
 Ber. What time a day? | *Kath.* The houre that fooles should aske. 617
 And *Rosaline* they call her, aske for her: 932
 Rosa. It is not so. Aske them how manie inches 2086
 Long. I know the reason (Lady) why you aske. 2155
 Quee. Doth this man serue God? | *Bero.* Why aske you? 2469

ASPECT = 1
    Should rauish dooters with a false aspect: 1609
ASSE = 3*1
    *Boy. A message well simpathisd, a Horse to be embassa-|doure
    for an Asse.   819
    *Boy. Marrie sir, you must send the Asse vpon the Horse,   822
    Boyet. Therefore as he is, an Asse, let him go: 2577
    Bero. For the Asse to the Iude: giue it him. Iudas away.   2580
ASSIST = 1*1
    Boy. My fathers wit, and my mothers tongue assist me.   399
    *manager is in loue; yea he loueth. Assist me some extempo-|rall   484
ASSISTANCE = 1
    acquainted you withall, to the ende to craue your assistance.   1848
ASSISTANTS = *1
    *assistants the Kinges commaund, and this most gallant
    il-|lustrate   1853
ASSURE = *5
    *sweetly varried like a scholler at the least: but sir I assure ye   1159
    *well culd, chose, sweete, & apt I do assure you sir, I do assure.   1827
    *I do assure ye very good friende: for what is inwarde   1830
    *You cannot beg vs sir, I can assure you sir, we know what   2433
AT = 44*17
ATEES = *1
    *Bero. Pompey is mooued more Ates more Atees stir them, | or
    stir them on.   2644
ATES = *1
    *Bero. Pompey is mooued more Ates more Atees stir them, | or
    stir them on.   2644
ATH = 1
    Armatho ath toothen side, o a most daintie man,   1142
ATHE = 1
    Mar. Wide a'the bow hand, yfaith your hand is out.   1124
ATHWART = 1
    Nor neuer lay his wreathed armes athwart   1472
ATOTHER = 1
    And his Page atother side, that handfull of wit,   1146
ATTACH = 1
    Then homeward euery man attach the hand   1726
ATTAINDER = 1
    Standes in attainder of eternall shame.   168
ATTAINT = 1
    You are attaint with faultes and periurie: 2779
ATTEMPTED = *1
    *is falsely attempted? Loue is a familiar; Loue is a Diuell.   474
ATTENDE = 2
    Haste, signifie so much while we attende,   524
    Brag. Shall I tell you a thing? | Peda. We attende.   1876
ATTENDES = 1
    What humble suite attendes thy answere there,   2800
ATTENDING = 2
    Enter the Princesse of Fraunce, with three | attending Ladies and
    three Lordes.   490
    Shee (an attending Starre) scarce seene a light.   1580
ATTENTION = 1
    Ferd. Will you heare this Letter with attention?   226
AUAUNT = 1
    Quee. Auaunt perplexitie, What shall we do,   2221

AUCTHORITIE = 1
Saue base aucthoritie from others Bookes. 92
AUDACIOUSLY = 1
Yet feare not thou but speake audaciously. 1996
AUDATIOUS = *1
*wittie without affection, audatious without impudencie, 1743
AUDIENCE = 2*2
O dismisse this audience, and I shall tell you more. 1556
*Peda. Shall I haue audience? He shall present *Hercules* 1866
*Page. An excellent deuice: so if any of the audience hisse, 1869
*King. That she vouchsafe me audience for one word. 2238
AUGHT *see* ought
AUOYDE = 1
And therefore redd that would auoyde disprayse, 1613
AUSTERE = 1
If this Austere insociable life, | Change not your offer made in
heate of blood. 2759
AUTHORITIE = 1*1
*Arm. Most sweete *Hercules*: more authoritie deare Boy, 373
Long. O some authoritie how to proceede, 1636
AUTHOUR = 2
For where is any Authour in the worlde, 1662
Or for Mens sake, the authour of these Women: 1710
AWAIE = 1
Prin. You will the sooner that I were awaie, 607
AWAY *see also* way = 17*8
Ferd. Your othe is past, to passe away from these. 53
Clo. Come *Iaquenetta*, away. *Exeunt.* 448
Ar. Take away this villaine, shut him vp. 456
Boy. Come you transgressing slaue, away. 457
*tune, but a snip and away: these are complementes, these 790
Brag. The way is but short, away. | *Boy.* As swift as Lead sir. 824
Quee. Thou hast mistaken his letter. Come Lords away. 1090
*Away, the gentles are at their game, and we will to our re-
|creation. *Exeunt.* 1331
King. Soft, Whither away so fast? 1524
The treason and you goe in peace away togeather. 1534
King. Hence sirs, away. 1560
For feare their colours should be washt away. 1620
King. Away, away, no time shalbe omitted, 1732
Peda. Most *Dull,* honest *Dull,* to our sport: away. *Exeunt.* 1886
But while tis spoke each turne away his face. 2040
*And they wel mockt depart away with shame. *Sound Trom.* 2048
Bero. Take away the Conquerour, take away *Alisander.* 2527
*and a feard to speake? Run away for shame *Ali-|sander.* 2532
Bero. For the *Asse* to the *Iude*: giue it him. *Iudas* away. 2580
*wench is cast away: shee's quicke, the childe bragges in her |
bellie already: tis yours. 2632
Ber. Worthies away, the Scaene begins to cloude. 2679
Quee. Boyet prepare, I will away to nyght. 2685
But if they will not, throw away that spirrit, 2828
AY *see also* I = 3
King. Ay mee! 1354
Long. Ay mee! I am forsworne. 1379
Ay mee sayes one! O *Ioue* the other cryes! 1478
AYER = *1
Brag. Sweete Ayer, go tendernes of yeeres, take this Key, 775

AYRE = 2*1

   of thy health-geuing ayre: And as I am a Gentleman, betooke my   244

   Ayre (quoth he) thy cheekes may blow,   1446

   Ayre would I might triumph so.   1447

B = 1

   Kath. Faire as a text B in a Coppie booke.   1930

B = 1

BA = 1*1

   Peda. Ba, *puericia* with a horne added.   1787

   Pag. Ba most seely Sheepe, with a horne: you heare his | (learning.   1788

BABE = 1

   And when he was a babe, a childe, a shrimpe,   2543

BACHUS = 1

   Loues tongue proues daintie, *Bachus* grosse in taste,   1690

BACKE = 2*2

   *great carriage: for he carried the Towne-gates on his backe   377

   Prin. Faire I giue you backe againe, and welcome I haue   586

   And if you proue it, Ile repay it backe, | Or yeelde vp *Aquitaine.*   654

   And stand betweene her backe sir and the fier,   2415

BACKES = 2

   Page. A holy parcell of the fayrest dames that euer turnd their | backes to mortall viewes.   2055

   The Ladyes turne their backes to him.   2057

BACKWARD = 1

   is Ab speld backward with the horne on his head?   1786

BAD = 1 .

   Quee. Els your memorie is bad, going ore it erewhile.   1078

BADGE = 1

   King. O paradox, Blacke is the badge of Hell,   1603

BADGES = 1

   And by these badges vnderstand the King,   2712

BALLES = 1

   With two pitch balles stucke in her face for eyes.   963

BALLET = *2

   Ar. Is there not a Ballet Boy, of the King & the Begger?   413

   Boy. The worlde was very guiltie of such a Ballet some   415

BANCROUT = 1

   Make rich the ribbes, but bancrout quite the wits.   31

BANDIED = 1

   Quee. Well bandied both, a set of Wit well played.   1916

BANQUET = 1

   The minde shall banquet, though the body pine,   29

BARBARISME = 1

   And though I haue for barbarisme spoke more   121

BARBAROUS = *2

   Holo. Most barbarous intimation: yet a kind of insinua-|tion,   1163

   *barbarous. Do you not educate youth at the Charg-house   1816

BARD = *1

   Ber. Things hid & bard (you meane) from cammon sense.   62

BARGAINE = 2*1

   Clo. The Boy hath sold him a bargaine, a Goose, that's flat.   865

   To sell a bargaine well is as cunning as fast and loose: 867

   To make a world-without-end bargaine in: 2749

BARKE = 1

   Mar. Dumaine is mine as sure as barke on tree.   2206

19

BARRAINE = 2
O these are barraine taskes, too hard to keepe,   51
And therefore finding barraine practizers,   1676
BARREN = *1
*sensible in the duller partes: and such barren plantes are   1179
BASE = 5*5
Saue base aucthoritie from others Bookes.   92
*did I see that low spirited Swaine, that base Minow of thy myrth,   255
Boy. Which the base vulgar do call three.   356
*base for a Souldier to loue; so am I in loue with a base wench.   364
*Arm. I do affect the verie ground (which is base) where her   470
Not vttred by base sale of chapmens tongues: 507
welcome to the wide fieldes too base to be mine.   588
*Veni, vidi, vici: Which to annothanize in the vulgar, O base   1048
Kisses the base ground with obedient breast.   1574
BASER = 1*1
He throwes vppon the grosse worlds baser slaues   34
*shoo (which is baser) guided by her foote (which is basest)   471
BASEST = *1
*shoo (which is baser) guided by her foote (which is basest)   471
BASTARD = *1
*heauens were so pleased, that thou wart but my Ba-|stard;   1811
BATE = 1
That honour which shall bate his sythes keene edge,   10
BAYTED = 1
Quee. Alas poore Machabeus, how hath he bin bayted.   2585
BE see also shalbe, twilbe, wilbe = 89*35
BE = *2
BEAME = 1
But I a Beame do finde in each of three.   1499
BEAMED = 3
Page. Once to beholde with your Sunne beamed eyes,   2065
With your Sunne beamed eyes.   2066
You were best call it Daughter beamed eyes.   2068
BEAMES = 1
As thy eye beames, when their fresh rayse haue smot.   1360
BEARD = 2
Lon. Gods blessing on your beard.   702
Kath. A wife? a beard, faire health, and honestie,   2784
BEARE = 4*1
*lewe thereof, impose on thee nothing but this: Beare this   895
To see him walke before a Lady, and to beare her Fann.   1143
Thus must thou speake, and thus thy body beare.   1992
Of the olde rage: beare with me, I am sicke.   2350
But that it beare this tryall, and last Loue,   2763
BEARER = 1
Stand a side good bearer. Boyet you can carue,   1032
BEARES = 4*1
Rosa. Why she that beares the Bow. Finely put off.   1096
*Thy eie Ioues lightning beares, thy voyce his dreadful thu(n)der   1279
Mar. Follie in Fooles beares not so strong a note,   1965
A heauie hart beares not a humble tongue.   2695
And Thom beares Logges into the hall,   2881
BEARING = 1
good reput, carriage bearing, and estimation.   267
BEAST = 1
Bo. So you graunt pasture for me. | Lad. Not so gentle Beast.   724

BEASTES = *1
*selfe to walke: the time When? about the sixt houre, When
Beastes   245
BEAT = 1
Sweete chucks beat not the bones of the buried: 2618
BEATEN = 1
Bero. By heauen, all drie beaten with pure scoffe.   2180
BEAUTIE = 13
Queene. Good L.(ord) Boyet, my beautie though but meane,   504
Beautie is bought by iudgement of the eye,   506
Quee. I thanke my Beautie, I am faire that shoote,   985
Quee. See see, my beautie wilbe sau'd by merrit.   996
Rosa. Shall I teach you to know. | Boy. I my continent of beautie. 1094
Ah neuer fayth could hold, yf not to beautie vowed.   1268
Beautie doth varnish Age, as if new borne,   1593
That I may sweare Beautie doth beautie lacke,   1600
Without the beautie of a womans face?   1651
Teaches such beautie as a womans eye: 1663
Kath. A light condition in a beautie darke.   1907
Plaide fouleplay with our othes: your beautie Ladies   2714
BEAUTIES = 3
And beauties crest becomes the heauens well.   1605
Page. All haile, the richest Beauties on the earth.   2053
Berow. Beauties no richer then rich Taffata.   2054
BEAUTIFULL = *1
*thou art louelie: more fairer then faire, beautifull then
beau- | tious,   1043
BEAUTIOUS = 1*2
*true that thou art beautious, trueth it selfe that   1042
*thou art louelie: more fairer then faire, beautifull then
beau- | tious,   1043
Quee. Beautious as Incke: a good conclusion.   1929
BEAUTIS = 1
Of beautis tutors haue inritcht you with: 1674
BECAUSE = 4*3
Arma. Thou prettie because little.   332
Boy. Little prettie, because little: wherefore apt.   333
Arma. And therfore apt, because quicke.   334
*instant: by hart you loue her, because your hart cannot come   810
*by her: in hart you loue her, because your hart is in loue   811
*Iudas Machabeus; this Swaine (because of his great lim   1860
Pedan. I will not be put out of countenance. | Bero. Because thou
hast no face.   2560
BECOME = *1
*For as it would ill become me to be vaine, indiscreet, or a |
(foole,   1183
BECOMES = 1
And beauties crest becomes the heauens well.   1605
BECOMMING = 1
Within the limit of becomming mirth,   559
BECOMS = 1
Nothing becoms him ill that he would well.   538
BEDDES = 1
But seeke the weery beddes of people sicke.   2782
BEDECKING = 1
With such bedecking ornaments of praise.   571

21

BEDELL = *1
*A verie Bedell to a humerous sigh, a Critick, nay a night-|watch
Constable,   941
BEDRED = 1
To her decrepit, sicke, and bedred Father.   148
BEE *see also* Humble-Bee *l.*743 856 +2 856 +6 859 = 4
BEEN *see also* been, bin *l.*652 *939 1383 1474 *1742 *1776 1898
1998 2741 = 6*3
BEFALL = 1*2
Ber. Now faire befall your maske.   619
Berow. A tweluemonth? well; befall what will befall,   2831
BEFITTED = 1
That will be time and may by vs befitted.   1733
BEFORE = 9*5
Before the Birdes haue any cause to sing?   112
Before we enter his forbidden gates,   517
Before I came: Marrie thus much I haue learnt,   578
Submissiue fall his princely feete before,   1070
To see him walke before a Lady, and to beare her Fann.   1143
*set before vs, that we thankful should be: which we taste,   1180
*mine, where if (before repast) it shall please you to gratifie   1319
Peda. Sir, you shall present before her the Nine Worthies,   1850
*and learned Gentleman, before the Princesse: I say   1854
A better speach was neuer spoke before.   2002
Mar. Then die a Calfe, before your hornes do grow.   2169
Tolde our intentes before: which once disclosd,   2406
*And lay my Armes before the Leggs of this sweete Lasse of
France.*   2503
Before I saw you: and the worldes large tongue   2803
BEG = *1
*You cannot beg vs sir, I can assure you sir, we know what   2433
BEGETS = 1
His eye begets occasion for his wit,   561
BEGG = 1
Rosa. O vaine peticioner, begg a greater matter,   2106
BEGGE = 2
How I would make him fawne, and begge, and seeke,   1952
Thou bidst me begge, this begging is not strange.   2109
BEGGER = *6
Ar. Is there not a Ballet Boy, of the King & the Begger?   413
*Begger *Zenelophon*: and he it was that might rightly say,   1047
*To whom came he? to the Begger. What saw he? the   1053
*Begger. Who ouercame he? the Begger. The conclusion is   1054
*I am the King (for so standes the comparison) thou the
Beg-|ger,   1058
BEGGERS = *1
*whose side? the Beggers. The catastrophe is a Nuptiall, on   1056
BEGGING = 1
Thou bidst me begge, this begging is not strange.   2109
BEGIN = 4*2
Ar. Some enigma, some riddle, come, thy *Lenuoy* begin.   843
*Now will I begin your morrall, and do you follow with | my
lenuoy.   857
Ar. Come hither, come hither: How did this argument | (begin?   869
And to begin Wench, so God helpe me law,   2346
Pedan. Begin sir, you are my elder.   2558
B. Ver begin.   2858

22

BEGINS = 2
Page. Peace, the peale begins.   1783
Ber. Worthies away, the Scaene begins to cloude.   2679
BEGON *see also* gon = 1
Ber. Is this your perfectnes? begon you rogue.   2070
BEGOT = 1*1
*Ideas, aprehentions, motions, reuolutions. These are begot in   1232
Whose influence is begot of that loose grace,   2820
BEGUYLE = 1
Light seeking light, doth light of light beguyle: 82
BEHALFE = 1
To know his pleasure, and in that behalfe   518
BEHAUIOUR = 1*1
*his   gate   maiesticall,   and   his   generall   behauiour   vaine,
redicu- | lous,   1750
Bero. See where it comes. Behauiour what wert thou?   2263
BEHAUIOURS = 1
Prin. Your reason. | *Bo.* Why all his behauiours did make their
retire,   737
BEHOLDE = 6
Do but beholde the teares that swell in me,   1368
Toward that shade I might beholde addrest,   1984
Not to beholde. | Berow. Once to beholde, rogue.   2063
Page. Once to beholde with your Sunne beamed eyes,   2065
Beholde the window of my hart, mine eye: 2799
BEHOLDEST = *1
*ebon coloured Incke, which here thou viewest, beholdest, suruayest,
or*   252
BEING *l.*458 626 *812 856 +3 856 +7 860 958 959 1187 1398 1400
2360 2729 2731 = 13*1
BELEEUE = 1
But I beleeue although I seeme so loth,   170
BELIKE = 2
Prin. Some merrie mocking Lord belike, ist so?   544
Boy. And if my hand be out, then belike your hand is in.   1127
BELLIE = 1
*wench is cast away: shee's quicke, the childe bragges in her |
bellie already: tis yours.   2632
BELLY = *1
Bero. I, if a'haue no more mans blood in his belly then wil |
suppe a Flea.   2647
BELONG = 1
Rosa. But that you take what doth to you belong,   2308
BELONGES = 1
To thinges of sale, a sellers prayse belonges: 1589
BELONGING = 1
Bo. Belonging to whom? | *La.* To my fortunes and mee.   727
BEND = 1
We bend to that, the working of the hart.   1008
BENE = 2
But *omne bene* say I, being of an olde Fathers minde,   1187
*Curat. Laus deo, bene intelligo. | * Peda. Bome boon for boon
prescian,* a litle scratcht, twil serue.   1766
BENT = 1
Which not to anger bent, is musique, and sweete fier.   1281

BEPRAY = *1
  *Ile flash, Ile do it by the Sword: I bepray you let me bor-|row
  my Armes againe.   2651
BER = 63*12
BERO = 1
  Boy. Farewell to me sir, and welcome to you. *Exit Bero.*   714
BERO = 47*13
BEROW = 20*4
BEROWNE see also Be., Ber., Bero., Berow. = 26*5
  Enter Ferdinand K.(ing) of Nauar, Berowne, | *Longauill, and*
  Dumaine.   2
  You three, *Berowne, Dumaine,* and *Longauill,*   19
  Longa. You swore to that *Berowne,* and to the rest.   57
  Ferd. Berowne is like an enuious sneaping Frost,   109
  Ferd. Well, sit you out: go home *Berowne*: adue.   119
  My Lord *Berowne,* see him deliuered ore,   300
  Enter *Nauar, Longauill, Dumaine, & Berowne.*   583
  Enter Berowne.   708
  Lady Maria. That last is *Berowne,* the merrie madcap L.(ord)   715
  Enter Berowne.   909
  Clow. I haue a Letter from Monsier *Berowne,* | to one Ladie
  Rosaline.   1029
  Clow. From my Lord *Berowne,* a good Maister of mine,   1088
  Iag. I sir from one mounsier *Berowne,* one of the strange |
  Queenes Lordes.   1294
  Your Ladiships in all desired imployment, Berowne.   1301
  Ped. Sir *Holofernes,* this *Berowne* is one of the Votaries   1302
  Enter Berowne with a paper in his hand, alone.   1333
  O would the *King, Berowne,* and *Longauill,*   1460
  What will *Berowne* say when that he shall heare   1482
  King. Berowne reade it ouer. *He reades the letter.*   1537
  Ber. My eyes are then no eyes, nor I *Berowne.*   1581
  King. Then leaue this chat, and good *Berowne* now proue   1633
  Nay I haue Vearses too, I thanke *Berowne,*   1922
  That same *Berowne* ile torture ere I go.   1950
  So shall *Berowne* take me for *Rosaline.*   2025
  This pert *Berowne* was out of countnance quite.   2191
  Quee. Berowne did sweare him selfe out of all suite.   2194
  Quee. And quicke *Berowne* hath plighted Fayth to me.   2204
  And Lord *Berowne* (I thanke him) is my deare.   2396
  King. Berowne, they will shame vs: let them not approch.   2453
  Berowne steps foorth.   2621
  Rosa. Oft haue I heard of you my Lord *Berowne,*   2802
BEROWNE = 3
BEROWNES = 1
  Dum. It is *Berownes* writing, and heere is his name.   1547
BESEDGED = *1
  Ferd. So it is besedged with sable coloured melancholie, I did   242
BESEECH = 5*4
  Clow. Of other mens secrets I beseech you.   241
  Longauill. I beseech you a word, What is she in the white?   695
  I beseech you read it.   1256
  I beseech your societie.   1324
  Iaque. I beseech your Grace let this Letter be read,   1535
  *betweene vs, let it passe. I do beseech thee remember thy   1831
  *curtesie. I beseech thee apparrell thy head: and among other   1832

BESEECH *cont.*
Brag. We will haue, if this fadge not, an Antique. I be-|seech
you follow. 1878
King. Madame Not so, I do beseech you stay. 2686
BESEEMETH = 1
To teach a teacher ill beseemeth mee. 603
BESHROW = 1
Quee. A Poxe of that iest, and I beshrow all Shrowes, 1934
BESIDE = 2*1
And but one meale on euery day beside: 44
When she did starue the generall world beside, 502
*the Moone is neuer but a month olde: and I say beside 1205
BESIEDGE = 1
Like one that comes heere to besiedge his Court, 580
BEST = 8*6
*most grase, *Birdes best peck, and Men sit downe to that*
nourishment 246
Ber. This is not so well as I looked for, but the best that | euer I
heard. 275
Fer. I the best, for the worst. But sirra, What say you to this? 277
Boy. As I haue read sir, and the best of them too. 390
As our best mouing faire soliciter: 520
*for the best ward of mine honour, is rewarding | my dependants.
Moth, follow. 897
You were best call it Daughter beamed eyes. 2068
Rosa. In priuat then. | *King.* I am best pleasd with that. 2133
With eies best seeing, heauens fierie eie: 2302
That sport best pleases, that doth best know how: 2460
Bero. My hat to a halfe-pennie, *Pompey* prooues the best |
Worthie. 2509
Boye. No, he is best indued in the small. 2597
Bero. Honest plaine words, best pearce the eare of griefe, 2711
BESTOW = 1*1
By Fauours seuerall, which they did bestow. 2017
*But I will forward with my deuice; sweete royaltie bestow | on
me the sence of hearing. 2619
BETIME *see* time
BETOOKE = *1
*of thy health-geuing ayre: And as I am a Gentleman, betooke my 244
BETRAIE = *1
*are humours, these betraie nice wenches that would be-|traied 792
BETRAIED = *1
*are humours, these betraie nice wenches that would be-|traied 792
BETRAY = 1
Ar. I do betray my selfe with blushing: Maide. | *Maide.* Man. 436
BETRAYED = 3
Are we betrayed thus to thy ouer-view? 1513
Ber. Not you by mee, but I betrayed to you. 1514
I am betrayed by keeping companie 1517
BETTER = 7*4
Boy. To be whipt: and yet a better loue then my maister. 424
This ciuill warre of wittes were much better vsed 730
Clow. Gardon, O sweete gardon, better then remuneratio(n). 935
*a leuenpence-farthing better: most sweete gardon. I will 936
*What vaine? What Wethercock? Did you euer heare better? 1075
If so our Copper byes no better treasure. 1737
A better speach was neuer spoke before. 2002

BETTER *cont.*

Ros. Well, better wits haue worne plaine statute Caps,   2202

King. Consture my speaches better, if you may.   2267

Quee. Then wish me better, I will giue you leaue.   2268

That hid the worse, and shewed the better face.   2317

BETWEENE = 2*1

Betweene L.(ord) *Perigort* and the bewtious heire | Of *Iaques*
Fauconbridge solemnized.   533

*betweene vs, let it passe. I do beseech thee remember thy   1831

And stand betweene her backe sir and the fier,   2415

BEWARE *see* ware

BEWTIOUS = 2

Betweene L.(ord) *Perigort* and the bewtious heire | Of *Iaques*
Fauconbridge solemnized.   533

To the snow-white hand of the most bewtious Lady Rosaline.   1297

BIAS *see* byas

BID = 3

Rosa. Why that they haue, and bid them so be gon.   2080

Duma. Please it you, as much in priuat, & ile bid adieu.   2152

Bero. Goe bid them prepare. (*Exit.*   2450

BIDE = 1

And bide the pennance of each three yeeres day.   124

BIDS = 1

And manie miles: the Princesse bids you tell,   2090

BIDST = 1

Thou bidst me begge, this begging is not strange.   2109

BIEN = *1

bien venuto, where I will proue those Verses to be very
vn- | learned,   1322

BIG = *1

*that worthies thumbe, he is not so big as the end of his Club.   1864

BIGGE = 2

Clow. I Pompey *am*, Pompey *surnamde the bigge.* | *Duma.* The
great.   2497

Long. His Legge is too bigge for *Hectors.* | *Duman.* More Calfe
certaine.   2595

BIN *l.*129 371 856 *1902 1903 2247 2422 2585 = 7*1

BIRDBOLT = 1

him with thy Birdbolt vnder the left papp: in fayth secrets.   1356

BIRDES = 2*1

Before the Birdes haue any cause to sing?   112

*most grase, Birdes best peck, and Men sit downe to that
'nourishment*   246

And Birdes sit brooding in the Snow,   2890

BIRTH *see also* byrth = *1

*What was a month old at *Cains* birth, that's not fiue weeks | old
as yet?   1190

BIS = *1

Holo. Twice sodd simplicitie, bis coctus, O thou monster   1172

BITES = 1

That bites the first borne infants of the Spring.   110

BITS = 1

Fat paunches haue leane pates: and daynty bits   30

BITTER = 2

King. Too bitter is thy iest.   1512

Bero. Thou greeuest my gall. | *Quee.* Gall, bitter, | *Bero.*
Therefore meete.   2144

BLACKE = 7*1
*commende the blacke oppressing humour to the most holsome
phisicke   243
King. By heauen, thy Loue is blacke as Ebonie.   1596
No face is fayre that is not full so blacke.   1602
King. O paradox, Blacke is the badge of Hell,   1603
O if in blacke my Ladyes browes be deckt,   1607
And therefore is she borne to make blacke fayre.   1610
Paintes it selfe blacke, to imitate her brow.   1614
Ile change my blacke Gowne for a faithfull frend.   2795
BLACK-MOORES = 1
Enter Black-moores with musicke, the Boy with a | speach, and the
rest of the Lordes disguysed.   2051
BLAKE = 1
Duma. To looke like her are Chimnie-sweepers blake.   1615
BLAME = 1
Then if she feare or be to blame, | By this you shall not know,   407
BLEACH = 1
And Maidens bleach their summer smockes: 2872
BLEAT = 1
Mar. Bleat softly then, the Butcher heares you crie.   2171
BLESSE = 3
Prin. God blesse my Ladyes, are they all in loue?   569
Iaqu. God blesse the King. Enter Iaquenetta and Clowne.   1528
They did not blesse vs with one happie word.   2297
BLESSED = 1
King. Blessed are cloudes, to do as such cloudes do.   2103
BLESSING = 1
Lon. Gods blessing on your beard.   702
BLEW = 1
The Song. | When Dasies pied, and Violets blew,   2859
BLIND = 2
Bowes not his vassall head, and strooken blind.   1573
Nor woo in rime like a blind harpers songue.   2337
BLINDE = 2
Doth falsely blinde the eye-sight of his looke: 81
A Louers eyes will gaze an Eagle blinde.   1685
BLINDED = 2
And giue him light that it was blinded by.   88
That is not blinded by her maiestie?   1577
BLISTER = 1
King. A blister on his sweete tongue with my hart,   2260
BLOOD = 12*2
*graces Farborough: But I would see his owne person | in flesh
and blood. | Ber. This is he.   196
*Arma. I do say thou art quicke in answeres. Thou heatst | my
blood.   340
Ros. Alacke, let it blood.   683
The poore Deares blood, that my hart meanes no ill.   1010
*Ped. The Deare was (as you know) sanguis in blood, ripe   1153
Raignes in my blood, and will remembred be.   1432
Ber. A Feuer in your blood, why then incision   1433
As true we are as flesh and blood can be,   1563
Young blood doth not obay an olde decree.   1565
For natiue blood is counted paynting now: 1612
Rosa. The blood of youth burnes not with such excesse,   1963

27

BLOOD *cont.*

*Bero. I, if a'haue no more mans blood in his belly then wil |
suppe a Flea. 2647
If this Austere insociable life, | Change not your offer made in
heate of blood. 2759
When Blood is nipt, and wayes be full, 2883
BLOODES = 1
Brag. Sweete bloodes, I both may and will. 2663
BLOSSOME = 1
Spied a blossome passing faire, 1440
BLOSSOMES = 1
Nip not the gaudie blossomes of your Loue: 2762
BLOT = 1
She passes prayse, then prayse too short doth blot. 1590
BLOW = 5
Ayre (quoth he) thy cheekes may blow, 1446
Blow like sweete Roses, in this sommer aire. 2215
Quee. How blow? how blow? Speake to be vnderstood. 2216
When all aloude the winde doth blow, 2888
BLOWES = 2
And leape for ioy, though they are lame with blowes: 2213
And Dicke the Sheepheard blowes his naile: 2880
BLOWNE = 2
Are Angels varling cloudes, or Roses blowne. 2220
Haue blowne me full of maggot ostentation. 2341
BLUNT = 1
Is a sharpe Wit matcht with too blunt a Will: 541
BLUSH = 3
You may looke pale, but I should blush I know, 1466
King. Come sir, you blush: as his, your case is such. 1468
And markt you both, and for you both did blush. 1475
BLUSHING = 1
Ar. I do betray my selfe with blushing: Maide. | *Maide.* Man. 436
BLUSH-IN = 1
For blush-in cheekes by faultes are bred, 405
BO = 9*5
BOAST = 1
Bero. Well, say I am, why should proude Sommer boast, 111
BODIES = *1
*Nauar, my soules earthes God, and bodies fostring patrone: 232
BODKIN = 1
Duma. The head of a Bodkin. 2564
BODY = 2
The minde shall banquet, though the body pine, 29
Thus must thou speake, and thus thy body beare. 1992
BOLD = 1*1
Bold of your worthines, we single you, 519
*And sin to breake it: but pardon me, I am too sodaine bold, 601
BOLDE = 1
Making the bolde wagg by their prayses bolder. 2000
BOLDER = 1
Making the bolde wagg by their prayses bolder. 2000
BOMBAST = 1
As bombast and as lyning to the time: 2739
BOME = *1
Curat. Laus deo, bene intelligo. | **Peda. Bome boon for boon
prescian,* a litle scratcht, twil serue. 1766

28

BONE = 2
To shew his teeth as white as Whales bone,   2257
Duma. The carud-bone face on a Flaske.   2568
BONES = 1
Sweete chucks beat not the bones of the buried: 2618
BOOKE = 7*1
As paynefully to poare vpon a Booke,   79
Nath. Sir he hath neuer fed of the dainties that are bred | in a
booke.   1174
Studie his byas leaues, and makes his booke thine eyes.   1272
O who can giue an oth? Where is a booke?   1599
In that each of you haue forsworne his Booke.   1647
Curat. A most singuler and choyce Epithat, | *Draw-out his*
Table-booke.   1754
Page. Yes yes, he teaches boyes the Horne-booke: What   1785
Kath. Faire as a text B in a Coppie booke.   1930
BOOKES = 4
Saue base aucthoritie from others Bookes.   92
They are the Ground, the Bookes, the Achadems,   1653
And in that Vow we haue forsworne our Bookes: 1670
They are the Bookes, the Artes, the Achademes,   1703
BOOKE-MATES = 1
A Phantasime a Monarcho, and one that makes sport | To the
Prince and his Booke-mates.   1080
BOOKMEN = 1
On *Nauar* and his Bookmen, for heere tis abused.   731
BOOK-MEN = *1
Dul. You two are book-men, Can you tel me by your wit,   1189
BOON = *2
Curat. Laus deo, bene intelligo. | *Peda. Bome boon for boon*
prescian, a litle scratcht, twil serue.   1766
BOORD = 1
Boy. I was as willing to grapple as he was to boord.   719
BOOTELES = 1
And spend his prodigall wittes in booteles rimes,   1954
BORE = *1
*Well, she hath one a'my Sonnets already, the Clowne bore   1348
BORNE = 8*1
That bites the first borne infants of the Spring.   110
For euery man with his affectes is borne,   162
In high borne wordes the worth of many a Knight: 183
Berow. Ah you whoreson loggerhead, you were borne to | do me
shame.   1548
We can not crosse the cause why we were borne: 1566
Beautie doth varnish Age, as if new borne,   1593
And therefore is she borne to make blacke fayre.   1610
Kath. And *Longauill* was for my seruice borne.   2205
If ouerboldly we haue borne our selues,   2692
BORROW = *1
*Ile flash, Ile do it by the Sword: I bepray you let me bor-|row
my Armes againe.   2651
BOSOME = 2
Through the transparent bosome of the deepe,   1363
His louing bosome, to keepe downe his hart.   1473
BOTH = 9*5
Lon. To heare meekely sir, and to laugh moderatly, or | to
forbeare both.   209

29

BOTH *cont.*

**Arma.* I confesse both, they are both the varnish of a com-|pleat
man.   351
*whose side? the Kinges: no, on both in one, or one in both.   1057
Clo. By my troth most plesant, how both did fit it.   1118
**Mar.* A marke marueilous wel shot, for they both did hit.   1119
And markt you both, and for you both did blush.   1475
Writ a both sides the leafe, margent and all,   1895
Quee. Well bandied both, a set of Wit well played.   1916
Berow. Neither of either: I remit both twaine.   2398
Brag. Sweete bloodes, I both may and will.   2663
To those that make vs both faire Ladies you,   2732

BOUGHT = 3
Beautie is bought by iudgement of the eye,   506
Then the boyes fat *Lenuoy*, the Goose that you bought,   875
Rosa. Then cannot we be bought: and so adue,   2130

BOUND = 4*1
**Clo.* I am more bound to you then your fellowes, for they | are
but lightly rewarded.   454
One part of *Aquitaine* is bound to vs,   631
Where that and other specialties are bound: 662
*Enfreedoming thy person: thou wert emured, restrained, |
captiuated, bound.   890
Breake vp this Capon. | *Boyet* I am bound to serue.   1034

BOW = 3
But come, the Bow: Now Mercie goes to kill,   999
Rosa. Why she that beares the Bow. Finely put off.   1096
Mar. Wide a'the bow hand, yfaith your hand is out.   1124

BOWED = *1
*Those thoughts to me were Okes, to thee like Osiers bowed   1270

BOWES = 1
Bowes not his vassall head, and strooken blind.   1573

BOWLE = 1*1
**Cl.* Shes to hard for you at pricks, sir challeng her to bowle   1133
When roasted Crabbs hisse in the bowle,   2892

BOWLER = *1
*good neighbour fayth, and a very good Bowler: but for   2535

BOY see also B. = 12*9
**Armado.* Boy, What signe is it when a man of great spi-|rite
growes melancholy?   312
*I should outsweare *Cupid.* Comfort mee Boy, what great   370
**Arm.* Most sweete *Hercules*: more authoritie deare Boy,   373
**Ar.* Is there not a Ballet Boy, of the King & the Begger?   413
*example my digression by some mightie presedent. Boy,   420
Ar. Sing Boy, My spirit growes heauie in loue.   426
*not; his disgrace is to be called Boy, but his glorie is to sub-|due   482
Boy. Proud of imployment, willingly I go. *Exit Boy.*   526
Enter *Braggart* and his *Boy.*   770
Brag. By hart, and in hart boy.   805
**Clo.* The Boy hath sold him a bargaine, a Goose, that's flat.   865
*A domineering pedant ore the Boy, then whom no mor-|tall so
magnificent.   943
This wimpled whyning purblind wayward Boy,   945
*was a man when King *Pippen* of Fraunce was a litle boy, as |
touching the hit it.   1109
Enter *Bragart, Boy.*   1769
For he hath been fiue thousand yeere a Boy.   1898

BOY cont.
The Boy replyde, An Angell is not euill: 1997
Enter Black-moores with musicke, the Boy with a | speach, and the
rest of the Lordes disguysed.   2051
*Bero. The Pedant, the Bragart, the Hedge-Priest, the | Foole,
and the Boy,   2485
Enter Pedant for Iudas, and the Boy for Hercules.   2540
Keepe some state in thy exit, and vanish. Exit Boy.   2547
BOY = 64*25
BOYE = 1*1
BOYES = 3*1
Then the boyes fat *Lenuoy*, the Goose that you bought,   875
And *Nestor* play at push-pin with the boyes,   1506
* *Page.* Yes yes, he teaches boyes the Horne-booke: What   1785
Nor to the motion of a Schoole-boyes tongue: 2335
BOYET see also Bo., Boy. = 13*1
Queene. Good L.(ord) *Boyet*, my beautie though but meane,   504
But now to taske the tasker, good *Boyet*,   511
Lord. Heere comes *Boyet. Enter Boyet.*   572
Boyet you can produce acquittances,   657
Prin. Come, to our Pauilion, *Boyet* is disposde.   754
Stand a side good bearer. *Boyet* you can carue,   1032
* *Maria.* You still wrangle with her *Boyet*, and she strikes | at the
brow.   1104
Enter Boyet.   1969
Quee. Heere comes *Boyet*, and myrth is in his face.   1970
Quee. Thy newes *Boyet?* | *Boy.* Prepare Maddame, prepare.   1972
Rosal. What would these strangers? | Know their mindes *Boyet.*   2071
Pay him the due of honie-tonged *Boyet.*   2259
Quee. Boyet prepare, I will away to nyght.   2685
BOYET = 22*5
BRA = *2
BRABANT = 2
Berowne. Did not I dance with you in *Brabant* once?   609
Kather. Did not I dance with you in *Brabant* once? | *Ber.* I know
you did.   610
BRACE = 1
sweete breath, as will vtter a brace of wordes.   2468
BRAG = 33*12
BRAGART = 2*1
Enter Bragart, Boy.   1769
Enter Bragart.   2466
*Bero. The Pedant, the Bragart, the Hedge-Priest, the | Foole,
and the Boy,   2485
BRAGGART see also Bra., Brag. = 3
Enter *Braggart* and his *Boy.*   770
Enter Braggart.   2587
Enter Braggart.   2841
BRAGGART = *1
BRAGGES = *1
*wench is cast away: shee's quicke, the childe bragges in her |
bellie already: tis yours.   2632
BRAINE = 4
That hath a mint of phrases in his braine: 176
Other slow Artes intirely keepe the braine: 1675
Liues not alone emured in the braine: 1679
To weede this wormewood from your fructfull braine,   2808

BRANCH = 1
That violates the smallest branch herein. 25
BRANNE = 1
Fer. Sir I will pronounce your sentence: You shall fast a | weeke
with Branne and Water. 295
BRASSE = 1
Can anie face of brasse hold longer out? 2327
BRAUE = 3
Therefore braue Conquerours, for so you are, 12
Boyet. Full merely hath this braue nuage, this carreere | bin run. 2421
Quee. Speake braue *Hector*, we are much delighted. 2622
BRAULE = *1
Boy. Maister, will you win your loue with a french braule? 779
BRAWLING = 1
Brag. How meanest thou? brawling in French. 780
BRAZEN = 1
Liue registred vpon our brazen Tombes, 6
BREACH = 1
As honor (without breach of honor) may, 667
BREAD = *1
*haue it to buy Ginger bread: Holde, there is the verie 1808
BREAK = *2
Rosa. Not one word more my Maides, break off, break off. 2178
BREAKE = 11*1
Studie to breake it, and not breake my troth. 71
Ber. This Article my liedge your selfe must breake, 143
If I breake fayth, this word shall speake for me, 164
Prin. Why, will shall breake it will, and nothing els. 595
*And sin to breake it: but pardon me, I am too sodaine bold, 601
Breake vp this Capon. | *Boyet* I am bound to serue. 1034
Breake the necke of the Waxe, and euery one giue eare. 1039
You would for Parradise breake Fayth and troth, 1480
To breake the vow I am ingaged in. 1516
The vertue of your eie must breake my oth. 2274
King. Despise me when I breake this Oth of mine. 2379
BREAKES = 2
And he that breakes them in the least degree, 167
For vertues office neuer breakes mens troth. 2276
BREAKING = 1*1
*and sodaine breaking out of myrth (as it were) I haue 1847
So much I hate a breaking cause to be 2281
BREAST = 1
Kisses the base ground with obedient breast. 1574
BREATH = 7*2
Thendeuour of this present breath may buy: 9
Vowes are but breath, and breath a vapoure is. 1401
Wish himselfe the heauens breath. 1445
That charge their breath against vs? Say scout say. 1980
sweete breath, as will vtter a brace of wordes. 2468
Brag. For mine owne part I breath free breath: I haue 2680
In the conuerse of breath (your gentlenes 2693
BREATHED = 2
A man so breathed, that certaine he would fight; yea, 2608
+When he breathed he was a man: 2618 +1
BREATHS = *1
Boye. Tapers they are with your sweete breaths puft out. 2185

BRED = 1*1
For blush-in cheekes by faultes are bred,   405
*Nath. Sir he hath neuer fed of the dainties that are bred | in a
booke.   1174
BREEDE = 1
Are these the breede of Wits so wondered at?   2184
BREEDING = *1
*Ber. The Spring is neare when greene geese are a bree-|(ding.   103
BREST = 3*1
A yeelding gainst some reason in my brest,   647
And where my Liedges? all about the brest. | A Caudle hou!   1510
*hand, a foote, a face, an eye: a gate, a state, a brow, a brest,   1522
Hence hermite then my hart, is in thy brest.   2776
BRIGHT = 4
Nor shines the siluer Moone one halfe so bright,   1362
Long. And since her time are Colliers counted bright.   1616
As bright Appolos Lute, strung with his haire.   1694
Vouchsafe bright Moone, and these thy Starrs to shine,   2104
BRING = 2*2
*thy Lawes furie, and shall at the least of thy sweete notice, bring   271
*giue enlargement to the Swaine, bring him festinatly hither,   776
Marcad. I am sorrie Madame for the newes I bring   2675
King. No Madame, we will bring you on your way.   2834
BRINGES = 1
Pag. They do not marke me, and that bringes me out.   2069
BRITTAINE = *1
*woman when queene Guinouer of Brittaine was a litle wench | as
toching the hit it.   1112
BROKE = 3*1
Fell ouer the threshold, and broke my shin.   883
Vowes for thee broke deserue not punishment.   1396
If by mee broke, What foole is not so wise,   1405
*Quee. Peace peace, forbeare: your Oth once broke, you | force
not to forsweare.   2377
BROKEN = 3*1
*Pag. A wonder Maister, Heers a Costard broken in a shin.   841
Boy. By saying that a Costard was broken in a shin.   871
Ar. But tel me, How was there a Costard broken in a shin?   877
If broken then, it is no fault of mine: 1404
BROOCH = 2
Bero. Saint Georges halfe cheeke in a Brooch.   2569
Duma. I and in a Brooch of Lead.   2570
BROODING = 1
And Birdes sit brooding in the Snow,   2890
BROOKE = 1
Many can brooke the weather, that loue not the winde.   1188
BROUGHT = 1
Haue brought about the annuall reckoning.   2758
BROW = 6*1
A whitly wanton, with a veluet brow,   962
Where faire is not, praise cannot mend the brow.   992
*Maria. You still wrangle with her Boyet, and she strikes | at the
brow.   1104
*hand, a foote, a face, an eye: a gate, a state, a brow, a brest,   1522
Dares looke vpon the heauen of her brow,   1576
Paintes it selfe blacke, to imitate her brow.   1614
And though the mourning brow of progenie   2702

33

BROWES = 1*1
O if in blacke my Ladyes browes be deckt,   1607
*_Rosa._ Helpe holde his browes, heele sound: why looke | you
pale?   2323
BRUSE = 1
Bruse me with scorne, confound me with a flout.   2329
BUCKE = 1
it was a Bucke of the first head.   1160
BUD = 1
Boy. Faire Ladies maskt, are Roses in their bud: 2218
BUDDS = 1
And Cuckow-budds of yellow hew: 2861
BULLET = 1
He reputes me a Cannon, and the Bullet thats hee: 833
BULLETS = *1
*Fleeter then Arrowes, bullets wind thought swifter thinges.   2177
BURIED = 1
Sweete chucks beat not the bones of the buried: 2618
BURNES = 1
Rosa. The blood of youth burnes not with such excesse,   1963
BUSH = 2
Then Forrester my friend, Where is the Bush   981
I haue been closely shrowded in this bush,   1474
BUSINES = 1
On serious busines crauing quicke dispatch,   522
BUT _l._28 31 37 40 44 46 77 97 116 163 170 172 186 191 *196 *236
237 *253 261 *275 *277 281 *391 *416 *433 455 *465 *475 *482
504 511 558 *601 626 628 634 637 670 *698 716 717 729 753 *755
763 *781 *790 797 *800 801 823 824 847 856 +3 856 +7 860 877
*895 928 959 977 995 999 1072 1077 *1097 1106 *1121 *1159 1187
*1205 1217 1226 *1234 *1243 *1286 *1288 *1291 *1315 *1342
*1344 1366 1368 1370 1397 1401 1426 1431 1448 1455 1466 1495
1496 1499 1514 1582 1631 1664 1678 1680 1719 *1807 *1811
*1834 *1837 *1841 *1842 1893 1917 1920 1935 1951 1996 2011
2029 2031 2037 2040 2046 2077 2079 2102 2107 *2108 *2114 2119
2190 2203 2287 2298 2305 2308 2367 2392 2408 2428 2429 *2444
2449 *2474 *2507 *2535 *2536 2575 2592 2593 *2619 *2668 *2673
2709 2740 2754 2763 2782 2783 2796 2828 *2848 = 114*48
BUTCHER = 1
Mar. Bleat softly then, the Butcher heares you crie.   2171
BUTSHAFT = *1
*seduced, and he had a very good wit. _Cupids_ Butshaft is too   478
BUTT = *1
*_Lon._ Looke how you butt your selfe in these sharpe mocks,   2166
BUTTON = *1
*_Page._ Maister, let me take you a button hole lower. Do   2656
BUY = 5*1
Thendeuour of this present breath may buy: 9
As Iewels in Christall for some Prince to buy.   747
Did poynt you to buy them along as you past.   749
I will neuer buy and sell out of this word.   907
a man buy for a remuneration?   912
*haue it to buy Ginger bread: Holde, there is the verie   1808
BUYES _see also_ byes = *1
*_King._ Prise you your selues: What buyes your company?   2127
BY = 86*33, 1
That by and by disguysd they will be heere.   1988

BYAS = 1
Studie his byas leaues, and makes his booke thine eyes. 1272
BYES = 1
If so our Copper byes no better treasure. 1737
BYRTH = 2
Why should I ioy in any abhortiue byrth? 113
When great thinges labouring perish in their byrth. 2464
BYTH = 1
Do not you know my Ladies foote by'th squier? 2413
CADENCE = *1
*facilitie, and golden cadence of poesie *caret*: *Ouiddius* 1287
CAESARS = 1
Boyet. The pummel of *Caesars* Fauchion. 2567
CAINS = *1
*What was a month old at *Cains* birth, that's not fiue weeks | old
as yet? 1190
CALD = 2
Then cald you for the *Lenuoy*. 872
cald the Deare: the Princesse kild a Pricket. 1209
CALDE = 2
To a Ladie of France, that he calde *Rosaline*. 1089
And trow you what he calde me? | *Quee*. Qualme perhaps. 2198
CALFE = 4*2
*not det: he clepeth a Calfe, Cauſe: halfe, haufe: neighbour 1761
* *Mar*. Veale quoth the Dutch-man: is not veale a Calfe? 2159
Long. A Calfe faire Ladie. 2161
Mar. No, a faire Lorde Calfe. 2162
Mar. Then die a Calfe, before your hornes do grow. 2169
Long. His Legge is too bigge for *Hectors*. | *Duman*. More Calfe
certaine. 2595
CALL = 10*1
Boy. Which the base vulgar do call three. 356
Berowne they call him, but a merrier man, 558
And *Rosaline* they call her, aske for her: 932
Do not call it sinne in me, 1452
to od as it were, too peregrinat as I may call it. 1752
*which he would call abbominable, it insinuateth me of in-|famie: 1763
of this day, which the rude multitude call the after-noone. 1823
You were best call it Daughter beamed eyes. 2068
Mende him who can, the Ladies call him sweete. 2254
I dare not call them fooles; but this I thinke, 2298
ende of our shew. | *King*. Call them foorth quickly, we will do so. 2851
CALLED = *4
which is called Supper: So much for the time When. Now for the 247
* *Ferd*. For* Iaquenetta (*so is the weaker vessell called*) *which I* 269
*not; his disgrace is to be called Boy, but his glorie is to sub-|due 482
*who is intituled, nominated, or called, *Don Adriano de
Ar-|matho.* 1746
CALST = 1
Brag. Calst thou my loue Hobbi-horse. 799
CAME = 7*5
Before I came: Marrie thus much I haue learnt, 578
+ *Pag*. Vntill the Goose came out of doore, 856 +8
 Arm. Vntill the Goose came out of doore, 861
* *Clow*. True, and I for a Plantan, thus came your argument | (in, 873
*and obscure vulgar; *videliset*, He came, see, and ouercame: 1049
*He came, one; see, two; ouercame, three. Who came? the 1050

CAME *cont.*
*To whom came he? to the Begger. What saw he? the	1053
And rought not to fiue-weeks when he came to fiuescore.	1198
Rosa. Madame, came nothing els along with that?	1892
Kath. Lord *Longauill* said I came ore his hart:	2197
King. We came to visite you, and purpose now,	2269

CAMMON = *1
Ber. Things hid & bard (you meane) from cammon sense.	62

CAN *l.*37 98 122 141 468 *473 657 1032 1117 1188 *1189 1276 1373
1436 1443 1563 1566 1599 1644 1648 1716 1729 2126 2129 2140
2209 2248 2252 2254 2327 2359 *2433 = 29*3
CANARIE = *1
*the tongues ende, canarie to it with your feete, humour it	782

CANDLES = *1
Duma. Darke needes no Candles now, for darke is light.	1618

CANGENET = 1
accent. Let me superuise the cangenet.	1285

CANNON = 1*1
*thy established proclaymed Edict and continent Cannon: Which	260
He reputes me a Cannon, and the Bullet thats hee:	833

CANNOT = 10*6
Ber. I cannot stay thankes-giuing. *Exit.*	690
*instant: by hart you loue her, because your hart cannot come	810
that you cannot enioy her.	813
Where faire is not, praise cannot mend the brow.	992
Boy. And I cannot, cannot, cannot: and I cannot, an other |	
(can,	1116
Gainst whom the world cannot holde argument,	1394
Rosa. Then cannot we be bought: and so adue,	2130
Ber. I cannot giue you lesse.	2312
*You cannot beg vs sir, I can assure you sir, we know what	2433
Cannot picke out fiue such, take each one in his vaine.	2488
Bero. This cannot be *Hector.*	2598
It cannot be, it is impossible.	2817
Mirth cannot moue a soule in agonie.	2818

CANST *l.**318 1114 1115 = 2*1
CANUS = 1
Whose Clubb kilde Cerberus *that three headed* Canus,	2542

CANZONET *see* cangenet
CAP = 1
Thou makest the triumpherie, the corner cap of societie,	1385

CAPABLE = *1
*want no instruction: If their Daughters be capable, I will	1242

CAPACITIE = 1*1
Holo. God comfort thy capacitie, I say th'allusion holdes | in the	
Exchange.	1202
By light we loose light, your capacitie	2303

CAPERD = 1
The thirde he caperd and cryed, All goes well.	2005

CAPON = 1
Breake vp this Capon. | *Boyet* I am bound to serue.	1034

CAPP = 1
Bero. Whats her name in the capp? | *Boy. Katherin* by good happ.	709

CAPPE = 1
Bero. I and worne in the cappe of a Tooth-drawer:	2571

CAPS = 1
Ros. Well, better wits haue worne plaine statute Caps,	2202

CAPTIUATED = 1
*Enfreedoming thy person: thou wert emured, restrained, |
captiuated, bound.   890
CAPTIUE = *1
*victorie: On whose side? the King: the captiue is inricht, on   1055
CARE = 2*2
*care a pin, if the other three were in. Heere comes one with   1351
Kath. You waigh me not, O thats you care not for me.   1914
Ros. Great reason: for past care, is still past cure.   1915
Clow. We wil turne it finely off sir, we wil take some care.   2451
CARET = *1
*facilitie, and golden cadence of poesie *caret*: *Ouiddius*   1287
CARNATION = *1
Clow. Pray you sir, How much Carnation Ribbon may   911
CARREERE = 1
Boyet. Full merely hath this braue nuage, this carreere | bin run. 2421
CARRIAGE = 3*2
good reput, carriage bearing, and estimation.   267
*name more; and sweete my childe let them be men of good |
repute and carriage.   374
Boy. Sampson Maister, he was a man of good carriage,   376
*great carriage: for he carried the Towne-gates on his backe   377
And their rough carriage so rediculous,   2229
CARRIE = 1*1
Brag. Fetch hither the Swaine, he must carrie me a letter.   817
No drop but as a Coach doth carrie thee: 1366
CARRIED = *1
*great carriage: for he carried the Towne-gates on his backe   377
CARRIES = *1
*i.d. no, Ile giue you a remuneration: Why? it carries it
re-|muneration: 905
CARRY = 1
Some carry tale, some please-man, some sleight saine: 2402
CARUD-BONE = 1
Duma. The carud-bone face on a Flaske.   2568
CARUE = 2
Stand a side good bearer. *Boyet* you can carue,   1032
A can carue to, and lispe: Why this is hee   2248
CARYING = *1
*thee in my rapier, as much as thou didst me in carying gates.   380
CASE = 2
King. Come sir, you blush: as his, your case is such.   1468
Rosa. There, then, that Vizard, that superfluous case,   2316
CASES = 1
Rosa. They were all in lamentable cases,   2192
CAST = *1
*wench is cast away: shee's quicke, the childe bragges in her |
bellie already: tis yours.   2632
CATASTROPHE = *1
*whose side? the Beggers. The catastrophe is a Nuptiall, on   1056
CATCH = 1
For euery obiect that the one doth catch,   562
CATCHT = 1
Quee. None are so surely caught, when they are catcht,   1959
CAUDLE = 1
And where my Liedges? all about the brest. | A Caudle hou!   1510

CAUFE = *1
*not det: he clepeth a Calfe, Caufe: halfe, haufe: neighbour   1761
CAUGHT = 2
Quee. None are so surely caught, when they are catcht,   1959
They haue the Plague, and caught it of your eyes,   2354
CAUSE = 4*2
Before the Birdes haue any cause to sing?   112
Bero. Well sir, be it as the stile shall giue vs cause to clime | in
the merrines.   211
*Spaniards Rapier: The first and second cause will not serue   480
We can not crosse the cause why we were borne: 1566
So much I hate a breaking cause to be   2281
If for my Loue (as there is no such cause)   2752
CAUSER = 1
And studie too, the causer of your vow.   1661
CAUSES = 1
All causes to the purpose of his speede: 2699
CEDER = 1
Duma. As vpright as the Ceder.   1423
CELESTIALL = 2
Celestiall as thou art, Oh pardon loue this wrong,   1282
There stay vntill the twelue Celestiall Signes   2757
CELO = *1
*of *Celo* the skie, the welken the heauen, & anon falleth like   1155
CERBERUS = 1
Whose Clubb kilde Cerberus *that three headed* Canus,   2542
CERTAINE = 5*2
and as a certaine Father saith   1313
Peda. I do dine to day at the fathers of a certaine pupill of   1318
There is no certaine Princesse that appeares.   1493
King. What present hast thou there? | *Clow.* Some certaine
treason.   1529
*let that passe. By the world I recount no fable, some certaine   1838
Long. His Legge is too bigge for *Hectors.* | *Duman.* More Calfe
certaine.   2595
A man so breathed, that certaine he would fight; yea,   2608
CERTES = 1
Peda. And certes the text most infallibly concludes it.   1328
CHAINE = 1
The Chaine were longer, and the Letter short.   1946
CHALLENG = *1
Cl. Shes to hard for you at pricks, sir challeng her to bowle   1133
CHALLENGE = 5*1
Quee. When she shall challenge this, you wil reiect her.   2374
Duma. Hector will challenge him.   2646
Brag. By the North Pole I do challenge thee.   2649
Duma. You may not deny it, *Pompey* hath made the chal- | (lenge.   2661
Come challenge me, challenge me by these desertes: 2765
CHANCE = *1
Rosa. Since you are strangers, and come here by chance,   2120
CHANGE = 6*3
And change you Fauours two, so shall your Loues   2026
King. Then in our measure, do but vouchsafe one change,   2108
Not yet no daunce: thus change I like the Moone.   2111
Duman. Will you vouchsafe with me to change a word? | *Maria.*
Name it.   2147
Therefore change Fauours, and when they repaire,   2214

CHANGE *cont.*

The Ladies did change Fauours; and then wee   2407
*first shew thriue, these foure will change habites, and present |
the other fiue.   2481
If this Austere insociable life, | Change not your offer made in
heate of blood.   2759
Ile change my blacke Gowne for a faithfull frend.   2795
CHANGED = *1
*Ro. You tooke the moone at ful, but now shee's changed?   2114
CHANGING = 1
Kath. But in this changing, What is your intent?   2029
CHAPMENS = 1
Not vttred by base sale of chapmens tongues: 507
CHARGE = 1
That charge their breath against vs? Say scout say.   1980
CHARG-HOUSE = *1
*barbarous. Do you not educate youth at the Charg-house   1816
CHARITIE = 3
Long. Dumaine thy Loue is farre from charitie,   1464
For Charitie it selfe fulfilles the Law: 1715
And who can seuer Loue from Charitie.   1716
CHARLES = 1
For such a summe from speciall officers, | Of *Charles* his father.   658
CHAST = 1
Will you giue hornes chast Lady? do not so.   2168
CHAT = 1*1
King. Then leaue this chat, and good *Berowne* now proue   1633
King. If you denie to daunce, lets holde more chat.   2132
CHAUNCE = 1
And trauailing along this coast I heere am come by chaunce,   2502
CHEATE = 1
Some tricks, some quillets, how to cheate the diuell.   1637
CHECKE = 1
To checke their follie pashions solembe teares.   2010
CHEEKE = 3
Do meete as at a faire in her faire cheeke,   1584
That smyles, his cheeke in yeeres, and knowes the trick   2404
Bero. Saint *Georges* halfe cheeke in a Brooch.   2569
CHEEKES = 4
For blush-in cheekes by faultes are bred,   405
For still her cheekes possesse the same, | Which natiue she doth
owe   409
The night of dew that on my cheekes downe flowes.   1361
Ayre (quoth he) thy cheekes may blow,   1446
CHI *see* que
CHIDE = 1
You chide at him, offending twice as much.   1469
CHIDES = 1
That when he playes at Tables chides the Dice   2251
CHIEFE = 1
Are not you the chiefe woman? You are the thickest heere.   1027
CHILD = 1*2
Ar. Sweet inuocation of a child, most pretty & pathetical.   401
Bra. Warble child, make passionate my sense of hearing. | *Boy.*
Concolinel.   772
Ber. Stoope I say, her shoulder is with child.   1424

CHILDE = 3*5
    This childe of Fancie that *Armado* hight,   181
    Ferd. With a childe of our Grandmother Eue, *a female; or for thy*   263
    *name more; and sweete my childe let them be men of good | repute and carriage.   374
    *the parentes of the foresaid childe or pupill, vndertake your   1321
    *Page. Offerd by a childe to an old man: which is wit-old.   1798
    And when he was a babe, a childe, a shrimpe,   2543
    *wench is cast away: shee's quicke, the childe bragges in her | bellie already: tis yours.   2632
    All wanton as a childe, skipping and vaine.   2719
CHIMNIE-SWEEPERS = 1
    Duma. To looke like her are Chimnie-sweepers blake.   1615
CHIRRA = 2
    Brag. Chirra. | *Peda. Quari* Chirra, not Sirra?   1772
CHOAKE = 1
    Rosal. Why thats the way to choake a gibing spirrit,   2819
CHOLER *see* coller
CHOOSE = *1
    Rosa. If we choose by the hornes, your selfe come not   1102
CHOSE = 1*1
    Haue chose as vmpier of their mutenie.   180
    *well culd, chose, sweete, & apt I do assure you sir, I do assure.   1827
CHOYCE = 1
    Curat. A most singuler and choyce Epithat, | *Draw-out his Table-booke.*   1754
CHRISTAL = 1
    One her haires were Golde, Christal the others eyes.   1479
CHRISTALL = 1
    As Iewels in Christall for some Prince to buy.   747
CHRISTMAS = 2
    At Christmas I no more desire a Rose,   114
    To dash it lik a Christmas Comedie: 2401
CHUCK = *1
    *(sweete chuck) with some delightfull ostentation, or show,   1844
CHUCKS = 1
    Sweete chucks beat not the bones of the buried: 2618
CIPHER *see* cypher
CITA = *1
    *about your Infamie *vnu(m) cita* a gigge of a Cuckolds horne.   1805
CITTERNE *see* cytterne
CIUILL = 1
    This ciuill warre of wittes were much better vsed   730
CL = *1
CLAMOURS = 1
    Deaft with the clamours of their owne deare grones,   2825
CLAPT = 1
    With that all laught, and clapt him on the shoulder,   1999
CLAW = *1
    Dull. If a talent be a claw, looke how he clawes him | with a talent.   1228
CLAWES = *1
    Dull. If a talent be a claw, looke how he clawes him | with a talent.   1228
CLEANE = 1
    King. I thinke *Hector* was not so cleane timberd.   2594

CLEAUING = 1
Clo. Then will she get the vpshoot by cleauing the is in.   1129
CLEPETH = *1
*not det: he clepeth a Calfe, Caufe: halfe, haufe: neighbour   1761
CLIME = *1
Bero. Well sir, be it as the stile shall giue vs cause to clime | in
the merrines.   211
CLIPT = 1
Dum. Iudas Machabeus *clipt, is plaine* Iudas.   2552
CLO = 10*14
CLOAKE = 1
A woman that is like a Iermane Cloake,   956
CLOCKS = 1
And merrie Larkes are Ploughmens Clocks: 2870
CLOSE = 2*1
I thought to close mine eyes some halfe an houre: 1982
*Your Lion that holdes his Polax sitting on a close stoole,   2530
The sodaine hand of death close vp mine eye.   2775
CLOSELY = 1
I haue been closely shrowded in this bush,   1474
CLOTH = *1
*you will be scrapt out of the painted cloth for this.   2529
CLOUDE = 2
Ber. Worthies away, the Scaene begins to cloude.   2679
Let not the cloude of Sorrow iustle it   2706
CLOUDED = 1
Rosa. My face is but a Moone, and clouded too.   2102
CLOUDES = 4
King. Blessed are cloudes, to do as such cloudes do.   2103
(Those cloudes remooued) vpon our waterie eyne.   2105
Are Angels varling cloudes, or Roses blowne.   2220
CLOUEN = 1
Long. Stucke with Cloues. | *Dum.* No clouen.   2604
CLOUES = 1
Long. Stucke with Cloues. | *Dum.* No clouen.   2604
CLOUT = *1
Clo. Indeed a'must shoot nearer, or hele neare hit the clout.   1125
CLOW = 23*25
CLOWN = *2
CLOWNE see also Cl., Clo., Clow., Clown. = 7*2
Enter *Clowne, Constable,* and *Wench.*   430
Enter *Page* and *Clowne.*   840
Enter Clowne.   1016
Clo. By my soule a Swaine, a most simple Clowne.   1137
Enter Iaquenetta and the Clowne.   1245
*Well, she hath one a'my Sonnets already, the Clowne bore   1348
*it, the Foole sent it, and the Lady hath it: sweete Clowne,   1349
Iaqu. God blesse the King. *Enter Iaquenetta and Clowne.*   1528
Enter Clowne.   2424
CLOWNE = 2*1
CLUB = *1
*that worthies thumbe, he is not so big as the end of his Club.   1864
CLUBB = 1*1
*hard for *Hercules* Clubb, and therefore too much oddes for a   479
Whose Clubb kilde Cerberus *that three headed* Canus,   2542
CLYMBE = 1
Clymbe ore the house to vnlocke the little gate.   118

CLYMING = 1
Still clyming trees in the *Hesperides*.   1692
COACH = 1
No drop but as a Coach doth carrie thee: 1366
COAST = 1
And trauailing along this coast I heere am come by chaunce,   2502
COATE = 1
His faces owne margent did coate such amazes,   750
COCKELL = 1
Ber. Alone alone sowed Cockell, reapt no Corne,   1734
COCKLED = 1
Then are the tender hornes of Cockled Snayles.   1689
COCTUS = *1
Holo. Twice sodd simplicitie, bis coctus, O thou monster   1172
CODPEECES = 1
Dread Prince of Placcats, King of Codpeeces.   950
COFFING = 1
And coffing drownes the Parsons saw;   2889
COGG = 1
Quee. Seuenth sweete adue, since you can cogg,   2140
COLLER = 1
Lon. Nay my coller is ended. She is a most sweet Ladie. | *Exit*
Longauil.   705
COLLIERS = 1
Long. And since her time are Colliers counted bright.   1616
COLLUSION = *1
Dul. Tis true in deede, the Collusion holdes in the Ex- | (change.   1200
COLOUR = *2
Arm. Greene in deede is the colour of Louers: but to   391
*haue a loue of that colour, mee thinkes *Sampson* had small   392
COLOURABLE = *1
Ped. Sir tell not mee of the Father, I do feare colourable   1314
COLOURD = 1
Ber. An amber colourd Rauen was well noted.   1422
COLOURED = *2
Ferd. So it is besedged with sable coloured melancholie, I did
ebon coloured Incke, which here thou viewest, beholdest, suruayest,
or   252
COLOURES = 1*1
And weare his coloures like a Tumblers hoope.   954
*coloures. But to returne to the Verses, Did they please you | sir
Nathaniel?   1315
COLOURS = 2
Boy. Most maculate thoughts Maister, are maskt vnder | such
colours.   396
For feare their colours should be washt away.   1620
COLT = *1
Boy. No Maister, the Hobbi-horse is but a colt, and your   800
COLUMBINE *see* Cullambine
COMBAT = 1*1
*you not see, *Pompey* is vncasing for the Combat: What   2657
Brag. Gentlemen and Souldiers, pardon me, I will not | combat
in my shyrt.   2659
COME = 25*16
Ber. Item, That no woman shall come within a myle of   128
These othes and lawes will proue an idle scorne. | Surra, Come
on.   304

COME *cont.*

Clo. Come *Iaquenetta*, away. *Exeunt.*	448
Boy. Come you transgressing slaue, away.	457
It should none spare, that come within his power.	˙543
Boyet. So please your Grace, the packet is not come,	661
You may not come (faire Princesse) within my gates,	669
Prin. Come, to our Pauilion, *Boyet* is disposde.	754
*instant: by hart you loue her, because your hart cannot come	810
Ar. Some enigma, some riddle, come, thy *Lenuoy* begin.	843
Ar. Come hither, come hither: How did this argument | (begin?	869
Clow. I will come to your worship to morrow morning.	926
But come, the Bow: Now Mercie goes to kill,	999
King. Why did he come? to see. Why did he see? to ouer-|come.	1051
Quee. Thou hast mistaken his letter. Come Lords away.	1090
Rosa. If we choose by the hornes, your selfe come not	1102
Rosa. Shall I come vpon thee with an olde saying, that	1108
Ma. Come come, you talke greasely, your lips grow fowle.	1131
King. Come sir, you blush: as his, your case is such.	1468
Ber. Your Mistresses dare neuer come in raine,	1619
Yf Fayrings come thus plentifully in.	1889
Cried *via* we will doo't come what wil come.	2004
Quee. But what, but what, come they to visite vs?	2011
Rosa. Come on then, weare the Fauours most in sight.	2028
Boy. The Trompet soundes, be maskt, the maskers come.	2049
Boy. If to come hither, you haue measurde miles,	2089
Kin. Wil you not daunce? How come you thus estranged?	2112
Rosa. Since you are strangers, and come here by chance,	2120
Nor neuer come in vizard to my friend,	2336
Whether the three Worthis shall come in or no?	2427
King. I say they shall not come.	2458
And trauailing along this coast I heere am come by chaunce,	2502
Ergo, *I come with this Appologie.*	2546
Duma. Though my mockes come home by me, I will | now be merrie.	2590
Come challenge me, challenge me by these desertes:	2765
Come when the King doth to my Lady come:	2789
King. Come sir, it wants a tweluemonth an'aday, | And then twill ende.	2838

COMEDIE = 2

To dash it lik a Christmas Comedie:	2401
Might well haue made our sport a Comedie.	2837

COMES = 11 *3

For well you know here comes in Embassaie,	144
Or vainely comes th'admired Princesse hither.	150
Lord. Heere comes *Boyet. Enter Boyet.*	572
Like one that comes heere to besiedge his Court,	580
Bo. Heere comes *Nauar.*	584
The Princesse comes to hunt here in the Parke,	929
Boyet. Here comes a member of the common wealth.	1017
*When it comes so smoothly off, so obscenly as it were, so fit.	1140
*care a pin, if the other three were in. Heere comes one with	1351
Sweete leaues shade follie. Who is he comes heere?	1375
Berow. Why he comes in like a periure, wearing papers.	1380
Quee. Heere comes *Boyet*, and myrth is in his face.	1970
Bero. See where it comes. Behauiour what wert thou?	2263
Ber. Hide thy head *Achilles*, here comes *Hector* in Armes.	2588

COMFORT = *3

*I should outsweare *Cupid.* Comfort mee Boy, what great   370
Holo. God comfort thy capacitie, I say th'allusion holdes | in the
Exchange.   1202
Ber. I could put thee in comfort, not by two that I know,   1384
COMISERATION = *1

*truer then trueth it selfe: haue comiseration on thy   1044
COMMANDE = *1

*for so witnesseth thy lowlines. Shall I commande thy   1059
COMMANDER = *2

Curat. *When in the world I liud, I was the worldes commander:*   2512
Cura. *When in the worlde I liued, I was the worldes commander.*   2522
COMMAUND = *1

*assistants the Kinges commaund, and this most gallant
il-|lustrate   1853
COMMAUNDE = *1

Boyet. Gone to her Tent. Please it your Maiestie com-|maunde   2236
COMMEND = 3

Ber. Ladie I will commend you to my none hart.   677
And to her white hand see thou do commend   933
Well learned is that tongue, that well can thee commend.   1276
COMMENDATIONS = *1

Ros. Pray you, do my commendations, I would be glad | to see
it.   678
COMMENDE = *1

*commende the blacke oppressing humour to the most holsome
phisicke   243
COMMENDES = 1

Const. Signeour *Arme Arme* commendes you: 199
COMMING = 3*1

Vouchsafe to read the purpose of my comming,   604
Sea sicke I thinke comming from *Muscouie.*   2325
*are Worthies a comming will speake their minde in some | other
sort. *Exit Curat.*   2537
Excuse me so comming too short of thankes,   2696
COMMIXTURE = 1

Dismaskt, their dammaske sweete commixture showne,   2219
COMMON *see also* cammon = 4

When Mistresses from common sense are hid.   69
My lippes are no Common, though seuerall they be.   726
Boyet. Here comes a member of the common wealth.   1017
*Daughters profite very greatly vnder you: you are a good |
member of the common wealth.   1239
COMMONWEALTH *see* common

COMON = 1

Bero. Com'on then, I will sweare to study so,   64
COMPANIE = 3

Ar. I say sing. | *Boy.* Forbeare till this companie be past.   428
Long. By whom shall I send this (companie?) Stay.   1411
I am betrayed by keeping companie   1517
COMPANION = *1

*conuerse this quondam day with a companion of the kings,   1745
COMPANIONS = 1*1

*phantasims, such insociable and poynt deuise companions,   1758
The King and his companions warely,   1985
COMPANY = 1*1

King. Prise you your selues: What buyes your company?   2127

COMPANY *cont.*
To haue one show worse then the Kings and his company. 2456
COMPARDE = 1
I am comparde to twentie thousand fairs. 1925
COMPARISON = *1·
*I am the King (for so standes the comparison) thou the Beg-|ger, 1058
COMPARISONS = 1
Full of comparisons and wounding floutes: 2805
COMPETTITOURS = 1
And he and his compettitours in oth, | Were all addrest to meete you gentle Lady 576
COMPILE = 1
Did neuer Sonnet for her sake compile, 1471
COMPILED = *1
*that the two Learned men haue compiled, in prayse of the 2849
COMPLAINE = 1
Let vs complaine to them what fooles were heare, 2225
COMPLEAT = *1
*Arma. I confesse both, they are both the varnish of a com-|pleat man. 351
COMPLEMENT = *1
*concerne much: stay not thy complement, I forgiue thy | dewtie, adue. 1307
COMPLEMENTES = *1
*tune, but a snip and away: these are complementes, these 790
COMPLEMENTS = 1*1
A man of complements whom right and wrong 179
*hir to tryall. Thine in all complements of deuoted and hartburning 272
COMPLET = 1*1
A Maide of grace and complet maiestie, | About surrender vp of Aquitaine, 146
*Boy. No my complet Maister, but to Iigge off a tune at 781
COMPLEXION = 3
Boy. A Woman, Maister. | Arm. Of what complexion? 383
Arm. Tell me precisely of what complexion? | Boy. Of the sea-water Greene sir. 387
King. And Aethiops of their sweete complexion crake. 1617
COMPLEXIONS = 2
Arm. Is that one of the foure complexions? 389
Of all complexions the culd soueraigntie, 1583
COMPREHEND = *1
*Where all those pleasures liue, that Art would comprehend. 1273
COMPYLED = 1
A hudge translation of hipocrisie, | Vildly compyled, profound simplicitie. 1941
COMS = 1*1
*Kin. The Ship is vnder sayle, and heere she coms amaine. 2489
And Milke coms frozen home in paile: 2882
CONCEAUE = 1
Quee. Faire in all Haile is foule, as I conceaue. 2266
CONCEIT = 1*1
*Nath. Of persing a Hogshead, a good luster of conceit 1251
Cut me to peeces with thy keene conceit. 2331
CONCEITES = 2
Which his fayre tongue (conceites expositer) 564
Seemeth their conference, their conceites haue winges, 2176

CONCERNE = *1
  *concerne much: stay not thy complement, I forgiue thy | dewtie,
  adue. 1307
CONCERNING = 1*1
  Clow. The matter is to me sir, as concerning *Iaquenetta*: 213
  *Sir *Holofernes*, as concerning some entertainement of time, 1851
CONCLUDES = 2
  Peda. And certes the text most infallibly concludes it. 1328
  Pag. The Sheepe, the other two concludes it o u. 1794
CONCLUSION = 1*1
  *Begger. Who ouercame he? the Begger. The conclusion is 1054
  Quee. Beautious as Incke: a good conclusion. 1929
CONCOLINEL = 1
  * *Bra.* Warble child, make passionate my sense of hearing. | *Boy.*
  Concolinel. 772
COND = 1
  That well by hart hath cond his embassage 1990
CONDIGNE = 1
  Arma. In thy condigne praise. 336
CONDITION = 1
  Kath. A light condition in a beautie darke. 1907
CONDUCT = 2
  Prin. I wilbe welcome then, Conduct me thither. 591
  Ber. First from the Parke let vs conduct them thither, 1725
CONFERENCE = 2
  Importuous personall conference with his grace. 523
  Seemeth their conference, their conceites haue winges, 2176
CONFESSE = 6*2
  Clo. Sir I confesse the Wench. 279
  Clo. I do confesse much of the hearing it, but little of the |
  marking of it. 281
  * *Arma.* I confesse both, they are both the varnish of a com-|pleat
  man. 351
  * *Arm.* I will hereupon confesse I am in loue: and as it is 363
  In so vnseeming to confesse receit, 651
  Guiltie my Lord, guiltie: I confesse, I confesse. 1550
  Duman. Let vs confesse and turne it to a iest. 2320
CONFESSION = 1
  Quee. The fairest is confession. 2366
CONFIDENT = 1
  Yet confident Ile keepe what I haue sworne, 123
CONFIRME = 1
  Rosal. By heauen you did; and to confirme it plaine, 2391
CONFLICT = 1
  In conflict that you get the Sunne of them. 1720
CONFOUND = 1
  Bruse me with scorne, confound me with a flout. 2329
CONFOUNDED = 1
  Their forme confounded, makes most forme in myrth, 2463
CONFRONTED = 1
  We foure in deede confronted were with foure, 2294
CONGRATULATE = *1
  *to congratulate the Princesse at her Pauilion, in the *posteriors* 1822
CONGRUENT = *2
  * *Arm.* I spoke it tender iuuenal, as a congruent apethaton 324
  *congruent, and measurable for the after noone: the worde is 1826

CONQUERING = 1
By East, West, North, and South, I spred my conquering might: 2514
CONQUEROR = *1
*Qu. The conqueror is dismaid: proceed good *Alexander.* 2520
CONQUEROUR = *3
*Bero. Take away the Conquerour, take away *Alisander.* 2527
*Clow. O sir, you haue ouerthrowne *Alisander* the Conque-|rour: 2528
**will be geuen to *Aiax.* He wilbe the ninth Worthie: a
Con-|querour, 2531
CONQUEROURS = 1
Therefore braue Conquerours, for so you are, 12
CONSCIENCE = 1
*Nat. Very reuerent sport truly, and done in the testimonie | of a
good conscience. 1151
CONSCIENCES = 1
And consciences that will not die in debt, 2258
CONSENT = 1
I see the tricke ant: here was a consent, 2399
CONSIDER = 2
Consider who the King your father sendes: 493
Consider what you first did sweare vnto: 1641
CONSONANT = 1
Peda. Quis quis thou Consonant? 1790
CONSORT = *1
*Pri. Sweete health and faire desires consort your grace. 675
CONSORTED = *1
*hight Costard, (*Clow.* O mee) *sorted and consorted contrary to* 259
CONST = 1*1
CONSTAB = 1*1
CONSTABLE see also Const., Constab. = 3
Enter a Constable with Costard with a letter. 192
Enter *Clowne, Constable,* and *Wench.* 430
*A verie Bedell to a humerous sigh, a Critick, nay a night-|watch
Constable, 941
CONSTURE = 1
King. Consture my speaches better, if you may. 2267
CONTAINE = 1
That shew, containe, and nourish all the worlde. 1704
CONTEMPLATION = 1
In leaden contemplation haue found out 1672
CONTEMPLATYUE = 1
Still and contemplatyue in lyuing art. 18
CONTEMPT = 1
Boy. Why that contempt will kill the speakers hart, 2041
CONTEMPTS = 1
Clowne. Sir the Contempts thereof are as touching me. 201
CONTENT = 1
Where zeale striues to content, and the contentes 2461
CONTENTES = 1*1
*Vnder pardon sir, What are the contentes? or rather as *Hor-|race* 1262
Where zeale striues to content, and the contentes 2461
CONTINENT = 1*1
*thy established proclaymed Edict and continent Cannon: Which 260
Rosa. Shall I teach you to know. | *Boy.* I my continent of beautie. 1094
CONTINUALL = 1
Small haue continuall plodders euer wonne, 91

CONTINUE = 1
Will heare your idle scornes; continue then, 2826
CONTRARIE = 1*1
*Boy. He speakes the meer contrarie, crosses loue not him. 344
Woo contrarie, deceyued by these remoues. 2027
CONTRARY = *1
*hight Costard, (Clow. O mee) sorted and consorted contrary to 259
CONUERSE = 2*1
*conuerse this quondam day with a companion of the kings, 1745
In the conuerse of breath (your gentlenes 2693
Visite the speachlesse sicke, and still conuerse, 2812
CONUINCE = 1
The holy suite which faine it would conuince, 2704
COOLE = 1
Boy. Vnder the coole shade of a Siccamore, 1981
COPHETUA = *1
*King Cophetua set eie vpon the pernicious and indubitate 1046
COPPER = 1
If so our Copper byes no better treasure. 1737
COPPICE = 1
Forr. Heereby vpon the edge of yonder Coppice, 983
COPPIE = 1
Kath. Faire as a text B in a Coppie booke. 1930
CORMORANT = 1
When spight of cormorant deuouring Time, 8
CORNE = 1*1
*Lon. He weedes the corne, & still lets grow the weeding. 101
Ber. Alone alone sowed Cockell, reapt no Corne, 1734
CORNER = 1*1
*East from the West corner of thy curious knotted garden; There 254
Thou makest the triumpherie, the corner cap of societie, 1385
CORPORALL = 2
And I to be a Corporall of his fielde, 953
Ber. By earth she is not, corporall, there you ly. 1420
CORRECTION = 1*2
*Clow. As it shall follow in my correction, and God defend | the
right. 224
Clow. Not so sir, vnder correction sir, I hope it is not so. 2432
*Clow. Vnder correction sir we know where-vntill it doth |
amount. 2436
COST = 5*1
COSTARD see also Cost. = 12*4
Lon. Costard the swaine and he, shalbe our sport, 190
Enter a Constable with Costard with a letter. 192
*hight Costard, (Clow. O mee) sorted and consorted contrary to 259
with the rational hinde Costard: she deserues well. 422
*Constab. Sir, the Dukes pleasure is that you keepe Costard 431
*Pag. A wonder Maister, Heers a Costard broken in a shin. 841
Boy. By saying that a Costard was broken in a shin. 871
Ar. But tel me, How was there a Costard broken in a shin? 877
I Costard running out, that was safely within, 882
Arm. Sirra Costard, I will infranchise thee. 886
Pag. Like the sequell I. Signeur Costard adew. Exit. 899
Ber. O my good knaue Costard, exceedingly well met. 910
*it was geuen me by Costard, and sent me from Don Armatho: 1255
Mayd. Good Costard go with me: sir God saue your life. 1309
King. Where hadst thou it? | Iaqu. Of Costard. 1538

COSTARD cont.
 Bero. Pompey the great. | *Clow.* Your seruant and *Costard.*   2525
COSTART = 1
 Cost. Not a worde of *Costart* yet. | *Ferd. So it is*   234
COTE = 1
 Long. So did our lookes. | *Rosa.* We did not cote them so.   2744
COTED = 2
 Duma. Her Amber heires for foule hath amber coted.   1421
 Which partie coted presence of loose loue   2724
COUCHES = 1
 Your eyes do make no couches in your teares.   1492
COUERS = 1
 Kath. Faire fall the face it couers.   620
COULD *l.*1268 *1384 2701 = 2*1
COULDE = *1
 *loue? I may. Shall I enforce thy loue? I coulde. Shall I en-|treate   1060
COUNSAILE = 2
 This seald-vp counsaile. Ther's thy guerdon: goe.   934
 And in our mayden counsaile rated them,   2737
COUNSAILES = 1
 Their seuerall counsailes they vnboosome shall,   2033
COUNTED = 3
 Then you much willing to be counted wise,   509
 For natiue blood is counted paynting now: 1612
 Long. And since her time are Colliers counted bright.   1616
COUNTENANCE = 3
 Pedan. I will not be put out of countenance. | *Bero.* Because thou
 hast no face.   2560
 And now forward, for we haue put thee in countenance.   2572
 Peda. You haue put me out of countenance.   2573
COUNTNANCE = 1
 This pert *Berowne* was out of countnance quite.   2191
COUNTREY = *2
 *I do loue, that Countrey girle that I tooke in the Parke   421
 *significant to the countrey Maide *Iaquenetta*: there is
 remu-|neration,   896
COUPPLEMENT *see* cupplement
COURSE = 1
 Therefore to's seemeth it a needfull course,   516
COURSES = 1
 Courses as swift as thought in euery power,   1681
COURSING = 1
 I am coursing my selfe.   1335
COURT = 13*2
 Our Court shalbe a lytlle Achademe,   17
 And stay heere in your Court for three yeeres space.   56
 my Court. Hath this bin proclaymed?   129
 shame as the rest of the Court can possible deuise.   141
 Ferd. I that there is, our Court you know is haunted   173
 No Woman may approch his silent Court: 515
 Like one that comes heere to besiedge his Court,   580
 Nauar. Faire Princesse, Welcome to the court of *Nauar.*   585
 *not yet: the roofe of this Court is too high to be yours, and   587
 Nau. You shalbe welcome Madame to my Court.   590
 To the court of his eye, peeping thorough desier.   739
 **Boy.* This *Armado* is a *Spaniard* that keepes here in court,   1079
 Their purpose is to parlee, to court, and daunce,   2014

COURT *cont.*
And then the King will court thee for his Deare: 2023
To leade you to our Court, vouchsafe it then. 2270
COURTECIE = 2
Forbid the smyling courtecie of Loue, 2703
At courtshyp pleasant iest and courtecie, 2738
COURTESIE *see also* curtesie = 1
Iacke hath not Gill: these Ladies courtesie 2836
COURTIER = *1
*Desire prisoner, and ransome him to anie French Courtier 367
COURTISIE = 1
That kist his hand, a way in courtisie. 2249
COURTSHIP = 1
Trim gallants, full of Courtship and of state. 2290
COURTSHYP = 1
At courtshyp pleasant iest and courtecie, 2738
COWARDES = 1
Or hide your heades like Cowardes, and flie hence. 1978
COXCOMBE = 1
Berow. O most prophane coxcombe. 1418
COYNE = 1
Long. The face of an olde Roman coyne, scarce seene. 2566
CRAB = 1
a Crab on the face of *Terra*, the soyle, the land, the earth. 1156
CRABBS = 1
When roasted Crabbs hisse in the bowle, 2892
CRACKE = 1
My loue to thee is sound, *sance* cracke or flaw. 2347
CRADLES = 1
And giues the Crutch the Cradles infancie. 1594
CRAKE = 1
King. And *Aethiops* of their sweete complexion crake. 1617
CRAMBD = 1
As would be crambd vp in a sheete of paper 1894
CRAUE = 1
acquainted you withall, to the ende to craue your assistance. 1848
CRAUING = 1
On serious busines crauing quicke dispatch, 522
CREDITE = 1
Thus will I saue my Credite in the shoote, 1001
CREDO = 3*1
Holo. Sir *Nathaniel*, haud credo. 1161
Dul. Twas not a *haud credo*, twas a Pricket. 1162
to insert again my *haud credo* for a Deare. 1168
**Dul.* I said the Deare was not a *haud credo*, twas a Pricket. 1170
CREST = 1
And beauties crest becomes the heauens well. 1605
CRIE = 1
Mar. Bleat softly then, the Butcher heares you crie. 2171
CRIED = 1
Cried *via* we will doo't come what wil come. 2004
CRIMES = 1
Glorie growes guyltie of detested crimes, 1006
CRITICK = *1
*A verie Bedell to a humerous sigh, a Critick, nay a night-|watch
Constable, 941

CRITTICK = 1
And *Crittick Tymon* laugh at idle toyes.   1507
CROSSE = 2
   We can not crosse the cause why we were borne: 1566
   Quee. The effect of my intent is to crosse theirs: 2030
CROSSES = *1
   Boy. He speakes the meer contrarie, crosses loue not him.   344
CROST = 1*1
   Boy. I am answerd sir. | *Arma.* I loue not to be crost.   342
   *your eyes, with your armes crost on your thinbellies doblet   787
CROWNE = *1
   *Why? it is a fayrer name then French-Crowne.   906
CROWNES = 3
   The payment of a hundred thousand Crownes,   625
   A hundred thousand Crownes, and not demaunds   639
   One paiment of a hundred thousand Crownes,   640
CRUSSHEST = *1
   *you may cry, Well done *Hercules,* now thou crusshest the   1870
CRUTCH = 1
   And giues the Crutch the Cradles infancie.   1594
CRY = *1
   *you may cry, Well done *Hercules,* now thou crusshest the   1870
CRYED = 1
   The thirde he caperd and cryed, All goes well.   2005
CRYES = 1
   Ay mee sayes one! O *Ioue* the other cryes!   1478
CUCKOLDS = *1
   *about your Infamie *vnu(m) cita* a gigge of a Cuckolds horne.   1805
CUCKOW = 9*1
   *Owle and the Cuckow? it should haue followed in the   2850
   *This *Ver,* the Spring: The one maynteined by the Owle, | th'other
    by the Cuckow.   2856
   The Cuckow then on euerie tree,   2864
   Mocks married men; for thus singes hee, | Cuckow.   2865
   Cuckow, Cuckow: O word of feare, | Vnpleasing to a married
   ear.   2867
   The Cuckow then on euerie tree,   2873
   Mockes married men, for thus singes he, | Cuckow.   2874
   Cuckow, cuckow: O word of feare,   2876
CUCKOW-BUDDS = 1
   And Cuckow-budds of yellow hew: 2861
CULD = 1*1
   Of all complexions the culd soueraigntie,   1583
   *well culd, chose, sweete, & apt I do assure you sir, I do assure.   1827
CULLAMBINE = 1
   I am that Flower. | *Dum.* That Mint. | *Long.* That Cullambine.   2610
CUNNING = 1
   To sell a bargaine well is as cunning as fast and loose: 867
CUP = *1
   *welcome the sower Cup of prosperitie, affliccio(n) may one day   308
CUPID = 4*2
   *I should outsweare *Cupid.* Comfort mee Boy, what great   370
   This signior *Iunios* gyant dwarffe, dan *Cupid,*   946
   That *Cupid* will impose for my neglect,   968
   Be. Shot by heauen, proceed sweet *Cupid,* thou hast thumpt   1355
   King. Saint *Cupid* then and Souldiers to the fielde.   1717
   Quee. Saint *Dennis* to S.(aint) *Cupid*: What are they,   1979

CUPIDS = 2*2
*seduced, and he had a very good wit. *Cupids* Butshaft is too   478
Lad. 2. He is *Cupids* Graundfather, and learnes newes | of him.   760
Ber. O Rimes are gardes on wanton *Cupids* hose, | Disfigure not
his Shop.   1390
That he was faine to seale on *Cupids* name.   1896
CUPPLEMENT = 1
*to *Fortuna delaguar*, I wish you the peace of mind most royall |
cupplement. *Exit.*   2475
CURA = *1
**Cura*. When in the worlde I liued, I was the worldes commander.*   2522
CURAT = 2
Enter the Pedant, the Curat, and Dull.   1739
*are Worthies a comming will speake their minde in some | other
sort. *Exit Curat.*   2537
CURAT = 3*3
CURATE see also Curat., Curat.Nath. = 1*2
*that the Curate and your sweete selfe, are good at such
erup-|tions,   1846
*parish Curate *Alexander, Armadoes* Page *Hercules*, the Pe-|dant   2479
Enter Curate for Alexander.   2511
CURATNATH = *1
CURE = 1
Ros. Great reason: for past care, is still past cure.   1915
CURES = 1
Thy grace being gainde, cures all disgrace in mee.   1400
CURIOUS = *1
**East from the West corner of thy curious knotted garden; There*   254
CURSIE = *1
*for a new deuisde cursie. I thinke scorne to sigh, mee thinks   368
CURST = 1
Boy. Do not curst wiues hold that selfe-soueraigntie   1011
CURTESIE = 1*1
*curtesie. I beseech thee apparrell thy head: and among other   1832
My Ladie (to the maner of the dayes) | In curtesie giues
vndeseruing praise.   2292
CURTSIE = 1
Curtsie sweete hartes, and so the Measure endes.   2124
CUT = 2
Whose edge hath power to cut whose will still wils,   542
Cut me to peeces with thy keene conceit.   2331
CUTTING = 1
Cutting a smaller haire then may be seene,   2174
CYPHER = 1
Arm. A most fine Figure. | *Boy.* To proue you a Cypher.   361
CYTTERNE = 1
Pedan. What is this? | *Boyet.* A Cytterne head.   2562
DAINTIE = 3
Armatho ath toothen side, o a most daintie man,   1142
Her feete were much too daintie for such tread.   1628
Loues tongue proues daintie, *Bachus* grosse in taste,   1690
DAINTIES = *1
**Nath.* Sir he hath neuer fed of the dainties that are bred | in a
booke.   1174
DALLIE = *1
*my poore shoulder, and with his royall finger thus dallie   1836

DAMES = *1
   *Page. A holy parcell of the fayrest dames that euer turnd their |
   backes to mortall viewes.   2055
DAMMASKE = 1
   Dismaskt, their dammaske sweete commixture showne,   2219
DAMOSELLA = *1
   *the Ape his keeper, the tyred Horse his rider: But Damosella   1291
DAMSEL see also Demsel = 2
   Fer. Well, it was proclaimed Damsel.   287
   Clo. This was no Damsel neither sir, she was a Virgin.   288
DAMSELL = *1
   *but a' must fast three dayes a weeke: for this Damsell   433
DAN = 1
   This signior Iunios gyant dwarffe, dan Cupid,   946
DANCE = 4
   Berowne. Did not I dance with you in Brabant once?   609
   Kather. Did not I dance with you in Brabant once? | Ber. I know
   you did.   610
   the Taber to the worthies, and let them dance the hey.   1885
   Ros. But shall we dance, if they desire vs toot?   2037
DANGEROUS = 1*1
   A dangerous law against gentletie.   138
   *A dangerous rime maister against the reason of white & red.   411
DARE = 2
   Ber. Your Mistresses dare neuer come in raine,   1619
   I dare not call them fooles; but this I thinke,   2298
DARES = 2
   Clow. Be to me, and euerie man that dares not fight. | Ferd. No
   wordes.   239
   Dares looke vpon the heauen of her brow,   1576
DARKE = 4*4
   And make a darke nyght too of halfe the day: 49
   Your light growes darke by loosing of your eyes.   84
   *Duma. Darke needes no Candles now, for darke is light.   1618
   *Ros. Whats your darke meaning mouce, of this light word?   1905
   Kath. A light condition in a beautie darke.   1907
   Ros. Looke what you do, you do it still i'th darke.   1911
   *Boyet. A light for Mounsier Iudas, it growes darke, he | may
   stumble.   2583
DARKLY = 1
   Therefore Ile darkly ende the argument.   1910
DARKNES = 1
   So ere you finde where light in darknes lyes,   83
DART = 1
   Heere stand I, Ladie dart thy skill at me,   2328
DASH = 1
   To dash it lik a Christmas Comedie: 2401
DASHT = *1
   *honest man; looke you, and soone dasht. He is a marueylous   2534
DASIES = 1
   The Song. | When Dasies pied, and Violets blew,   2859
DAUGHTER = 4
   The French kinges daughter with your selfe to speake: 145
   Tell him, the Daughter of the King of France   521
   Lon. Pray you sir, Whose daughter?   700
   You were best call it Daughter beamed eyes.   2068

DAUGHTERS = *2
   *Daughters profite very greatly vnder you: you are a good |
   member of the common wealth.   1239
   *want no instruction: If their Daughters be capable, I will   1242
DAUNCE = 5*2
   *Dull. Ile make one in a daunce, or so: or I will play on   1884
   Their purpose is to parlee, to court, and daunce,   2014
   Not yet no daunce: thus change I like the Moone.   2111
   *Kin. Wil you not daunce? How come you thus estranged?   2112
   Weele not be nice, take handes, we will not daunce.   2121
   King. If you denie to daunce, lets holde more chat.   2132
   And I will wish thee neuer more to daunce,   2332
DAUNCES = 1
   For Reuels, Daunces, Maskes, and merrie houres,   1730
DAUNCING = 1
   wordes, the dauncing Horse will tell you.   360
DAWES = 1
   When Turtles tread and Rookes and Dawes,   2871
DAY see also aday = 19*7
   And one day in a weeke to touch no foode: 43
   And but one meale on euery day beside: 44
   And not be seene to wincke of all the day.   47
   And make a darke nyght too of halfe the day: 49
   And bide the pennance of each three yeeres day.   124
   *welcome the sower Cup of prosperitie, affliccio(n) may one day   308
   *I must keepe her at the Parke, she is alowde for the Day |
   womand. Fare you well.   434
   Ber. What time a day? | Kath. The houre that fooles should aske. 617
   Well Lords, to day we shall haue our dispatch,   979
   Here sweete, put vp this, twilbe thine annother day.   1091
   *Peda. I do dine to day at the fathers of a certaine pupill of 1318
   Duma. As faire as day.   1425
   On a day, alacke the day: 1438
   O, but for my Loue, day would turne to night,   1582
   Ile finde a fayrer face not washt to day.   1622
   Ber. Ile proue her faire, or talke till doomse-day heere.   1623
   *conuerse this quondam day with a companion of the kings, 1745
   of this day, which the rude multitude call the after-noone.   1823
   *Peda. The posterior of the day, most generous sir, is liable, 1825
   *some show in the posterior of this day, to be rended by our 1852
   King. All haile sweete Madame, and faire time of day.   2265
   *seene the day of wrong through the litle hole of discretion, 2681
   Kath. Not so my Lord, a tweluemonth and a day,   2787
   You shall this tweluemonth terme from day to day,   2811
DAYES = 5*3
   Long. Foure dayes ago.   131
   *apperteining to thy young dayes, which we may nominate |
   tender.   325
   *but a' must fast three dayes a weeke: for this Damsell   433
   *Clo. Well, if euer I do see the merry dayes of desolation   462
   O heresy in faire, fit for these dayes,   997
   Ber. I as some dayes, but then no Sunne must shine.   1426
   Her fauour turnes the fashion of the dayes,   1611
   My Ladie (to the maner of the dayes) | In curtesie giues
   vndeseruing praise.   2292
DAYNTY = 1
   Fat paunches haue leane pates: and daynty bits   30

DAZLING = 1
Who dazling so, that eye shalbe his heed,   87
DE *l.*274 1067 *1746 = 2*1
DEAD = 3
   Brag. The sweete War-man is dead and rotten,   2617
   quicke by him, and hangd for *Pompey* that is dead by him.   2637
   is heauie in my tongue. The King your father | *Quee*. Dead for
   my life.   2676
DEADLIE = 1
   Tis deadlie sinne to keepe that oath my Lord,   600
DEAFT = 1
   Deaft with the clamours of their owne deare grones,   2825
DEALING = 1
   Long. Now to plaine dealing, Lay these glozes by,   1721
DEARE = 16*5
   So much deare Liedge, I haue already sworne,   38
   Ar. Why? sadnes is one & the selfe same thing deare imp.   315
   Arm. Most sweete *Hercules*: more authoritie deare Boy,   373
   I am in loue too. Who was *Sampsons* loue my deare Moth?   381
   Be now as prodigall of all Deare grace,   500
   As Nature was in making Graces deare,   501
   Nau. Heare me deare Lady, I haue sworne an oth,   592
   Deare Princesse were not his requestes so farr   645
   Rosa. Well then I am the shooter. | *Boy*. And who is your Deare?   1100
   Ped. The Deare was (as you know) sanguis in blood, ripe   1153
   to insert again my *haud credo* for a Deare.   1168
   Dul. I said the Deare was not a *haud credo*, twas a Pricket.   1170
   *on the death of the Deare, and to humour the igno-|rault   1208
   cald the Deare: the Princesse kild a Pricket.   1209
   Berow. The King he is hunting the Deare,   1334
   Duma. I neuer knew man holde vile stuffe so deare.   1625
   And then the King will court thee for his Deare: 2023
   Rosa. Madame, he swore that he did hold me deare,   2382
   And Lord *Berowne* (I thanke him) is my deare.   2396
   Full of deare guiltines, and therefore this,   2751
   Deaft with the clamours of their owne deare grones,   2825
DEARES = 1
   The poore Deares blood, that my hart meanes no ill.   1010
DEAREST = 2
   Boyet. Now Maddame summon vp your dearest spirrits,   492
   Thine in the dearest designe of industri, | Don Adriana de
   Armatho.   1066
DEATH = 5*2
   And then grace vs, in the disgrace of death: 7
   *on the death of the Deare, and to humour the igno-|rault   1208
   That the Louer sicke to death,   1444
   Quee. No, to the death we will not moue a foot,   2038
   For the remembraunce of my Fathers death.   2770
   The sodaine hand of death close vp mine eye.   2775
   Berow. To moue wilde laughter in the throate of death?   2816
DEATHS = 1
   Bero. A deaths face in a Ring.   2565
DEBATE = 1
   From tawnie Spaine lost in the worldes debate.   184
DEBT = 1*2
   *should say doubt; det, when he shold pronounce debt; debt, 1760
   And consciences that will not die in debt,   2258

DEBTOR = *1
  Ros. Ware pensalls, How? Let me not die your debtor,   1931
DECEAUE = 1
  Deceaue me not now, *Nauar* is infected.   734
DECEIUED = 2
  Boy. I am much deceiued, but I remember the stile.   1077
  King. You are deceiued, tis not so.   2484
DECEYUED = 1
  Woo contrarie, deceyued by these remoues.   2027
DECIDES = 1
  And often at his very loose decides   2700
DECKT = 1
  O if in blacke my Ladyes browes be deckt,   1607
DECLARES = 1
  My Scutchion plaine declares that I am Alisander.   2515
DECREE = 2
  Fer. We must of force dispence with this Decree,   158
  Young blood doth not obay an olde decree.   1565
DECREES = 1
  And to the strictest decrees Ile write my name.   126
DECREPIT = 1
  To her decrepit, sicke, and bedred Father.   148
DEED = *1
  Naso was the man. And why in deed *Naso*, but for smel-|ling   1288
DEEDE = 6*3
  Studie me how to please the eye in deede,   85
  Arm. Greene in deede is the colour of Louers: but to   391
  I and by heauen, one that will do the deede,   964
  neare. Finely put on in deede.   1103
  Dul. Tis true in deede, the Collusion holdes in the Ex-|(change.   1200
  *deede too: but let that passe, for I must tell thee it will   1834
  Ros. In deede I waigh not you, and therefore light.   1913
  Out | Boy. True, out in deede.   2060
  We foure in deede confronted were with foure,   2294
DEEME = 1
  As you shall deeme your selfe lodgd in my hart.   671
DEEPE = 3
  Subscribe to your deepe othes, and keepe it to.   27
  That will not be deepe searcht with sawcie lookes: 90
  Through the transparent bosome of the deepe,   1363
DEFENCE = 1
  Muster your Wits, stande in your owne defence,   1977
DEFEND = *1
  Clow. As it shall follow in my correction, and God defend | the
  right.   224
DEFILE = *1
  *that defiles; defile, a foule worde: Well, set thee downe   1337
DEFILES = *1
  *that defiles; defile, a foule worde: Well, set thee downe   1337
DEFINE = 2
  Ar. Define, define, well educated infant.   398
DEFORMED = 2
  ignorance, How deformed doost thou looke.   1173
  Hath much deformed vs, fashioning our humours   2715
DEGREE = 1*1
  And he that breakes them in the least degree,   167
  *the great: for mine owne part I know not the degree of the   2448

DEGREES = 1
Ile leaue it by degrees; soft, let vs see,   2351
DEITIE = 1
Bero. This is the lyuer veine, which makes flesh a deitie.   1407
DELAGUAR = *1
*to *Fortuna delaguar*, I wish you the peace of mind most royall |
cupplement. *Exit.*   2475
DELIGHT = 3*1
And traine our intelects to vaine delight.   76
How you delight my Lords I know not I,   185
*safe, and you must suffer him to take no delight, nor no
pe-|nance,   432
Do paint the Meadowes with delight: 2863
DELIGHTED = 1
Quee. Speake braue *Hector*, we are much delighted.   2622
DELIGHTES = 1
Bero. Why? all delightes are vaine, but that most vaine   77
DELIGHTFULL = *1
*(sweete chuck) with some delightfull ostentation, or show,   1844
DELIGHTS = 1
Nor God nor I delights in periurd men.   2272
DELIUER = *2
*deliuer me from the reprobate thought of it, I would take   366
*deliuer this Paper into the royall hand of the King, it may   1306
DELIUERED = 1*1
My Lord *Berowne*, see him deliuered ore,   300
*and deliuered vpon the mellowing of occasion: But the   1234
DELIUERS = 1
Deliuers in such apt and gracious wordes,   565
DELYGHTS = 1
The grosser manner of these worldes delyghts: 33
DEMAUND = 1*1
For here he doth demaund to haue repaide,   638
Ber. Where, when, what Vizard? why demaund you this?   2314
DEMAUNDS = 1
A hundred thousand Crownes, and not demaunds   639
DEMIE = 1
Like a demie God, here sit I in the skie,   1413
DEMONSTRATION = *1
Boy. By a familier demonstration of the working, my | tough
signeor.   320
DEMSEL = *1
Clo. I was taken with none sir, I was taken with a Demsel.   285
DEN = 1*1
Clo. God dig-you-den al, pray you which is the head lady?   1018
Foode for his rage, repasture for his den.   1073
DENIDE = 1
Though so denide faire harbour in my house,   672
DENIE = 3*1
Clo. If it were, I denie her Virginitie: I was taken with a | Maide. 291
And denie himselfe for *Ioue*,   1456
King. If you denie to daunce, lets holde more chat.   2132
King. If this, or more then this, I would denie,   2773
DENNIS = 1
Quee. Saint *Dennis* to S.(aint) *Cupid*: What are they,   1979
DENY = 2
Duma. You may not deny it, *Pompey* hath made the chal-|(lenge. 2661

LOVE'S LABOUR'S LOST

DENY *cont.*
If this thou do deny, let our handes part,   2771
DEO = 1
Curat. Laus deo, bene intelligo. | *Peda. Bome boon for boon prescian,* a litle scratcht, twil serue.   1766
DEPART = 2*1
Which we much rather had depart withall,   642
Quee. Sweete hartes we shalbe rich ere we depart,   1888
*And they wel mockt depart away with shame. *Sound Trom.*   2048
DEPENDANTS = 1
*for the best ward of mine honour, is rewarding | my dependants. *Moth,* follow.   897
DEPUTIE = *1
*Ferd. Great Deputie the welkins Vizgerent, and sole dominatur of   231
DERIUE = 2
From womens eyes this doctrine I deriue,   1652
From womens eyes this doctrine I deriue.   1701
DESCRIED = *1
King. We were descried, theyle mock vs now dounright.   2318
DESCRIPTION = 1
Bero. A right description of our sport my Lord.   2465
DESERTES = 1
Come challenge me, challenge me by these desertes: 2765
DESERUE = 2
Vowes for thee broke deserue not punishment.   1396
Are pick-purses in Loue, and we deserue to die.   1555
DESERUES = 1
with the rational hinde *Costard*: she deserues well.   422
DESIER = 1
To the court of his eye, peeping thorough desier.   739
DESIGNE = 1
Thine in the dearest designe of industri, | Don Adriana de Armatho.   1066
DESIGNES = *1
*importunt and most serious designes, and of great import in   1833
DESIRE = 4*2
At Christmas I no more desire a Rose,   114
*Desire prisoner, and ransome him to anie French Courtier   367
Lon. Perchance light in the light. I desire her name?   697
Bo. She hath but one for her selfe, to desire that were a | (shame.   698
Pag. A good *Lenuoy*, ending in the Goose: woulde you | desire more?   863
Ros. But shall we dance, if they desire vs toot?   2037
DESIRED = 1
Your Ladiships in all desired imployment, Berowne.   1301
DESIRES = 1*1
And the hudge armie of the worldes desires.   14
Pri. Sweete health and faire desires consort your grace.   675
DESIRST = 1
That in loues griefe desirst societie: 1465
DESOLATION = 1*1
Clo. Well, if euer I do see the merry dayes of desolation   462
King. O you haue liu'd in desolation heere,   2283
DESPIGHT = 1
Despight of sute, to see a Ladies face.   2021
DESPISE = 1
King. Despise me when I breake this Oth of mine.   2379

58

DET = *2
  *should say doubt; det, when he shold pronounce debt; debt,   1760
  *not det: he clepeth a Calfe, Caufe: halfe, haufe: neighbour   1761
DETESTED = 1
  Glorie growes guyltie of detested crimes,   1006
DEUICE = 1*2
  *Page. An excellent deuice: so if any of the audience hisse,   1869
  And shape his seruice wholly to my deuice,   1955
  *But I will forward with my deuice; sweete royaltie bestow | on
  me the sence of hearing.   2619
DEUILL see also Diuel, Diuell = 1
  I should haue feard her had shee been a deuill.   1998
DEUILLS see also diuels
DEUINE = 2
  Duma. O most deuine *Kate.*   1417
  Berow. Is Ebonie like her? O word deuine!   1597
DEUISD = 1
  Who deuis'd this penaltie? | *Long.* Marrie that did I.   134
DEUISDE = *1
  *for a new deuisde cursie. I thinke scorne to sigh, mee thinks   368
DEUISE = 2*2
  shame as the rest of the Court can possible deuise.   141
  *God of Rime, for I am sure I shall turne Sonnet. Deuise   485
  King. And winn them too, therefore let vs deuise,   1723
  *phantasims, such insociable and poynt deuise companions,   1758
DEUOTED = *1
  *hir to tryall. Thine in all complements of deuoted and hartburning   272
DEUOURING = 1
  When spight of cormorant deuouring Time,   8
DEUOUT = 1
  But more deuout then this our respectes,   2740
DEUS-ACE = 1
  summe of deus-ace amountes to.   354
DEW = 2
  Faire payment for foule wordes, is more then dew.   994
  The night of dew that on my cheekes downe flowes.   1361
DEWTIE = 1
  *concerne much: stay not thy complement, I forgiue thy | dewtie,
  adue.   1307
DEY see day
DIALOGUE = *1
  *But most esteemed greatnes, will you heare the Dialogue   2848
DIAMONDES = *1
  *A Ladie walde about with Diamondes: Looke you, what I | haue
  from the louing King.   1890
DICE = 2
  Methegline, Wort, and Malmsey; well runne dice: 2138
  That when he playes at Tables chides the Dice   2251
DICK = 1
  Some mumble newes, some trencher Knight, some Dick   2403
DICKE = 1
  And Dicke the Sheepheard blowes his naile: 2880
DICTIMA = 1
  Dul. What is *dictima?* | *Nath.* A title to *Phebe,* to *Luna,* to the
  Moone.   1194
DICTISIMA = 2
  Holo. Dictisima goodman *Dull, dictisima* goodman *Dull.*   1192

DID *l*.135 *242 *250 *255 280 502 609 610 611 738 743 744 749 750
    *869 *1051 *1075 1118 *1119 1219 *1315 1393 1471 1475 1483
    1486 1498 *1545 *1568 *1570 1621 1641 *1744 1938 1991 2007
    2017 2194 2297 2372 2373 2381 2382 2383 2391 2393 2395 2407
    2500 2544 2744 2745 = 40*13
DIDST = *1
 *thee in my rapier, as much as thou didst me in carying gates. 380
DIE = 8*1
 To loue, to wealth, to pompe, I pine and die, 35
 Are pick-purses in Loue, and we deserue to die. 1555
 Ros. Ware pensalls, How? Let me not die your debtor, 1931
 Mar. Then die a Calfe, before your hornes do grow. 2169
 Long. One word in priuate with you ere I die. 2170
 And consciences that will not die in debt, 2258
 That he would wed me, or els die my Louer. 2385
 Die when you will, a Smocke shalbe your shroude. 2418
 Thou shalt die. 2635
DIED = 1*1
 *And so she died: had she bin Light like you, of such a mery 1902
 nimble stiring spirit, she might a bin Grandam ere she died. 1903
DIES = 1
 Dies in the zeale of that which it presentes: 2462
DIGEST = 1
 They will digest this harsh indignitie. 2210
DIGNITIE = 1
 Where seuerall worthies make one dignitie, 1585
DIGRESSION = *1
 *example my digression by some mightie presedent. Boy, 420
DIG-YOU-DEN = *1
 Clo. God dig-you-den al, pray you which is the head lady? 1018
DINE = 1*1
 As thus, to study where I well may dine, 66
 Peda. I do dine to day at the fathers of a certaine pupill of 1318
DINNER = *1
 Curat. I prayse God for you sir, your reasons at Dinner 1741
DIRECTED = 1
 virgin, Was this directed to you? 1292
DISBURSED = 1
 Disbursed by my father in his warres. 627
DISCLOSD = 1*1
 Bo. But to speak that in words, which his eie hath disclosd. 755
 Tolde our intentes before: which once disclosd, 2406
DISCLOSED = 1
 By the hartes still rethoricke, disclosed with eyes. 733
DISCOURSE = 1*2
 So sweete and voluble is his discourse. 568
 A. No Page, it is an epilogue or discourse to make plaine, 855
 *discourse peremptorie: his tongue fyled, his eye ambitious, 1749
DISCRETION = *2
 *purse of wit, thou Pidgin-egge of discretion. O and the 1810
 *seene the day of wrong through the litle hole of discretion, 2681
DISFIGURE = 1
 Ber. O Rimes are gardes on wanton *Cupids* hose, | Disfigure not
 his Shop. 1390
DISGRACE = 2*1
 And then grace vs, in the disgrace of death: 7
 *not; his disgrace is to be called Boy, but his glorie is to sub-|due 482

DISGRACE *cont.*
Thy grace being gainde, cures all disgrace in mee.   1400
DISGUYSD = 3
Against your Peace Loue doth approch, disguysd: 1975
That by and by disguysd they will be heere.   1988
Disguysd like *Muscouites* in shapeles geare: 2226
DISGUYSDE = 2
Lets mocke them still as well knowne as disguysde: 2224
Were not you here but euen now, disguysde? | *King.* Madame, I
was.   2367
DISGUYSED = 1
Enter Black-moores with musicke, the Boy with a | speach, and the
rest of the Lordes disguysed.   2051
DISH *see* dysh
DISHCLOUTE = *1
*Linnen: since when, Ile be sworne he wore none, but a
dish-|cloute   2668
DISMAID = *1
Qu. The conqueror is dismaid: proceed good *Alexander.*   2520
DISMASKT = 1
Dismaskt, their dammaske sweete commixture showne,   2219
DISMISSE = 1
O dismisse this audience, and I shall tell you more.   1556
DISPATCH = 2
On serious busines crauing quicke dispatch,   522
Well Lords, to day we shall haue our dispatch,   979
DISPENCE = 1
Fer. We must of force dispence with this Decree,   158
DISPENSATION = 1
Then seeke a dispensation for his oth: 581
DISPLAYDE = 1
With Visages displayde to talke and greete.   2036
DISPOSD = 1
To make my Lady laugh, when shees disposd: 2405
DISPOSDE = 1
Prin. Come, to our Pauilion, *Boyet* is disposde.   754
DISPRAYSE = 1
And therefore redd that would auoyde disprayse,   1613
DISPUTES = *1
Peda. Thou disputes like an Infant: goe whip thy Gigg.   1802
DIUEL = 1
King. No Diuel will fright thee then so much as shee.   1624
DIUELL = 1*1
*is falsely attempted? Loue is a familiar; Loue is a Diuell.   474
Some tricks, some quillets, how to cheate the diuell.   1637
DIUELS = 1
Ber. Diuels soonest tempt resembling spirites of light.   1606
DIUINE *see* deuine
DIUORCE = 1
And quite diuorce his memorie from his part.   2042
DO *1.*26 155 281 *340 346 356 *379 *421 436 *451 *462 *470 546
550 649 653 *678 684 764 766 *793 853 *857 919 922 933 937 964
1011 *1314 *1318 *1329 *1341 *1343 1365 1368 1370 1452 1463
1470 1492 1499 1549 1584 1668 *1816 1820 *1827 *1830 *1831
*1842 1872 1911 1912 2012 2031 2043 2069 2073 2099 2103 *2108
2110 2119 2168 2169 2221 2342 2356 2362 2413 2419 2576 2623
2649 *2651 2654 *2656 2686 2753 2771 2852 2863 = 66*24

DOBLET = *1
  *your eyes, with your armes crost on your thinbellies doblet   787
DOCTRINE = 2
  From womens eyes this doctrine I deriue,   1652
  From womens eyes this doctrine I deriue.   1701
DOE *l.*1181 *1344 2361 = 1*2
DOGGES = 1
  The Dogges did yell, put ell to Sore, | then Sorell iumps from
  thicket: 1219
DOMINATUR = *1
  *Ferd. *Great Deputie the welkins Vizgerent, and sole dominatur of*   231
DOMINE = 1*1
  *Nath. Let me heare a staffe, a stanze, a verse, *Lege domine.*   1265
  ne inteligis domine, to make frantique lunatique?   1764
DOMINEERING = *1
  *A domineering pedant ore the Boy, then whom no mor-|tall so
  magnificent.   943
DOMINICALL = 1
  My red Dominicall, my golden letter,   1932
DON *see also* Dun = 4*2
  heate of duetie. | Don Adriano de Armado.   273
  Fer. And *Don Armado* shall be your keeper.   299
  Thine in the dearest designe of industri, | Don Adriana de
  Armatho.   1066
  *it was geuen me by *Costard,* and sent me from *Don Armatho*:   1255
  *who is intituled, nominated, or called, *Don Adriano de
  Ar-| matho.   1746
  Bero. Loe, he is tilting straight. Peace, I haue don.   2423
DONE *see also* don *l.*718 920 924 927 *1151 *1312 *1870 2505 = 5*3
DOOMSE-DAY = 1
  Ber. Ile proue her faire, or talke till doomse-day heere.   1623
DOORE = 2
  + *Pag.* Vntill the Goose came out of doore,   856 +8
  Arm. Vntill the Goose came out of doore,   861
DOOST *l.*1173 1372 *1402 = 2*1
DOOT = 1
  Cried *via* we will doo't come what wil come.   2004
DOOTE = 1
  Not wounding, pittie would not let me doote.   1002
DOOTERS = 1
  Should rauish dooters with a false aspect: 1609
DOOTH *l.*2241 = 1
DOSEN = 1
  There's halfe a dosen sweetes.   2139
DOST *l.*1068 1542 1945 2578 2634 = 5
DOTE = 2
  For none offende, where all alike do dote.   1463
  As foolrie in the Wise, when Wit doth dote: 1966
DOTH *l.*73 78 81 82 154 155 178 355 410 *472 513 562 624 638 *850
  *1259 *1290 1364 1366 1565 1586 1590 1593 1600 1654 1966 1967
  1975 2091 2244 2308 2387 *2436 *2443 2460 2469 2722 2789 2835
  2887 2888 2896 = 36*6
DOUBLE = 3
  And giues to euery power a double power,   1682
  Long. You haue a double tongue within your Maske,   2157
  Quee. I vnderstand you not, my griefes are double.   2710

DOUBT = 2*1
    *should say doubt; det, when he shold pronounce debt; debt,   1760
    And euer and anon they made a doubt,   1993
    Quee. Therefore I do it, and I make no doubt,   2043
DOUNRIGHT = *1
    **King.* We were descried, theyle mock vs now dounright.   2318
DOUT = *1
    *such rackers of ortagriphie, as to speake dout fine, when he   1759
DOWNE = 7*3
    That his owne hand may strike his honour downe,   24
    most grase, Birdes best peck, and Men sit downe to that
    nourishment   246
    smile againe, and till then sit thee downe sorrow. *Exeunt.*   309
    Lord, Lord, how the Ladies and I haue put him downe.   1138
    *that defiles; defile, a foule worde: Well, set thee downe   1337
    The night of dew that on my cheekes downe flowes.   1361
    His louing bosome, to keepe downe his hart.   1473
    Pell, mell, downe with them: but be first aduisd,   1719
    The fourth turnd on the tooe, and downe he fell: 2006
    **Bero.* Thus pooure the Starres downe plagues for periurie.   2326
DOWRIE = 1
    Then *Aquitaine* a Dowrie for a Queene.   499
DRAWEN = 1
    O he hath drawen my picture in his letter. | *Quee.* Any thing like?   1926
DRAWER = 1
    Bero. I and worne in the cappe of a Tooth-drawer: 2571
DRAWETH = *2
    ** & most propostrous euent that draweth fro(m) my snowhite pen*
    the   251
    **Peda.* He draweth out the thred of his verbositie, finer   1756
DRAWING = *1
    *If drawing my Sword against the humor of affection, would   365
DRAW-OUT = 1
    Curat. A most singular and choyce Epithat, | *Draw-out his*
    Table-booke.   1754
DREAD = 2
    Bero. Sweete Lord and why? | *Long.* To fright them hence with
    that dread penaltie.   136
    Dread Prince of Placcats, King of Codpeeces.   950
DREADFUL = *1
    *Thy eie *Ioues* lightning beares, thy voyce his dreadful thu(n)der   1279
DREADFULL = 1
    Of his almightie dreadfull little might.   969
DREAME = 1
    Can you still dreame and poare and thereon looke.   1648
DRIE = 2
    Bero. By heauen, all drie beaten with pure scoffe.   2180
    Bero. This iest is drie to me, gentle sweete,   2300
DRINKE = 1
    When they are thirstie, fooles would faine haue drinke.   2299
DROP = 2
    No drop but as a Coach doth carrie thee: 1366
    How shall she know my griefes? Ile drop the paper.   1374
DROPPS = 1
    To those fresh morning dropps vpon the Rose,   1359
DROWNES = 1
    And coffing drownes the Parsons saw;   2889

DROWSIE = 1
Make heauen drowsie with the harmonie.   1696
DRUM = *1
*men. Adue Valoure, rust Rapier, be still Drum, for your   483
DRUNKARD = 1
Ber. One drunkard loues an other of the name.   1382
DRUNKE = *1
*He hath not eate paper as it were: he hath not drunke inck.   1176
DUE *see also* dew = 1
Pay him the due of honie-tonged *Boyet.*   2259
DUELLA = *1
*my turne: *Passado* he respects not, the *Duella* he regards   481
DUETIE = 2*1
duetie prickes me on) haue sent to thee, to receiue the meede of
pu-|nishment   265
heate of duetie.| Don Adriano de Armado.   273
Our duetie is so rich, so infinite,   2098
DUKE = 2*1
Ar. I haue promised to studie three yeeres with the duke.   345
*Who are the Votaries my louing Lordes, that are vowfel-|lowes
with this vertuous Duke?   528
I saw him at the Duke *Alansoes* once,   553
DUKES = 1*1
Constab. Which is the Dukes owne person?   193
Constab. Sir, the Dukes pleasure is that you keepe *Costard*   431
DUL = 2*4
DULL see also Dul. = 8*2
by thy sweete Graces Officer Anthonie Dull, *a man of*   266
Antho. Me ant shall please you? I am *Anthony Dull.*   268
Brag. The meaning prettie ingenius, is not Lead a mettal |
heauie, dull, and slow?   826
Enter *Dull, Holofernes,* the *Pedant* and *Nathaniel.*   1150
Holo. Dictisima goodman *Dull, dictisima* goodman *Dull.*   1192
Enter the Pedant, the Curat, and Dull.   1739
Peda. Via good-man *Dull,* thou hast spoken no worde all | this
while.   1880
Peda. Most *Dull,* honest *Dull,* to our sport: away. *Exeunt.*   1886
DULL = 1*2
DULLER = *1
*sensible in the duller partes: and such barren plantes are   1179
DUM = 13
DUMA = 34*2
DUMAINE see also Dum., Duma., Duman. = 13*1
Enter Ferdinand K.(ing) of Nauar, Berowne,| *Longauill, and
Dumaine.*   2
You three, *Berowne, Dumaine,* and *Longauill,*   19
Dumaine. My louing Lord, *Dumaine* is mortefied,   32
2. Lad. The young *Dumaine,* a well accomplisht youth,   548
Enter *Nauar, Longauill, Dumaine,* & *Berowne.*   583
Enter Dumaine.   691
Enter Dumaine.   1410
Dumaine transformed, foure Woodcocks in a dysh.   1416
Dumaine reades his Sonnet.   1437
Long. Dumaine thy Loue is farre from charitie,   1464
Where lies thy griefe, o tell me good *Dumaine*?   1508
But *Katherine* what was sent to you | From faire *Dumaine*?   1935
Mar. Dumaine was at my seruice, and his sword,   2195

DUMAINE cont.
   Mar. Dumaine is mine as sure as barke on tree.   2206
DUMAINE = 1
DUMAN = 2*1
DUN = 2
   King. Where hadst thou it? | *Cost.* Of *Dun Adramadio, Dun*
   Adramadio.   1540
DUNGHEL = 1
   Peda. Oh I smell false Latine, *dunghel* for *vnguem.*   1814
DUNGIL = *1
   *Go to, thou hast it *ad dungil* at the fingers ends, as they say.   1813
DUNGIONS = 1
   The hue of dungions, and the Schoole of night: 1604
DURANCE = *1
   Arm. I giue thee thy libertie, set thee from durance, and in   894
DURING = 1
   As motion and long during action tyres   1657
DURST = 1
   Neuer durst Poet touch a pen to write,   1697
DUTCH-MAN = *1
   Mar. Veale quoth the Dutch-man: is not veale a Calfe?   2159
DWARFFE = 1
   This signior *Iunios* gyant dwarffe, dan *Cupid,*   946
DYSH = 1
   Dumaine transformed, foure Woodcocks in a dysh.   1416
E = 1
   Peda. I will repeate them: a e I.   1793
EACH = 7
   But like of each thing that in season growes.   116
   And bide the pennance of each three yeeres day.   124
   Which each to other hath so strongly sworne.   302
   But I a Beame do finde in each of three.   1499
   In that each of you haue forsworne his Booke.   1647
   But while tis spoke each turne away his face.   2040
   Cannot picke out fiue such, take each one in his vaine.   2488
EAGLE = 1
   A Louers eyes will gaze an Eagle blinde.   1685
EAGLE-SIGHTED = 1
   What peromptorie Eagle-sighted eye   1575
EARE = 9*2
   Breake the necke of the Waxe, and euery one giue eare.   1039
   *as the Pomwater, who now hangeth like a Iewel in the eare   1154
   What *Longauill,* and reading: listen eare.   1377
   A Louers eare will heare the lowest sound.   1686
   Boyet. Madame, and prettie mistresses giue eare.   2207
   What did you whisper in your Ladies eare?   2372
   What did the *Russian* whisper in your eare?   2381
   Bero. Honest plaine words, best pearce the eare of griefe,   2711
   A iestes prosperitie lies in the eare,   2822
   Cuckow, Cuckow: O word of feare, | Vnpleasing to a married
   eare.   2867
   Vnpleasing to a married eare.   2877
EARES = 4
   That aged eares play treuant at his tales,   566
   O then his lines would rauish sauage eares,   1699
   Our eares vouchsafe it. | *King.* But your legges should do it.   2118
   Of him that makes it: then if sickly eares   2824

EARTH = 3*2
a Crab on the face of *Terra*, the soyle, the land, the earth.   1156
*in a turph of Earth, Fier enough for a Flint, Pearle enough   1252
*Then thou faire Sunne, which on my earth doost shine,   1402
Ber. By earth she is not, corporall, there you ly.   1420
Page. All haile, the richest Beauties on the earth.   2053
EARTHES = *1
*Nauar, *my soules earthes God, and bodies fostring patrone:*   232
EARTHLY = 3
These earthly Godfathers of heauens lights,   93
That singes heauens prayse, with such an earthly tong.   1283
My Vow was earthly, thou a heauenly Loue.   1399
EASELY = 1
For my great sute, so easely obtainde.   2697
EASIE = *1
*three studied ere yele thrice wincke: and how easie it is to   358
EASIER = 1
Thou art easier swallowed then a flapdragon.   1781
EASLIE = 1
The measure then of one is easlie tolde.   2088
EAST = 2*2
**seest. But to the place Where? It standeth North North-east & by*   253
**East from the West corner of thy curious knotted garden; There*   254
At the first opning of the gorgious East,   1572
By East, West, North, and South, I spred my conquering might: 2514
EATE = *1
*He hath not eate paper as it were: he hath not drunke inck.   1176
EATEN = *1
*I maruaile thy M.(aister) hath not eaten thee for a worde, for
thou   1779
EBB = 1
The Sea will ebb and flow, heauen shew his face: 1564
EBON = *1
**ebon coloured Incke, which here thou viewest, beholdest, suruayest,*
or   252
EBONIE = 2
King. By heauen, thy Loue is blacke as Ebonie.   1596
Berow. Is Ebonie like her? O word deuine!   1597
ECLIPED = 1
Iudas *I am, ecliped* Machabeus.   2551
EDGE = 4
That honour which shall bate his sythes keene edge,   10
Whose edge hath power to cut whose will still wils,   542
Forr. Heereby vpon the edge of yonder Coppice,   983
Boyet. The tongues of mocking Wenches are as keene | As is the
Rasors edge inuisible: 2172
EDICT = 1*1
Our late edict shall strongly stand in force,   15
**thy established proclaymed Edict and continent Cannon: Which*   260
EDUCATE = *1
*barbarous. Do you not educate youth at the Charg-house   1816
EDUCATED = 1
Ar. Define, define, well educated infant.   398
EELE = 3
Boy. I will praise an Eele with the same praise.   337
Arma. What? that an Eele is ingenious.   338
Boy. That an Eele is quicke.   339

EFFECT = 1
  Quee. The effect of my intent is to crosse theirs: 2030
EGGE = *1
  *purse of wit, thou Pidgin-egge of discretion. O and the   1810
EGMA = *1
  Clo. No egma, no riddle, no *lenuoy*, no salue, in thee male sir.   845
EIE = 6*3
  Bo. But to speak that in words, which his eie hath disclosd.   755
  I onelie haue made a mouth of his eie,   756
  *King *Cophetua* set eie vpon the pernicious and indubitate   1046
  *Thy eie *Ioues* lightning beares, thy voyce his dreadful thu(n)der   1279
  The vertue of your eie must breake my oth.   2274
  With eies best seeing, heauens fierie eie: 2302
  Rosa. This proues you wise and rich: for in my eie.   2306
  And laugh vpon the apple of her eie?   2414
  You leere vpon me, do you: ther's an eie | Woundes like a leaden
  sword.   2419
EIES = 1
  With eies best seeing, heauens fierie eie: 2302
EITHER = 1
  Berow. Neither of either: I remit both twaine.   2398
EL = 1
  If Sore be sore, then el to Sore, | makes fiftie sores o sorell: 1223
ELAMENTES = 1
  But with the motion of all elamentes,   1680
ELBOW = 1
  One rubbd his elbow thus, and fleerd, and swore,   2001
ELDER = 2
  Pedan. Begin sir, you are my elder.   2558
  Bero. Well folowed, *Iudas* was hanged on an Elder.   2559
ELEGANCIE = *1
  Nath. Here are onely numbers ratefied, but for the ele-|gancie   1286
ELEUENPENCE *see* leuenpence
ELL = 1
  The Dogges did yell, put ell to Sore, | then Sorell iumps from
  thicket: 1219
ELS = 8
  Prin. Why, will shall breake it will, and nothing els.   595
  Quee. Els your memorie is bad, going ore it erewhile.   1078
  Or Pricket-sore, or els Sorell, | the people fall a hooting.   1221
  This will I send, and something els more plaine.   1458
  Els none at all in ought proues excellent.   1705
  Or els we loose our selues, to keepe our othes: 1713
  Rosa. Madame, came nothing els along with that?   1892
  That he would wed me, or els die my Louer.   2385
ELSE = *1
  Ferd. Why that to know which else we should not know.   60
EMBASSADOURE = *1
  Boy. A message well simpathisd, a Horse to be embassa-|doure
  for an Asse.   819
EMBASSADOURS = 1
  Your Fauours, embassadours of Loue.   2736
EMBASSAGE = 1
  That well by hart hath cond his embassage   1990
EMBASSAIE = 1
  For well you know here comes in Embassaie,   144

EMBASSIE = 1
To whom he sendes, and whats his Embassie.   494
EMPERATOR = 1
Sole Emperator and great generall | Of trotting Parrators (O my
litle hart.)   951
EMPLOY *see also* imploy = 2
Ber. O stay slaue, I must employ thee.   917
Ped. Alone, we will employ thee.   1883
EMPLOYMENT *see* imployment
EMPRESSE = 1
O sweete *Maria*, Empresse of my Loue,   1388
EMPTIE = 1
And I shall finde you emptie of that fault, | Right ioyfull of your
reformation.   2829
EMURED = 1*1
*Enfreedoming thy person: thou wert emured, restrained, |
captiuated, bound.   890
Liues not alone emured in the braine: 1679
ENCHANTED *see* inchaunted
ENCHANTING *see* inchaunting
ENCOUNTER *see* incounter
ENCOUNTERS *see* incounters
ENCOUNTRED *see* incontred
END = 1*1
*that worthies thumbe, he is not so big as the end of his Club.   1864
To make a world-without-end bargaine in: 2749
ENDE = 11*1
What is the ende of study, let me know?   59
*the tongues ende, canarie to it with your feete, humour it   782
acquainted you withall, to the ende to craue your assistance.   1848
Therefore Ile darkly ende the argument.   1910
And wonder what they were, and to what ende   2227
Bero. Speake for your selues, my wit is at an ende.   2363
Duma. For the latter ende of his name.   2579
Euen to the opposed ende of our ententes.   2716
Longauill. What saies *Maria?* | *Mari.* At the tweluemonths ende, 2793
Berow. Our wooing doth not ende like an olde Play: 2835
King. Come sir, it wants a tweluemonth an'aday, | And then twill
ende.   2838
ende of our shew. | *King.* Call them foorth quickly, we will do so. 2851
ENDED = 2
Lon. Nay my coller is ended. She is a most sweet Ladie. | *Exit*
Longauil.   705
and he ended the market.   876
ENDES = 1
Curtsie sweete hartes, and so the Measure endes.   2124
ENDEUOUR = 2
Thendeuour of this present breath may buy: 9
With all the fierce endeuour of your wit,   2814
ENDEUOURS = 1
For all your faire endeuours and intreat: 2688
ENDING = *1
Pag. A good *Lenuoy*, ending in the Goose: woulde you | desire
more?   863
ENDS = *1
*Go to, thou hast it *ad dungil* at the fingers ends, as they say. 1813

ENDURE *see also* indure = 1
A worlde of tormentes though I should endure, 2279
ENFORCE = 1*1
*loue? I may. Shall I enforce thy loue? I coulde. Shall I en-|treate 1060
To enforce the pained impotent to smile. 2815
ENFORCEST *see* inforcest
ENFRANCHISE *see* infranchise
ENFREEDOMING = *1
*Enfreedoming thy person: thou wert emured, restrained,|
captiuated, bound. 890
ENGAGED *see* ingaged
ENGENDERS *see* ingenders
ENIGMA = *1
*Ar. Some enigma, some riddle, come, thy *Lenuoy* begin. 843
ENIOY = 1
that you cannot enioy her. 813
ENIOYNED *see* inioyned
ENLARGEMENT = *1
*giue enlargement to the Swaine, bring him festinatly hither, 776
ENOUGH = *4
*in a turph of Earth, Fier enough for a Flint, Pearle enough 1252
*Curat. Where will you finde men worthie enough to pre-|sent
them? 1857
*Brag. Pardon sir, error: He is not quantitie enough for 1863
ENRICHT *see* inricht, inritcht
ENROLLED = 3
Which I hope well is not enrolled there. 42
The which I hope is not enrolled there. 45
Which I hope well is not enrolled there. 50
ENTENDED = 1
So shall we stay mocking entended game, 2047
ENTENTES = 1
Euen to the opposed ende of our ententes. 2716
ENTER = 38*1
Enter Ferdinand K.(ing) of Nauar, Berowne,| *Longauill, and
Dumaine.* 2
Enter a Constable with Costard with a letter. 192
Enter Armado and Moth his page. 311
Enter *Clowne, Constable,* and *Wench.* 430
*Enter the Princesse of Fraunce, with three| attending Ladies and
three Lordes.* 490
Before we enter his forbidden gates, 517
Lord. Heere comes *Boyet. Enter Boyet.* 572
To let you enter his vnpeeled house. 582
Enter *Nauar, Longauill, Dumaine, & Berowne.* 583
Enter Dumaine. 691
Enter Berowne. 708
Enter *Braggart* and his *Boy.* 770
Enter *Page* and *Clowne.* 840
Enter Berowne. 909
Enter the Princesse, a Forrester, her Ladyes,| and her Lordes. 973
Enter Clowne. 1016
Enter *Dull, Holofernes,* the *Pedant* and *Nathaniel.* 1150
Enter Iaquenetta and the Clowne. 1245
Enter Berowne with a paper in his hand, alone. 1333
Enter Longauill. The King steps a side. 1376
Enter Dumaine. 1410

ENTER *cont.*
Iaqu. God blesse the King. *Enter Iaquenetta and Clowne.*   1528
Enter the Pedant, the Curat, and Dull.   1739
Enter Bragart, Boy.   1769
*in minoritie: his enter and exit shalbe strangling a Snake;   1867
Enter the Ladyes.   1887
Enter Boyet.   1969
*Enter Black-moores with musicke, the Boy with a | speach, and the
rest of the Lordes disguysed.*   2051
Enter the King and the rest.   2234
Enter the Ladies.   2262
Enter Clowne.   2424
Enter Bragart.   2466
Enter Pompey.   2490
Enter Curate for Alexander.   2511
Enter Pedant for Iudas, and the Boy for Hercules.   2540
Enter Braggart.   2587
Enter a Messenger Mounsier Marcade.   2671
Enter Braggart.   2841
Enter all.   2854
ENTERTAINEMENT = *1
*Sir *Holofernes,* as concerning some entertainement of time,   1851
ENTERTEINMENT = 1
Some enterteinment for them in their Tentes.   1724
ENTERUIEW = 1
Ferd. It shall suffise me; at which enteruiew,   664
ENTIRE *see* intire
ENTIRELY *see* intirely
ENTITLE *see* intitle
ENTITULED *see* intitled, intituled
ENTREATE *see also* intreat, intreate = *1
*loue? I may. Shall I enforce thy loue? I coulde. Shall I en-|treate   1060
ENTRETH = 1
He standes a side. The King entreth.   1353
ENUIOUS = 1
Ferd. Berowne is like an enuious sneaping Frost,   109
ENUOY *see* lenuoy
EPILOGUE = *1
A. No Page, it is an epilogue or discourse to make plaine,   855
EPITHAT = 1
Curat. A most singular and choyce Epithat, | *Draw-out his
Table-booke.*   1754
EPITHETON *see* apethaton
EPYTAPH = *1
Holo. Sir *Nathaniel,* will you heare an extemporall Epy-|taph   1207
EPYTHAT = 1
Boyet. They will not answere to that Epythat.   2067
EPYTHITHES = *1
Curat.Nath. Truely M.(aister) *Holofernes,* the epythithes are   1158
EQUALL = 1
And Iustice alwayes whirles in equall measure: 1735
ERE = 6*2
So ere you finde where light in darknes lyes,   83
*three studied ere yele thrice wincke: and how easie it is to   358
Ar. Villaine, thou shalt fast for thy offences ere thou be |
pardoned.   449
Quee. Who ere a was, a showd a mounting minde.   978

ERE *cont.*
 Quee. Sweete hartes we shalbe rich ere we depart,   1888
 nimble stiring spirit, she might a bin Grandam ere she died.   1903
 That same *Berowne* ile torture ere I go.   1950
 Long. One word in priuate with you ere I die.   2170
EREWHILE = 1
 Quee. Els your memorie is bad, going ore it erewhile.   1078
ERGO = 1
 Ergo, *I come with this Appologie.*   2546
ERROR = 1*1
 Brag. Pardon sir, error: He is not quantitie enough for   1863
 We are againe forsworne in will and error.   2410
ERROUR = 1
 Our loue being yours, the errour that Loue makes   2729
ERUPTIONS = *1
 *that the Curate and your sweete selfe, are good at such
 erup-|tions,   1846
ESTABLISHED = *1
 thy established proclaymed Edict and continent Cannon: Which   260
ESTEEMD = 1
 A man of soueraigne peerelesse he is esteemd: 536
ESTEEME = 1
 Your selfe, helde precious in the worldes esteeme,   495
ESTEEMED = *2
 more sweete vnderstanding a Woman: him, I (as my euer esteemed   264
 *But most esteemed greatnes, will you heare the Dialogue   2848
ESTETES = 1
 Which you on all estetes will execute,   2806
ESTIMATION = 1
 good reput, carriage bearing, and estimation.   267
ESTRANGED = *1
 Kin. Wil you not daunce? How come you thus estranged?   2112
ET *l.1771* = 1
ETERNALL = 1
 Standes in attainder of eternall shame.   168
ETERNITIE = 1
 And make vs heires of all eternitie.   11
EUE = 1*1
 Ferd. With a childe of our Grandmother Eue, *a female; or for thy*   263
 Had he bin *Adam* he had tempted *Eue.*   2247
EUEN = 5
 Duma. Now the number is euen.   1557
 Were not you here but euen now, disguysde?| *King.* Madame, I
 was.   2367
 Marcad. Euen so: my tale is tolde.   2678
 Euen to the opposed ende of our ententes.   2716
 And euen that falshood in it selfe a sinne,   2733
EUENT = *1
 *& most propostrous euent that draweth fro(m) my snowhite pen
 the*   251
EUER = 9*5
 Small haue continuall plodders euer wonne,   91
 Bero. How low so euer the matter, I hope in God for high |
 (words.   204
 more sweete vnderstanding a Woman: him, I (as my euer esteemed   264
 Ber. This is not so well as I looked for, but the best that | euer I
 heard.   275

EUER *cont.*
  Clo. Well, if euer I do see the merry dayes of desolation   462
Still a repairing: euer out of frame,   957
  *What vaine? What Wethercock? Did you euer heare better?   1075
Loue, whose Month is euer May: 1439
For all the wealth that euer I did see,   1486
And euer and anon they made a doubt,   1993
  Page. A holy parcell of the fayrest dames that euer turnd their |
backes to mortall viewes.   2055
  Page. That euer turnde their eyes to mortall viewes.   2059
Or euer but in vizards shew their faces.   2190
By being once falce, for euer to be true   2731
EUERIE = 6
  Clow. Be to me, and euerie man that dares not fight. | *Ferd.* No
wordes.   239
thy picture, and my hart on thy euerie part.   1064
Thou shinst in euerie teare that I do weepe,   1365
For euerie one pursents three.   2430
The Cuckow then on euerie tree,   2864
The Cuckow then on euerie tree,   2873
EUERMORE = 1
  Ber. So Studie euermore is ouershot,   153
EUERY = 16
And but one meale on euery day beside: 44
That giue a name to euery fixed Starre,   94
And euery Godfather can giue a name.   98
For euery man with his affectes is borne,   162
For euery obiect that the one doth catch,   562
That euery one her owne hath garnished,   570
  Na. Thy owne wish wish I thee in euery place. *Exit.*   676
  Boy. And euery iest but a word.   717
Breake the necke of the Waxe, and euery one giue eare.   1039
Courses as swift as thought in euery power,   1681
And giues to euery power a double power,   1682
Then homeward euery man attach the hand   1726
And euery one his Loue-feat will aduance,   2015
For Ladies; we will euery one be maskt,   2019
This is the floure that smyles on euery one.   2256
To euery varied obiect in his glaunce: 2723
EUERYONE *see* euerie, euery
EUILL = 1*1
  *There is no euill angel but Loue, yet was *Sampson* so temp-|ted,   475
The Boy replyde, An Angell is not euill: 1997
EUNUCH = 1
Though *Argus* were her eunuch and her garde.   965
EUYLL = 1
  Duma. I marie there, some flatterie for this euyll.   1635
EXAMPLE = 2*1
  *example my digression by some mightie presedent. Boy,   420
  +I will example it.   856 +1
Were Louers too, ill to example ill,   1461
EXCEEDING = 1
For I protest, the Schoolemaister is exceeding fantasticall,   2473
EXCEEDINGLY = 1
  Ber. O my good knaue *Costard,* exceedingly well met.   910
EXCEL = *1
  Arm. O wel knit *Sampson,* strong ioynted *Sampson;* I do excel   379

EXCELL = 1
O Queene of queenes, how farre doost thou excell, 1372
EXCELLENCE = 1
Haue found the ground of Studies excellence, 1650
EXCELLENT = 1*2
*and he had an excellent strength: Yet was *Salomon* so 476
Els none at all in ought proues excellent. 1705
Page. An excellent deuice: so if any of the audience hisse, 1869
EXCESSE = 1
Rosa. The blood of youth burnes not with such excesse, 1963
EXCHANGE = 2*3
*thy loue? I will. What, shalt thou exchange for raggs 1061
Th'allusion holdes in the Exchange. 1199
Dul. Tis true in deede, the Collusion holdes in the Ex-|(change. 1200
Holo. God comfort thy capacitie, I say th'allusion holdes | in the
Exchange. 1202
Dul. And I say the polusion holdes in the Exchange: for 1204
EXCREMENT = *1
*with my excrement, with my mustachie: but sweete hart 1837
EXCUSE = 4
Your owne good thoughts excuse me, and farewell. 673
King. Teach vs sweet Madame, for our rude transgression | Some
faire excuse. 2364
In your rich wisedome to excuse, or hide, 2690
Excuse me so comming too short of thankes, 2696
EXE = *1
King. Farewel mad Wenches, you haue simple wits. *Exe.* 2181
EXECUTE = 1
Which you on all estetes will execute, 2806
EXEUNT see also Exe. = 8
smile againe, and till then sit thee downe sorrow. *Exeunt.* 309
Clo. Come *Iaquenetta*, away. *Exeunt.* 448
Boy. You are too hard for mee. *Exeunt omnes.* 768
Sowla, sowla. *Exeunt.* Shoot within. 1148
*Away, the gentles are at their game, and we will to our re-
|creation. *Exeunt.* 1331
Peda. Most *Dull*, honest *Dull*, to our sport: away. *Exeunt.* 1886
Quee. Whip to our Tents as Roes runs ore land. *Exeunt.* 2232
and I will right my selfe like a Souldier. *Exeunt Worthys* 2682
EXHALST = 1
Exhalst this vapour-vow in thee it is: 1403
EXIT = 17*2
as an other man, & therfore I can be quiet. *Exit.* 468
*Wit, write Pen, for I am for whole volumes in folio. *Exit.* 486
Boy. Proud of imployment, willingly I go. *Exit Boy.* 526
Na. Thy owne wish wish I thee in euery place. *Exit.* 676
Ber. I cannot stay thankes-giuing. *Exit.* 690
Dum. A gallant Lady *Mounsir*, fare you wel. *Exit.* 694
Lon. Nay my coller is ended. She is a most sweet Ladie. | *Exit
Longauil.* 705
Boy. Farewell to me sir, and welcome to you. *Exit Bero.* 714
Pag. Like the sequell I. Signeur *Costard* adew. *Exit.* 899
do it sir in print: gardon remuneration. | *Exit.* 937
Thou canst not hit it my good man. *Exit.* 1115
Cost. Haue with thee my girle. *Exit.* 1311
*in minoritie: his enter and exit shalbe strangling a Snake; 1867
Boy. I will, and so will she, I know my Lord. *Exit.* 2239

EXIT *cont.*

Bero. Goe bid them prepare. (*Exit.*	2450
*to *Fortuna delaguar,* I wish you the peace of mind most royall | cupplement. *Exit.*	2475
*are Worthies a comming will speake their minde in some | other sort. *Exit Curat.*	2537
Keepe some state in thy exit, and vanish. Exit Boy.	2547

EXPECTING = *1

*roabes, for tittles tytles, for thy selfe, mee. Thus expecting	1062

EXPENCE = *1

**Brag.* Annoynted, I implore so much expence of thy royal	2467

EXPERIENCE = 1

Brag. How hast thou purchased this experience?	795

EXPIRATION = 1

Then at the expiration of the yeere,	2764

EXPLICATION = *1

*as it were *in via,* in way of explication *facere*: as it were	1164

EXPOSITER = 1

Which his fayre tongue (conceites expositer)	564

EXPRESSE = 1

That shall expresse my trueloues fasting paine.	1459

EXPRESSED = 1

Proud with his forme, in his eye pride expressed.	741

EXPRESSELY = 1

When I to fast expressely am forbid.	67

EXPREST = 1

Hencefoorth my wooing minde shalbe exprest	2344

EXTEMPORALL = *2

*manager is in loue; yea he loueth. Assist me some extempo-|rall	484
**Holo.* Sir *Nathaniel,* will you heare an extemporall Epy-|taph	1207

EXTRAUAGANT = *1

*extrauagant spirit, full of formes, figures, shapes, obiectes,	1231

EXTREAME = 1

King. The extreame partes of time extreamly formes,	2698

EXTREAMLY = 1

King. The extreame partes of time extreamly formes,	2698

EY = 1

And wretched fooles secrets heedfully ore ey.	1414

EYE *see also* eie = 22*4

Studie me how to please the eye in deede,	85
By fixing it vppon a fayrer eye,	86
Who dazling so, that eye shalbe his heed,	87
Beautie is bought by iudgement of the eye,	506
His eye begets occasion for his wit,	561
Ber. Will you prickt with your eye. | *Ros. No poynt,* with my knife.	686
To the court of his eye, peeping thorough desier.	739
Proud with his forme, in his eye pride expressed.	741
Mee thought all his senses were lokt in his eye,	746
*I will not. O but her eye: by this light, but for her eye, I	1342
As thy eye beames, when their fresh rayse haue smot.	1360
Did not the heauenly Rethorique of thine eye,	1393
Duma. By heauen the woonder in a mortall eye.	1419
*hand, a foote, a face, an eye: a gate, a state, a brow, a brest,	1522
What peromptorie Eagle-sighted eye	1575
Might shake off fiftie, looking in her eye:	1592
If that she learne not of her eye to looke:	1601

EYE *cont.*

Teaches such beautie as a womans eye:	1663
It addes a precious seeing to the eye:	1684
*discourse peremptorie: his tongue fyled, his eye ambitious,	1749
Formd by the eye, and therefore like the eye.	2720
Varying in subiectes as the eye doth roule,	2722
The sodaine hand of death close vp mine eye.	2775
Beholde the window of my hart, mine eye:	2799

EYES = 28*3

Your light growes darke by loosing of your eyes.	84
By the hartes still rethoricke, disclosed with eyes.	733
That all eyes saw his eyes inchaunted with gazes.	751
*your eyes, with your armes crost on your thinbellies doblet	787
With two pitch balles stucke in her face for eyes.	963
*thy replie, I prophane my lippes on thy foote, my eyes on	1063
Studie his byas leaues, and makes his booke thine eyes.	1272
*would not loue her; yes for her two eyes. Well, I do nothing	1343
One her haires were Golde, Christal the others eyes.	1479
Your eyes do make no couches in your teares.	1492
Ber. My eyes are then no eyes, nor I *Berowne.*	1581
Ber O if the streetes were paued with thine eyes,	1627
From womens eyes this doctrine I deriue,	1652
You haue in that forsworne the vse of eyes:	1660
Then when our selues we see in Ladies eyes, | With our selues.	1666
Such fierie Numbers as the prompting eyes,	1673
But Loue first learned in a Ladies eyes,	1678
A Louers eyes will gaze an Eagle blinde.	1685
From womens eyes this doctrine I deriue.	1701
I thought to close mine eyes some halfe an houre:	1982
Berow. Their eyes villaine, their eyes.	2058
Page. That euer turnde their eyes to mortall viewes.	2059
Page. Once to beholde with your Sunne beamed eyes,	2065
With your Sunne beamed eyes.	2066
You were best call it Daughter beamed eyes.	2068
They haue the Plague, and caught it of your eyes,	2354
Put on by vs, if in your heauenly eyes,	2725
Those heauenly eyes that looke into these faultes,	2727

EYE-SIGHT = 1

Doth falsely blinde the eye-sight of his looke:	81

EYLIDS = *1

*with turning vp your eylids, sigh a note and sing a note som-|time	783

EYNE = 1

(Those cloudes remooued) vpon our waterie eyne.	2105

EY-SIGHT = 2

Did stumble with haste in his ey-sight to bee,	743
As precious ey-sight, and did value me	2383

FA = *1

*Who vnderstandeth thee not, loues thee not, *vt re sol la mi fa*:	1261

FABLE = *1

*let that passe. By the world I recount no fable, some certaine	1838

FACE = 25*1

Ar. I will tell thee wonders. | *Ma.* With that face.	442
Kath. Faire fall the face it couers.	620
By thy fauour sweete Welkin, I must sigh in thy face:	837
With two pitch balles stucke in her face for eyes.	963
a Crab on the face of *Terra*, the soyle, the land, the earth.	1156

FACE *cont.*

As doth thy face through teares of mine giue light:	1364
*hand, a foote, a face, an eye: a gate, a state, a brow, a brest,	1522
The Sea will ebb and flow, heauen shew his face:	1564
No face is fayre that is not full so blacke.	1602
Ile finde a fayrer face not washt to day.	1622
Long. Looke, heer's thy loue, my foote and her face see.	1626
Without the beautie of a womans face?	1651
Now for not looking on a womans face,	1659
And if my face were but as faire as yours,	1920
O that your face were not so full of Oes.	1933
Quee. Heere comes *Boyet*, and myrth is in his face.	1970
Despight of sute, to see a Ladies face.	2021
But while tis spoke each turne away his face.	2040
Vouchsafe to shew the sunshine of your face,	2100
Rosa. My face is but a Moone, and clouded too.	2102
That hid the worse, and shewed the better face.	2317
Can anie face of brasse hold longer out?	2327
Pedan. I will not be put out of countenance. | *Bero.* Because thou hast no face.	2560
Bero. A deaths face in a Ring.	2565
Long. The face of an olde Roman coyne, scarce seene.	2566
Duma. The carud-bone face on a Flaske.	2568

FACERE = *1

*as it were *in via*, in way of explication *facere*: as it were	1164

FACES = 4

His faces owne margent did coate such amazes,	750
Or euer but in vizards shew their faces.	2190
Bero. False, we haue giuen thee faces.	2574
Duma. Hee's a God or a Painter: for he makes faces.	2599

FACILE = *1

Nath. Facile precor gellida, quando pecas omnia sub vmbra ru-|minat,	1257

FACILITIE = *2

Holo. I wil somthing affect the letter, for it argues facilitie.	1213
*facilitie, and golden cadence of poesie *caret*: *Ouiddius*	1287

FADGE = *1

Brag. We will haue, if this fadge not, an Antique. I be-|seech you follow.	1878

FAINE = 3

That he was faine to seale on *Cupids* name.	1896
When they are thirstie, fooles would faine haue drinke.	2299
The holy suite which faine it would conuince,	2704

FAIRE = 46*6

Ar. And so farewell. | *Ma.* Faire weather after you.	446
As our best mouing faire soliciter:	520
Boyet. Nauar had notice of your faire approch,	575
Nauar. Faire Princesse, Welcome to the court of *Nauar.*	585
Prin. Faire I giue you backe againe, and welcome I haue	586
Nau. Not for the worlde faire Madame, by my will.	594
Ber. Now faire befall your maske.	619
Kath. Faire fall the face it couers.	620
And holde faire friendship with his Maiestie,	636
From reasons yeelding, your faire selfe should make	646
You may not come (faire Princesse) within my gates,	669
Though so denide faire harbour in my house,	672
Pri. Sweete health and faire desires consort your grace.	675

FAIRE *cont.*
To feele only looking on fairest of faire:	745
Quee. I thanke my Beautie, I am faire that shoote,	985
O short liu'd pride. Not faire? alacke for woe | *For.* Yes Madam	
faire.	989
Where faire is not, praise cannot mend the brow.	992
Faire payment for foule wordes, is more then dew.	994
For. No thing but faire is that which you inherrit.	995
O heresy in faire, fit for these dayes,	997
A giuing hand, though fowle, shall haue faire praise.	998
*Boyet | *reedes.* By heauen, that thou art faire, is most infallible:	1041
*thou art louelie: more fairer then faire, beautifull then beau-|tious,	1043
*Then thou faire Sunne, which on my earth doost shine,	1402
Duma. As faire as day.	1425
Spied a blossome passing faire,	1440
Do meete as at a faire in her faire cheeke,	1584
Ber. Ile proue her faire, or talke till doomse-day heere.	1623
Of his faire Mistres, in the after noone	1727
Forerunne faire Loue, strewing her way with flowers.	1731
And if my face were but as faire as yours,	1920
Kath. Faire as a text B in a Coppie booke.	1930
But *Katherine* what was sent to you | From faire *Dumaine?*	1935
Duma. Faire Ladie.	2149
*Mar. Say you so? Faire Lord, take that for your faire Lady	2150
Long. A Calfe faire Ladie.	2161
Mar. No, a faire Lorde Calfe.	2162
Boy. Faire Ladies maskt, are Roses in their bud:	2218
King. Faire sir, God saue you: Wher's the Princesse?	2235
King. All haile sweete Madame, and faire time of day.	2265
Quee. Faire in all Haile is foule, as I conceaue.	2266
*King. Teach vs sweet Madame, for our rude transgression | Some faire excuse.	2364
Quee. And were you well aduisde? | *King.* I was faire Madame.	2369
Ber. Welcome pure wit, thou partst a faire fray.	2425
Brag. That is al one my faire sweete honie monarch,	2472
For all your faire endeuours and intreat:	2688
For your faire sakes, haue we neglected time.	2713
To those that make vs both faire Ladies you,	2732
Kath. A wife? a beard, faire health, and honestie,	2784

FAIRER = *1
*thou art louelie: more fairer then faire, beautifull then beau-|tious,	1043

FAIRES = 1
At Wakes and Wassels, meetings, markets, Faires.	2243

FAIREST = 4
To feele only looking on fairest of faire:	745
A Stand where you may make the fairest shoote.	984
And thereupon thou speakst the fairest shoote.	986
Quee. The fairest is confession.	2366

FAIRS = 1
I am comparde to twentie thousand fairs.	1925

FAITH *see also* yfaith = 2*1
Kath. Yes in good faith.	2200
King. My faith and this, the Princesse I did giue,	2393
*Clow. Faith vnlesse you play the honest *Troyan,* the poore	2631

FAITHFULL = 2
  Some thousand Verses of a faithfull Louer.   1940
  Ile change my blacke Gowne for a faithfull frend.   2795
FAITHFULLY = 1
  Of that which hath so faithfully been paide.   652
FALCE = 1
  By being once falce, for euer to be true   2731
FALCONBRIDGE *see also* Fauconbridge = *1
  Bo. Good sir be not offended, She is an heire of *Falcon-| (bridge.* 703
FALL = 3
  Kath. Faire fall the face it couers.   620
  Submissiue fall his princely feete before,   1070
  Or Pricket-sore, or els Sorell, | the people fall a hooting. 1221
FALLETH = *1
  *of *Celo* the skie, the welken the heauen, & anon falleth like 1155
FALSE = 5
  Perswade my hart to this false periurie?   1395
  Should rauish dooters with a false aspect: 1609
  Peda. Oh I smell false Latine, *dunghel* for *vnguem.*   1814
  Bero. False, we haue giuen thee faces.   2574
  Is likewise yours: we to our selues proue false,   2730
FALSEHOOD = *1
  *of falsehood) if I loue. And how can that be true loue, which 473
FALSELY = 1 *1
  Doth falsely blinde the eye-sight of his looke: 81
  *is falsely attempted? Loue is a familiar; Loue is a Diuell. 474
FALSHOOD = 1
  And euen that falshood in it selfe a sinne,   2733
FAME = 3
  Ferdinand. | Let Fame, that all hunt after in their lyues,   4
  Too much to know, is to know nought but fame: 97
  You are not ignorant all telling fame   512
FAMES = 1
  When for Fames sake, for praise an outward part,   1007
FAMILIAR = *1
  *is falsely attempted? Loue is a familiar; Loue is a Diuell. 474
FAMILIER = *2
  Boy. By a familier demonstration of the working, my | tough
signeor.   320
  Brag. Sir, the King is a noble Gentleman, and my fami-|lier, 1829
FANATTICALL *see* phanatticall
FANCIE = 1 *1
  This childe of Fancie that *Armado* hight,   181
  *out the odoriferous flowers of fancie? the ierkes of in-|uention 1289
FANGLED = 1
  Then wish a Snow in Mayes new fangled showes: 115
FANN = 1
  To see him walke before a Lady, and to beare her Fann. 1143
FANTASTICALL = 1
  For I protest, the Schoolemaister is exceeding fantasticall, 2473
FAR = 1
  Brag. This Hector *far surmounted* Hanniball.   2626
FARBOROUGH = *1
  *graces Farborough: But I would see his owne person | in flesh
and blood. | *Ber.* This is he.   196

FARE = 3
  *I must keepe her at the Parke, she is alowde for the Day |
  womand. Fare you well.   434
  Dum. A gallant Lady *Mounsir*, fare you wel. *Exit.*   694
  Clow. Well, I will do it sir: Fare you well.   922
FARES = 1
  King. How fares your Maiestie?   2684
FAREWEL = *1
  King. Farewel mad Wenches, you haue simple wits. *Exe.*   2181
FAREWELL = 4
  Ar. And so farewell. | *Ma.* Faire weather after you.   446
  Your owne good thoughts excuse me, and farewell.   673
  Boy. Farewell to me sir, and welcome to you. *Exit Bero.*   714
  Was guyltie of it.) Farewell worthy Lord: 2694
FARR = 1
  Deare Princesse were not his requestes so farr   645
FARRE = 2
  O Queene of queenes, how farre doost thou excell,   1372
  Long. Dumaine thy Loue is farre from charitie,   1464
FARTHING = 1*1
  Ber. O what is a remuneration? | *Cost.* Marie sir, halfepennie
  farthing.   913
  *a leuenpence-farthing better: most sweete gardon. I will   936
FARTHINGS = *2
  *Remuneration, O that's the latine word for three-farthings: 903
  *Three-farthings remuneration, What's the price of this yncle?   904
FASHION = 3*1
  A man in all the worldes new fashion planted,   175
  *vntrained, or rather vnlettered, or ratherest vnconfirmed
  fa-|shion,   1167
  I heard your guyltie Rimes, obserude your fashion: 1476
  Her fauour turnes the fashion of the dayes,   1611
FASHIONING = 1
  Hath much deformed vs, fashioning our humours   2715
FASHIONS = 1
  A man of fier new wordes, Fashions owne knight.   189
FASHYON = 1
  In their owne fashyon like a merriment.   2742
FAST = 10*3
  Longauill. I am resolued, tis but a three yeeres fast: 28
  Not to see Ladyes, study, fast, not sleepe.   52
  When I to fast expressely am forbid.   67
  Fer. Sir I will pronounce your sentence: You shall fast a | weeke
  with Branne and Water.   295
  *but a' must fast three dayes a weeke: for this Damsell   433
  Ar. Villaine, thou shalt fast for thy offences ere thou be |
  pardoned.   449
  Clo. Let me not be pent vp sir, I will fast being loose.   458
  Boy. No sir, that were fast and loose: thou shalt to prison.   460
  Ber. Your wit's too hot, it speedes too fast, twill tire.   615
  To sell a bargaine well is as cunning as fast and loose: 867
  King. Soft, Whither away so fast?   1524
  To fast, to study, and to see no woman: 1642
  Say, Can you fast? your stomacks are too young: 1644
FASTES = 1
  If frostes and fastes, hard lodging, and thin weedes,   2761

FASTING = 1
That shall expresse my trueloues fasting paine.   1459
FAT = 7
Fat paunches haue leane pates: and daynty bits   30
Sir, your penny-worth is good, and your Goose be fat.   866
Let me see a fat *Lenuoy*, I thats a fat Goose.   868
Then the boyes fat *Lenuoy*, the Goose that you bought,   875
Rosa. Wel-liking Wits they haue grosse grosse, fat fat.   2187
FATE = 1
That he should be my foole, and I his fate.   1958
FATHER = 10*3
To her decrepit, sicke, and bedred Father.   148
Consider who the King your father sendes: 493
Ferd. Madame, your father heere doth intimate,   624
Disbursed by my father in his warres.   627
If then the King your father will restore,   633
And haue the money by our father lent,   643
Prin. You do the King my father too much wrong,   649
For such a summe from speciall officers, | Of *Charles* his father.   658
**Lad.* 3. Then was *Venus* like her mother, for her father is | but
grim.   762
and as a certaine Father saith   1313
**Ped.* Sir tell not mee of the Father, I do feare colourable   1314
*What a ioyfull father wouldest thou make me?   1812
is heauie in my tongue. The King your father | *Quee.* Dead for
my life.   2676
FATHERS = 3*1
Boy. My fathers wit, and my mothers tongue assist me.   399
But *omne bene* say I, being of an olde Fathers minde,   1187
**Peda.* I do dine to day at the fathers of a certaine pupill of 1318
For the remembraunce of my Fathers death.   2770
FAUCHION = 1
Boyet. The pummel of *Caesars* Fauchion.   2567
FAUCONBRIDGE = 1
Betweene L.(ord) *Perigort* and the bewtious heire | Of *Iaques*
Fauconbridge solemnized.   533
FAULT = 5
If broken then, it is no fault of mine: 1404
It were a fault to snatch wordes from my tongue.   2309
**Clo.* Tis not so much worth: but I hope I was perfect. I | made a
litle fault in great.   2507
And I will haue you, and that fault withall.   2827
And I shall finde you emptie of that fault, | Right ioyfull of your
reformation.   2829
FAULTES = 4
Her faultes will nere be knowne: 404
For blush-in cheekes by faultes are bred,   405
Those heauenly eyes that looke into these faultes,   2727
You are attaint with faultes and periurie: 2779
FAUOUR = 8
By thy fauour sweete Welkin, I must sigh in thy face: 837
As thou wilt win my fauour, good my knaue,   918
Her fauour turnes the fashion of the dayes,   1611
But *Rosaline*, you haue a Fauour too?   1917
My Fauour were as great, be witnesse this,   1921
Holde *Rosaline*, this Fauour thou shalt weare,   2022
*of *Iaquenettaes*, and that a weares next his hart for a | Fauour.   2669

FAUOUR *cont.*
Therefore if you my fauour meane to get,   2780
FAUOURS = 7
  By Fauours seuerall, which they did bestow.   2017
  And change you Fauours two, so shall your Loues   2026
  Rosa. Come on then, weare the Fauours most in sight.   2028
  Pag. Out of your fauours heauenly spirites vouchsafe   2062
  Therefore change Fauours, and when they repaire,   2214
  The Ladies did change Fauours; and then wee   2407
  Your Fauours, embassadours of Loue.   2736
FAWNE = 1
  How I would make him fawne, and begge, and seeke,   1952
FAYRE = 4
  The onely soyle of his fayre vertues glose,   539
  Which his fayre tongue (conceites expositer)   564
  No face is fayre that is not full so blacke.   1602
  And therefore is she borne to make blacke fayre.   1610
FAYRER = 2*1
  By fixing it vppon a fayrer eye,   86
  *Why? it is a fayrer name then French-Crowne.   906
  Ile finde a fayrer face not washt to day.   1622
FAYREST = 1*1
  I were the fayrest Goddesse on the ground.   1924
  * *Page. A holy parcell of the fayrest dames that euer turnd their |*
  backes to mortall viewes.   2055
FAYRINGS = 1
  Yf Fayrings come thus plentifully in.   1889
FAYTH = 7*1
  If I breake fayth, this word shall speake for me,   164
  Ah neuer fayth could hold, yf not to beautie vowed.   1268
  him with thy Birdbolt vnder the left papp: in fayth secrets.   1356
  You would for Parradise breake Fayth and troth,   1480
  Fayth infringed, which such zeale did sweare.   1483
  Our louing lawfull, and our fayth not torne.   1634
  Quee. And quicke *Berowne* hath plighted Fayth to me.   2204
  *good neighbour fayth, and a very good Bowler: but for   2535
FAYTHFULL = 1
  Though to my selfe forsworne, to thee Ile faythfull proue.   1269
FAYTHFULLY = 1
  Duma. Ile serue thee true and faythfully till then.   2791
FEARD = 1*1
  I should haue feard her had shee been a deuill.   1998
  *and a feard to speake? Run away for shame *Ali-| sander.*   2532
FEARE = 5*5
  Then if she feare or be to blame, | By this you shall not know,   407
  * *Bo.* I feare too much rubbing: good night my good owle.   1135
  * *Holo.* Sir you haue done this in the feare of God verie
  reli-|giously: 1312
  * *Ped.* Sir tell not mee of the Father, I do feare colourable   1314
  * *Long.* I feare these stubborne lines lacke power to moue.   1387
  * *Ber.* A toy my Leedge, a toy: your grace needs not feare it.   1543
  For feare their colours should be washt away.   1620
  Yet feare not thou but speake audaciously.   1996
  Cuckow, Cuckow: O word of feare, | Vnpleasing to a married
  eare.   2867
  Cuckow, cuckow: O word of feare,   2876

FEARES = 1
And feares by pale white showne: 406
FEAST = 1*1
 1. *Lady.* I know him Maddame at a marriage feast, 532
 Boy. They haue been at a great feast of Languages, and | stolne the scraps. 1776
FEAT = 1
And euery one his Loue-feat will aduance, 2015
FED = *1
 Nath. Sir he hath neuer fed of the dainties that are bred | in a booke. 1174
FEEDE = 1
No Sheepe (sweete Lambe) vnlesse we feede on your lippes. 722
FEELDE = 1*1
He rather meanes to lodge you in the feelde, 579
 Quee. This Feelde shall holde me, and so hold your vow: 2271
FEELE = 1
To feele only looking on fairest of faire: 745
FEELING = 1*2
 Clow. Thou hast no feeling of it *Moth*, I will speake that | (*Lenuoy.* 880
 *and feeling, are for those partes that doe fructifie in vs | more then he. 1181
Loues feeling is more soft and sensible, 1688
FEETE = 3*1
 *the tongues ende, canarie to it with your feete, humour it 782
Submissiue fall his princely feete before, 1070
Her feete were much too daintie for such tread. 1628
The staires as he treades on them kisse his feete. 2255
FELICITIE = 1
A wife of such wood were felicitie. 1598
FELL = 2
Fell ouer the threshold, and broke my shin. 883
The fourth turnd on the tooe, and downe he fell: 2006
FELLOW = 4*2
My fellow Schollers, and to keepe those statutes 21
Ber. This fellow, What would'st? 194
 Que. Thou shalt know her fellow by the rest that haue no | (heads. 1020
Quee. Thou fellow, a worde. 1082
Berow. This fellow peckes vp Wit as Pidgions Pease, 2240
 Clow. Fellow *Hector*, she is gone; she is two months on | her way. 2628
FELLOWES = *1
 Clo. I am more bound to you then your fellowes, for they | are but lightly rewarded. 454
FELLOWSHIP = 1
Long. In loue I hope, sweete fellowship in shame. 1381
FEMALE = *1
 Ferd. With a childe of our Grandmother Eue, *a female; or for thy* 263
FEMININE = *1
 *put it to them. But *Vir sapis qui pauca loquitur*, a soule Femi-|nine saluteth vs. 1243
FER = 7*3
FERD = 15*6

FERDINAND see also Fer., Ferd. = 1
    Enter Ferdinand K.(ing) of Nauar, Berowne, | *Longauill, and*
    Dumaine.   2
FERDINAND = 1
FESTINATLY = *1
    *giue enlargement to the Swaine, bring him festinatly hither,   776
FETCH = *1
    Brag. Fetch hither the Swaine, he must carrie me a letter.   817
FETHERS = *1
    Quee. What plume of fethers is he that indited this letter?   1074
FEUER = 2
    Duma. I would forget her, but a Feuer shee   1431
    Ber. A Feuer in your blood, why then incision   1433
FEW = 2
    few haue the grace to do it.   1872
    Mari. The liker you, few taller are so young.   2797
FIE = 1
    Fie paynted Rethoricke, O shee needes it not,   1588
FIELDE = 3
    And I to be a Corporall of his fielde,   953
    King. Saint *Cupid* then and Souldiers to the fielde.   1717
    That oft in fielde with Targ and Shield did make my foe to sweat,   2500
FIELDES = 1
    welcome to the wide fieldes too base to be mine.   588
FIER = 4*1
    A man of fier new wordes, Fashions owne knight.   189
    *in a turph of Earth, Fier enough for a Flint, Pearle enough   1252
    Which not to anger bent, is musique, and sweete fier.   1281
    They sparcle still the right promethean fier,   1702
    And stand betweene her backe sir and the fier,   2415
FIERCE = 1
    With all the fierce endeuour of your wit,   2814
FIERD = 1
    Is that Lead slow which is fierd from a Gunne?   831
FIERIE = 2
    Such fierie Numbers as the prompting eyes,   1673
    With eies best seeing, heauens fierie eie: 2302
FIERWORKE = *1
    *or pageant, or antique, or fierworke: Now vnderstanding   1845
FIFT = 1
    Pag. The last of the fiue Vowels if You repeate them, | or the fift
    if I.   1791
FIFTIE = 2
    If Sore be sore, then el to Sore, | makes fiftie sores o sorell: 1223
    Might shake off fiftie, looking in her eye: 1592
FIGHT = 2*1
    Clow. Be to me, and euerie man that dares not fight. | *Ferd.* No
    wordes.   239
    A man so breathed, that certaine he would fight; yea,   2608
    Clow. I will not fight with a Pole like a Northren man;   2650
FIGURE = 3
    Arm. A most fine Figure. | *Boy.* To proue you a Cypher.   361
    Peda. What is the figure? What is the figure? | *Page.* Hornes.   1800
FIGURES = 1*1
    *extrauagant spirit, full of formes, figures, shapes, obiectes,   1231
    Figures pedanticall, these sommer flies,   2340

FILED *see* fyled
FILL = 1
   How manie inches doth fill vp one mile? 2091
FINDE = 7*2
   So ere you finde where light in darknes lyes, 83
   Pedan. You finde not the apostraphas, and so misse the 1284
   All vnseene, can passage finde: 1443
   But I a Beame do finde in each of three. 1499
   Ile finde a fayrer face not washt to day. 1622
   Lets vs once loose our othes to finde our selues, 1712
   Curat. Where will you finde men worthie enough to pre-|sent
   them? 1857
   Ros. We neede more light to finde your meaning out. 1908
   And I shall finde you emptie of that fault, | Right ioyfull of your
   reformation. 2829
FINDING = 1
   And therefore finding barraine practizers, 1676
FINE = 3*1
   Or studie where to meete some Mistris fine. 68
   Arm. A most fine Figure. | *Boy.* To proue you a Cypher. 361
   *such rackers of ortagriphie, as to speake dout fine, when he 1759
   Ber. What, are there but three? | *Clow.* No sir, but it is vara fine, 2428
FINELY = 3*1
   Rosa. Why she that beares the Bow. Finely put off. 1096
   hang me by the necke, if horns that yeere miscarrie. | Finely put
   on. 1098
   neare. Finely put on in deede. 1103
   Clow. We wil turne it finely off sir, we wil take some care. 2451
FINER = *1
   Peda. He draweth out the thred of his verbositie, finer 1756
FINGER *see also* fynger = 1*1
   *my poore shoulder, and with his royall finger thus dallie 1836
   Brag. I will kisse thy royall finger, and take leaue. 2845
FINGERS = *1
   *Go to, thou hast it *ad dungil* at the fingers ends, as they say. 1813
FINIS *l.*2901 = 1
FINISH = *1
   La. You Sheepe and I pasture: shall that finish the iest? 723
FIRE = 2
   Tis won as townes with fire, so won so lost. 157
   From whence doth spring the true *Promethean* fire. 1654
FIRST = 11*3
   That bites the first borne infants of the Spring. 110
   *Spaniards Rapier: The first and second cause will not serue 480
   Ber. Why villaine, thou must know first. 925
   Quee. What, what? First praise mee, and againe say no. 988
   it was a Bucke of the first head. 1160
   Long. Am I the first that haue been periurd so? 1383
   At the first opning of the gorgious East, 1572
   Consider what you first did sweare vnto: 1641
   But Loue first learned in a Ladies eyes, 1678
   Pell, mell, downe with them: but be first aduisd, 1719
   Ber. First from the Parke let vs conduct them thither, 1725
   *first shew thriue, these foure will change habites, and present |
   the other fiue. 2481
   Bero. There is fiue in the first shew. 2483
   Yet since Loues argument was first on foote, 2705

FIT = 5*1
 Duma. How followes that? | *Ber.* Fit in his place and tyme.   105
O heresy in faire, fit for these dayes,   997
One a these Maides girdles for your waste should be fit.   1026
 Clo. By my troth most plesant, how both did fit it.   1118
 *When it comes so smoothly off, so obscenly as it were, so fit.   1140
none so fit as to present the nine Worthies.   1855
FITTED = 1
Well fitted in artes, glorious in armes: 537
FITTETH = *1
 Arm. I am ill at reckning, it fitteth the spirit of a Tapster.   349
FIUE = 5*2
 *What was a month old at *Cains* birth, that's not fiue weeks | old
as yet?   1190
A witherd Hermite fiue score winters worne,   1591
 * *Pag.* The last of the fiue Vowels if You repeate them, | or the fift
if I.   1791
For he hath been fiue thousand yeere a Boy.   1898
 *first shew thriue, these foure will change habites, and present |
the other fiue.   2481
 Bero. There is fiue in the first shew.   2483
Cannot picke out fiue such, take each one in his vaine.   2488
FIUESCORE = 1
And rought not to fiue-weeks when he came to fiuescore.   1198
FIUE-WEEKS = 1
And rought not to fiue-weeks when he came to fiuescore.   1198
FIXED = 1
That giue a name to euery fixed Starre,   94
FIXING = 1
By fixing it vppon a fayrer eye,   86
FLAPDRAGON = 1
Thou art easier swallowed then a flapdragon.   1781
FLASH = *1
 *Ile flash, Ile do it by the Sword: I bepray you let me bor-|row
my Armes againe.   2651
FLASKE = 1
 Duma. The carud-bone face on a Flaske.   2568
FLAT = 1*1
 * *Clo.* The Boy hath sold him a bargaine, a Goose, that's flat.   865
Flat treason gainst the kingly state of youth.   1643
FLATTER = 1
To flatter vp these powers of mine with rest,   2774
FLATTERIE = 1
 Duma. I marie there, some flatterie for this euyll.   1635
FLAW = 1
My loue to thee is sound, *sance* cracke or flaw.   2347
FLEA = 1
 * *Bero.* I, if a'haue no more mans blood in his belly then wil |
suppe a Flea.   2647
FLEE = 1
 Boy. Thump then, and I flee.   835
FLEERD = 1
One rubbd his elbow thus, and fleerd, and swore,   2001
FLEETER = *1
 *Fleeter then Arrowes, bullets wind thought swifter thinges.   2177

FLESH = 3*2
*graces Farborough: But I would see his owne person | in flesh
and blood. | *Ber.* This is he.   196
Clow. Such is the simplicitie of man to harken after the flesh   228
Clow. My sweete ounce of mans flesh, my in-conie Iew: 901
Bero. This is the lyuer veine, which makes flesh a deitie.   1407
As true we are as flesh and blood can be,   1563
FLIE = 1
Or hide your heades like Cowardes, and flie hence.   1978
FLIES = 1
Figures pedanticall, these sommer flies,   2340
FLINT = *1
*in a turph of Earth, Fier enough for a Flint, Pearle enough   1252
FLORISH = 2
Needes not the painted florish of your prayse: 505
Lend me the florish of all gentle tongues,   1587
FLOURE = 1
This is the floure that smyles on euery one.   2256
FLOUT = 2
Quee. O pouertie in wit, Kingly poore flout.   2188
Bruse me with scorne, confound me with a flout.   2329
FLOUTES = 1
Full of comparisons and wounding floutes: 2805
FLOW = 1
The Sea will ebb and flow, heauen shew his face: 1564
FLOWER = 1
I am that Flower. | *Dum.* That Mint. | *Long.* That Cullambine.   2610
FLOWERS = 1*1
*out the odoriferous flowers of fancie? the ierkes of in-|uention   1289
Forerunne faire Loue, strewing her way with flowers.   1731
FLOWES = 1
The night of dew that on my cheekes downe flowes.   1361
FOE = 1
That oft in fielde with Targ and Shield did make my foe to sweat,   2500
FOLDE = 1
With three folde loue I wish you all these three.   2785
FOLDED = 1
Regent of Loue-rimes, Lord of folded armes,   947
FOLIO = *1
*Wit, write Pen, for I am for whole volumes in folio. *Exit.*   486
FOLKE = *1
Clow. Walke aside the true folke, and let the traytors stay.   1561
FOLLIE = 4
Sweete leaues shade follie. Who is he comes heere?   1375
As Wit turnde Foole, follie in Wisedome hatcht: 1960
Mar. Follie in Fooles beares not so strong a note,   1965
To checke their follie pashions solembe teares.   2010
FOLLOW = 2*2
Clow. As it shall follow in my correction, and God defend | the
right.   224
*Now will I begin your morrall, and do you follow with | my
lenuoy.   857
*for the best ward of mine honour, is rewarding | my dependants.
Moth, follow.   897
Brag. We will haue, if this fadge not, an Antique. I be-|seech
you follow.   1878

86

FOLLOWED = *1
   *Owle and the Cuckow? it should haue followed in the   2850
FOLLOWES = 1
   Duma. How followes that? | *Ber.* Fit in his place and tyme.   105
FOLLOWING = 1*2
   *vppon the Forme, and taken following her into the Parke: 218
   *which put togeather, is in manner and forme following.   219
   Ber. For the following sir.   223
FOLOWED = 1
   Bero. Well folowed, *Iudas* was hanged on an Elder.   2559
FOLOWING = 2
   Clow. In manner and forme folowing sir all those three.   216
   Folowing the signes, wood but the signe of shee.   2408
FOODE = 2
   And one day in a weeke to touch no foode: 43
   Foode for his rage, repasture for his den.   1073
FOOLE = 10*5
   Ros. Is the foole sicke. | *Ber.* Sicke at the hart.   681
   *For as it would ill become me to be vaine, indiscreet, or a |
   (foole,   1183
   *sorrow; for so they say the foole sayd, and so say I, and I the   1338
   *foole: Well proued wit. By the Lord this Loue is as madd   1339
   *it, the Foole sent it, and the Lady hath it: sweete Clowne,   1349
   *sweeter Foole, sweetest Lady. By the worlde, I woulde not   1350
   Berow. Now in thy likenesse, one more foole appeare.   1378
   If by mee broke, What foole is not so wise,   1405
   * *King.* What? | * *Ber.* That you three fooles, lackt me foole, to
   make vp the | (messe.   1551
   That he should be my foole, and I his fate.   1958
   As Wit turnde Foole, follie in Wisedome hatcht: 1960
   And Wits owne grace to grace a learned Foole.   1962
   Bero. I am a foole, and full of pouertie.   2307
   Ber. O, I am yours and all that I possesse. | *Rosa.* All the foole
   mine.   2310
   * *Bero.* The Pedant, the Bragart, the Hedge-Priest, the | Foole,
   and the Boy,   2485
FOOLES = 10*1
   Ber. What time a day? | *Kath.* The houre that fooles should aske.   617
   And wretched fooles secrets heedfully ore ey.   1414
   * *King.* What? | * *Ber.* That you three fooles, lackt me foole, to
   make vp the | (messe.   1551
   Then fooles you were, these women to forsweare: 1706
   Or keeping what is sworne, you will proue fooles,   1707
   Ros. They are worse fooles to purchase mocking so.   1949
   Mar. Follie in Fooles beares not so strong a note,   1965
   Let vs complaine to them what fooles were heare,   2225
   I dare not call them fooles; but this I thinke,   2298
   When they are thirstie, fooles would faine haue drinke.   2299
   Which shallow laughing hearers giue to fooles,   2821
FOOLISH = 2*2
   * *Nath.* This is a gyft that I haue simple: simple, a foolish   1230
   Your wits makes wise thinges foolish when we greete   2301
   Wise thinges seeme foolish, and rich thinges but poore.   2305
   *There ant shall please you a foolish mylde man, an   2533
FOOLRIE = 2
   O what a Scaene of foolrie haue I seene,   1500
   As foolrie in the Wise, when Wit doth dote: 1966

FOORTH = 3*1

*and so foorth. Ah good olde *Mantuan*, I may speake	1258
Bero. Now step I foorth to whip hipocrisie.	1488
Berowne steps foorth.	2621
ende of our shew. | *King.* Call them foorth quickly, we will do so.	2851

FOOT = 1

Quee. No, to the death we will not moue a foot,	2038

FOOTE = 4*3

*shoo (which is baser) guided by her foote (which is basest)	471
*thy replie, I prophane my lippes on thy foote, my eyes on	1063
*hand, a foote, a face, an eye: a gate, a state, a brow, a brest,	1522
Long. Looke, heer's thy loue, my foote and her face see.	1626
Do not you know my Ladies foote by'th squier?	2413
Boyet. Loues her by the foote.	2624
Yet since Loues argument was first on foote,	2705

FOR *l.*12 20 56 121 122 144 162 164 182 187 *195 *204 *206 *220
221 223 *247 *250 *263 *269 *275 *277 290 *306 *364 *368 *377
393 394 405 409 417 *433 *434 *449 *454 *466 *479 *483 *485
*486 499 549 551 561 562 581 594 608 638 658 *698 724 731 747
753 *762 768 821 823 851 872 *873 *897 *903 912 919 932 963
966 967 968 987 989 993 994 997 1004 1007 1009 1012 1014 1026
*1058 *1059 *1061 *1062 1073 *1119 *1133 1168 *1181 *1183
*1204 *1213 1236 *1237 *1238 *1252 1253 *1286 *1288 *1298
1317 *1326 *1338 *1342 *1343 1371 1396 1421 1450 1453 1454
1456 1457 1463 1471 1475 1480 1481 1486 1491 1520 1582 1612
*1618 1620 1621 1628 1635 1638 1649 1659 1662 1671 1691 1708
1709 1710 1715 1724 1730 *1741 *1767 *1779 1814 1819 *1826
*1830 *1834 *1863 1868 1873 1898 1904 1912 1914 1915 1995
2019 2023 2025 2032 2097 *2150 2156 2193 2205 2209 2213 2238
2273 2276 2306 *2326 2356 2359 2361 2363 *2364 2430 2438
*2443 *2448 2449 2473 2511 *2516 *2529 *2532 *2535 2540 2555
2572 2579 2580 *2583 2595 2599 *2614 *2636 2637 2653 *2657
2666 *2667 *2669 2675 2677 *2680 2688 2697 2713 2731 2752
2753 2770 2795 2801 2804 2840 2847 2865 2874 = 159*78

FOR = 2

FORBEARE = 3*1

Ber. To heare, or forbeare hearing.	208
**Lon.* To heare meekely sir, and to laugh moderatly, or | to forbeare both.	209
Ar. I say sing. | *Boy.* Forbeare till this companie be past.	428
**Quee.* Peace peace, forbeare: your Oth once broke, you | force not to forsweare.	2377

FORBID = 3

To know the thing I am forbid to know:	65
When I to fast expressely am forbid.	67
Forbid the smyling courtecie of Loue,	2703

FORBIDDEN = 1

Before we enter his forbidden gates,	517

FORCE = 3

Our late edict shall strongly stand in force,	15
Fer. We must of force dispence with this Decree,	158
**Quee.* Peace peace, forbeare: your Oth once broke, you | force not to forsweare.	2377

FOREHEAD = 1

Would from my forehead wipe a periurde note:	1462

FORERUNNE = 1

Forerunne faire Loue, strewing her way with flowers.	1731

FORESAID = *1
*the parentes of the foresaid childe or pupill, vndertake your 1321
FORESTALL = 1
Forestall our sport, to make vs thus vntrue? 2412
FOREUER see euer
FORFAIT = 2
Berow. Our states are forfait, seeke not to vndoo vs. 2358
That you stand forfait, being those that sue. 2360
FORGET = 2
It doth forget to do the thing it should: 155
Duma. I would forget her, but a Feuer shee 1431
FORGIUE = *1
*concerne much: stay not thy complement, I forgiue thy | dewtie,
adue. 1307
FORGOT = 2*1
Ferd. What say you Lordes? why, this was quite forgot. 151
Boy. The Hobbie-horse is forgot. 798
loue perhaps, a hacknie: But haue you forgot your Loue? 801
FORLORNE = 1
To some forlorne and naked Hermytage, 2755
FORMD = 1
Formd by the eye, and therefore like the eye. 2720
FORME = 7*2
Clow. In manner and forme folowing sir all those three. 216
*vppon the Forme, and taken following her into the Parke: 218
*which put togeather, is in manner and forme following. 219
to a woman, for the forme in some forme. 221
Proud with his forme, in his eye pride expressed. 741
This is the Ape of Forme, Mounsier the nice, 2250
Their forme confounded, makes most forme in myrth, 2463
FORMES = 2*1
*extrauagant spirit, full of formes, figures, shapes, obiectes, 1231
King. The extreame partes of time extreamly formes, 2698
Full of straying shapes, of habites and of formes: 2721
FORR = 3
FORRAGE = 1
And he from forrage will incline to play. 1071
FORRESTER see also For., Forr. = 2
Enter the Princesse, a Forrester, her Ladyes, | and her Lordes. 973
Then Forrester my friend, Where is the Bush 981
FORSOTH = *1
Ber. O and I forsoth in loue, I that haue been loues whip? 939
FORSWEARE = 3
Then fooles you were, these women to forsweare: 1706
I do forsweare them, and I here protest, 2342
Quee. Peace peace, forbeare: your Oth once broke, you | force
not to forsweare. 2377
FORSWORE = 2
A Woman I forswore, but I will proue, 1397
Thou being a Goddesse, I forswore not thee. 1398
FORSWORNE = 16*1
Ber. Necessitie will make vs all forsworne 160
I am forsworne on meere necessitie. 165
*doth tread. I shall be forsworne (which is a great argument 472
Prin. Our Lady helpe my Lord, he'le be forsworne. 593
If Loue make me forsworne, how shall I sweare to loue? 1267
Though to my selfe forsworne, to thee Ile faythfull proue. 1269

FORSWORNE *cont.*

Long. Ay mee! I am forsworne.	1379
That I am forsworne for thee:	1453
Therefore of all handes must we be forsworne.	1567
Ber. O nothing so sure, and thereby all forsworne.	1632
In that each of you haue forsworne his Booke.	1647
You haue in that forsworne the vse of eyes:	1660
And in that Vow we haue forsworne our Bookes:	1670
It is Religion to be thus forsworne.	1714
Light Wenches may proue plagues to men forsworne,	1736
We are againe forsworne in will and error.	2410
Kath. Yet sweare not, least ye be forsworne agen.	2792

FORT = 1

Bero. What reason haue you fort.	2664

FORTUNA = *1

*to *Fortuna delaguar*, I wish you the peace of mind most royall | cupplement. *Exit.*	2475

FORTUNES = 1

Bo. Belonging to whom? | *La.* To my fortunes and mee.	727

FORWARD = 1*1

And now forward, for we haue put thee in countenance.	2572
*But I will forward with my deuice; sweete royaltie bestow | on me the sence of hearing.	2619

FOSTRING = *1

*Nauar, *my soules earthes God, and bodies fostring patrone:*	232

FOULE = 3*1

Faire payment for foule wordes, is more then dew.	994
*that defiles; defile, a foule worde: Well, set thee downe	1337
Duma. Her Amber heires for foule hath amber coted.	1421
Quee. Faire in all Haile is foule, as I conceaue.	2266

FOULEPLAY = 1

Plaide fouleplay with our othes: your beautie Ladies	2714

FOUND = 4*1

*three ages since, but I thinke now tis not to be found: or if it	416
You found his Moth, the King your Moth did see:	1498
Haue found the ground of Studies excellence,	1650
In leaden contemplation haue found out	1672
As to reioyce at friendes but newly found.	2709

FOURE = 8*3

Long. Foure dayes ago.	131
Boy. Of all the foure, or the three, or the two, or one of | the foure.	385
Arm. Is that one of the foure complexions?	389
+And staied the oddes by adding foure.	856 +9
Staying the oddes by adding foure.	862
Dumaine transformed, foure Woodcocks in a dysh.	1416
We foure in deede confronted were with foure,	2294
Iudas Machabeus: And if these foure Worthies in their	2480
*first shew thriue, these foure will change habites, and present | the other fiue.	2481

FOURTH = 1

The fourth turnd on the tooe, and downe he fell:	2006

FOWER = *1

Bero. True true, we are fower: will these turtles be gon?	1558

FOWLE = 1*1

A giuing hand, though fowle, shall haue faire praise.	998
Ma. Come come, you talke greasely, your lips grow fowle.	1131

FOX = 1
+The Fox, the Ape, and the Humble-Bee,   856 +2
FOXE = 2
    +*Ar.* The Foxe, the Ape, and the Humble-Bee,   856 +6
    The Foxe, the Ape, and the Humble-Bee,   859
FRAME = 1
    Still a repairing: euer out of frame,   957
FRAMED = *1
    *with the King, and here he hath framed a letter to a sequent   1303
FRANCE = 3*1
    Tell him, the Daughter of the King of France   521
    And go well satisfied to France againe.   648
    To a Ladie of France, that he calde *Rosaline.*   1089
    *And lay my Armes before the Leggs of this sweete Lasse of
    France.*   2503
FRANCIS = *1
    Clow. O marrie me to one Francis, I smell some *Lenuoy,*   887
FRANTIQUE = 1
    ne inteligis domine, to make frantique lunatique?   1764
FRAUNCE = 3*1
    *Enter the Princesse of Fraunce, with three | attending Ladies and
    three Lordes.*   490
    Ore Saterday we will returne to Fraunce.   980
    *was a man when King *Pippen* of Fraunce was a litle boy, as |
    touching the hit it.   1109
    Shall we resolue to woe these gyrles of Fraunce?   1722
FRAY = 1
    Ber. Welcome pure wit, thou partst a faire fray.   2425
FREE = 3*1
    Brag. A most acute Iuuenall, volable and free of grace,   836
    These Lordes are visited, you are not free,   2355
    Quee. No, they are free that gaue these tokens to vs.   2357
    Brag. For mine owne part I breath free breath: I haue   2680
FRENCH = 2*2
    The French kinges daughter with your selfe to speake: 145
    *Desire prisoner, and ransome him to anie French Courtier   367
    Boy. Maister, will you win your loue with a french braule?   779
    Brag. How meanest thou? brawling in French.   780
FRENCH-CROWNE = *1
    *Why? it is a fayrer name then French-Crowne.   906
FREND = 1
    Ile change my blacke Gowne for a faithfull frend.   2795
FRESH = 2
    To those fresh morning dropps vpon the Rose,   1359
    As thy eye beames, when their fresh rayse haue smot.   1360
FRIEND = 2*1
    Then Forrester my friend, Where is the Bush   981
    Que. O thy letter, thy letter: He's a good friend of mine.   1031
    Nor neuer come in vizard to my friend,   2336
FRIENDE = *1
    *I do assure ye very good friende: for what is inwarde   1830
FRIENDES = 4*1
    Ros. Youle neare be friendes with him, a kild your sister.   1900
    King. Why take we handes then? | *Rosa.* Onely to part friendes. 2122
    Ber. Well said old mocker, I must needes be friendes with |
    (thee.   2495
    From what it purposd, since to wayle friendes lost,   2707

FRIENDES *cont.*
As to reioyce at friendes but newly found. 2709
FRIENDSHIP = 1
And holde faire friendship with his Maiestie, 636
FRIGHT = 2
Bero. Sweete Lord and why? | *Long.* To fright them hence with
that dread penaltie. 136
King. No Diuel will fright thee then so much as shee. 1624
FROM *l.*53 *62 69 92 127 184 203 *251 *254 *366 646 658 689 *748
831 *894 1029 1071 1086 1087 1088 1220 *1255 *1294 1449 1462
1464 1477 1526 1652 1654 1701 1716 1725 *1815 1891 1936 2042
2309 2325 2609 2707 2756 2808 2811 = 36*9
FROST = 1
Ferd. Berowne is like an enuious sneaping Frost, 109
FROSTES = 1
If frostes and fastes, hard lodging, and thin weedes, 2761
FROZEN = 2
Quee. Twentie adieus my frozen Muskouits. 2183
And Milke coms frozen home in paile: 2882
FRUCTFULL = 1
To weede this wormewood from your fructfull braine, 2808
FRUCTIFIE = *1
*and feeling, are for those partes that doe fructifie in vs | more
then he. 1181
FUL = *1
Ro. You tooke the moone at ful, but now shee's changed? 2114
FULFILLES = 1
For Charitie it selfe fulfilles the Law: 1715
FULL = 12*2
Clo. Well sir I hope when I do it, I shall do it on a full |
stomacke. 451
*extrauagant spirit, full of formes, figures, shapes, obiectes, 1231
No face is fayre that is not full so blacke. 1602
O that your face were not so full of Oes. 1933
Trim gallants, full of Courtship and of state. 2290
Bero. I am a foole, and full of pouertie. 2307
Haue blowne me full of maggot ostentation. 2341
Boyet. Full merely hath this braue nuage, this carreere | bin run. 2421
As Loue is full of vnbefitting straines, 2718
Full of straying shapes, of habites and of formes: 2721
Quee. We haue receiud your Letters, full of Loue: 2735
Full of deare guiltines, and therefore this, 2751
Full of comparisons and wounding floutes: 2805
When Blood is nipt, and wayes be full, 2883
FUNCTIONS = 1
Aboue their functions and their offices. 1683
FURIE = 1*1
*thy Lawes furie, and shall at the least of thy sweete notice, bring 271
King. What zeale, what furie, hath inspirde thee now? 1578
FYLED = *1
*discourse peremptorie: his tongue fyled, his eye ambitious, 1749
FYNGER = 1
Another with his fynger and his thume, 2003
GAINDE = 1
Thy grace being gainde, cures all disgrace in mee. 1400
GAINE = 1
If studies gaine be thus, and this be so, 72

GAINST = 4
A yeelding gainst some reason in my brest,   647
Gainst thee thou Lambe, that standest as his pray: 1069
Gainst whom the world cannot holde argument,   1394
Flat treason gainst the kingly state of youth.   1643
GALL = 2
Bero. Thou greeuest my gall. | *Quee.* Gall, bitter, | *Bero.*
Therefore meete.   2144
GALLANT = 2*2
Dum. A gallant Lady *Mounsir*, fare you wel. *Exit.*   694
*assistants the Kinges commaund, and this most gallant
il-|lustrate   1853
* *Peda. Iosua*, your selfe, my selfe, and this gallant Gentle-|man   1859
This Gallant pins the Wenches on his sleeue.   2246
GALLANTS = 3
Quee. And will they so? the Gallants shalbe taskt: 2018
Boyet. Ladies, withdraw: the gallants are at hand,   2231
Trim gallants, full of Courtship and of state.   2290
GALLOPS = 1
A true man, or a theefe, that gallops so.   1525
GALLOWES = 1
Kath. I and a shrowde vnhappie gallowes too.   1899
GAME = 2*1
*Away, the gentles are at their game, and we will to our re-
|creation. *Exeunt.*   1331
So shall we stay mocking entended game,   2047
We haue had pastimes here and pleasant game,   2286
GAMSTER = 1
Boy. You are a Gentleman and a Gamster sir.   350
GARDE = 1
Though *Argus* were her eunuch and her garde.   965
GARDEN = *1
* *East from the West corner of thy curious knotted garden; There*   254
GARDES = 1
Ber. O Rimes are gardes on wanton *Cupids* hose, | Disfigure not
his Shop.   1390
GARDON = 1*3
* *Clow.* Gardon, O sweete gardon, better then remuneratio(n).   935
*a leuenpence-farthing better: most sweete gardon. I will   936
do it sir in print: gardon remuneration. | *Exit.*   937
GARNISHED = 1
That euery one her owne hath garnished,   570
GATE = 1*2
Clymbe ore the house to vnlocke the little gate.   118
*hand, a foote, a face, an eye: a gate, a state, a brow, a brest,   1522
*his gate maiesticall, and his generall behauiour vaine,
redicu-|lous,   1750
GATED = 1
for he is verie slow gated: but I go.   823
GATES = 2*2
*great carriage: for he carried the Towne-gates on his backe   377
*thee in my rapier, as much as thou didst me in carying gates.   380
Before we enter his forbidden gates,   517
You may not come (faire Princesse) within my gates,   669
GAUDIE = 1
Nip not the gaudie blossomes of your Loue: 2762

GAUDIO = 1
   Curat. Vides ne quis venit? | *Peda. Video, et gaudio.*   1770
GAUE = 6
   And prodigally gaue them all to you.   503
   Who gaue thee this letter? | *Clow.* I tolde you, my Lord.   1083
   Quee. No, they are free that gaue these tokens to vs.   2357
   You gaue me this: but take it sir againe.   2392
   Braggart. The Armipotent Mars, *of Launces the almightie,* | *gaue*
Hector *a gift.*   2600
   Gaue Hector *a gift, the heir of Illion,*   2607
GAZE = 1
   A Louers eyes will gaze an Eagle blinde.   1685
GAZES = 1
   That all eyes saw his eyes inchaunted with gazes.   751
GEARE = 1
   Disguysd like *Muscouites* in shapeles geare: 2226
GEESE = *1
   Ber. The Spring is neare when greene geese are a bree- | (ding.   103
GELDED *see* guelded
GELLIDA = *1
   *Nath. Facile precor gellida, quando pecas omnia sub vmbra
ru-* | *minat,*   1257
GENERALL = 2*1
   When she did starue the generall world beside,   502
   Sole Emperator and great generall | Of trotting Parrators (O my
litle hart.)   951
   *his gate maiesticall, and his generall behauiour vaine,
redicu-* | *lous,*   1750
GENEROUS = 1*1
   Peda. The *posterior* of the day, most generous sir, is liable,   1825
   Pedan. This is not generous, not gentle, not humble.   2582
GENTLE = 10
   And he and his compettitours in oth, | Were all addrest to meete
you gentle Lady   576
   Bo. So you graunt pasture for me. | *Lad.* Not so gentle Beast.   724
   And in her traine there is a gentle Ladie: 930
   And gentle *Longauill,* where lies thy paine?   1509
   Lend me the florish of all gentle tongues,   1587
   Berow. Nothing but peace, and gentle visitation.   2077
   Rosa. What would they, say they? | *Boy.* Nothing but peace, and
gentle visitation.   2078
   Bero. This iest is drie to me, gentle sweete,   2300
   Pedan. This is not generous, not gentle, not humble.   2582
   Duma. O shall I say, I thanke you gentle Wife?   2786
GENTLEMAN = 2*4
   of thy health-geuing ayre: And as I am a Gentleman, betooke my
Boy. You are a Gentleman and a Gamster sir.   244
   Boy. You are a Gentleman and a Gamster sir.   350
   Brag. Sir, the King is a noble Gentleman, and my fami- | lier,   1829
   *and learned Gentleman, before the Princesse: I say   1854
   Peda. Iosua, your selfe, my selfe, and this gallant Gentle- | man   1859
   Page. Thrice worthie Gentleman.   1875
GENTLEMEN = *1
   Brag. Gentlemen and Souldiers, pardon me, I will not | combat
in my shyrt.   2659
GENTLENES = 1
   In the conuerse of breath (your gentlenes   2693

GENTLES = 1*1
Prin. Good witts will be iangling, but gentles agree, 729
*Away, the gentles are at their game, and we will to our re-
|creation. *Exeunt.* 1331
GENTLETIE = 1
A dangerous law against gentletie. 138
GEORGES = 1
Bero. Saint *Georges* halfe cheeke in a Brooch. 2569
GERMANE *see* Iermane
GESSE = 1
Boy. They do, they do; and are appariled thus, | Like *Muscouites,*
or *Russians,* as I gesse. 2012
GET = 3*1
Clo. Then will she get the vpshoot by cleauing the is in. 1129
In conflict that you get the Sunne of them. 1720
Clow. O Lord sir, it were pittie you should get your liuing | by
reckning sir. 2439
Therefore if you my fauour meane to get, 2780
GEUEN = *2
*it was geuen me by *Costard,* and sent me from *Don Armatho*: 1255
*will be geuen to *Aiax.* He wilbe the ninth Worthie: a
Con-|querour, 2531
GEUING = *1
*of thy health-geuing ayre: And as I am a Gentleman, betooke my 244
GIANT *see* gyant
GIBING = 1
Rosal. Why thats the way to choake a gibing spirrit, 2819
GIFT *see also* gyft = 3
*Braggart. The Armipotent Mars, of Launces the almightie, | gaue
Hector *a gift.* 2600
Duma. A gift Nutmegg. | *Bero.* A Lemmon. 2602
Gaue Hector *a gift, the heir of Illion,* 2607
GIGG = *1
Peda. Thou disputes like an Infant: goe whip thy Gigg. 1802
GIGGE = 1*1
To see great *Hercules* whipping a Gigge, 1504
*about your Infamie *vnu(m) cita* a gigge of a Cuckolds horne. 1805
GILL = 1
Iacke hath not Gill: these Ladies courtesie 2836
GINGER = *1
*haue it to buy Ginger bread: Holde, there is the verie 1808
GIRDLES = 1
One a these Maides girdles for your waste should be fit. 1026
GIRLE = 1*2
*with *Iaquenetta,* and *Iaquenetta* is a trew girle, and therefore 307
*I do loue, that Countrey girle that I tooke in the Parke 421
Cost. Haue with thee my girle. *Exit.* 1311
GIRLES *see also* gyrles = 1
Quee. We are wise girles to mocke our Louers so. 1948
GIUE = 23*6
And giue him light that it was blinded by. 88
That giue a name to euery fixed Starre, 94
And euery Godfather can giue a name. 98
Giue me the paper, let me reade the same, 125
Bero. Well sir, be it as the stile shall giue vs cause to clime | in
the merrines. 211
Prin. Faire I giue you backe againe, and welcome I haue 586

GIUE *cont.*
We will giue vp our right in *Aquitaine,*   635
Ile giue you *Aquitaine,* and all that is his,   752
And you giue him for my sake but one louing kisse.   753
*giue enlargement to the Swaine, bring him festinatly hither,   776
Arm. I giue thee thy libertie, set thee from durance, and in   894
*i.d. no, Ile giue you a remuneration: Why? it carries it
re-|muneration: 905
Breake the necke of the Waxe, and euery one giue eare.   1039
Quee. To whom shouldst thou giue it?| *Clow.* From my Lord to
my Ladie.   1085
Iaquenetta. God giue you good morrow M.(aister) Person.   1246
a paper, God giue him grace to grone.   1352
As doth thy face through teares of mine giue light: 1364
O who can giue an oth? Where is a booke?   1599
Holde take thou this my sweete, and giue mee thine,   2024
Will you giue hornes chast Lady? do not so.   2168
Boyet. Madame, and prettie mistresses giue eare.   2207
Quee. Then wish me better, I will giue you leaue.   2268
Ber. I cannot giue you lesse.   2312
Quee. God giue thee ioy of him: the Noble Lord   2386
King. My faith and this, the Princesse I did giue,   2393
Bero. For the *Asse* to the *Iude:* giue it him. *Iudas* away.   2580
Long. I must rather giue it the raine: for it runnes against|
Hector.   2614
Then if I haue much loue, Ile giue you some.   2790
Which shallow laughing hearers giue to fooles,   2821
GIUEN *see also* geuen = 1
Bero. False, we haue giuen thee faces.   2574
GIUES = 5
Most rude melancholie, Valour giues thee place.   838
King. So sweete a kisse the golden Sunne giues not,   1358
And giues the Crutch the Cradles infancie.   1594
And giues to euery power a double power,   1682
My Ladie (to the maner of the dayes)| In curtesie giues
vndeseruing praise.   2292
GIUING *see also* geuing = 2
Ber. I cannot stay thankes-giuing. *Exit.*   690
A giuing hand, though fowle, shall haue faire praise.   998
GLAD = *1
Ros. Pray you, do my commendations, I would be glad| to see
it.   678
GLASSE = 1
Heere (good my glasse) take this for telling trew: 993
GLASSES = 1
My teares for glasses, and still make me weepe.   1371
GLAST = 1
*Who tendring their owne worth from where they were| (glast,   748
GLAUNCE = 1
To euery varied obiect in his glaunce: 2723
GLORIE = 2*1
*not; his disgrace is to be called Boy, but his glorie is to sub-|due   482
Glorie growes guyltie of detested crimes,   1006
And they thy glorie through my griefe will show: 1369
GLORIOUS = 2
Studie is lyke the heauens glorious Sunne,   89
Well fitted in artes, glorious in armes: 537

GLOSE = 2
The onely soyle of his fayre vertues glose,   539
If vertues glose will staine with any soyle,   540
GLOUE = 2
Kath. Madame, this Gloue.   1937
By this white Gloue (how white the hand God knowes)   2343
GLOZES = 1
Long. Now to plaine dealing, Lay these glozes by,   1721
GNAT = 1
To see a King transformed to a Gnat.   1503
GO = 11*2
Ferd. Well, sit you out: go home *Berowne*: adue.   119
Boy. Proud of imployment, willingly I go. *Exit Boy.*   526
And go well satisfied to France againe.   648
Brag. Sweete Ayer, go tendernes of yeeres, take this Key,   775
for he is verie slow gated: but I go.   823
But being watcht, that it may still go right.   959
To pray for her, go to: it is a plague   967
Mayd. Good *Costard* go with me: sir God saue your life.   1309
Long. This same shall go. *He reades the Sonnet.*   1392
Ber. I post from Loue, good Louer let me go.   1526
*Go to, thou hast it *ad dungil* at the fingers ends, as they say. 1813
That same *Berowne* ile torture ere I go.   1950
Boyet. Therefore as he is, an Asse, let him go: 2577
GOD = 21*10
Bero. How low so euer the matter, I hope in God for high |
(words.   204
Lon. A high hope for a low heauen. God grant vs patience   206
Clow. As it shall follow in my correction, and God defend | the
right.   224
Nauar, my soules earthes God, and bodies fostring patrone: 232
*therfore I will say nothing: I thanke God I haue as little
pa-|tience   467
*God of Rime, for I am sure I shall turne Sonnet. Deuise   485
Prin. God blesse my Ladyes, are they all in loue?   569
Ber. Now God saue thy life. | *Ros.* And yours from long liuing. 688
Cost. I thanke your worship, God be wy you.   916
Clo. God dig-you-den al, pray you which is the head lady?   1018
Holo. God comfort thy capacitie, I say th'allusion holdes [in the
Exchange.   1202
Iaquenetta. God giue you good morrow M.(aister) Person.   1246
Mayd. Good *Costard* go with me: sir God saue your life.   1309
Holo. Sir you haue done this in the feare of God verie
reli-|giously: 1312
a paper, God giue him grace to grone.   1352
God amende vs, God amende, we are much out a th'way.   1409
Like a demie God, here sit I in the skie,   1413
Iaqu. God blesse the King. *Enter Iaquenetta and Clowne.*   1528
Curat. I prayse God for you sir, your reasons at Dinner   1741
Quee. Will they returne? | *Boy.* They will they will, God knowes, 2211
King. Faire sir, God saue you: Wher's the Princesse?   2235
And vtters it againe when God dooth please.   2241
Nor God nor I delights in periurd men.   2272
By this white Gloue (how white the hand God knowes)   2343
And to begin Wench, so God helpe me law,   2346
Quee. God giue thee ioy of him: the Noble Lord   2386
Quee. Doth this man serue God? | *Bero.* Why aske you?   2469

GOD *cont.*

    Quee. A speakes not like a man of God his making.   2471
    Duma. Hee's a God or a Painter: for he makes faces.   2599
    Marcad. God saue you Madame.   2672

GODDES = 1

    And when Loue speakes, the voyce of all the Goddes,   1695

GODDESSE = 3

    Thou being a Goddesse, I forswore not thee.   1398
    A greene Goose, a Goddesse, pure pure ydolatarie.   1408
    I were the fayrest Goddesse on the ground.   1924

GODFATHER = 1

    And euery Godfather can giue a name.   98

GODFATHERS = 1

    These earthly Godfathers of heauens lights,   93

GODS = 1

    Lon. Gods blessing on your beard.   702

GOD-HEAD = 1

    Rosa. That was the way to make his god-head Wax: 1897

GOD-LIKE = 1

    Ferd. I, that is studies god-like recompence.   63

GOE = 8*2

    And goe we Lordes to put in practise that,   301
    This seald-vp counsaile. Ther's thy guerdon: goe.   934
    *of progression, hath miscarried. Trip and goe my sweete,   1305
    The treason and you goe in peace away togeather.   1534
    * *Peda.* Thou disputes like an Infant: goe whip thy Gigg.   1802
    Quee. Goe sicknes as thou art.   2201
    You put our Page out: goe, you are aloude.   2417
    Bero. Goe bid them prepare. (*Exit.*   2450
    I goe Woolward for pennance.   2666
    Your oth I will not trust, but goe with speede   2754

GOES = 3*1

    But come, the Bow: Now Mercie goes to kill,   999
    * *Boy.* My Lady goes to kill hornes, but if thou marrie,   1097
    Duma. O vile, then as she goes what vpward lyes?   1629
    The thirde he caperd and cryed, All goes well.   2005

GOING = 2

    And neuer going a right, being a Watch: 958
    Quee. Els your memorie is bad, going ore it erewhile.   1078

GOLDE = 1

    One her haires were Golde, Christal the others eyes.   1479

GOLDEN = 2*1

    *facilitie, and golden cadence of poesie *caret: Ouiddius*   1287
    King. So sweete a kisse the golden Sunne giues not,   1358
    My red Dominicall, my golden letter,   1932

GON = 3*1

    Ber. Nay then will I be gon.   623
    * *Bero.* True true, we are fower: will these turtles be gon?   1558
    Rosa. Why that they haue, and bid them so be gon.   2080
    Boy. She saies you haue it, and you may be gon.   2081

GONE = 3*2

    Boy. What then, do you see? | *Lad.* I, our way to be gone.   766
    Of manie weerie miles you haue ore gone,   2095
    * *Boyet.* Gone to her Tent. Please it your Maiestie com-|maunde   2236
    The partie is gone.   2627
    * *Clow.* Fellow *Hector,* she is gone; she is two months on | her
    way.   2628

GOOD = 35*22

Dum. Proceeded well, to stop all good proceeding.	100
Bero. No my good Lord, I haue sworne to stay with you.	120
good reput, carriage bearing, and estimation.	267
Bero. Ile lay my Head to any good mans Hat,	303
*name more; and sweete my childe let them be men of good | repute and carriage.	374
Boy. Sampson Maister, he was a man of good carriage,	376
*seduced, and he had a very good wit. *Cupids* Butshaft is too	478
Queene. Good L.(ord) *Boyet*, my beautie though but meane,	504
But now to taske the tasker, good *Boyet*,	511
For he hath wit to make an ill shape good,	551
And much too little of that good I saw,	554
Your owne good thoughtes excuse me, and farewell.	673
Ber. Would that do it good? | *Ros.* My Phisicke saies I.	684
Bo. Good sir be not offended, She is an heire of *Falcon-* | *(bridge.*	703
Bero. Whats her name in the capp? | *Boy.* *Katherin* by good happ.	709
Prin. Good witts will be iangling, but gentles agree,	729
Pag. A good *Lenuoy*, ending in the Goose: woulde you | desire more?	863
Sir, your penny-worth is good, and your Goose be fat.	866
Ber. O my good knaue *Costard*, exceedingly well met.	910
As thou wilt win my fauour, good my knaue,	918
Heere (good my glasse) take this for telling trew:	993
Que. O thy letter, thy letter: He's a good friend of mine.	1031
Stand a side good bearer. *Boyet* you can carue,	1032
Clow. From my Lord *Berowne*, a good Maister of mine,	1088
Thou canst not hit it my good man. *Exit.*	1115
Bo. I feare too much rubbing: good night my good owle.	1135
Nat. Very reuerent sport truly, and done in the testimonie | of a good conscience.	1151
Nath. *Perge*, good M.(aister) *Holofernes perge*, so it shall please | you to abrogate squirilitie.	1211
*gyft is good in those whom it is acute, and I am thankfull | for it.	1235
*Daughters profite very greatly vnder you: you are a good | member of the common wealth.	1239
Iaquenetta. God giue you good morrow M.(aister) Person.	1246
Nath. Of persing a Hogshead, a good luster of conceit	1251
Iaque. Good M.(aister) Parson be so good as read me this letter,	1254
*and so foorth. Ah good olde *Mantuan*, I may speake	1258
Mayd. Good *Costard* go with me: sir God saue your life.	1309
King. And mine too good Lord.	1429
Ber. Amen, so I had mine: Is not that a good word?	1430
Ah good my Leidge, I pray thee pardon mee.	1489
Good hart, What grace hast thou thus to reproue	1490
Where lies thy griefe, o tell me good *Dumaine*?	1508
Ber. I post from Loue, good Louer let me go.	1526
King. Twere good yours did: for sir to tell you plaine,	1621
King. Then leaue this chat, and good *Berowne* now proue	1633
*I do assure ye very good friende: for what is inwarde	1830
*that the Curate and your sweete selfe, are good at such erup-|tions,	1846
Quee. Beautious as Incke: a good conclusion.	1929
The King was weeping ripe for a good word.	2193
Kath. Yes in good faith.	2200
Rosa. Good Madame, if by me youle be aduisde,	2223

99

GOOD *cont.*
Quee. Nay my good Lord let me ore'rule you now.   2459
King. Heere is like to be a good presence of Worthies: 2477
* *Qu.* The conqueror is dismaid: proceed good *Alexander.*   2520
*good neighbour fayth, and a very good Bowler: but for   2535
Quee. Stand aside good *Pompey.*   2539
GOODMAN = 2
Holo. Dictisima goodman *Dull, dictisima* goodman *Dull.*   1192
GOODNIGHT *see* good
GOOD-MAN = *1
* *Peda. Via* good-man *Dull,* thou hast spoken no worde all | this
while.   1880
GOOSE = 7*2
+ *Pag.* Vntill the Goose came out of doore,   856 +8
Arm. Vntill the Goose came out of doore,   861
* *Pag.* A good *Lenuoy,* ending in the Goose: woulde you | desire
more?   863
* *Clo.* The Boy hath sold him a bargaine, a Goose, that's flat.   865
Sir, your penny-worth is good, and your Goose be fat.   866
Let me see a fat *Lenuoy,* I thats a fat Goose.   868
Then the boyes fat *Lenuoy,* the Goose that you bought,   875
some Goose in this.   888
A greene Goose, a Goddesse, pure pure ydolatarie.   1408
GORGIOUS = 1
At the first opning of the gorgious East,   1572
GOWNE = 1
Ile change my blacke Gowne for a faithfull frend.   2795
GRACE = 25*4
And then grace vs, in the disgrace of death: 7
I onely swore to study with your grace,   55
A Maide of grace and complet maiestie, | About surrender vp of
Aquitaine,   146
Not by might mastred, but by speciall grace.   163
Be now as prodigall of all Deare grace,   500
Importuous personall conference with his grace.   523
And shape to win grace though he had no wit.   552
I heare your grace hath sworne out Houskeeping: 599
Boyet. So please your Grace, the packet is not come,   661
* *Pri.* Sweete health and faire desires consort your grace.   675
Brag. A most acute Iuuenall, volable and free of grace,   836
*the table with a Grace, I will on my priuiledge I haue with   1320
a paper, God giue him grace to grone.   1352
Thy grace being gainde, cures all disgrace in mee.   1400
Good hart, What grace hast thou thus to reproue   1490
Iaque. I beseech your Grace let this Letter be read,   1535
* *Ber.* A toy my Leedge, a toy: your grace needs not feare it.   1543
*please his Grace (by the worlde) sometime to leane vpon   1835
few haue the grace to do it.   1872
And Wits owne grace to grace a learned Foole.   1962
Boyet. O I am stable with laughter, Wher's her Grace?   1971
And not a man of them shall haue the grace   2020
Nor to their pend speach render we no grace: 2039
Haue not the grace to grace it with such show.   2245
Thus purifies it selfe and turns to grace.   2734
No no my Lord, your Grace is periurde much,   2750
Whose influence is begot of that loose grace,   2820

GRACES = 2*2
*graces Farborough: But I would see his owne person | in flesh
and blood. | *Ber.* This is he.   196
**by thy sweete Graces Officer* Anthonie Dull, *a man of*   266
As Nature was in making Graces deare,   501
Brag. I do adore thy sweete Graces Slipper.   2623
GRACIOUS = 3*1
Deliuers in such apt and gracious wordes,   565
My Loue (her Mistres) is a gracious Moone,   1579
*Snake; that is the way to make an offence gracious, though   1871
Quee. Prepare I say: I thanke you gracious Lords   2687
GRANDAM = 1
nimble stiring spirit, she might a bin Grandam ere she died.   1903
GRANDMOTHER = *1
**Ferd. With a childe of our Grandmother* Eue, *a female; or for thy* 263
GRANT = *1
**Lon.* A high hope for a low heauen. God grant vs patience   206
GRAPPLE = 1
Boy. I was as willing to grapple as he was to boord.   719
GRASE = *1
**most grase, Birdes best peck, and Men sit downe to that
nourishment*   246
GRASSE = 2
To treade a Measure with her on this grasse.   2083
To tread a Measure with you on this grasse.   2085
GRATIFIE = *1
*mine, where if (before repast) it shall please you to gratifie   1319
GRAUITIES = 2
As grauities reuolt to wantons be.   1964
Haue misbecombd our othes and grauities.   2726
GRAUNDFATHER = *1
**Lad.* 2. He is *Cupids* Graundfather, and learnes newes | of him. 760
GRAUNT = 2
Bo. So you graunt pasture for me. | *Lad.* Not so gentle Beast. 724
King. Now at the latest minute of the houre, | Graunt vs your
loues.   2746
GRAUNTED = 1
But is there no quicke recreation graunted?   172
GREASELY = *1
**Ma.* Come come, you talke greasely, your lips grow fowle.   1131
GREASIE = 2
While greasie Ione doth keele the pot.   2887
While greasie Ione doth keele the pot.   2896
GREAT = 19*14
**Ferd. Great Deputie the welkins Vizgerent, and sole dominatur of* 231
**Armado.* Boy, What signe is it when a man of great spi-|rite
growes melancholy?   312
Boy. A great signe sir that he will looke sadd.   314
*I should outsweare *Cupid.* Comfort mee Boy, what great   370
*great carriage: for he carried the Towne-gates on his backe   377
Boy. And thats great maruaile, louing a light Wench.   427
*doth tread. I shall be forsworne (which is a great argument   472
Is my report to his great worthines.   555
Sole Emperor and great generall | Of trotting Parrators (O my
litle hart.)   951
To see great *Hercules* whipping a Gigge,   1504

GREAT *cont.*

Boy. They haue been at a great feast of Languages, and | stolne
the scraps.   1776
*importunt and most serious designes, and of great import in   1833
Iudas Machabeus; this Swaine (because of his great lim   1860
or ioynt) shall passe *Pompey* the great, the Page *Hercules.*   1861
Ros. Great reason: for past care, is still past cure.   1915
My Fauour were as great, be witnesse this,   1921
*am (as they say, but to parfect one man in one poore man) |
Pompion the great sir.   2444
*the great: for mine owne part I know not the degree of the   2448
When great thinges labouring perish in their byrth.   2464
*He presents *Hector* of *Troy,* the Swaine *Pompey* the great, the   2478
Clow. I *Pompey am,* Pompey *surnamde the bigge.* | *Duma.* The
great.   2497
Clow. It is great sir, Pompey *surnamd the great.*   2499
Lady. Great thankes great *Pompey.*   2506
Clo. Tis not so much worth: but I hope I was perfect. I | made a
litle fault in great.   2507
Bero. Pompey the great. | *Clow.* Your seruant and *Costard.*   2525
Peda. Great *Hercules is presented by this Impe,*   2541
Bero. Greater then great, great, great, great *Pompey: Pom-|pey*
the hudge.   2641
For my great sute, so easely obtainde.   2697
GREATER = 1*1
Rosa. O vaine peticioner, begg a greater matter,   2106
Bero. Greater then great, great, great, great *Pompey: Pom-|pey*
the hudge.   2641
GREATEST = 1
Clow. Which is the greatest Ladie, the highest?   1022
GREATLY = *1
*Daughters profite very greatly vnder you: you are a good |
member of the common wealth.   1239
GREATNES = *2
*special honours it pleaseth his greatnes to impart to *Armado*   1839
*But most esteemed greatnes, will you heare the Dialogue   2848
GREENE = 3*2
Ber. The Spring is neare when greene geese are a bree-|(ding.   103
Arm. Tell me precisely of what complexion? | *Boy.* Of the sea-
water Greene sir.   387
Arm. Greene in deede is the colour of Louers: but to   391
Boy. It was so sir, for she had a greene wit.   394
A greene Goose, a Goddesse, pure pure ydolatarie.   1408
GREETE = 2
With Visages displayde to talke and greete.   2036
Your wits makes wise thinges foolish when we greete   2301
GREEUEST = 1
Bero. Thou greeuest my gall. | *Quee.* Gall, bitter, | *Bero.*
Therefore meete.   2144
GREYHOUND = 1
Dum. I and *Hector*'s a Greyhound.   2616
GRIEFE = 3*1
And they thy glorie through my griefe will show: 1369
That in loues griefe desirst societie: 1465
Where lies thy griefe, o tell me good *Dumaine*?   1508
Bero. Honest plaine words, best pearce the eare of griefe,   2711

GRIEFES = 2
How shall she know my griefes? Ile drop the paper. 1374
Quee. I vnderstand you not, my griefes are double. 2710
GRIM = 1
Lad. 3. Then was *Venus* like her mother, for her father is | but
grim. 762
GRONE = 4
Ber. I would you heard it grone. 680
Well, I will loue, write, sigh, pray, shue, grone, 970
a paper, God giue him grace to grone. 1352
Or grone for Ione? or spende a minutes time, 1520
GRONES = 2
Of sighes, of grones, of sorrow, and of teene: 1501
Deaft with the clamours of their owne deare grones, 2825
GRONING = 1
With groning wretches: and your taske shall be, 2813
GROONES = 1
Th'annoynted soueraigne of sighes and groones: 948
GROSSE = 5*1
He throwes vppon the grosse worlds baser slaues 34
Boy. Then I am sure you know how much the grosse 353
Loues tongue proues daintie, *Bachus* grosse in taste, 1690
Rosa. Wel-liking Wits they haue grosse grosse, fat fat. 2187
And we that sell by grosse, the Lord doth know, 2244
GROSSER = 1
The grosser manner of these worldes delyghts: 33
GROUND = 5*2
*ground Which? which I meane I walkt vpon, it is ycliped Thy
Park.* 248
Arm. I do affect the verie ground (which is base) where her 470
Kisses the base ground with obedient breast. 1574
Haue found the ground of Studies excellence, 1650
They are the Ground, the Bookes, the Achadems, 1653
I were the fayrest Goddesse on the ground. 1924
With that they all did tumble on the ground, 2007
GROW = 3*2
Lon. He weedes the corne, & still lets grow the weeding. 101
Prin. Such short liued wits do wither as they grow. 546
Ma. Come come, you talke greasely, your lips grow fowle. 1131
Ber. Nay then two treyes, an if you grow so nice, 2137
Mar. Then die a Calfe, before your hornes do grow. 2169
GROWES = 5*1
Your light growes darke by loosing of your eyes. 84
But like of each thing that in season growes. 116
Armado. Boy, What signe is it when a man of great spi-|rite
growes melancholy? 312
Ar. Sing Boy, My spirit growes heauie in loue. 426
Glorie growes guyltie of detested crimes, 1006
Boyet. A light for Mounsier *Iudas*, it growes darke, he | may
stumble. 2583
GUARD *see* garde
GUARDES *see* gardes
GUELDED = 1
Then *Aquitaine*, so guelded as it is. 644
GUERDON = 1
This seald-vp counsaile. Ther's thy guerdon: goe. 934

GUESSE *see* gesse
GUEST = 1
    I would not yeelde to be your houses guest: 2280
GUIDED = *1
    *shoo (which is baser) guided by her foote (which is basest)   471
GUILTIE = 2*1
    Boy. The worlde was very guiltie of such a Ballet some   415
    Guiltie my Lord, guiltie: I confesse, I confesse.   1550
GUILTINES = 1
    Full of deare guiltines, and therefore this,   2751
GUINOUER = *1
    *woman when queene *Guinouer* of Brittaine was a litle wench | as
    toching the hit it.   1112
GUNNE = 1
    Is that Lead slow which is fierd from a Gunne?   831
GUYLTIE = 3
    Glorie growes guyltie of detested crimes,   1006
    I heard your guyltie Rimes, obserude your fashion: 1476
    Was guyltie of it.) Farewell worthy Lord: 2694
GYANT = 1
    This signior *Iunios* gyant dwarffe, dan *Cupid*,   946
GYFT = *2
    Nath. This is a gyft that I haue simple: simple, a foolish   1230
    *gyft is good in those whom it is acute, and I am thankfull | for
    it.   1235
GYRLES = 1
    Shall we resolue to woe these gyrles of Fraunce?   1722
HA *l*.821 = 2
HABITE = 2
    In *Russian* habite: heere they stayed an houre,   2295
    Nor neuer more in Russian habite waite.   2333
HABITES = 1*1
    *first shew thriue, these foure will change habites, and present |
    the other fiue.   2481
    Full of straying shapes, of habites and of formes: 2721
HACKNIE = 1
    loue perhaps, a hacknie: But haue you forgot your Loue?   801
HAD *l*.*297 *392 394 *476 *478 552 575 642 803 1427 1428 1430
    *1807 *1809 *1902 1998 2247 2286 2505 = 13*7
HADST *l*.1538 1540 = 2
HAILE = 3
    Page. All haile, the richest Beauties on the earth.   2053
    King. All haile sweete Madame, and faire time of day,   2265
    Quee. Faire in all Haile is foule, as I conceaue.   2266
HAIRE = 3
    It mournes, that painting vsurping haire   1608
    As bright *Appolos* Lute, strung with his haire.   1694
    Cutting a smaller haire then may be seene,   2174
HAIRES *see also* heires = 1
    One her haires were Golde, Christal the others eyes.   1479
HALFE = 11*1
    And make a darke nyght too of halfe the day: 49
    Being but the one halfe of, of an intire summe,   626
    But that one halfe which is vnsatisfied,   634
    Nor shines thē siluer Moone one halfe so bright,   1362
    *not det: he clepeth a Calfe, Caufe: halfe, haufe: neighbour   1761
    The Letter is too long by halfe a mile.   1944

HALFE *cont.*

I thought to close mine eyes some halfe an houre:	1982
Twice to your Visore, and halfe once to you.	2131
There's halfe a dosen sweetes.	2139
And would afforde my speachles vizard halfe.	2158
Long. Let's part the word? | *Mar.* No, Ile not be your halfe:	2163
Bero. Saint *Georges* halfe cheeke in a Brooch.	2569

HALFEPENNIE = 1*1

Ber. O what is a remuneration? | *Cost.* Marie sir, halfepennie farthing.	913
*Remuneration I had of thy Maister, thou halfepennie	1809

HALFE-PENNIE = *1

Bero. My hat to a halfe-pennie, *Pompey* prooues the best | Worthie.	2509

HALL = 1

And Thom beares Logges into the hall,	2881

HAND = 16*3

That his owne hand may strike his honour downe,	24
Meane time receiue such welcome at my hand,	666
And to her white hand see thou do commend	933
A giuing hand, though fowle, shall haue faire praise.	998
Mar. Wide a'the bow hand, yfaith your hand is out.	1124
Boy. And if my hand be out, then belike your hand is in.	1127
*To see him kisse his hand, & how most sweetly a wil sweare:	1144
To the snow-white hand of the most bewtious Lady Rosaline.	1297
*deliuer this Paper into the royall hand of the King, it may	1306
Enter Berowne with a paper in his hand, alone.	1333
But alacke my hand is sworne,	1448
*hand, a foote, a face, an eye: a gate, a state, a brow, a brest,	1522
Then homeward euery man attach the hand	1726
Boyet. Ladies, withdraw: the gallants are at hand,	2231
That kist his hand, a way in courtisie.	2249
By this white Gloue (how white the hand God knowes)	2343
The sodaine hand of death close vp mine eye.	2775

HANDED = *1

Berow. White handed Mistres, one sweet word with thee.	2135

HANDES = 5*1

*like a Rabbet on a spit, or your handes in your pocket like a	788
Therefore of all handes must we be forsworne.	1567
Marg. I, or I would these handes might neuer part.	1947
Weele not be nice, take handes, we will not daunce.	2121
King. Why take we handes then? | *Rosa.* Onely to part friendes.	2122
If this thou do deny, let our handes part,	2771

HANDFULL = 1

And his Page atother side, that handfull of wit,	1146

HANG = 3*1

hang me by the necke, if horns that yeere miscarrie. | Finely put on.	1098
*againe a my side. I will not loue; if I do hang mee: I'fayth	1341
Peda. What meane you sir? | *Boyet.* To make *Iudas* hang him selfe.	2556
Winter. | When Isacles hang by the wall,	2878

HANGD = 1

quicke by him, and hangd for *Pompey* that is dead by him.	2637

HANGE = 1

Will they not (thinke you) hange them selues to nyght?	2189

HANGED = 1
  Bero. Well folowed, *Iudas* was hanged on an Elder.   2559
HANGES = 1
  The shape of Loues Tiburne, that hanges vp Simplicitie.   1386
HANGETH = *1
  *as the Pomwater, who now hangeth like a Iewel in the eare   1154
HANNIBALL = 1
  Brag. *This* Hector *far surmounted* Hanniball.   2626
HAPP = 1
  Bero. Whats her name in the capp? | *Boy. Katherin* by good happ.   709
HAPPIE = 1
  They did not blesse vs with one happie word.   2297
HAPPINES = 1
  Nath. And thanke you to: for societie (saith the text) | is the
  happines of life.   1326
HARBOUR = 1
  Though so denide faire harbour in my house,   672
HARD = 7*2
  O these are barraine taskes, too hard to keepe,   51
  Or hauing sworne too hard a keeping oth,   70
  *hard for *Hercules* Clubb, and therefore too much oddes for a   479
  Boy. You are too hard for mee. *Exeunt omnes.*   768
  Quee. Was that the king that spurd his horse so hard,   975
  Cl. Shes to hard for you at pricks, sir challeng her to bowle   1133
  To be ore-hard and taken napping so.   1467
  And ouer hard, what you shall ouer heare: 1987
  If frostes and fastes, hard lodging, and thin weedes,   2761
HARKE = 1
  Harke slaue, it is but this: 928
HARKEN = *1
  Clow. Such is the simplicitie of man to harken after the flesh   228
HARME = 2
  When I was wont to thinke no harme all nyght,   48
  Most power to do most harme, least knowing ill: 550
HARMONIE = 2
  Doth rauish like inchaunting harmonie: 178
  Make heauen drowsie with the harmonie.   1696
HARPERS = 1
  Nor woo in rime like a blind harpers songue.   2337
HARSH = 1*1
  They will digest this harsh indignitie.   2210
  *The wordes of Mercurie, are harsh after the | songes of Apollo.   2897
HART = 24*10
  As you shall deeme your selfe lodgd in my hart.   671
  Ber. Ladie I will commend you to my none hart.   677
  Ros. Is the foole sicke. | *Ber.* Sicke at the hart.   681
  His hart like an Agot with your print impressed,   740
  Brag. Almost I had. | *Boy.* Negligent student, learne her by hart.   803
  Brag. By hart, and in hart boy.   805
  Boy. And out of hart Maister: all those three I will | proue.   806
  *instant: by hart you loue her, because your hart cannot come   810
  *by her: in hart you loue her, because your hart is in loue   811
  *with her: and out of hart you loue her, being out of hart   812
  Sole Emperator and great generall | Of trotting Parrators (O my
  litle hart.)   951
  We bend to that, the working of the hart.   1008
  The poore Deares blood, that my hart meanes no ill.   1010

HART *cont.*

thy picture, and my hart on thy euerie part.	1064
Perswade my hart to this false periurie?	1395
His louing bosome, to keepe downe his hart.	1473
Good hart, What grace hast thou thus to reproue	1490
*with my excrement, with my mustachie: but sweete hart	1837
*let that passe; the very all of all is: but sweet hart, I do implore	1842
And so may you: For a light hart liues long.	1904
Quee. I thinke no lesse: Dost thou not wish in hart	1945
That well by hart hath cond his embassage	1990
Boy. Why that contempt will kill the speakers hart,	2041
Kath. Lord *Longauill* said I came ore his hart:	2197
King. A blister on his sweete tongue with my hart,	2260
*of *Iaquenettaes,* and that a weares next his hart for a	Fauour.	2669
A heauie hart beares not a humble tongue.	2695
Neither intitled in the others hart.	2772
Hence hermite then my hart, is in thy brest.	2776
Beholde the window of my hart, mine eye:	2799

HARTBURNING = *1

hir to tryall. Thine in all complements of deuoted and hartburning	272

HARTES = 4

By the hartes still rethoricke, disclosed with eyes.	733
Quee. Sweete hartes we shalbe rich ere we depart,	1888
Curtsie sweete hartes, and so the Measure endes.	2124
They are infected, in their hartes it lyes:	2353

HARUEST = 1

Scarce shew a haruest of their heauie toyle.	1677

HAST *l.*795 *880 *1090 *1355 1490 1529 *1813 *1880 2561 = 4*5

HASTE = 2

Haste, signifie so much while we attende,	524
Did stumble with haste in his ey-sight to bee,	743

HAT = 1*2

Bero. Ile lay my Head to any good mans Hat,	303
*smelling loue with your hat penthouse like ore the shop of	786
Bero. My hat to a halfe-pennie, *Pompey* prooues the best		
Worthie.	2509

HATCHT = 1

As Wit turnde Foole, follie in Wisedome hatcht:	1960

HATE = 1

So much I hate a breaking cause to be	2281

HATEFULL = 1

Youle not be periurde, tis a hatefull thing:	1494

HATH *l.*129 156 176 302 513 542 551 570 599 652 *698 *755 856
*865 *1174 *1176 *1303 *1305 *1345 *1348 *1349 1421 1578
*1779 *1841 1898 1926 1961 1990 2204 2421 2585 2661 2715 2717
2836 = 24*13

HAUD = 3*1

Holo. Sir *Nathaniel, haud credo.*	1161
Dul. Twas not a *haud credo,* twas a Pricket.	1162
to insert again my *haud credo* for a Deare.	1168
Dul. I said the Deare was not a *haud credo,* twas a Pricket.	1170

HAUE *see also* a, a'haue *l.*20 30 38 91 95 112 *120 121 123 154 180
*265 *345 371 390 *392 *419 463 *467 557 578 *586 592 628 638
641 643 663 701 756 801 920 924 *939 979 998 *1020 1029 *1044
1106 1123 1138 *1230 1311 *1312 *1320 *1336 1360 1383 1415
1435 1474 1487 1500 1502 1640 1646 1647 1650 1660 1669 1670
1672 1674 *1742 *1776 *1778 *1808 *1843 *1847 *1866 1868 1872

HAUE   *cont.*
*1878 1891 1917 1922 1998 2020 2080 2081 2082 2084 2087 2089
2095 2157 2176 *2181 2187 2202 2245 *2275 2283 2286 2299 2341
2349 2352 2354 2361 2397 2423 2456 *2528 2572 2573 2574 2575
2664 2665 *2680 2692 2713 2726 2735 2741 2758 2790 2802 2827
2837 2846 *2849 *2850 = 97*28
HAUFE = *1
*not det: he clepeth a Calfe, Caufe: halfe, haufe: neighbour   1761
HAUING = 1
Or hauing sworne too hard a keeping oth,   70
HAUNTED = 1
Ferd. I that there is, our Court you know is haunted   173
HAY *see* hey
HE *see also* a', a'haue = 71*45
HEAD = 10*4
Bero. Ile lay my Head to any good mans Hat,   303
Clo. God dig-you-den al, pray you which is the head lady?   1018
it was a Bucke of the first head.   1160
Bowes not his vassall head, and strooken blind.   1573
The streete should see as she walkt ouer head.   1630
When the suspitious head of theft is stopt.   1687
*art not so long by the head as honorificabilitudinitatibus: 1780
is Ab speld backward with the horne on his head?   1786
*curtesie. I beseech thee apparrell thy head: and among other   1832
Rosa. That was the way to make his god-head Wax: 1897
Clow. I Pompey *am*, | *Boyet.* With Libbards head on knee.   2493
Pedan. What is this? | *Boyet.* A Cytterne head.   2562
Duma. The head of a Bodkin.   2564
Ber. Hide thy head *Achilles*, here comes *Hector* in Armes.   2588
HEADED = 1
Whose Clubb kilde Cerberus *that three headed* Canus,   2542
HEADES = 1
Or hide your heades like Cowardes, and flie hence.   1978
HEADS = 1
Que. Thou shalt know her fellow by the rest that haue no |
(heads.   1020
HEALTH = 1*1
Pri. Sweete health and faire desires consort your grace.   675
Kath. A wife? a beard, faire health, and honestie,   2784
HEALTH-GEUING = *1
of thy health-geuing ayre: And as I am a Gentleman, betooke my   244
HEARD *see* hard = 8
Ber. This is not so well as I looked for, but the best that | euer I
heard.   275
Ar. I loue thee. | *Ma.* So I heard you say.   444
Was there with him, if I haue heard a trueth.   557
Ferd. I do protest I neuer heard of it: 653
Ber. I would you heard it grone.   680
Bo. Her mothers, I haue heard.   701
I heard your guyltie Rimes, obserude your fashion: 1476
Rosa. Oft haue I heard of you my Lord *Berowne*,   2802
HEARE = 16*9
But I protest I loue to heare him lie,   186
Ber. To heare, or forbeare hearing.   208
Lon. To heare meekely sir, and to laugh moderatly, or | to
forbeare both.   209
Ferd. Will you heare this Letter with attention?   226

HEARE *cont.*

Bero. As we would heare an Oracle.	227
Fer. Did you heare the Proclamation?	280
I am lesse proude to heare you tell my worth,	508
Nau. Heare me deare Lady, I haue sworne an oth,	592
I heare your grace hath sworne out Houskeeping:	599
Boy. Do you heare my mad Wenches? | *Lad.* No.	764
Thus dost thou heare the nemean Lion roare,	1068
*What vaine? What Wethercock? Did you euer heare better?	1075
Holo. Sir *Nathaniel*, will you heare an extemporall Epy-|taph	1207
Nath. Let me heare a staffe, a stanze, a verse, *Lege domine.*	1265
*and heere is part of my Rime, and heare my mallicholie.	1347
What will *Berowne* say when that he shall heare	1482
*In pruning mee when shall you heare that I will prayse a	1521
Long. It did moue him to passion, & therfore lets heare it.	1545
A Louers eare will heare the lowest sound.	1686
Pag. Ba most seely Sheepe, with a horne: you heare his | (learning.	1788
And ouer hard, what you shall ouer heare:	1987
But will you heare; the King is my Loue sworne.	2203
Let vs complaine to them what fooles were heare,	2225
Will heare your idle scornes; continue then,	2826
*But most esteemed greatnes, will you heare the Dialogue	2848

HEARERS = 1

Which shallow laughing hearers giue to fooles,	2821

HEARES = 3

Berow. Tell her we measure them by weerie steps. | *Boy.* She heares her selfe.	2092
Mar. Bleat softly then, the Butcher heares you crie.	2171
Of him that heares it, neuer in the tongue	2823

HEARING = 3*1

Ber. To heare, or forbeare hearing.	208
Clo. I do confesse much of the hearing it, but little of the | marking of it.	281
Bra. Warble child, make passionate my sense of hearing. | *Boy.* Concolinel.	772
*But I will forward with my deuice; sweete royaltie bestow | on me the sence of hearing.	2619

HEARINGES = 1

And younger hearinges are quite rauished.	567

HEART *see* hart

HEARTBURNING *see* hartburning

HEARTES *see* hartes

HEATE = 2

heate of duetie. | Don Adriano de Armado.	273
If this Austere insociable life, | Change not your offer made in heate of blood.	2759

HEATST = *1

Arma. I do say thou art quicke in answeres. Thou heatst | my blood.	340

HEAUELY = 1

Ar. Thou shalt be heauely punished.	453

HEAUEN = 9*4

Lon. A high hope for a low heauen. God grant vs patience	206
I and by heauen, one that will do the deede,	964
Boyet | reedes. By heauen, that thou art faire, is most infallible:	1041
*of *Celo* the skie, the welken the heauen, & anon falleth like	1155

HEAUEN cont.

*in the world but lie, and lie in my throate. By heauen I doe	1344
*Be. Shot by heauen, proceed sweet *Cupid*, thou hast thumpt	1355
Duma. By heauen the woonder in a mortall eye.	1419
The Sea will ebb and flow, heauen shew his face:	1564
Dares looke vpon the heauen of her brow,	1576
King. By heauen, thy Loue is blacke as Ebonie.	1596
Make heauen drowsie with the harmonie.	1696
Bero. By heauen, all drie beaten with pure scoffe.	2180
Rosal. By heauen you did; and to confirme it plaine,	2391

HEAUENLY = 6*1

Did not the heauenly Rethorique of thine eye,	1393
My Vow was earthly, thou a heauenly Loue.	1399
Ber. Did they quoth you? Who sees the heauenly *Rosaline*,	1570
Pag. Out of your fauours heauenly spirites vouchsafe	2062
Of heauenly Othes vowed with integritie.	2282
Put on by vs, if in your heauenly eyes,	2725
Those heauenly eyes that looke into these faultes,	2727

HEAUENS = 8*1

Studie is lyke the heauens glorious Sunne,	89
These earthly Godfathers of heauens lights,	93
Ah heauens, it is most patheticall nit.	1147
That singes heauens prayse, with such an earthly tong.	1283
More Sacks to the myll. O heauens I haue my wysh,	1415
Wish himselfe the heauens breath.	1445
And beauties crest becomes the heauens well.	1605
*heauens were so pleased, that thou wart but my Ba-|stard;	1811
With eies best seeing, heauens fierie eie:	2302

HEAUIE = 6

Ar. Sing Boy, My spirit growes heauie in loue.	426
Brag. The meaning prettie ingenius, is not Lead a mettal	
heauie, dull, and slow?	826
Scarce shew a haruest of their heauie toyle.	1677
Kath. He made her melancholie, sad, and heauie,	1901
is heauie in my tongue. The King your father | *Quee.* Dead for	
my life.	2676
A heauie hart beares not a humble tongue.	2695

HEAUING = *1

*my spleene, the heauing of my lunges prouokes me to	
redi-|culous	849

HECTOR = 12*4

*He presents *Hector* of *Troy*, the Swaine *Pompey* the great, the	2478
Ber. Hide thy head *Achilles*, here comes *Hector* in Armes.	2588
King. Hector was but a *Troyan* in respect of this.	2592
Boyet. But is this *Hector*?	2593
King. I thinke *Hector* was not so cleane timberd.	2594
Bero. This cannot be *Hector*.	2598
Braggart. The Armipotent Mars, *of Launces the almightie,* | *gaue*	
Hector *a gift.*	2600
Gaue Hector *a gift, the heir of Illion,*	2607
Long. I must rather giue it the raine: for it runnes against |	
Hector.	2614
Quee. Speake braue *Hector*, we are much delighted.	2622
Brag. This Hector *far surmounted* Hanniball.	2626
Clow. Fellow *Hector*, she is gone; she is two months on | her	
way.	2628
Clow. Then shall *Hector* be whipt for *Iaquenetta* that is	2636

HECTOR *cont.*
   Dum. Hector trembles.   2643
   Duma. Hector will challenge him.   2646
   Queen. Was not that *Hector?* | *Duma.* The worthie Knight of
   Troy.   2843
HECTORS = 2
   Long. His Legge is too bigge for *Hectors.* | *Duman.* More Calfe
   certaine.   2595
   Dum. I and *Hector's* a Greyhound.   2616
HEDGE-PRIEST = *1
   **Bero.* The Pedant, the Bragart, the Hedge-Priest, the | Foole,
   and the Boy,   2485
HEE *l.*833 1554 2248 2865 = 5
HEED = 1
   Who dazling so, that eye shalbe his heed,   87
HEEDFULLY = 1
   And wretched fooles secrets heedfully ore ey.   1414
HEELE *l.**2323 = *1
HEERE = 24*4
   That is, to lyue and study heere three yeeres.   39
   And stay heere in your Court for three yeeres space.   56
   Shee must lie heere on meere necessitie.   159
   Arma. True. | **Boy.* Why sir is this such a peece of studie? Now
   heere is   357
   Lord. Heere comes *Boyet. Enter Boyet.*   572
   Like one that comes heere to besiedge his Court,   580
   Bo. Heere comes *Nauar.*   584
   Ferd. Madame, your father heere doth intimate,   624
   On *Nauar* and his Bookmen, for heere tis abused.   731
   Heere (good my glasse) take this for telling trew: 993
   Are not you the chiefe woman? You are the thickest heere. 1027
   This letter is mistooke: it importeth none heere.   1036
   *and heere is part of my Rime, and heare my mallicholie. 1347
   *care a pin, if the other three were in. Heere comes one with
   Sweete leaues shade follie. Who is he comes heere?   1351
                                                   1375
   King. What makes treason heere? | *Clow.* Nay it makes nothing
   sir.   1531
   Dum. It is *Berownes* writing, and heere is his name.   1547
   Ber. Ile proue her faire, or talke till doomse-day heere. 1623
   Quee. Heere comes *Boyet,* and myrth is in his face.   1970
   That by and by disguysd they will be heere.   1988
   Immediatly they will againe be heere,   2208
   King. O you haue liu'd in desolation heere,   2283
   In *Russian* habite: heere they stayed an houre,   2295
   Heere stand I, Ladie dart thy skill at me,   2328
   Quee. When you then were heere,   2371
   King. Heere is like to be a good presence of Worthies: 2477
   **Kin.* The Ship is vnder sayle, and heere she coms amaine. 2489
   And trauailing along this coast I heere am come by chaunce, 2502
HEEREBY = 1
   Forr. Heereby vpon the edge of yonder Coppice,   983
HEERS = 1 *1
   **Pag.* A wonder Maister, Heers a *Costard* broken in a shin. 841
   Long. Looke, heer's thy loue, my foote and her face see. 1626
HEES = 2
   Ferd. How well hees read to reason against reading.   99
   Duma. Hee's a God or a Painter: for he makes faces. 2599

111

HEIR = 1
Gaue Hector *a gift, the heir of Illion,*   2607
HEIRE = 2*1
Betweene L.(ord) *Perigort* and the bewtious heire | Of *Iaques*
Fauconbridge solemnized.   533
Boyet. The heire of *Alanson, Rosalin* her name.   693
*Bo. Good sir be not offended, She is an heire of *Falcon-* | (*bridge.*   703
HEIRES = 2
And make vs heires of all eternitie.   11
Duma. Her Amber heires for foule hath amber coted.   1421
HELDE = 1
Your selfe, helde precious in the worldes esteeme,   495
HELE = 1*1
Prin. Our Lady helpe my Lord, he'le be forsworne.   593
*Clo. Indeed a'must shoot nearer, or hele neare hit the clout.   1125
HELL *see also* ell = 1
King. O paradox, Blacke is the badge of Hell,   1603
HELPE = 3*1
Prin. Our Lady helpe my Lord, he'le be forsworne.   593
Hath Wisedomes warrant, and the helpe of Schoole,   1961
*Rosa. Helpe holde his browes, heele sound: why looke | you
pale?   2323
And to begin Wench, so God helpe me law,   2346
HENCE = 4
Bero. Sweete Lord and why? | *Long.* To fright them hence with
that dread penaltie.   136
King. Hence sirs, away.   1560
Or hide your heades like Cowardes, and flie hence.   1978
Hence hermite then my hart, is in thy brest.   2776
HENCEFOORTH = 1
Hencefoorth my wooing minde shalbe exprest   2344
HER *see also* hir *l.*132 148 *217 *218 *291 393 404 409 *434 *470
*471 570 693 *696 697 *698 701 709 712 *762 804 *810 *811 *812
813 930 931 932 933 963 965 966 967 973 974 *1020 *1104 1106
*1133 1143 *1342 *1343 1421 1424 1431 1434 1471 1479 1576
1577 1579 1584 1592 1597 1601 1611 1614 1615 1616 1623 1626
1628 1731 *1822 *1850 1901 1971 1998 2082 2083 2092 2093
*2236 2237 2373 *2374 2394 2414 2415 2624 2629 *2632
2847 = 67*28
HERALD = 1
My Herald is returnd.   839
HERALDE = 1
Their Heralde is a prettie knauish Page: 1989
HERCLE = *1
*Nath. Me hercle, yf their Sonnes be ingenous, they shal   1241
HERCULES = 6*5
men haue bin in loue? | *Boy. Hercules* Maister.   371
*Arm. Most sweete *Hercules*: more authoritie deare Boy,   373
*hard for *Hercules* Clubb, and therefore too much oddes for a   479
To see great *Hercules* whipping a Gigge,   1504
For Valoure, is not Loue a *Hercules*?   1691
or ioynt) shall passe *Pompey* the great, the Page *Hercules.*   1861
*Peda. Shall I haue audience? He shall present *Hercules*   1866
*you may cry, Well done *Hercules*, now thou crusshest the   1870
*parish Curate *Alexander, Armadoes* Page *Hercules*, the Pe-| dant   2479
Enter Pedant for Iudas, and the Boy for Hercules.   2540
Peda. Great Hercules *is presented by this Impe,*   2541

HERE *see also* heare = 12*6
That are recorded in this sedule here.	22
For well you know here comes in Embassaie,	144
ebon coloured Incke, which here thou viewest, beholdest, suruayest, or	252
For here he doth demaund to haue repaide,	638
But here without you shalbe so receiude,	670
The Princesse comes to hunt here in the Parke,	929
Boyet. Here comes a member of the common wealth.	1017
Boy. This *Armado* is a *Spaniard* that keepes here in court,	1079
Here sweete, put vp this, twilbe thine annother day.	1091
Nath. Here are onely numbers ratefied, but for the ele-|gancie	1286
*with the King, and here he hath framed a letter to a sequent	1303
Like a demie God, here sit I in the skie,	1413
Rosa. Since you are strangers, and come here by chance,	2120
We haue had pastimes here and pleasant game,	2286
I do forsweare them, and I here protest,	2342
Were not you here but euen now, disguysde? | *King.* Madame, I was.	2367
I see the tricke ant: here was a consent,	2399
Ber. Hide thy head *Achilles*, here comes *Hector* in Armes.	2588

HEREBY = 1
Maid. Thats hereby. | *Ar.* I know where it is situate.	439

HEREIN = 1
That violates the smallest branch herein.	25

HERESIE = *1
*learned without opinion, and strange without heresie: I did	1744

HERESY = 1
O heresy in faire, fit for these dayes,	997

HEREUPON = *1
Arm. I will hereupon confesse I am in loue: and as it is	363

HERMITE = 2
A witherd Hermite fiue score winters worne,	1591
Hence hermite then my hart, is in thy brest.	2776

HERMYTAGE = 1
To some forlorne and naked Hermytage,	2755

HEROICALL = *1
*heroicall Vassall. The magnanimous and most illustrate	1045

HERSELFE *see* selfe
HES = *1
Que. O thy letter, thy letter: He's a good friend of mine.	1031

HESPERIDES = 1
Still clyming trees in the *Hesperides*.	1692

HEW = 1
And Cuckow-budds of yellow hew:	2861

HEY = 1
the Taber to the worthies, and let them dance the hey.	1885

HIBERBOLES = 1
Three pilde Hiberboles, spruce affection:	2339

HID = 4*1
Ber. Things hid & bard (you meane) from cammon sense.	62
When Mistresses from common sense are hid.	69
Berow. All hid, all hid, an olde infant play,	1412
That hid the worse, and shewed the better face.	2317

HIDE = 2*1
Or hide your heades like Cowardes, and flie hence.	1978
Ber. Hide thy head *Achilles*, here comes *Hector* in Armes.	2588

HIDE *cont.*
  In your rich wisedome to excuse, or hide,   2690
HIEMS = 1
  Brag. This side is *Hiems*, Winter.   2855
HIGH = 2*3
  In high borne wordes the worth of many a Knight: 183
  *Bero. How low so euer the matter, I hope in God for high |
  (words.   204
  *Lon. A high hope for a low heauen. God grant vs patience   206
  Like humble visage Suters his high will.   525
  *not yet: the roofe of this Court is too high to be yours, and   587
HIGHEST = 1
  Clow. Which is the greatest Ladie, the highest?   1022
HIGHNES = *1
  *Quee. Amazde my Lord? Why lookes your highnes sad?   2321
HIGHT = 1*1
  This childe of Fancie that *Armado* hight,   181
  *hight Costard, (*Clow.* O mee) *sorted and consorted contrary to*   259
HILL = 2
  Against the steepe vp rising of the hill?   976
  on the top of the Mountaine? | *Peda.* Or *Mons* the hill.   1817
HIM *l.*88 186 187 *264 300 *344 *367 *432 456 521 532 538 553 557
  558 716 718 753 761 *776 777 *865 1138 1143 *1144 *1185 *1228
  1352 1356 1469 1487 *1545 1900 1952 1956 1991 1994 1999 2057
  2194 2254 2259 2386 2396 2449 2557 2577 2580 2637 2646 *2667
  2823 2824 = 44*11
HIMSELFE *see also* selfe = 2
  Wish himselfe the heauens breath.   1445
  And denie himselfe for *Ioue*,   1456
HINDE = 1
  with the rational hinde *Costard*: she deserues well.   422
HINDER = 1
  Ferd. These be the stopps that hinder studie quit,   75
HIPOCRISIE = 2
  Bero. Now step I foorth to whip hipocrisie.   1488
  A hudge translation of hipocrisie, | Vildly compyled, profound
  simplicitie.   1941
HIR *l.**270 *272 = *2
HIS *l.*10 24 81 87 106 162 171 176 177 *195 *196 311 *377 *482 494
  515 517 518 523 525 539 543 545 555 561 564 566 568 576 580 581
  582 597 598 627 636 641 645 659 718 731 738 739 740 741 742 743
  746 750 751 752 *755 756 770 902 953 954 969 975 1069 1070
  1073 1081 *1090 *1144 1146 *1165 *1166 *1178 1263 1272 *1279
  *1290 *1291 1333 1391 1437 1468 1472 1473 1484 1498 1547 1564
  1573 1647 1694 1698 1699 1727 *1748 *1749 *1750 1755 *1756
  *1757 1786 *1788 *1835 *1836 *1839 *1860 *1864 *1867 1897
  1926 1954 1955 1957 1958 1970 1985 1990 2001 2003 2015 2016
  2023 2040 2042 2195 2197 2242 2246 2249 2255 2257 2260 2261
  *2323 2387 2404 2456 2471 2488 *2518 *2530 2544 2579 2595
  2609 *2647 *2669 2699 2700 2723 2880 = 126*36
HISSE = 1*1
  *Page. An excellent deuice: so if any of the audience hisse,   1869
  When roasted Crabbs hisse in the bowle,   2892
HIT = 8*2
  Boyet. But she her selfe is hit lower: Haue I hit her now?   1106
  *was a man when King *Pippen* of Fraunce was a litle boy, as |
  touching the hit it.   1109

HIT *cont.*
*woman when queene *Guinouer* of Brittaine was a litle wench | as
toching the hit it.   1112
Rosa. Thou canst not hit it, hit it, hit it,   1114
Thou canst not hit it my good man. *Exit.*   1115
* Mar. A marke marueilous wel shot, for they both did hit.   1119
*Clo. Indeed a'must shoot nearer, or hele neare hit the clout.   1125
HITHER = 2*4
Or vainely comes th'admired Princesse hither.   150
*giue enlargement to the Swaine, bring him festinatly hither,   776
*Brag. Fetch hither the Swaine, he must carrie me a letter.   817
*Ar. Come hither, come hither: How did this argument | (begin?   869
Boy. If to come hither, you haue measurde miles,   2089
HOBBIE-HORSE = 1
Boy. The Hobbie-horse is forgot.   798
HOBBI-HORSE = 1*1
Brag. Calst thou my loue Hobbi-horse.   799
*Boy. No Maister, the Hobbi-horse is but a colt, and your   800
HOGGSHEAD = *1
*Clo. Marrie M.(aister) Scholemaster, he that is liklest to a
hoggs-|(head.   1249
HOGSHEAD = *1
*Nath. Of persing a Hogshead, a good luster of conceit   1251
HOLD = 4*1
Boy. Do not curst wiues hold that selfe-soueraigntie   1011
Ah neuer fayth could hold, yf not to beautie vowed.   1268
*Quee. This Feelde shall holde me, and so hold your vow: 2271
Can anie face of brasse hold longer out?   2327
Rosa. Madame, he swore that he did hold me deare,   2382
HOLDE = 8*3
And holde faire friendship with his Maiestie,   636
Gainst whom the world cannot holde argument,   1394
I that am honest, I that holde it sinne   1515
Duma. I neuer knew man holde vile stuffe so deare.   1625
*haue it to buy Ginger bread: Holde, there is the verie   1808
Holde *Rosaline*, this Fauour thou shalt weare,   2022
Holde take thou this my sweete, and giue mee thine,   2024
King. If you denie to daunce, lets holde more chat.   2132
*Quee. This Feelde shall holde me, and so hold your vow: 2271
*Rosa. Helpe holde his browes, heele sound: why looke | you
pale?   2323
To holde the Plough for her sweete loue three yeere.   2847
HOLDES = 1*4
Th'allusion holdes in the Exchange.   1199
*Dul. Tis true in deede, the Collusion holdes in the Ex-|(change.   1200
*Holo. God comfort thy capacitie, I say th'allusion holdes | in the
Exchange.   1202
*Dul. And I say the polusion holdes in the Exchange: for   1204
*Your Lion that holdes his Polax sitting on a close stoole,   2530
HOLDING = 1
Holding a trencher, iesting merrilie?   2416
HOLDSOME = 1
Is not by much so holdsome profitable,   2708
HOLE = *2
*Page. Maister, let me take you a button hole lower. Do   2656
*seene the day of wrong through the litle hole of discretion,   2681

HOLLA = 1
Brag. Holla. Approch. 2853
HOLO = 3*8
HOLOFERNES see also Holo. = 1*4
Enter *Dull, Holofernes,* the *Pedant* and *Nathaniel.* 1150
Curat.Nath. Truely M.(aister) *Holofernes,* the epythithes are 1158
Nath. Perge, good M.(aister) *Holofernes perge,* so it shall please |
you to abrogate squirilitie. 1211
Ped. Sir *Holofernes,* this *Berowne* is one of the Votaries 1302
*Sir *Holofernes,* as concerning some entertainement of time, 1851
HOLSOME = *1
*commende the blacke oppressing humour to the most holsome
phisicke* 243
HOLY = 1*1
*Page. A holy parcell of the fayrest dames that euer turnd their |
backes to mortall viewes.* 2055
The holy suite which faine it would conuince, 2704
HOME = 3*1
Ferd. Well, sit you out: go home *Berowne:* adue. 119
home, it reioiceth my intellect, true wit. 1797
Duma. Though my mockes come home by me, I will | now be
merrie. 2590
And Milke coms frozen home in paile: 2882
HOMEWARD = 1
Then homeward euery man attach the hand 1726
HOMINUM = *1
Ped. Noui hominum tanquam te, His humour is loftie, his 1748
HONEST = 4*3
Boy. Minnime honest Maister, or rather Maister no. 828
I that am honest, I that holde it sinne 1515
Peda. Most *Dull,* honest *Dull,* to our sport: away. *Exeunt.* 1886
In russet yeas, and honest kersie noes. 2345
*honest man; looke you, and soone dasht. He is a marueylous 2534
Clow. Faith vnlesse you play the honest *Troyan,* the poore 2631
Bero. Honest plaine words, best pearce the eare of griefe, 2711
HONESTIE = 1
Kath. A wife? a beard, faire health, and honestie, 2784
HONIE = 2
Quee. Honie, and Milke, and Suger: there is three. 2136
Brag. That is al one my faire sweete honie monarch, 2472
HONIE-TONGED = 1
Pay him the due of honie-tonged *Boyet.* 2259
HONOR = 2
As honor (without breach of honor) may, 667
HONORABLE = 1
In honorable tearmes; nay he can sing 2252
HONORIFICABILITUDINITATIBUS = *1
*art not so long by the head as honorificabilitudinitatibus: 1780
HONOUR = 4*1
That honour which shall bate his sythes keene edge, 10
That his owne hand may strike his honour downe, 24
*for the best ward of mine honour, is rewarding | my dependants.
Moth, follow. 897
Now by my maiden honour yet as pure, | As the vnsallied Lilly I
protest, 2277
King. Vpon mine honour no. 2376

HONOURABLIE = 1
Most honourablie doth vphold his word,   2387
HONOURS = *1
*special honours it pleaseth his greatnes to impart to *Armado*   1839
HOOPE = 1
And weare his coulers like a Tumblers hoope.   954
HOOTING = 1
Or Pricket-sore, or els Sorell, | the people fall a hooting.   1221
HOPE = 6*4
Which I hope well is not enrolled there.   42
The which I hope is not enrolled there.   45
Which I hope well is not enrolled there.   50
Bero. How low so euer the matter, I hope in God for high |
(words.   204
Lon. A high hope for a low heauen. God grant vs patience   206
Clo. Well sir I hope when I do it, I shall do it on a full |
stomacke.   451
Long. In loue I hope, sweete fellowship in shame.   1381
Clow. Not so sir, vnder correction sir, I hope it is not so.   2432
we know: I hope sir three times thrice sir. | *Bero*. Is not nine.   2434
Clo. Tis not so much worth: but I hope I was perfect. I | made a
litle fault in great.   2507
HORNE = 2*3
is Ab speld backward with the horne on his head?   1786
Peda. Ba, *puericia* with a horne added.   1787
Pag. Ba most seely Sheepe, with a horne: you heare his |
(learning.   1788
Pag. Lende me your Horne to make one, and I will whip   1804
*about your Infamie *vnu(m)* *cita* a gigge of a Cuckolds horne.   1805
HORNES = 4*2
Boy. My Lady goes to kill hornes, but if thou marrie,   1097
Rosa. If we choose by the hornes, your selfe come not   1102
Then are the tender hornes of Cockled Snayles.   1689
Peda. What is the figure? What is the figure? | *Page*. Hornes.   1800
Will you giue hornes chast Lady? do not so.   2168
Mar. Then die a Calfe, before your hornes do grow.   2169
HORNE-BOOKE = *1
Page. Yes yes, he teaches boyes the Horne-booke: What   1785
HORNS = 1
hang me by the necke, if horns that yeere miscarrie. | Finely put
on.   1098
HORRACE = *1
*Vnder pardon sir, What are the contentes? or rather as *Hor-| race*   1262
HORSE = 4*4
wordes, the daucing Horse will tell you.   360
Boy. The Hobbie-horse is forgot.   798
Brag. Calst thou my loue Hobbi-horse.   799
Boy. No Maister, the Hobbi-horse is but a colt, and your   800
Boy. A message well simpathisd, a Horse to be embassa-|doure
for an Asse.   819
Boy. Marrie sir, you must send the Asse vpon the Horse,   822
Quee. Was that the king that spurd his horse so hard,   975
*the Ape his keeper, the tyred Horse his rider: But *Damosella*   1291
HOSE = 1
Ber. O Rimes are gardes on wanton *Cupids* hose, | Disfigure not
his Shop.   1390

HOSPITALL = 1

Ile iest a tweluemonth in an Hospitall.   2832

HOT = 2

Ber. Your wit's too hot, it speedes too fast, twill tire.   615

Lady Ka. Two hot Sheepes marie. | *Bo.* And wherefore not
Shipps?   720

HOU = 1

And where my Liedges? all about the brest. | A Caudle hou!   1510

HOUND = *1

*imitarie is nothing: So doth the Hound his maister,   1290

HOURE = 6*1

*selfe to walke: the time When? about the sixt houre, When
Beastes*   245

Boy. You may do it in an houre sir. | *Arma.* Impossible.   346

Ber. What time a day? | *Kath.* The houre that fooles should aske.   617

I thought to close mine eyes some halfe an houre: 1982

In *Russian* habite: heere they stayed an houre,   2295

And talkt apace: and in that houre (my Lord)   2296

King. Now at the latest minute of the houre, | Graunt vs your
loues.   2746

HOURES = 3

And then to sleepe but three houres in the nyght,   46

I neuer spent an houres talke withall.   560

For Reuels, Daunces, Maskes, and merrie houres,   1730

HOUSE = 4*2

Clymbe ore the house to vnlocke the little gate.   118

*I was seene with her in the Manner house, sitting with her   217

To let you enter his vnpeeled house.   582

Though so denide faire harbour in my house,   672

*barbarous. Do you not educate youth at the Charg-house   1816

My wofull selfe vp in a mourning house, | Rayning the teares of
lamentation,   2768

HOUSES = 1

I would not yeelde to be your houses guest: 2280

HOUSKEEPING = 1

I heare your grace hath sworne out Houskeeping: 599

HOW = 39*13

Studie me how to please the eye in deede,   85

Ferd. How well hees read to reason against reading.   99

Duma. How followes that? | *Ber.* Fit in his place and tyme.   105

Fer. How well this yeelding rescewes thee from shame.   127

How you delight my Lords I know not I,   185

Bero. How low so euer the matter, I hope in God for high |
(words.   204

Arm. How canst thou part sadnes and melancholy, my | tender
Iuuenall?   318

Boy. How meane you sir, I prettie, and my saying apt?   330

Boy. How many is one thrice tolde?   348

Boy. Then I am sure you know how much the grosse   353

*three studied ere yele thrice wincke: and how easie it is to   358

Ma. Lord how wise you are.   441

*of falsehood) if I loue. And how can that be true loue, which   473

Kath. How needles was it then to aske the question?   612

Brag. How meanest thou? brawling in French.   780

Brag. How hast thou purchased this experience?   795

Ar. Come hither, come hither: How did this argument | (begin?   869

Ar. But tel me, How was there a *Costard* broken in a shin?   877

HOW *cont.*
Clow. Pray you sir, How much Carnation Ribbon may	911
Clo. By my troth most plesant, how both did fit it.	1118
Lord, Lord, how the Ladies and I haue put him downe.	1138
*To see him kisse his hand, & how most sweetly a wil sweare:	1144
ignorance, How deformed doost thou looke.	1173
Dull. If a talent be a claw, looke how he clawes him | with a talent.	1228
If Loue make me forsworne, how shall I sweare to loue?	1267
O Queene of queenes, how farre doost thou excell,	1372
How shall she know my griefes? Ile drop the paper.	1374
Ber. Once more Ile marke how Loue can varrie Wit.	1436
How will he scorne, how will he spende his wit?	1484
How will he triumph, leape, and laugh at it?	1485
Kin. How now, What is in you? Why dost thou teare it?	1542
Long. O some authoritie how to proceede,	1636
Some tricks, some quillets, how to cheate the diuell.	1637
Ros. Ware pensalls, How? Let me not die your debtor,	1931
How I would make him fawne, and begge, and seeke,	1952
Rosa. It is not so. Aske them how manie inches	2086
How manie inches doth fill vp one mile?	2091
Rosa. How manie weerie steps,	2094
Kin. Wil you not daunce? How come you thus estranged?	2112
Lon. Looke how you butt your selfe in these sharpe mocks,	2166
Quee. How blow? how blow? Speake to be vnderstood.	2216
King. How Madame? *Russians?* | *Quee.* I in trueth My Lord.	2288
By this white Gloue (how white the hand God knowes)	2343
Rosa. It is not so, for how can this be true,	2359
Bero. How much is it?	2441
That sport best pleases, that doth best know how:	2460
Alisander, alas you see how tis a little oreparted, but there	2536
Bero. A kissing traytour. How art thou proud *Iudas?*	2553
Quee. Alas poore *Machabeus,* how hath he bin bayted.	2585
King. How fares your Maiestie?	2684

HUDGE = 4
And the hudge armie of the worldes desires.	14
A hudge translation of hipocrisie, | Vildly compyled, profound simplicitie.	1941
Is of that nature, that to your hudge stoore,	2304
Bero. Greater then great, great, great, great *Pompey: Pom-|pey* the hudge.	2641

HUE *see also* hew = 1
The hue of dungions, and the Schoole of night:	1604

HUMBLE = 4
Like humble visage Suters his high will.	525
Pedan. This is not generous, not gentle, not humble.	2582
A heauie hart beares not a humble tongue.	2695
What humble suite attendes thy answere there,	2800

HUMBLE-BEE = 3
+The Fox, the Ape, and the Humble-Bee,	856 +2
+*Ar.* The Foxe, the Ape, and the Humble-Bee,	856 +6
The Foxe, the Ape, and the Humble-Bee,	859

HUMEROUS = *1
*A verie Bedell to a humerous sigh, a Critick, nay a night-|watch Constable,	941

HUMILITIE = 1
And plant in Tyrants milde humilitie.	1700

HUMOR = *1
*If drawing my Sword against the humor of affection, would   365
HUMORS = 1
Lad. They say so most, that most his humors know.   545
HUMOUR = *4
*commende the blacke oppressing humour to the most holsome
phisicke*   243
*the tongues ende, canarie to it with your feete, humour it   782
*on the death of the Deare, and to humour the igno-|rault   1208
* *Ped. Noui hominum tanquam te*, His humour is loftie, his   1748
HUMOURS = 1*1
*are humours, these betraie nice wenches that would be-|traied   792
Hath much deformed vs, fashioning our humours   2715
HUNDRED = 5
The payment of a hundred thousand Crownes,   625
A hundred thousand more, in suretie of the which,   630
A hundred thousand Crownes, and not demaunds   639
One paiment of a hundred thousand Crownes,   640
Of one sore I an hundred make | by adding but one more l.   1225
HUNT = 2
Ferdinand. | Let Fame, that all hunt after in their lyues,   4
The Princesse comes to hunt here in the Parke,   929
HUNTETH = 1
And when it hath the thing it hunteth most,   156
HUNTING = 1
Berow. The King he is hunting the Deare,   1334
HUSHERING = 1
A meane most meanely, and in hushering.   2253
HYPERBOLES *see* Hiberboles
HYPOCRISIE *see* hipocrisie
I = 316*167, 19*3
Ferd. I, that is studies god-like recompence.   63
Ferd. I that there is, our Court you know is haunted   173
* *Fer.* I the best, for the worst. But sirra, What say you to this?   277
Ber. Would that do it good? | *Ros.* My Phisicke saies I.   684
Boy. What then, do you see? | *Lad.* I, our way to be gone.   766
Let me see a fat *Lenuoy*, I thats a fat Goose.   868
I and by heauen, one that will do the deede,   964
Rosa. Shall I teach you to know. | *Boy.* I my continent of beautie.   1094
Holo. I sir, and very learned.   1264
* *Iag.* I sir from one mounsier *Berowne*, one of the strange |
Queenes Lordes.   1294
Ber. I as some dayes, but then no Sunne must shine.   1426
Duma. I marie there, some flatterie for this euyll.   1635
* *Pag.* The last of the fiue Vowels if You repeate them, | or the fift
if I.   1791
Peda. I will repeate them: a e I.   1793
Kath. I and a shrowde vnhappie gallowes too.   1899
Marg. I, or I would these handes might neuer part.   1947
King. How Madame? *Russians?* | *Quee.* I in trueth My Lord.   2288
Duma. I and in a Brooch of Lead.   2570
Bero. I and worne in the cappe of a Tooth-drawer: 2571
Dum. I and *Hector*'s a Greyhound.   2616
* *Bero.* I, if a'haue no more mans blood in his belly then wil |
suppe a Flea.   2647
Queen. I sweete my Lord, and so I take my leaue.   2833

IACKE = 1
Iacke hath not Gill: these Ladies courtesie 2836
IANGLING = 1
Prin. Good witts will be iangling, but gentles agree, 729
IAQ = *1
IAQU = 2
IAQUE = 1*1
IAQUENETTA see also Iaq., Iaqu., Iaque. = 6*5
Clow. The matter is to is sir, as concerning *Iaquenetta*: 213
Ferd. For Iaquenetta (*so is the weaker vessell called*) *which I* 269
*with *Iaquenetta*, and *Iaquenetta* is a trew girle, and therefore 307
Clo. Come *Iaquenetta*, away. *Exeunt.* 448
*significant to the countrey Maide *Iaquenetta*: there is remu-|neration, 896
It is writ to *Iaquenetta*. 1037
Enter Iaquenetta and the Clowne. 1245
Iaqu. God blesse the King. *Enter Iaquenetta and Clowne.* 1528
Clow. Then shall *Hector* be whipt for *Iaquenetta* that is 2636
I am a Votarie; I haue vowde to *Iaquenetta* 2846
IAQUENETTA = 1
IAQUENETTAES = *1
*of *Iaquenettaes*, and that a weares next his hart for a | Fauour. 2669
IAQUES = 1
Betweene L.(ord) *Perigort* and the bewtious heire | Of *Iaques Fauconbridge* solemnized. 533
ICICLES *see* Isacles
ID = *1
*i.d. no, Ile giue you a remuneration: Why? it carries it re-|muneration: 905
IDEAS = *1
*Ideas, aprehentions, motions, reuolutions. These are begot in 1232
IDLE = 3
These othes and lawes will proue an idle scorne. | Surra, Come on. 304
And *Crittick Tymon* laugh at idle toyes. 1507
Will heare your idle scornes; continue then, 2826
IDOLATRIE *see* ydolatarie
IERKES = *1
*out the odoriferous flowers of fancie? the ierkes of in-|uention 1289
IERMANE = 1
A woman that is like a Iermane Cloake, 956
IEST = 11*1
Bero. By yea and nay sir, than I swore in iest. 58
The other turnes to a mirth-moouing iest, 563
Not a word with him but a iest. 716
Boy. And euery iest but a word. 717
La. You Sheepe and I pasture: shall that finish the iest? 723
King. Too bitter is thy iest. 1512
Quee. A Poxe of that iest, and I beshrow all Shrowes, 1934
Bero. This iest is drie to me, gentle sweete, 2300
Duman. Let vs confesse and turne it to a iest. 2320
At courtshyp pleasant iest and courtecie, 2738
Dum. Our letters madame, shewed much more then iest. 2743
Ile iest a tweluemonth in an Hospitall. 2832

IESTES = 3
O my troth most sweete iestes, most inconie vulgar wit,   1139
And make him proude to make me proude that iestes,   1956
A iestes prosperitie lies in the eare,   2822
IESTING = 1
Holding a trencher, iesting merrilie?   2416
IEW = *1
*Clow. My sweete ounce of mans flesh, my in-conie Iew: 901
IEWEL = *1
*as the Pomwater, who now hangeth like a Iewel in the eare   1154
IEWELL = 2
I knew her by this Iewell on her sleeue.   2394
Quee. Pardon me sir, this Iewell did she weare,   2395
IEWELS = 1
As Iewels in Christall for some Prince to buy.   747
IF see also yf l.26 72 164 *236 *291 *365 407 *416 *462 *473 540
557 606 608 633 654 732 *784 *785 *809 1003 1072 *1097 1098
*1102 1123 1127 1223 *1228 *1242 *1247 1267 1275 *1319 *1341
*1351 1404 1405 1593 1601 1607 1627 1737 *1791 1792 *1869
*1878 1920 2037 2073 2087 2089 2132 2137 2222 2223 2267 2362
*2480 2505 *2647 2692 2725 2752 2759 2761 2771 2773 2780 2790
2824 2828 = 50*22
IFAYTH see also yfaith = *1
*againe a my side. I will not loue; if I do hang mee: I'fayth   1341
IGNORANCE = 3
Where now his knowledge must proue ignorance.   598
ignorance, How deformed doost thou looke.   1173
Thrust thy sharpe wit quite through my ignorance,   2330
IGNORANT = 2
You are not ignorant all telling fame   512
All ignorant that soule, that sees thee without wonder.   1277
IGNORAULT = *1
*on the death of the Deare, and to humour the igno-|rault   1208
IGNORAUNCE = 1
Prin. Were my Lord so, his ignoraunce were wise,   597
IGNORAUNT = 1
Nau. Your Ladishyp is ignoraunt what it is.   596
IIGGE = 1*1
*Boy. No my complet Maister, but to Iigge off a tune at   781
And profound Sallomon to tune a Iigge.   1505
IILL see Gill
ILE l.123 126 303 654 752 *905 1269 1374 1435 1436 1622 1623
*1884 1910 1950 2141 2152 2164 2351 *2651 2654 *2668 2788
2790 2791 2795 2796 2832 = 24*5
ILL = 8*2
*Arm. I am ill at reckning, it fitteth the spirit of a Tapster.   349
Nothing becoms him ill that he would well.   538
Most power to do most harme, least knowing ill: 550
For he hath wit to make an ill shape good,   551
To teach a teacher ill beseemeth mee.   603
And shooting well, is then accounted ill: 1000
The poore Deares blood, that my hart meanes no ill.   1010
*For as it would ill become me to be vaine, indiscreet, or a |
(foole,   1183
Were Louers too, ill to example ill,   1461
ILLION = 1
Gaue Hector a gift, the heir of Illion,   2607

ILLUSTRATE = *2
   *heroicall Vassall. The magnanimous and most illustrate   1045
   *assistants the Kinges commaund, and this most gallant
   il-|lustrate   1853
ILLUSTRIOUS = 1
   Bero. Armado is a most illustrious wight,   188
IMBRACE = 1
   Ber. Sweete Lords, sweete Louers, O let vs imbrace,   1562
IMITARIE = *1
   *imitarie is nothing: So doth the Hound his maister,   1290
IMITATE = 1
   Paintes it selfe blacke, to imitate her brow.   1614
IMMACULATE *see also* maculate = 1
   Arm. My loue is most immaculate white and red.   395
IMMEDIATLY = 1
   Immediatly they will againe be heere,   2208
IMMURED *see* emured
IMP = *1
   Ar. Why? sadnes is one & the selfe same thing deare imp.   315
IMPACIENT = 1
   His tongue all impacient to speake and not see,   742
IMPART = *1
   *special honours it pleaseth his greatnes to impart to *Armado*   1839
IMPE = 1
   Peda. Great Hercules *is presented by this Impe,*   2541
IMPLORE = *2
   *let that passe; the very all of all is: but sweet hart, I do implore   1842
   Brag. Annoynted, I implore so much expence of thy royal   2467
IMPLOY = 1
   I must imploy him in a letter to my loue.   777
IMPLOYMENT = 2
   Boy. Proud of imployment, willingly I go. *Exit Boy.*   526
   Your Ladiships in all desired imployment, Berowne.   1301
IMPORT = *1
   *important and most serious designes, and of great import in   1833
IMPORTETH = 1
   This letter is mistooke: it importeth none heere.   1036
IMPORTUNT = *1
   *important and most serious designes, and of great import in   1833
IMPORTUOUS = 1
   Importuous personall conference with his grace.   523
IMPOSE = 2*1
   *lewe thereof, impose on thee nothing but this: Beare this   895
   That *Cupid* will impose for my neglect,   968
   Impose some seruice on me for thy Loue.   2801
IMPOSSIBLE = 2
   Boy. You may do it in an houre sir. | *Arma.* Impossible.   346
   It cannot be, it is impossible.   2817
IMPOTENT = 1
   To enforce the pained impotent to smile.   2815
IMPRESSED = 1
   His hart like an Agot with your print impressed,   740
IMPRISONMENT = *1
   Fer. It was proclaymed a yeeres imprisonment to be ta-|ken with
   a Wench.   283
IMPUDENCIE = *1
   *wittie without affection, audatious without impudencie,   1743

IN *see also* i' = 254*78
INCENSED = 1
  Duma. Roome for the incensed Worthies.   2653
INCHAUNTED = 1
  That all eyes saw his eyes inchaunted with gazes.   751
INCHAUNTING = 1
  Doth rauish like inchaunting harmonie: 178
INCHES = 2
  Rosa. It is not so. Aske them how manie inches   2086
  How manie inches doth fill vp one mile?   2091
INCISION = 1
  Ber. A Feuer in your blood, why then incision   1433
INCK = *1
  *He hath not eate paper as it were: he hath not drunke inck.   1176
INCKE = 2*1
  *ebon coloured Incke, which here thou viewest, beholdest, suruayest,
  or*   252
  Vntill his Incke were tempred with Loues sighes: 1698
  Quee. Beautious as Incke: a good conclusion.   1929
INCLINATION = *1
  *replication, or rather *ostentare*, to show as it were his
  inclina-|tion   1165
INCLINE = 1
  And he from forrage will incline to play.   1071
INCONIE *see also* in-conie = 1
  O my troth most sweete iestes, most inconie vulgar wit,   1139
INCONSIDERATE = *1
  *smyling: O pardone me my starres, doth the incon-|siderate   850
INCONSTANCIE = 1
  With men like men of inconstancie.   1518
INCONTRED = 1
  Brag. Men of peace well incontred. | *Ped.* Most millitarie sir
  salutation.   1774
INCOUNTER = *1
  *Then for the place Where? where I meane, I did incounter that
  ob-|seene*   250
INCOUNTERS = 1
  Arme Wenches arme, incounters mounted are,   1974
INDE = 1
  That (like a rude and sauadge man of *Inde*.)   1571
INDEED *see also* deed, deede = *1
  Clo. Indeed a'must shoot nearer, or hele neare hit the clout.   1125
INDIGNITIE = 1
  They will digest this harsh indignitie.   2210
INDISCREET = *1
  *For as it would ill become me to be vaine, indiscreet, or a |
  (foole,   1183
INDITED = *1
  Quee. What plume of fethers is he that indited this letter?   1074
INDUBITATE = *1
  *King *Cophetua* set eie vpon the pernicious and indubitate   1046
INDUED = 1
  Boye. No, he is best indued in the small.   2597
INDURE = *1
  *the tearme of three yeeres, he shall indure such publique   140

INDUSTRI = 1
Thine in the dearest designe of industri, | Don Adriana de
Armatho.   1066
INFALLIBLE = 1
 Boyet | reedes. By heauen, that thou art faire, is most infallible: 1041
INFALLIBLY = 1
 Peda. And certes the text most infallibly concludes it.   1328
INFAMIE = *2
 *which he would call abbominable, it insinuateth me of in-|famie: 1763
 *about your Infamie *vnu(m) cita* a gigge of a Cuckolds horne.   1805
INFAMONIZE = 1
 Brag. Dost thou infamonize me among potentates: 2634
INFANCIE = 1
 And giues the Crutch the Cradles infancie.   1594
INFANT = 2*1
 Ar. Define, define, well educated infant.   398
 Berow. All hid, all hid, an olde infant play,   1412
 Peda. Thou disputes like an Infant: goe whip thy Gigg.   1802
INFANTS = 1
 That bites the first borne infants of the Spring.   110
INFECTED = 2
 Deceaue me not now, *Nauar* is infected.   734
 They are infected, in their hartes it lyes: 2353
INFINITE = 1
 Our duetie is so rich, so infinite,   2098
INFLUENCE = 1
 Whose influence is begot of that loose grace,   2820
INFORCEST = *1
 Ar. By vertue thou inforcest laughter, thy sillie thought,   848
INFRANCHISE = 1
 Arm. Sirra *Costard,* I will infranchise thee.   886
INFRINGE = 1
 And *Ioue* for your Loue would infringe an oth.   1481
INFRINGED = 1
 Fayth infringed, which such zeale did sweare.   1483
INGAGED = 1
 To breake the vow I am ingaged in.   1516
INGENDERS = 1
 And abstinence ingenders maladies.   1645
INGENIOUS = 1
 Arma. What? that an Eele is ingenious.   338
INGENIUS = *1
 Brag. The meaning prettie ingenius, is not Lead a mettal |
heauie, dull, and slow?   826
INGENOUS = *1
 Nath. Me hercle, yf their Sonnes be ingenous, they shal   1241
INHERITE = 1
 Which with payne purchas'd, doth inherite payne,   78
INHERITOURE = 1
 To parlee with the sole inheritoure   496
INHERRIT = 1
 For. No thing but faire is that which you inherrit.   995
INIOYNED = *1
 Boy. True, and it was inioyned him in *Rome* for want of   2667
INKLE *see* yncle
INRICHT = *1
 *victorie: On whose side? the King: the captiue is inricht, on   1055

INRITCHT = 1
Of beautis tutors haue inritcht you with: 1674
INSERT = 1
to insert again my *haud credo* for a Deare.   1168
INSINUATETH = *1
*which he would call abbominable, it insinuateth me of in-|famie: 1763
INSINUATION = *1
Holo. Most barbarous intimation: yet a kind of insinua-|tion,   1163
INSOCIABLE = 1*1
*phantasims, such insociable and poynt deuise companions,   1758
If this Austere insociable life, | Change not your offer made in
heate of blood.   2759
INSPIRDE = 1
King. What zeale, what furie, hath inspirde thee now?   1578
INSTANCE = 1
I wilbe thine: and till that instance shutt   2767
INSTANT = *1
*instant: by hart you loue her, because your hart cannot come   810
INSTRUCTION = *1
*want no instruction: If their Daughters be capable, I will   1242
INT = 1
Let the mark haue a prick in't, to meate at, if it may be.   1123
INTEGRITIE = 1
Of heauenly Othes vowed with integritie.   2282
INTELECTS = 1
And traine our intelects to vaine delight.   76
INTELIGIS = 1
ne inteligis domine, to make frantique lunatique?   1764
INTELLECT = 1*2
*His intellect is not replenished, he is only an annimall, only   1178
*I will looke againe on the intellect of the letter, for the
no-|mination   1298
home, it reioiceth my intellect, true wit.   1797
INTELLIGO = 1
Curat. Laus deo, bene intelligo. | *Peda. Bome boon for boon
prescian*, a litle scratcht, twil serue.   1766
INTENDE = 1
Rosa. Nor shall not, if I do as I intende.   2362
INTENDED *see* entended
INTENT = 3
Kath. But in this changing, What is your intent?   2029
Quee. The effect of my intent is to crosse theirs: 2030
And mocke for mocke is onely my intent.   2032
INTENTES *see also* ententes = 1
Tolde our intentes before: which once disclosd,   2406
INTERIM = 1
For interim to our studies shall relate,   182
INTERRUPPTEST = *1
Quee. Welcome *Marcade*, but that thou interrupptest our |
merriment.   2673
INTERRUPT = 1
When lo to interrupt my purposed rest,   1983
INTERUIEW *see* enteruiew
INTIMATE = 1
Ferd. Madame, your father heere doth intimate,   624
INTIMATION = *1
Holo. Most barbarous intimation: yet a kind of insinua-|tion,   1163

INTIRE = 1
Being but the one halfe of, of an intire summe,   626
INTIRELY = 1
Other slow Artes intirely keepe the braine: 1675
INTITLE = 1
Prin. With what? | *Bo.* With that which we Louers intitle
Affected.   735
INTITLED = 1
Neither intitled in the others hart.   2772
INTITULED = *1
*who is intituled, nominated, or called, *Don Adriano de
Ar-| matho.*   1746
INTO *l.*218 *1306 1986 2727 2881 = 3*2
INTREAT = 1
For all your faire endeuours and intreat: 2688
INTREATE = 1
Do one thing for me that I shall intreate.   919
INUENTION = *2
*out the odoriferous flowers of fancie? the ierkes of in-|uention   1289
*neither sauouring of Poetrie, wit, nor inuention.   1323
INUISIBLE = 1
Boyet. The tongues of mocking Wenches are as keene | As is the
Rasors edge inuisible: 2172
INUITE = *1
*Sir I do inuite you too, you shall not say me nay: *pauca verba.*   1329
INUOCATION = *1
**Ar.* Sweet inuocation of a child, most pretty & pathetical.   401
INWARDE = *1
*I do assure ye very good friende: for what is inwarde   1830
IN-CONIE = *1
**Clow.* My sweete ounce of mans flesh, my in-conie Iew: 901
IONE = 4
Some men must loue my Ladie, and some Ione.   971
Or grone for Ione? or spende a minutes time,   1520
While greasie Ione doth keele the pot.   2887
While greasie Ione doth keele the pot.   2896
IOSUA = *1
**Peda. Iosua,* your selfe, my selfe, and this gallant Gentle-|man   1859
IOUE = 5
Thou for whom *Ioue* would sweare,   1454
And denie himselfe for *Ioue,*   1456
Ay mee sayes one! O *Ioue* the other cryes!   1478
And *Ioue* for your Loue would infringe an oth.   1481
Bero. By Ioue, I all wayes tooke three threes for nine.   2438
IOUES = *1
*Thy eie *Ioues* lightning beares, thy voyce his dreadful thu(n)der   1279
IOY = 3
Why should I ioy in any abhortiue byrth?   113
And leape for ioy, though they are lame with blowes: 2213
Quee. God giue thee ioy of him: the Noble Lord   2386
IOYFULL = 1*1
*What a ioyfull father wouldest thou make me?   1812
And I shall finde you emptie of that fault, | Right ioyfull of your
reformation.   2829
IOYNT = 1
or ioynt) shall passe *Pompey* the great, the Page *Hercules.*   1861

IOYNTED = *1
    *Arm. O wel knit *Sampson*, strong ioynted *Sampson*; I do excel   379
IS *see also* Hector's, heer's, hee's, he's, shee's, shes, that's, there's,
    ther's, tis, whats, wher's, wit's = 209*94, 1
    Clo. Then will she get the vpshoot by cleauing the is in.   1129
ISACLES = 1
    Winter. | When Isacles hang by the wall,   2878
ISCARIOT = 1
    Dum. A Iudas. | *Pedan. Not Iscariot sir.*   2549
IST = 1
    Prin. Some merrie mocking Lord belike, ist so?   544
IT *see also* ant, doo't, doote, fort, in't, ist, 't, tis, toot = 160*79
ITEM = *2
    Ber. Item, That no woman shall come within a myle of   128
    Item, Yf any man be seene to talke with a woman within   139
ITH = 1
    Ros. Looke what you do, you do it still i'th darke.   1911
ITSELFE *see* selfe
IUDAS = 12*3
    Iudas Machabeus; this Swaine (because of his great lim   1860
    Iudas Machabeus: And if these foure Worthies in their   2480
    Enter Pedant for Iudas, and the Boy for Hercules.   2540
    Peda. Iudas *I am.*   2548
    Dum. A Iudas. | *Pedan. Not Iscariot sir.*   2549
    Iudas *I am, ecliped* Machabeus.   2551
    Dum. Iudas Machabeus *clipt, is plaine* Iudas.   2552
    Bero. A kissing traytour. How art thou proud *Iudas*?   2553
    Peda. Iudas *I am.* | *Duma.* The more shame for you *Iudas.*   2554
    Peda. What meane you sir? | *Boyet.* To make *Iudas* hang him
    selfe.   2556
    Bero. Well folowed, *Iudas* was hanged on an Elder.   2559
    Bero. For the *Asse* to the *Iude*: giue it him. *Iudas* away.   2580
    Boyet. A light for Mounsier *Iudas*, it growes darke, he | may
    stumble.   2583
IUDE = 2
    And so adue sweete *Iude.* Nay, Why dost thou stay?   2578
    Bero. For the *Asse* to the *Iude*: giue it him. *Iudas* away.   2580
IUDGEMENT = 1
    Beautie is bought by iudgement of the eye,   506
IUMPS = 1
    The Dogges did yell, put ell to Sore, | then Sorell iumps from
    thicket: 1219
IUNIOS = 1
    This signior *Iunios* gyant dwarffe, dan *Cupid*,   946
IUNO = 1
    Iuno but an *Aethiop* were,   1455
IUSTICE = 1
    And Iustice alwayes whirles in equall measure: 1735
IUSTLE = 1
    Let not the cloude of Sorrow iustle it   2706
IUUENAL = *1
    Arm. I spoke it tender iuuenal, as a congruent apethaton   324
IUUENALL = 4
    Arm. How canst thou part sadnes and melancholy, my | tender
    Iuuenall?   318
    Boy. Why tender iuuenall? Why tender iuuenall?   323
    Brag. A most acute Iuuenall, volable and free of grace,   836

KA = 1
KATE = 1
Duma. O most deuine *Kate.* 1417
KATH = 21*1
KATHER = 1
KATHERIN = 1
Bero. Whats her name in the capp? | *Boy. Katherin* by good happ. 709
KATHERINE see also Ka., Kath., Kather. = 1
But *Katherine* what was sent to you | From faire *Dumaine*? 1935
KEELE = 2
While greasie Ione doth keele the pot. 2887
While greasie Ione doth keele the pot. 2896
KEENE = 3
That honour which shall bate his sythes keene edge, 10
Boyet. The tongues of mocking Wenches are as keene | As is the
Rasors edge inuisible: 2172
Cut me to peeces with thy keene conceit. 2331
KEEPE = 12*4
My fellow Schollers, and to keepe those statutes 21
Subscribe to your deepe othes, and keepe it to. 27
O these are barraine taskes, too hard to keepe, 51
Yet confident Ile keepe what I haue sworne, 123
I am the last that will last keepe his oth. 171
apprehended with the aforesayd Swaine, I keepe hir as a vessell of 270
Constab. Sir, the Dukes pleasure is that you keepe *Costard* 431
*I must keepe her at the Parke, she is alowde for the Day |
womand. Fare you well. 434
Tis deadlie sinne to keepe that oath my Lord, 600
*man after the olde painting, and keepe not too long in one 789
But do not loue thy selfe, then thou will keepe 1370
His louing bosome, to keepe downe his hart. 1473
Other slow Artes intirely keepe the braine: 1675
Or els we loose our selues, to keepe our othes: 1713
Quee. I will, and therefore keepe it. *Rosaline,* 2380
Keepe some state in thy exit, and vanish. Exit Boy. 2547
KEEPER = 1*1
Fer. And *Don Armado* shall be your keeper. 299
*the Ape his keeper, the tyred Horse his rider: But *Damosella* 1291
KEEPES = *1
Boy. This *Armado* is a *Spaniard* that keepes here in court, 1079
KEEPING = 3
Or hauing sworne too hard a keeping oth, 70
I am betrayed by keeping companie 1517
Or keeping what is sworne, you will proue fooles, 1707
KERSIE = 1
In russet yeas, and honest kersie noes. 2345
KEY = *1
Brag. Sweete Ayer, go tendernes of yeeres, take this Key, 775
KILD = 3
that, twas a Pricket that the Princesse kild. 1206
cald the Deare: the Princesse kild a Pricket. 1209
Ros. Youle neare be friendes with him, a kild your sister. 1900
KILDE = 1
Whose Clubb kilde Cerberus that three headed Canus, 2542
KILL = 3*1
But come, the Bow: Now Mercie goes to kill, 999
That more for praise, then purpose meant to kill. 1004

KILL   *cont.*
  *_Boy._ My Lady goes to kill hornes, but if thou marrie,   1097
  Boy. Why that contempt will kill the speakers hart,   2041
KILLS = *2
  *as _Aiax_, it kills Sheepe, it kills mee, I a Sheepe well prooued   1340
KIN = 1*2
KIND = *1
  *_Holo._ Most barbarous intimation: yet a kind of insinua-|tion,   1163
KING   *see also Kin.* = 24*10
  Enter Ferdinand K.(ing) of Nauar, Berowne,| _Longauill, and_
  Dumaine.   2
  *_Ar._ Is there not a Ballet Boy, of the King & the Begger?   413
  Consider who the King your father sendes: 493
  Tell him, the Daughter of the King of France   521
  If then the King your father will restore,   633
  Prin. You do the King my father too much wrong,   649
  Dread Prince of Placcats, King of Codpeeces.   950
  Quee. Was that the king that spurd his horse so hard,   975
  *King _Cophetua_ set eie vpon the pernicious and indubitate   1046
  *King. Why did he come? to see. Why did he see? to ouer-|come.   1051
  *victorie: On whose side? the King: the captiue is inricht, on   1055
  *I am the King (for so standes the comparison) thou the
  Beg-|ger,   1058
  *was a man when King _Pippen_ of Fraunce was a litle boy, as|
  touching the hit it.   1109
  *with the King, and here he hath framed a letter to a sequent   1303
  *deliuer this Paper into the royall hand of the King, it may   1306
  Berow. The King he is hunting the Deare,   1334
  He standes a side. The King entreth.   1353
  Enter Longauill. The King steps a side.   1376
  O would the _King, Berowne,_ and _Longauill,_   1460
  You found his Moth, the King your Moth did see: 1498
  To see a King transformed to a Gnat.   1503
  Iaqu. God blesse the King. _Enter Iaquenetta and Clowne._   1528
  *_Brag._ Sir, the King is a noble Gentleman, and my fami-|lier,   1829
  *secrecie, that the King would haue me present the Princesse   1843
  *A Ladie walde about with Diamondes: Looke you, what I| haue
  from the louing King.   1890
  The King and his companions warely,   1985
  For quoth the King, an Angell shalt thou see: 1995
  And then the King will court thee for his Deare: 2023
  The King was weeping ripe for a good word.   2193
  But will you heare; the King is my Loue sworne.   2203
  Enter the King and the rest.   2234
  is heauie in my tongue. The King your father| _Quee._ Dead for
  my life.   2676
  And by these badges vnderstand the King,   2712
  Come when the King doth to my Lady come: 2789
KING = 61*9
KINGES = 1*2
  The French kinges daughter with your selfe to speake: 145
  *whose side? the Kinges: no, on both in one, or one in both.   1057
  *assistants the Kinges commaund, and this most gallant
  il-|lustrate   1853
KINGLY = 2
  Flat treason gainst the kingly state of youth.   1643

KINGLY *cont.*
  Quee. O pouertie in wit, Kingly poore flout.   2188
KINGS = 1*2
  *conuerse this quondam day with a companion of the kings,   1745
  **Bra.* Sir, it is the Kings most sweete pleasur & affection,   1821
  To haue one show worse then the Kings and his company.   2456
KISSE = 4*1
  And you giue him for my sake but one louing kisse.   753
  *To see him kisse his hand, & how most sweetly a wil sweare: 1144
  King. So sweete a kisse the golden Sunne giues not,   1358
  The staires as he treades on them kisse his feete.   2255
  Brag. I will kisse thy royall finger, and take leaue.   2845
KISSES = 1
  Kisses the base ground with obedient breast.   1574
KISSING = 2
  Bero. A kissing traytour. How art thou proud *Iudas*?   2553
  And by this Virgin palme now kissing thine,   2766
KIST = 1
  That kist his hand, a way in courtisie.   2249
KNAUE = 2
  Ber. O my good knaue *Costard*, exceedingly well met.   910
  As thou wilt win my fauour, good my knaue,   918
KNAUISH = 1
  Their Heralde is a prettie knauish Page: 1989
KNEE = 1
  Clow. I Pompey *am,* | *Boyet.* With Libbards head on knee. 2493
KNEW = 4
  Duma. I neuer knew man holde vile stuffe so deare.   1625
  Ros. I would you knew.   1919
  O that I knew he were but in by th'weeke,   1951
  I knew her by this Iewell on her sleeue.   2394
KNIFE = 1
  Ber. Will you prickt with your eye. | *Ros. No poynt,* with my
  knife.   686
KNIGHT = 4*1
  In high borne wordes the worth of many a Knight: 183
  A man of fier new wordes, Fashions owne knight.   189
  Some mumble newes, some trencher Knight, some Dick   2403
  **Be.* Your nose smels no in his most tender smelling knight. 2518
  Queen. Was not that *Hector*? | *Duma.* The worthie Knight of
  Troy.   2843
KNIT = *1
  **Arm.* O wel knit *Sampson,* strong ioynted *Sampson*; I do excel 379
KNOTTED = *1
  **East from the West corner of thy curious knotted garden; There* 254
KNOW = 35*9
  What is the ende of study, let me know?   59
  **Ferd.* Why that to know which else we should not know.   60
  To know the thing I am forbid to know: 65
  Studie knowes that which yet it doth not know,   73
  Too much to know, is to know nought but fame: 97
  For well you know here comes in Embassaie,   144
  Ferd. I that there is, our Court you know is haunted   173
  How you delight my Lords I know not I,   185
  **Boy.* Then I am sure you know how much the grosse   353
  Then if she feare or be to blame, | By this you shall not know, 407

KNOW *cont.*

Maid. Thats hereby. | *Ar.* I know where it is situate.	439
To know his pleasure, and in that behalfe	518
Lor. Longauill is one. | *Princ.* Know you the man?	530
1. *Lady.* I know him Maddame at a marriage feast,	532
Lad. They say so most, that most his humors know.	545
Kather. Did not I dance with you in *Brabant* once? | *Ber.* I know you did.	610
By adding a tongue which I know will not lie.	757
Clow. I shall know sir when I haue done it.	924
Ber. Why villaine, thou must know first.	925
Forr. I know not, but I thinke it was not he.	977
*Que. Thou shalt know her fellow by the rest that haue no | (heads.	1020
Rosa. Shall I teach you to know. | *Boy.* I my continent of beautie.	1094
*Ped. The Deare was (as you know) sanguis in blood, ripe	1153
If knowledge be the marke, to know thee shall suffise.	1275
How shall she know my griefes? Ile drop the paper.	1374
*Ber. I could put thee in comfort, not by two that I know,	1384
You may looke pale, but I should blush I know,	1466
I would not haue him know so much by mee.	1487
Vnto his seuerall Mistres: which they'le know	2016
Rosal. What would these strangers? | Know their mindes *Boyet.*	2071
Know what they would?	2075
Long. I know the reason (Lady) why you aske.	2155
Boy. I will, and so will she, I know my Lord. *Exit.*	2239
And we that sell by grosse, the Lord doth know,	2244
Do not you know my Ladies foote by'th squier?	2413
Clow. O Lord sir, they would know,	2426
**You cannot beg vs sir, I can assure you sir, we know what	2433
we know: I hope sir three times thrice sir. | *Bero.* Is not nine.	2434
*Clow. Vnder correction sir we know where-vntill it doth | amount.	2436
**the great: for mine owne part I know not the degree of the	2448
That sport best pleases, that doth best know how:	2460

KNOWES = 4

Studie knowes that which yet it doth not know,	73
Quee. Will they returne? | *Boy.* They will they will, God knowes,	2211
By this white Gloue (how white the hand God knowes)	2343
That smyles, his cheeke in yeeres, and knowes the trick	2404

KNOWEST = 1

Ber. O thou knowest not what it is.	923

KNOWING = 2*1

*(Clowne. Mee?) *that vnlettered small knowing soule,* (*Clow.* Mee?)	257
Most power to do most harme, least knowing ill:	550
Knowing aforehand of our meriment,	2400

KNOWLEDGE = 3

Then for that Angell knowledge you can say,	122
Where now his knowledge must proue ignorance.	598
If knowledge be the marke, to know thee shall suffise.	1275

KNOWNE = 2

Her faultes will nere be knowne:	404
Lets mocke them still as well knowne as disguysde:	2224

L *see also* el = 1

Of one sore I an hundred make | by adding but one more l.	1225

LA *l.**1261 = *1
LA = 1*1
LABOURING = 1
  When great thinges labouring perish in their byrth.   2464
LACKE = 1*1
  **Long.* I feare these stubborne lines lacke power to moue.   1387
  That I may sweare Beautie doth beautie lacke,   1600
LACKT = *1
  **King.* What? | **Ber.* That you three fooles, lackt me foole, to
  make vp the | (messe.   1551
LAD = 5*4
LADIE = 15*1
  Ber. Ladie I will commend you to my none hart.   677
  Dum. Sir, I pray you a word, What Ladie is that same?   692
  Lon. Nay my coller is ended. She is a most sweet Ladie. | *Exit*
  Longauil.   705
  And in her traine there is a gentle Ladie: 930
  Some men must loue my Ladie, and some Ione.   971
  Clow. Which is the greatest Ladie, the highest?   1022
  Clow. I haue a Letter from Monsier *Berowne,* | to one Ladie
  Rosaline.   1029
  Quee. To whom shouldst thou giue it? | *Clow.* From my Lord to
  my Ladie.   1085
  Quee. From which Lord, to which Ladie?   1087
  To a Ladie of France, that he calde *Rosaline.*   1089
  *A Ladie walde about with Diamondes: Looke you, what I | haue
  from the louing King.   1890
  Duma. Faire Ladie.   2149
  Long. A Calfe faire Ladie.   2161
  My Ladie (to the maner of the dayes) | In curtesie giues
  vndeseruing praise.   2292
  Heere stand I, Ladie dart thy skill at me,   2328
  Berow. Studdies my Ladie? Mistres looke on me,   2798
LADIES = 17
  Enter the Princesse of Fraunce, with three | attending Ladies and
  three Lordes.   490
  Lord, Lord, how the Ladies and I haue put him downe.   1138
  Then when our selues we see in Ladies eyes, | With our selues.   1666
  But Loue first learned in a Ladies eyes,   1678
  For Ladies; we will euery one be maskt,   2019
  Despight of sute, to see a Ladies face.   2021
  Boy. Faire Ladies maskt, are Roses in their bud: 2218
  Boyet. Ladies, withdraw: the gallants are at hand,   2231
  Mende him who can, the Ladies call him sweete.   2254
  Enter the Ladies.   2262
  What did you whisper in your Ladies eare?   2372
  The Ladies did change Fauours; and then wee   2407
  Do not you know my Ladies foote by'th squier?   2413
  Plaide fouleplay with our othes: your beautie Ladies   2714
  Suggested vs to make, therefore Ladies   2728
  To those that make vs both faire Ladies you,   2732
  Iacke hath not Gill: these Ladies courtesie   2836
LADISHIPS = 1
  Your Ladiships in all desired imployment, Berowne.   1301
LADISHYP = 2
  Nau. Your Ladishyp is ignoraunt what it is.   596
  If your Ladishyp would say thankes Pompey, *I had done.*   2505

LADI-SMOCKES = 1
And Ladi-smockes all siluer white,   2862
LADY see also La., Lad., Lad.2., Lad.3., 1.Lady., 2.Lad.,
3.Lad. = 12*6
And he and his compettitours in oth, | Were all addrest to meete
you gentle Lady   576
Nau. Heare me deare Lady, I haue sworne an oth,   592
Prin. Our Lady helpe my Lord, he'le be forsworne.   593
Dum. A gallant Lady *Mounsir*, fare you wel. *Exit.*   694
To any Lady that subdewes a Lord.   1015
Clo. God dig-you-den al, pray you which is the head lady?   1018
Boy. My Lady goes to kill hornes, but if thou marrie,   1097
Bo. A mark, O mark but that mark: a mark saies my Lady.   1121
To see him walke before a Lady, and to beare her Fann.   1143
To the snow-white hand of the most bewtious Lady Rosaline.   1297
*it, the Foole sent it, and the Lady hath it: sweete Clowne,   1349
*sweeter Foole, sweetest Lady. By the worlde, I woulde not   1350
Mar. Say you so? Faire Lord, take that for your faire Lady   2150
Long. I know the reason (Lady) why you aske.   2155
Will you giue hornes chast Lady? do not so.   2168
I neuer swore this Lady such an oth.   2390
To make my Lady laugh, when shees disposd: 2405
Come when the King doth to my Lady come: 2789
LADY = 3*1
LADYES = 6
Not to see Ladyes, study, fast, not sleepe.   52
Prin. God blesse my Ladyes, are they all in loue?   569
Enter the Princesse, a Forrester, her Ladyes, | *and her Lordes.*   973
O if in blacke my Ladyes browes be deckt,   1607
Enter the Ladyes.   1887
The Ladyes turne their backes to him.   2057
LAMBE = 2
No Sheepe (sweete Lambe) vnlesse we feede on your lippes.   722
Gainst thee thou Lambe, that standest as his pray: 1069
LAME = 1
And leape for ioy, though they are lame with blowes: 2213
LAMENTABLE = 1
Rosa. They were all in lamentable cases,   2192
LAMENTATION = 1
My wofull selfe vp in a mourning house, | Rayning the teares of
lamentation,   2768
LAND = 2
a Crab on the face of *Terra*, the soyle, the land, the earth.   1156
Quee. Whip to our Tents as Roes runs ore land. *Exeunt.*   2232
LANGUAGE = 1
If they do speake our language, tis our will   2073
LANGUAGES = *1
Boy. They haue been at a great feast of Languages, and | stolne
the scraps.   1776
LARGE = 2
So to the Lawes at large I write my name,   166
Before I saw you: and the worldes large tongue   2803
LARKES = 1
And merrie Larkes are Ploughmens Clocks: 2870
LASSE = *1
*And lay my Armes before the Leggs of this sweete Lasse of
France.*   2503

LAST = 3*2
| | |
I am the last that will last keepe his oth. 171
*Lady Maria. That last is *Berowne*, the merrie madcap L.(ord) 715
*Pag. The last of the fiue Vowels if You repeate them, | or the fift
if I. 1791
But that it beare this tryall, and last Loue, 2763
LATE = 3
Our late edict shall strongly stand in force, 15
So you to studie now it is too late, 117
A messe of *Russians* left vs but of late. 2287
LATEST = 1
King. Now at the latest minute of the houre, | Graunt vs your
loues. 2746
LATINE = 1*1
*Remuneration, O that's the latine word for three-farthings: 903
Peda. Oh I smell false Latine, *dunghel* for *vnguem.* 1814
LATTER = 1
Duma. For the latter ende of his name. 2579
LAUGH = 4*1
*Lon. To heare meekely sir, and to laugh moderatly, or | to
forbeare both. 209
How will he triumph, leape, and laugh at it? 1485
And *Crittick Tymon* laugh at idle toyes. 1507
To make my Lady laugh, when shees disposd: 2405
And laugh vpon the apple of her eie? 2414
LAUGHING = 1
Which shallow laughing hearers giue to fooles, 2821
LAUGHT = 1
With that all laught, and clapt him on the shoulder, 1999
LAUGHTER = 2*2
*Ar. By vertue thou inforcest laughter, thy sillie thought, 848
Boyet. O I am stable with laughter, Wher's her Grace? 1971
With such a zelous laughter so profund, 2008
*Berow. To moue wilde laughter in the throate of death? 2816
LAUNCES = *2
*Braggart. The Armipotent Mars, of Launces the almightie, | gaue
Hector *a gift.* 2600
*Brag. Peace. The Armipotent Mars, of Launces the almighty, 2606
LAUS = 1
*Curat. Laus deo, bene intelligo. | *Peda. Bome boon for boon
prescian, a litle scratcht, twil serue. 1766
LAW = 3
A dangerous law against gentletie. 138
For Charitie it selfe fulfilles the Law: 1715
And to begin Wench, so God helpe me law, 2346
LAWES = 2*1
So to the Lawes at large I write my name, 166
*thy Lawes furie, and shall at the least of thy sweete notice, bring 271
These othes and lawes will proue an idle scorne. | Surra, Come
on. 304
LAWFULL = 1
Our louing lawfull, and our fayth not torne. 1634
LAY = 3*1
Bero. Ile lay my Head to any good mans Hat, 303
Nor neuer lay his wreathed armes athwart 1472
Long. Now to plaine dealing, Lay these glozes by, 1721

LAY *cont.*
  *And lay my Armes before the Leggs of this sweete Lasse of
  France.   2503
LEAD = 4*1
  Brag. The way is but short, away. | *Boy.* As swift as Lead sir. 824
  *Brag. The meaning prettie ingenius, is not Lead a mettal |
  heauie, dull, and slow?   826
  Brag. I say Lead is slow.   829
  Is that Lead slow which is fierd from a Gunne?   831
  Duma. I and in a Brooch of Lead.   2570
LEADE = 1
  To leade you to our Court, vouchsafe it then.   2270
LEADEN = 2
  In leaden contemplation haue found out   1672
  You leere vpon me, do you: ther's an eie | Woundes like a leaden
  sword.   2419
LEAFE = 1
  Writ a both sides the leafe, margent and all,   1895
LEANE = 1*1
  Fat paunches haue leane pates: and daynty bits   30
  **please his Grace (by the worlde) sometime to leane vpon 1835
LEAPE = 2
  How will he triumph, leape, and laugh at it?   1485
  And leape for ioy, though they are lame with blowes: 2213
LEARNE = 2
  Brag. Almost I had. | *Boy.* Negligent student, learne her by hart. 803
  If that she learne not of her eye to looke: 1601
LEARNED = 4*3
  Holo. I sir, and very learned.   1264
  Well learned is that tongue, that well can thee commend. 1276
  But Loue first learned in a Ladies eyes,   1678
  **learned without opinion, and strange without heresie: I did 1744
  **and learned Gentleman, before the Princesse: I say   1854
  And Wits owne grace to grace a learned Foole.   1962
  **that the two Learned men haue compiled, in prayse of the 2849
LEARNES = *1
  *Lad. 2. He is *Cupids* Graundfather, and learnes newes | of him. 760
LEARNING = 4*1
  **So were there a patch set on Learning, to see him in a schole. 1185
  Learning is but an adiunct to our selfe,   1664
  And where we are, our Learning likewise is.   1665
  Do we not likewise see our learning there?   1668
  *Pag. Ba most seely Sheepe, with a horne: you heare his |
  (learning.   1788
LEARNT = 1
  Before I came: Marrie thus much I haue learnt,   578
LEAST = 3*2
  And he that breakes them in the least degree,   167
  *thy Lawes furie, and shall at the least of thy sweete notice, bring 271
  Most power to do most harme, least knowing ill: 550
  **sweetly varried like a scholler at the least: but sir I assure ye 1159
  Kath. Yet sweare not, least ye be forsworne agen.   2792
LEAUE = 5*1
  Kath. Not till it leaue the rider in the mire.   616
  *King. Then leaue this chat, and good *Berowne* now proue 1633
  Quee. Then wish me better, I will giue you leaue.   2268
  Ile leaue it by degrees; soft, let vs see,   2351

LEAUE *cont.*
  Queen. I sweete my Lord, and so I take my leaue.   2833
  Brag. I will kisse thy royall finger, and take leaue.   2845
LEAUES = 3
  Studie his byas leaues, and makes his booke thine eyes.   1272
  Sweete leaues shade follie. Who is he comes heere?   1375
  Through the Veluet, leaues the wind,   1442
LEEDGE = 1*1
  Ber. A toy my Leedge, a toy: your grace needs not feare it.   1543
  For when would you (my Leedge) or you, or you?   1671
LEEGE = 1
  Hee, hee, and you: and you my Leege, and I,   1554
LEERE = 1
  You leere vpon me, do you: ther's an eie | Woundes like a leaden
  sword.   2419
LEFT = 2
  him with thy Birdbolt vnder the left papp: in fayth secrets.   1356
  A messe of *Russians* left vs but of late.   2287
LEGE = *1
  Nath. Let me heare a staffe, a stanze, a verse, *Lege domine.*   1265
LEGGE = 2
  a wast, a legge, a limme.   1523
  Long. His Legge is too bigge for *Hectors.* | *Duman.* More Calfe
  certaine.   2595
LEGGES = 1
  Our eares vouchsafe it. | *King.* But your legges should do it.   2118
LEGGS = *1
  And lay my Armes before the Leggs of this sweete Lasse of
  France.   2503
LEIDGE = 1
  Ah good my Leidge, I pray thee pardon mee.   1489
LEMMON = 1
  Duma. A gift Nutmegg. | *Bero.* A Lemmon.   2602
LEND = 1
  Lend me the florish of all gentle tongues,   1587
LENDE = *1
  Pag. Lende me your Horne to make one, and I will whip   1804
LENT = 1
  And haue the money by our father lent,   643
LENUOY = 10*6
  Ar. Some enigma, some riddle, come, thy *Lenuoy* begin.   843
  Clo. No egma, no riddle, no *lenuoy*, no salue, in thee male sir.   845
  *O sir, Plantan, a plaine Plantan: no *lenuoy*, no *lenuoy*, no Salue |
  sir, but a Plantan.   846
  take *salue* for *lenuoy*, and the word *lenuoy* for a *salue?*   851
  Pag. Do the wise thinke them other, is not *lenuoy* a *salue?*   853
  +Ther's the morrall: Now the *lenuoy.*   856 +4
  + *Pag.* I will adde the *lenuoy*, say the morrall againe.   856 +5
  *Now will I begin your morrall, and do you follow with | my
  lenuoy.   857
  * *Pag.* A good *Lenuoy*, ending in the Goose: woulde you | desire
  more?   863
  Let me see a fat *Lenuoy*, I thats a fat Goose.   868
  Then cald you for the *Lenuoy.*   872
  Then the boyes fat *Lenuoy*, the Goose that you bought,   875
  Clow. Thou hast no feeling of it *Moth*, I will speake that |
  (*Lenuoy.*   880

LENUOY cont.
  *Clow. O marrie me to one Francis, I smell some Lenuoy,   887
LESSE = 4
  Matchles Nauar, the plea of no lesse weight,   498
  I am lesse proude to heare you tell my worth,   508
  Quee. I thinke no lesse: Dost thou not wish in hart   1945
  Ber. I cannot giue you lesse.   2312
LET = 27*11
  Ferdinand. | Let Fame, that all hunt after in their lyues,   4
  Berow. Let me say no my liedge, and yf you please,   54
  What is the ende of study, let me know?   59
  Giue me the paper, let me reade the same,   125
  *name more; and sweete my childe let them be men of good |
  repute and carriage.   374
  Clo. Let me not be pent vp sir, I will fast being loose.   458
  To let you enter his vnpeeled house.   582
  Ros. Alacke, let it blood.   683
  Let me see a fat Lenuoy, I thats a fat Goose.   868
  *Clown. True, true, and now you wilbe my purgation, | and let me
  loose.   892
  Not wounding, pittie would not let me doote.   1002
  Let the mark haue a prick in't, to meate at, if it may be. 1123
  *Nath. Let me heare a staffe, a stanze, a verse, Lege domine. 1265
  accent. Let me superuise the cangenet.   1285
  Would let her out in Sawcers, sweete misprison.   1434
  Ber. I post from Loue, good Louer let me go.   1526
  Iaque. I beseech your Grace let this Letter be read,   1535
  *Clow. Walke aside the true folke, and let the traytors stay. 1561
  Ber. Sweete Lords, sweete Louers, O let vs imbrace,   1562
  King. And winn them too, therefore let vs deuise,   1723
  Ber. First from the Parke let vs conduct them thither,   1725
  *betweene vs, let it passe. I do beseech thee remember thy 1831
  *deede too: but let that passe, for I must tell thee it will 1834
  *let that passe. By the world I recount no fable, some certaine 1838
  *let that passe; the very all of all is: but sweet hart, I do implore 1842
  the Taber to the worthies, and let them dance the hey.   1885
  *Ros. Ware pensalls, How? Let me not die your debtor,   1931
  Ber. One word in secret. | Quee. Let it not be sweete.   2142
  Let vs complaine to them what fooles were heare,   2225
  Duman. Let vs confesse and turne it to a iest.   2320
  Ile leaue it by degrees; soft, let vs see,   2351
  *King. Berowne, they will shame vs: let them not approch. 2453
  Quee. Nay my good Lord let me ore'rule you now.   2459
  Boyet. Therefore as he is, an Asse, let him go: 2577
  *Ile flash, Ile do it by the Sword: I bepray you let me bor-|row
  my Armes againe.   2651
  *Page. Maister, let me take you a button hole lower. Do 2656
  Let not the cloude of Sorrow iustle it   2706
  If this thou do deny, let our handes part,   2771
LETS = 5*2
  *Lon. He weedes the corne, & still lets grow the weeding. 101
  Ber. Lets see the penaltie. On payne of loosing her tung. 132
  *Long. It did moue him to passion, & therfore lets heare it. 1545
  Lets vs once loose our othes to finde our selues,   1712
  King. If you denie to daunce, lets holde more chat.   2132
  Long. Let's part the word? | Mar. No, Ile not be your halfe: 2163
  Lets mocke them still as well knowne as disguysde: 2224

LETTER = 14*9
Enter a Constable with Costard with a letter. 192
Ther's villanie abrod, this letter will tell you more. 200
Fer. A letter from the magnifisent *Armado.* 203
Ferd. Will you heare this Letter with attention? 226
I must imploy him in a letter to my loue. 777
Brag. Fetch hither the Swaine, he must carrie me a letter. 817
Clow. I haue a Letter from Monsier *Berowne,* | to one Ladie
Rosaline. 1029
Que. O thy letter, thy letter: He's a good friend of mine. 1031
This letter is mistooke: it importeth none heere. 1036
Quee. What plume of fethers is he that indited this letter? 1074
Who gaue thee this letter? | *Clow.* I tolde you, my Lord. 1083
Quee. Thou hast mistaken his letter. Come Lords away. 1090
Holo. I wil somthing affect the letter, for it argues facilitie. 1213
Iaque. Good M.(aister) Parson be so good as read me this letter, 1254
*I will looke againe on the intellect of the letter, for the
no-|mination 1298
*with the King, and here he hath framed a letter to a sequent 1303
Iaque. I beseech your Grace let this Letter be read, 1535
King. Berowne reade it ouer. *He reades the letter.* 1537
O he hath drawen my picture in his letter. | *Quee.* Any thing like? 1926
My red Dominicall, my golden letter, 1932
The Letter is too long by halfe a mile. 1944
The Chaine were longer, and the Letter short. 1946
LETTERS = 3
Ros. Much in the letters, nothing in the praise. 1928
Quee. We haue receiud your Letters, full of Loue: 2735
Dum. Our letters madame, shewed much more then iest. 2743
LETTRED = 1
Brag. Mounsier, are you not lettred? 1784
LEUENPENCE-FARTHING = *1
*a leuenpence-farthing better: most sweete gardon. I will 936
LEWE = *1
*lewe thereof, impose on thee nothing but this: Beare this 895
LIABLE = *1
Peda. The *posterior* of the day, most generous sir, is liable, 1825
LIBBARDS = 1
Clow. I Pompey am, | *Boyet.* With Libbards head on knee. 2493
LIBERALL = 2
All liberall reason I will yeelde vnto. 665
The liberall opposition of our spirites, 2691
LIBERTIE = *2
Arm. By my sweete soule, I meane, setting thee at libertie. 889
Arm. I giue thee thy libertie, set thee from durance, and in 894
LIE *see also* ly = 5*2
Shee must lie heere on meere necessitie. 159
But I protest I loue to heare him lie, 186
By adding a tongue which I know will not lie. 757
*in the world but lie, and lie in my throate. By heauen I doe 1344
Clowne. I Pompey am. | *Bero.* You lie, you are not he. 2491
That lie within the mercie of your wit: 2807
LIEDGE *see also* Leedge, Leege, Leidge = 4
So much deare Liedge, I haue already sworne, 38
Berow. Let me say no my liedge, and yf you please, 54
Ber. This Article my liedge your selfe must breake, 143
Liedge of all loyterers and malecontents: 949

LIEDGES = 1
  And where my Liedges? all about the brest. | A Caudle hou!   1510
LIES *see also* lyes = 3
  Where lies thy griefe, o tell me good *Dumaine*?   1508
  And gentle *Longauill*, where lies thy paine?   1509
  A iestes prosperitie lies in the eare,   2822
LIEU *see* lewe
LIFE = 6
  Ber. Now God saue thy life. | *Ros.* And yours from long liuing.   688
  Mayd. Good *Costard* go with me: sir God saue your life.   1309
  Nath. And thanke you to: for societie (saith the text) | is the
  happines of life.   1326
  King. What meane you Madame: by my life my troth,   2388
  is heauie in my tongue. The King your father | *Quee.* Dead for
  my life.   2676
  If this Austere insociable life, | Change not your offer made in
  heate of blood.   2759
LIGHT *see also* lyght = 22*6
  Light seeking light, doth light of light beguyle: 82
  So ere you finde where light in darknes lyes,   83
  Your light growes darke by loosing of your eyes.   84
  And giue him light that it was blinded by.   88
  Boy. And thats great maruaile, louing a light Wench.   427
  Boyet. A woman sometimes, and you saw her in the light.   696
  Lon. Perchance light in the light. I desire her name?   697
  *I will not. O but her eye: by this light, but for her eye, I   1342
  As doth thy face through teares of mine giue light: 1364
  Shee (an attending Starre) scarce seene a light.   1580
  Ber. Diuels soonest tempt resembling spirites of light.   1606
  Duma. Darke needes no Candles now, for darke is light.   1618
  Light Wenches may proue plagues to men forsworne,   1736
  *And so she died: had she bin Light like you, of such a mery   1902
  And so may you: For a light hart liues long.   1904
  Ros. Whats your darke meaning mouce, of this light word?   1905
  Kath. A light condition in a beautie darke.   1907
  Ros. We neede more light to finde your meaning out.   1908
  Kath. Yole marre the light by taking it in snuffe: 1909
  Kath. So do not you, for you are a light Wench.   1912
  Ros. In deede I waigh not you, and therefore light.   1913
  By light we loose light, your capacitie   2303
  Boyet. A light for Mounsier *Iudas*, it growes darke, he | may
  stumble.   2583
LIGHTLY = 1
  Clo. I am more bound to you then your fellowes, for they | are
  but lightly rewarded.   454
LIGHTNING = *1
  *Thy eie *Ioues* lightning beares, thy voyce his dreadful thu(n)der   1279
LIGHTS = 1
  These earthly Godfathers of heauens lights,   93
LIK = 1
  To dash it lik a Christmas Comedie: 2401
LIKE *see also* lyke = 34*11
  Ferd. I, that is studies god-like recompence.   63
  Ferd. Berowne is like an enuious sneaping Frost,   109
  But like of each thing that in season growes.   116
  Doth rauish like inchaunting harmonie: 178
  like a Porter: and he was in loue.   378

LIKE *cont.*
Like humble visage Suters his high will.   525
Like one that comes heere to besiedge his Court,   580
His hart like an Agot with your print impressed,   740
*Lad. 3. Then was *Venus* like her mother, for her father is | but
grim.   762
*smelling loue with your hat penthouse like ore the shop of   786
*like a Rabbet on a spit, or your handes in your pocket like a   788
Pag. Like the sequell I. Signeur *Costard* adew. *Exit.*   899
And weare his coloures like a Tumblers hoope.   954
A woman that is like a Iermane Cloake,   956
*as the Pomwater, who now hangeth like a Iewel in the eare   1154
*of *Celo* the skie, the welken the heauen, & anon falleth like 1155
*sweetly varried like a scholler at the least: but sir I assure ye 1159
*Those thoughts to me were Okes, to thee like Osiers bowed   1270
Berow. Why he comes in like a periure, wearing papers.   1380
Like a demie God, here sit I in the skie,   1413
Tush, none but Minstrels like of Sonnetting.   1495
With men like men of inconstancie.   1518
That (like a rude and sauadge man of *Inde.*)   1571
Berow. Is Ebonie like her? O word deuine!   1597
Duma. To looke like her are Chimnie-sweepers blake.   1615
* *Peda.* Thou disputes like an Infant: goe whip thy Gigg.   1802
*And so she died: had she bin Light like you, of such a mery   1902
O he hath drawen my picture in his letter. | *Quee.* Any thing like? 1926
So perttaunt like would I ore'sway his state,   1957
Or hide your heades like Cowardes, and flie hence.   1978
Boy. They do, they do; and are appariled thus, | Like *Muscouites,*
or *Russians,* as I gesse.   2012
That we (like sauages) may worship it.   2101
Not yet no daunce: thus change I like the Moone.   2111
Blow like sweete Roses, in this sommer aire.   2215
Disguysd like *Muscouites* in shapeles geare: 2226
Nor woo in rime like a blind harpers songue.   2337
You leere vpon me, do you: ther's an eie | Woundes like a leaden
sword.   2419
Quee. A speakes not like a man of God his making.   2471
King. Heere is like to be a good presence of Worthies: 2477
* *Clow.* I will not fight with a Pole like a Northren man;   2650
and I will right my selfe like a Souldier. *Exeunt Worthys*   2682
Formd by the eye, and therefore like the eye.   2720
In their owne fashyon like a merriment.   2742
Berow. Our wooing doth not ende like an olde Play: 2835
LIKENESSE = 1
Berow. Now in thy likenesse, one more foole appeare.   1378
LIKER = 1
Mari. The liker you, few taller are so young.   2797
LIKEWISE = 3
And where we are, our Learning likewise is.   1665
Do we not likewise see our learning there?   1668
Is likewise yours: we to our selues proue false,   2730
LIKING = 1
Rosa. Wel-liking Wits they haue grosse grosse, fat fat.   2187
LIKLEST = *1
* *Clo.* Marrie M.(aister) Scholemaster, he that is liklest to a
hoggs- | (head.   1249

LILLY = 1
    Now by my maiden honour yet as pure, | As the vnsallied Lilly I
    protest,   2277
LIM = *1
    *Iudas Machabeus; this Swaine (because of his great lim   1860
LIMIT = 1
    Within the limit of becomming mirth,   559
LIMME = 1
    a wast, a legge, a limme.   1523
LINES = 1*2
    *Long. I feare these stubborne lines lacke power to moue.   1387
    *King. What, did these rent lines shew some loue of thine?   1568
    O then his lines would rauish sauage eares,   1699
LINING see lyning
LINNEN = *1
    *Linnen: since when, Ile be sworne he wore none, but a
    dish-|cloute   2668
LION see also lyon = 1*1
    Thus dost thou heare the nemean Lion roare,   1068
    *Your Lion that holdes his Polax sitting on a close stoole,   2530
LIPPES = 2*1
    No Sheepe (sweete Lambe) vnlesse we feede on your lippes.   722
    My lippes are no Common, though seuerall they be.   726
    *thy replie, I prophane my lippes on thy foote, my eyes on   1063
LIPS = *1
    *Ma. Come come, you talke greasely, your lips grow fowle.   1131
LISPE = 1
    A can carue to, and lispe: Why this is hee   2248
LISTEN = 1
    What Longauill, and reading: listen eare.   1377
LITLE = 2*4
    Sole Emperator and great generall | Of trotting Parrators (O my
    litle hart.)   951
    *was a man when King Pippen of Fraunce was a litle boy, as |
    touching the hit it.   1109
    *woman when queene Guinouer of Brittaine was a litle wench | as
    toching the hit it.   1112
    Curat. Laus deo, bene intelligo. | *Peda. Bome boon for boon
    prescian, a litle scratcht, twil serue.   1766
    *Clo. Tis not so much worth: but I hope I was perfect. I | made a
    litle fault in great.   2507
    *seene the day of wrong through the litle hole of discretion,   2681
LITTLE see also lyttle = 8*2
    Clymbe ore the house to vnlocke the little gate.   118
    Clo. I do confesse much of the hearing it, but little of the |
    marking of it.   281
    Arma. Thou prettie because little.   332
    Boy. Little prettie, because little: wherefore apt.   333
    *therfore I will say nothing: I thanke God I haue as little
    pa-|tience   467
    And much too little of that good I saw,   554
    But that it seemes he little purposeth: 637
    Of his almightie dreadfull little might.   969
    *Alisander, alas you see how tis a little oreparted, but there   2536
LIUD see also lyud = 2*1
    O short liu'd pride. Not faire? alacke for woe | For. Yes Madam
    faire.   989

LIUD *cont.*

King. O you haue liu'd in desolation heere,	2283
Curat. When in the world I liud, I was the worldes commander:	2512

LIUE *see also* lyue = 3*2

Liue registred vpon our brazen Tombes,	6
Haue sworne for three yeeres tearme, to liue with me:	20
To haue his title liue in *Aquitaine.*	641
Boy. A man, if I liue (and this) by, in, and without, vpon the	809
*Where all those pleasures liue, that Art would comprehend.	1273

LIUED = 1*1

Prin. Such short liued wits do wither as they grow.	546
Cura. When in the worlde I liued, I was the worldes commander.	2522

LIUER *see* lyuer

LIUES *see also* lyues = 2

Liues not alone emured in the braine:	1679
And so may you: For a light hart liues long.	1904

LIUING *see also* lyuing = 1*1

Ber. Now God saue thy life. | *Ros.* And yours from long liuing.	688
Clow. O Lord sir, it were pittie you should get your liuing | by reckning sir.	2439

LO = 1

When lo to interrupt my purposed rest,	1983

LODGD = 1

As you shall deeme your selfe lodgd in my hart.	671

LODGE = 2

Ar. I will visit thee at the Lodge.	438
He rather meanes to lodge you in the feelde,	579

LODGING = 1

If frostes and fastes, hard lodging, and thin weedes,	2761

LOE = 1

Bero. Loe, he is tilting straight. Peace, I haue don.	2423

LOFTIE = *1

Ped. Noui hominum tanquam te, His humour is loftie, his	1748

LOGGERHEAD = *1

Berow. Ah you whoreson loggerhead, you were borne to | do me shame.	1548

LOGGES = 1

And Thom beares Logges into the hall,	2881

LOKT = 1

Mee thought all his senses were lokt in his eye,	746

LON = 5*4

LONG = 8*4

Kath. Tis long of you that spur me with such questions.	614
Ber. Now God saue thy life. | *Ros.* And yours from long liuing.	688
*man after the olde painting, and keepe not too long in one	789
As motion and long during action tyres	1657
Clow. O they haue lyud long on the almsbasket of wordes.	1778
*art not so long by the head as honorificabilitudinitatibus:	1780
And so may you: For a light hart liues long.	1904
The Letter is too long by halfe a mile.	1944
Mari. O for your reason, quickly sir, I long?	2156
That, which long processe could not arbitrate.	2701
Long. Ile stay with patience, but the time is long.	2796
Berow. That's too long for a Play.	2840

LONG = 25*3

LONGA = 1

LONGAUIL = 1
   Lon. Nay my coller is ended. She is a most sweet Ladie. | *Exit*
   Longauil.   705
LONGAUILE = 2
   You do not loue *Maria? Longauile,*   1470
   Marg. This, and these Pearle, to me sent *Longauile.*   1943
LONGAUILL see also Lon., Long., Longa. = 12
   Enter Ferdinand K.(ing) of Nauar, Berowne, | *Longauill, and*
   Dumaine.   2
   You three, *Berowne, Dumaine,* and *Longauill,*   19
   Lor. Longauill is one. | *Princ.* Know you the man?   530
   In *Normandie* saw I this *Longauill,*   535
   Enter *Nauar, Longauill, Dumaine, & Berowne.*   583
   Enter Longauill. The King steps a side.   1376
   What *Longauill,* and reading: listen eare.   1377
   O would the *King, Berowne,* and *Longauill,*   1460
   And gentle *Longauill,* where lies thy paine?   1509
   Kath. Lord *Longauill* said I came ore his hart: 2197
   Kath. And *Longauill* was for my seruice borne. 2205
   Brag. Sweete Lord *Longauill* raine thy tongue. 2613
LONGAUILL = 2*1
LONGER = 2
   The Chaine were longer, and the Letter short.   1946
   Can anie face of brasse hold longer out?   2327
LOOKE = 13*7
   Doth falsely blinde the eye-sight of his looke: 81
   Boy. A great signe sir that he will looke sadd.   314
   Clo. Nay nothing M.(aster) *Moth,* but what they looke vppon. 465
   Now will I looke to his remuneration.   902
   ignorance, How deformed doost thou looke.   1173
   Dull. If a talent be a claw, looke how he clawes him | with a
   talent.   1228
   *I will looke againe on the intellect of the letter, for the
   no-|mination   1298
   You may looke pale, but I should blush I know, 1466
   Dares looke vpon the heauen of her brow,   1576
   If that she learne not of her eye to looke: 1601
   Duma. To looke like her are Chimnie-sweepers blake. 1615
. *Long.* Looke, heer's thy loue, my foote and her face see. 1626
   Can you still dreame and poare and thereon looke. 1648
   *A Ladie walde about with Diamondes: Looke you, what I | haue
   from the louing King.   1890
   Ros. Looke what you do, you do it still i'th darke. 1911
   Lon. Looke how you butt your selfe in these sharpe mocks, 2166
   Rosa. Helpe holde his browes, heele sound: why looke | you
   pale?   2323
   *honest man; looke you, and soone dasht. He is a marueylous 2534
   Those heauenly eyes that looke into these faultes, 2727
   Berow. Studdies my Ladie? Mistres looke on me, 2798
LOOKED = *1
   Ber. This is not so well as I looked for, but the best that | euer I
   heard.   275
LOOKES = 3*1
   That will not be deepe searcht with sawcie lookes: 90
   Quee. Amazde my Lord? Why lookes your highnes sad? 2321
   Long. So did our lookes. | *Rosa.* We did not cote them so. 2744
   And Marrians nose lookes red and raw: 2891

LOOKING = 3
    To feele only looking on fairest of faire: 745
    Might shake off fiftie, looking in her eye: 1592
    Now for not looking on a womans face,   1659
LOOSE = 12
    Clo. Let me not be pent vp sir, I will fast being loose.   458
    Boy. No sir, that were fast and loose: thou shalt to prison.   460
    To sell a bargaine well is as cunning as fast and loose: 867
    Clown. True, true, and now you wilbe my purgation, | and let me
    loose.   892
    To loose an oth, to winn a Parradise?   1406
    Lets vs once loose our othes to finde our selues,   1712
    Or els we loose our selues, to keepe our othes: 1713
    By light we loose light, your capacitie   2303
    meane you? you will loose your reputation.   2658
    And often at his very loose decides   2700
    Which partie coted presence of loose loue   2724
    Whose influence is begot of that loose grace,   2820
LOOSING = 2
    Your light growes darke by loosing of your eyes.   84
    Ber. Lets see the penaltie. On payne of loosing her tung. 132
LOQUITUR = *1
    *put it to them. But *Vir sapis qui pauca loquitur,* a soule Femi-
    |nine saluteth vs.   1243
LOR = 1
LORD *see also* lor = 43*9
    Dumaine. My louing Lord, *Dumaine* is mortefied,   32
    Bero. No my good Lord, I haue sworne to stay with you. 120
    Bero. Sweete Lord and why? | *Long.* To fright them hence with
    that dread penaltie.   136
    My Lord *Berowne,* see him deliuered ore,   300
    Boy. No no, O Lord sir no.   317
    Ma. Lord how wise you are.   441
    Queene. Good L.(ord) *Boyet,* my beautie though but meane, 504
    Betweene L.(ord) *Perigort* and the bewtious heire | Of *Iaques*
    Fauconbridge solemnized.   533
    Prin. Some merrie mocking Lord belike, ist so?   544
    Lord. Heere comes *Boyet. Enter Boyet.*   572
    Prin. Now, What admittance Lord?   574
    Prin. Our Lady helpe my Lord, he'le be forsworne.   593
    Prin. Were my Lord so, his ignoraunce were wise,   597
    Tis deadlie sinne to keepe that oath my Lord,   600
    Lady Maria. That last is *Berowne,* the merrie madcap L.(ord) 715
    Regent of Loue-rimes, Lord of folded armes,   947
    To any Lady that subdewes a Lord.   1015
    Who gaue thee this letter? | *Clow.* I tolde you, my Lord. 1083
    Quee. To whom shouldst thou giue it? | *Clow.* From my Lord to
    my Ladie.   1085
    Quee. From which Lord, to which Ladie?   1087
    Clow. From my Lord *Berowne,* a good Maister of mine, 1088
    Lord, Lord, how the Ladies and I haue put him downe.   1138
    Holo. Sir, I prayse the L.(ord) for you, and so may my
    parishi-|oners,   1237
    *foole: Well proued wit. By the Lord this Loue is as madd 1339
    King. And mine too good Lord.   1429
    Guiltie my Lord, guiltie: I confesse, I confesse.   1550
    For when would you my Lord, or you, or you,   1649

LORD *cont.*

Mar. Say you so? Faire Lord, take that for your faire Lady	2150
Kath. Lord *Longauill* said I came ore his hart:	2197
Boy. I will, and so will she, I know my Lord. *Exit.*	2239
And we that sell by grosse, the Lord doth know,	2244
Quee. Not so my Lord, it is not so I sweare,	2285
King. How Madame? *Russians?* | *Quee.* I in trueth My Lord.	2288
Rosa. Madame speake true: It is not so my Lord:	2291
And talkt apace: and in that houre (my Lord)	2296
Quee. Amazde my Lord? Why lookes your highnes sad?	2321
Write *Lord haue mercie on vs,* on those three,	2352
Quee. God giue thee ioy of him: the Noble Lord	2386
And Lord *Berowne* (I thanke him) is my deare.	2396
Clow. O Lord sir, they would know,	2426
Clow. O Lord sir, it were pittie you should get your liuing | by reckning sir.	2439
Clow. O Lord sir, the parties themselues, the actors sir	2442
Bero. We are shame proofe my Lord: & tis some policie	2455
Quee. Nay my good Lord let me ore'rule you now.	2459
Bero. A right description of our sport my Lord.	2465
Brag. Sweete Lord *Longauill* raine thy tongue.	2613
Was guyltie of it.) Farewell worthy Lord:	2694
No no my Lord, your Grace is periurde much,	2750
Kath. Not so my Lord, a tweluemonth and a day,	2787
Rosa. Oft haue I heard of you my Lord *Berowne,*	2802
Queen. I sweete my Lord, and so I take my leaue.	2833

LORDE = 1

Mar. No, a faire Lorde Calfe.	2162

LORDES = 9*2

Ferd. What say you Lordes? why, this was quite forgot.	151
And goe we Lordes to put in practise that,	301
Enter the Princesse of Fraunce, with three | *attending Ladies and three Lordes.*	490
*Who are the Votaries my louing Lordes, that are vowfel-|lowes with this vertuous Duke?	528
Enter the Princesse, a Forrester, her Ladyes, | *and her Lordes.*	973
Onely for praise sake, when they striue to be | Lords ore their Lordes?	1012
Iag. I sir from one mounsier *Berowne,* one of the strange | Queenes Lordes.	1294
And where that you haue vowd to studie (Lordes)	1646
O we haue made a Vow to studie, Lordes,	1669
Enter Black-moores with musicke, the Boy with a | *speach, and the rest of the Lordes disguysed.*	2051
These Lordes are visited, you are not free,	2355

LORDS = 7*1

How you delight my Lords I know not I,	185
Well Lords, to day we shall haue our dispatch,	979
Onely for praise sake, when they striue to be | Lords ore their Lordes?	1012
Quee. Thou hast mistaken his letter. Come Lords away.	1090
Ber. Sweete Lords, sweete Louers, O let vs imbrace,	1562
Berow. Aduaunce your standards, and vpon them Lords.	1718
For the Lords tokens on you do I see.	2356
Quee. Prepare I say: I thanke you gracious Lords	2687

LOSE *see* loose

LOSING *see* losing
LOST = 3
  Tis won as townes with fire, so won so lost.   157
  From tawnie Spaine lost in the worldes debate.   184
  From what it purposd, since to wayle friendes lost,   2707
LOTH = 1
  But I beleeue although I seeme so loth,   170
LOUE = 68*31
  To loue, to wealth, to pompe, I pine and die,   35
  But I protest I loue to heare him lie,   186
  Boy. I am answerd sir. | *Arma.* I loue not to be crost.   342
  Boy. He speakes the meer contrarie, crosses loue not him.   344
  Arm. I will hereupon confesse I am in loue: and as it is   363
  *base for a Souldier to loue; so am I in loue with a base wench.   364
  men haue bin in loue? | *Boy. Hercules* Maister.   371
  like a Porter: and he was in loue.   378
  I am in loue too. Who was *Sampsons* loue my deare Moth?   381
  *haue a loue of that colour, mee thinkes *Sampson* had small   392
  Arm. My loue is most immaculate white and red.   395
  *I do loue, that Countrey girle that I tooke in the Parke   421
  Boy. To be whipt: and yet a better loue then my maister.   424
  Ar. Sing Boy, My spirit growes heauie in loue.   426
  Ar. I loue thee. | *Ma.* So I heard you say.   444
  *of falsehood) if I loue. And how can that be true loue, which   473
  *is falsely attempted? Loue is a familiar; Loue is a Diuell.   474
  *There is no euill angel but Loue, yet was *Sampson* so temp-|ted,   475
  *manager is in loue; yea hee loueth. Assist me some extempo-|rall   484
  Of all that Vertue loue, for Vertue loued.   549
  Prin. God blesse my Ladyes, are they all in loue?   569
  I must imploy him in a letter to my loue.   777
  Boy. Maister, will you win your loue with a french braule?   779
  *through the throate, if you swallowed loue with sing-|ing   784
  *loue sometime through: nose as if you snufft vp loue by   785
  *smelling loue with your hat penthouse like ore the shop of   786
  Brag. Calst thou my loue Hobbi-horse.   799
  loue perhaps, a hacknie: But haue you forgot your Loue?   801
  *instant: by hart you loue her, because your hart cannot come   810
  *by her: in hart you loue her, because your hart is in loue   811
  *with her: and out of hart you loue her, being out of hart   812
  Ber. O and I forsoth in loue, I that haue been loues whip?   939
  What? I loue, I sue, I seeke a wife,   955
  And among three to loue the worst of all,   961
  Well, I will loue, write, sigh, pray, shue, grone,   970
  Some men must loue my Ladie, and some Ione.   971
  *loue? I may. Shall I enforce thy loue? I coulde. Shall I en-|treate   1060
  *thy loue? I will. What, shalt thou exchange for raggs   1061
  Many can brooke the weather, that loue not the winde.   1188
  If Loue make me forsworne, how shall I sweare to loue?   1267
  Celestiall as thou art, Oh pardon loue this wrong,   1282
  *foole: Well proued wit. By the Lord this Loue is as madd   1339
  *againe a my side. I will not loue; if I do hang mee: I'fayth   1341
  *would not loue her; yes for her two eyes. Well, I do nothing   1343
  *loue, and it hath taught me to rime, and to be mallicholie: 1345
  But do not loue thy selfe, then thou will keepe   1370
  Long. In loue I hope, sweete fellowship in shame.   1381
  O sweete *Maria,* Empresse of my Loue,   1388
  My Vow was earthly, thou a heauenly Loue.   1399

LOUE *cont.*
Ber. Once more Ile marke how Loue can varrie Wit.   1436
Loue, whose Month is euer May: 1439
Turning mortall for thy loue.   1457
Long. Dumaine thy Loue is farre from charitie,   1464
You do not loue *Maria*? *Longauile,*   1470
And *Ioue* for your Loue would infringe an oth.   1481
These Wormes for louing, that art most in loue?   1491
Ber. I post from Loue, good Louer let me go.   1526
Are pick-purses in Loue, and we deserue to die.   1555
*King. What, did these rent lines shew some loue of thine?   1568
My Loue (her Mistres) is a gracious Moone,   1579
O, but for my Loue, day would turne to night,   1582
King. By heauen, thy Loue is blacke as Ebonie.   1596
Long. Looke, heer's thy loue, my foote and her face see.   1626
King. But what of this, are we not all in loue?   1631
But Loue first learned in a Ladies eyes,   1678
For Valoure, is not Loue a *Hercules*?   1691
And when Loue speakes, the voyce of all the Goddes,   1695
For Wisedomes sake, a worde that all men loue: 1708
And who can seuer Loue from Charitie.   1716
Forerunne faire Loue, strewing her way with flowers.   1731
Quee. Nothing but this: yes as much loue in Rime,   1893
Against your Peace Loue doth approch, disguysd: 1975
But will you heare; the King is my Loue sworne.   2203
My loue to thee is sound, *sance* cracke or flaw.   2347
Forbid the smyling courtecie of Loue,   2703
As Loue is full of vnbefitting straines,   2718
Which partie coted presence of loose loue   2724
Our loue being yours, the errour that Loue makes   2729
Quee. We haue receiud your Letters, full of Loue: 2735
Your Fauours, embassadours of Loue.   2736
If for my Loue (as there is no such cause)   2752
Nip not the gaudie blossomes of your Loue: 2762
But that it beare this tryall, and last Loue,   2763
Berow. And what to me my Loue? and what to me?   2777
Duma. But what to me my Loue? but what to me?   2783
With three folde loue I wish you all these three.   2785
Then if I haue much loue, Ile giue you some.   2790
Impose some seruice on me for thy Loue.   2801
To holde the Plough for her sweete loue three yeere.   2847
LOUED = 1
Of all that Vertue loue, for Vertue loued.   549
LOUELIE = *1
*thou art louelie: more fairer then faire, beautifull then
beau-|tious,   1043
LOUER = 4
That the Louer sicke to death,   1444
Ber. I post from Loue, good Louer let me go.   1526
Some thousand Verses of a faithfull Louer.   1940
That he would wed me, or els die my Louer.   2385
LOUERS = 7*1
*Arm. Greene in deede is the colour of Louers: but to   391
Ber. And send you manie louers. | *Kath.* Amen, so you be none.   621
Prin. With what? | *Bo.* With that which we Louers intitle
Affected.   735
Were Louers too, ill to example ill,   1461

LOUERS cont.

Ber. Sweete Lords, sweete Louers, O let vs imbrace,	1562
A Louers eyes will gaze an Eagle blinde.	1685
A Louers eare will heare the lowest sound.	1686
Quee. We are wise girles to mocke our Louers so.	1948

LOUES = 14*2

Ber. O and I forsoth in loue, I that haue been loues whip?	939
*Who vnderstandeth thee not, loues thee not, *vt re sol la mi fa*:	1261
Ber. One drunkard loues an other of the name.	1382
The shape of Loues Tiburne, that hanges vp Simplicitie.	1386
That in loues griefe desirst societie:	1465
Loues feeling is more soft and sensible,	1688
Loues tongue proues daintie, *Bachus* grosse in taste,	1690
Vntill his Incke were tempred with Loues sighes:	1698
Or for Loues sake, a worde that loues all men.	1709
And change you Fauours two, so shall your Loues	2026
To Loues mistooke, and so be mockt withall.	2034
Boyet. Loues her by the foote.	2624
Yet since Loues argument was first on foote,	2705
Haue we not been, and therefore met your Loues,	2741
King. Now at the latest minute of the houre, | Graunt vs your loues.	2746

LOUETH = *1

*manager is in loue; yea he loueth. Assist me some extempo-|rall	484

LOUE-FEAT = 1

And euery one his Loue-feat will aduance,	2015

LOUE-MONGER = *1

Lad. Thou art an old Loue-monger, & speakest skilfully.	758

LOUE-RIMES = 1

Regent of Loue-rimes, Lord of folded armes,	947

LOUING = 7*1

Dumaine. My louing Lord, *Dumaine* is mortefied,	32
Boy. And thats great maruaile, louing a light Wench.	427
*Who are the Votaries my louing Lordes, that are vowfel-|lowes with this vertuous Duke?	528
And you giue him for my sake but one louing kisse.	753
His louing bosome, to keepe downe his hart.	1473
These Wormes for louing, that art most in loue?	1491
Our louing lawfull, and our fayth not torne.	1634
*A Ladie walde about with Diamondes: Looke you, what I | haue from the louing King.	1890

LOW = *3

Bero. How low so euer the matter, I hope in God for high | (words.	204
Lon. A high hope for a low heauen. God grant vs patience	206
*did I see that low spirited Swaine, that base Minow of thy myrth,	255

LOWER = 1*1

Boyet. But she her selfe is hit lower: Haue I hit her now?	1106
Page. Maister, let me take you a button hole lower. Do	2656

LOWEST = 1

A Louers eare will heare the lowest sound.	1686

LOWLINES = *1

*for so witnesseth thy lowlines. Shall I commande thy	1059

LOYTERERS = 1

Liedge of all loyterers and malecontents:	949

LUNA = 1
Dul. What is *dictima*? | *Nath.* A title to *Phebe*, to *Luna*, to the
Moone.   1194
LUNATIQUE = 1
ne inteligis domine, to make frantique lunatique?   1764
LUNGES = *1
*my spleene, the heauing of my lunges prouokes me to
redi-|culous   849
LUSTER = *1
Nath. Of persing a Hogshead, a good luster of conceit   1251
LUTE = 1
As bright *Appolos* Lute, strung with his haire.   1694
LY = 1
Ber. By earth she is not, corporall, there you ly.   1420
LYES = 4
So ere you finde where light in darknes lyes,   83
Bo. If my obseruation (which very seldome lyes   732
Duma. O vile, then as she goes what vpward lyes?   1629
They are infected, in their hartes it lyes: 2353
LYGHT = 1
To seeke the lyght of trueth, while trueth the whyle   80
LYKE = 1
Studie is lyke the heauens glorious Sunne,   89
LYNING = 1
As bombast and as lyning to the time: 2739
LYON = 1
Bero. And thou weart a̧ Lyon, we would do so.   2576
LYTLLE = 1
Our Court shalbe a lytlle Achademe,   17
LYUD = *1
Clow. O they haue lyud long on the almsbasket of wordes.   1778
LYUE = 1
That is, to lyue and study heere three yeeres.   39
LYUER = 1
Bero. This is the lyuer veine, which makes flesh a deitie.   1407
LYUES = 1
Ferdinand. | Let Fame, that all hunt after in their lyues,   4
LYUING = 2
Still and contemplatyue in lyuing art.   18
With all these lyuing in Philosophie.   36
MA = 4*1
MACHABEUS = 3*2
Iudas Machabeus; this Swaine (because of his great lim   1860
Iudas Machabeus: And if these foure Worthies in their   2480
Iudas *I am, ecliped* Machabeus.   2551
Dum. Iudas Machabeus *clipt, is plaine* Iudas.   2552
Quee. Alas poore *Machabeus*, how hath he bin bayted.   2585
MACULATE = *1
Boy. Most maculate thoughts Maister, are maskt vnder | such
colours.   396
MAD = 2*1
Boy. Do you heare my mad Wenches? | *Lad.* No.   764
King. Farewel mad Wenches, you haue simple wits. *Exe.*   2181
Till this mad man shewed thee, and what art thou now?   2264
MADAM = 2
Forr. Pardon me Madam, for I meant not so.   987

MADAM *cont.*

O short liu'd pride. Not faire? alacke for woe | *For.* Yes Madam
faire.   989

MADAME = 21*1

Nau. You shalbe welcome Madame to my Court.   590
Nau. Not for the worlde faire Madame, by my will.   594
Nau. Madame I will, if sodainelie I may.   606
Ferd. Madame, your father heere doth intimate,   624
Rosa. Madame, came nothing els along with that?   1892
Kath. Madame, this Gloue.   1937
Quee. Did he not send you twaine? | *Kath.* Yes Madame: and
moreouer,   1938
Boyet. Madame, and prettie mistresses giue eare.   2207
Rosa. Good Madame, if by me youle be aduisde,   2223
King. All haile sweete Madame, and faire time of day.   2265
King. How Madame? *Russians*? | *Quee.* I in trueth My Lord.   2288
Rosa. Madame speake true: It is not so my Lord: 2291
King. Teach vs sweet Madame, for our rude transgression | Some
faire excuse.   2364
Were not you here but euen now, disguysde? | *King.* Madame, I
was.   2367
Quee. And were you well aduisde? | *King.* I was faire Madame.   2369
Rosa. Madame, he swore that he did hold me deare,   2382
King. What meane you Madame: by my life my troth,   2388
Marcad. God saue you Madame.   2672
Marcad. I am sorrie Madame for the newes I bring   2675
King. Madame Not so, I do beseech you stay.   2686
Dum. Our letters madame, shewed much more then iest.   2743
King. No Madame, we will bring you on your way.   2834

MADCAP = *1

Lady Maria. That last is *Berowne*, the merrie madcap L.(ord)   715

MADD = *1

*foole: Well proued wit. By the Lord this Loue is as madd   1339

MADDAME = 3

Boyet. Now Maddame summon vp your dearest spirrits,   492
1. *Lady.* I know him Maddame at a marriage feast,   532
Quee. Thy newes *Boyet*? | *Boy.* Prepare Maddame, prepare.   1972

MADE = 13

Therefore this Article is made in vaine,   149
Boy. Yf she be made of white and red,   403
Doth noyse abroad *Nauar* hath made a Vow,   513
I onelie haue made a mouth of his eie,   756
Some say a Sore, but not a sore, | till now made sore with
shooting.   1217
O we haue made a Vow to studie, Lordes,   1669
Kath. He made her melancholie, sad, and heauie,   1901
And euer and anon they made a doubt,   1993
Maria. What, was your vizard made without a tongue?   2154
Clo. Tis not so much worth: but I hope I was perfect. I | made a
litle fault in great.   2507
Duma. You may not deny it, *Pompey* hath made the chal-|(lenge.   2661
If this Austere insociable life, | Change not your offer made in
heate of blood.   2759
Might well haue made our sport a Comedie.   2837

MAGGOT = 1

Haue blowne me full of maggot ostentation.   2341

MAGNANIMOUS = *1
   *heroicall Vassall. The magnanimous and most illustrate   1045
MAGNIFICENT = 1
   *A domineering pedant ore the Boy, then whom no mor-|tall so
   magnificent.   943
MAGNIFISENT = 1
   Fer. A letter from the magnifisent *Armado.*   203
MAID = 1
MAIDE see also Ma., Maid., Mayd. = 5*1
   A Maide of grace and complet maiestie, | About surrender vp of
   Aquitaine,   146
   Clo. If it were, I denie her Virginitie: I was taken with a | Maide.   291
   Fer. This Maide will not serue your turne sir.   293
   Clo. This Maide will serue my turne sir.   294
   Ar. I do betray my selfe with blushing: Maide. | *Maide.* Man.   436
   *significant to the countrey Maide *Iaquenetta*: there is
   remu-|neration,   896
MAIDE = 1
MAIDEN = 1
   Now by my maiden honour yet as pure, | As the vnsallied Lilly I
   protest,   2277
MAIDENS = 1
   And Maidens bleach their summer smockes: 2872
MAIDES = 1*1
   One a these Maides girdles for your waste should be fit.   1026
   Rosa. Not one word more my Maides, break off, break off.   2178
MAIESTICALL = 1*1
   *his gate maiesticall, and his generall behauiour vaine,
   redicu-|lous,   1750
   Presence maiesticall would put him out: 1994
MAIESTIE = 5*1
   A Maide of grace and complet maiestie, | About surrender vp of
   Aquitaine,   ·   146
   And holde faire friendship with his Maiestie,   636
   That is not blinded by her maiestie?   1577
   Boyet. Gone to her Tent. Please it your Maiestie com-|maunde   2236
   King. How fares your Maiestie?   2684
   Brag. Sweete Maiestie vouchsafe me.   2842
MAISTER = 7*18
   Boy. Speake you this in my praise Maister?   335
   men haue bin in loue? | *Boy. Hercules* Maister.   371
   Boy. Sampson Maister, he was a man of good carriage,   376
   Boy. A Woman, Maister. | *Arm.* Of what complexion?   383
   Boy. Most maculate thoughts Maister, are maskt vnder | such
   colours.   396
   *A dangerous rime maister against the reason of white & red.   411
   Boy. To be whipt: and yet a better loue then my maister.   424
   Boy. Maister, will you win your loue with a french braule?   779
   Boy. No my complet Maister, but to Iigge off a tune at   781
   Boy. No Maister, the Hobbi-horse is but a colt, and your   800
   Boy. And out of hart Maister: all those three I will | proue.   806
   Boy. Minnime honest Maister, or rather Maister no.   828
   Pag. A wonder Maister, Heers a *Costard* broken in a shin.   841
   Clow. From my Lord *Berowne*, a good Maister of mine,   1088
   Curat.Nath. Truely M.(aister) *Holofernes*, the epythithes are   1158
   Nath. Perge, good M.(aister) *Holofernes perge*, so it shall please |
   you to abrogate squirilitie.   1211

MAISTER *cont.*

Iaquenetta. God giue you good morrow M.(aister) Person. 1246
*Nath. Maister Person, *quasi* Person? And if one shoulde 1247
*Clo. Marrie M.(aister) Scholemaster, he that is liklest to a
hoggs-|(head. 1249
*Iaque. Good M.(aister) Parson be so good as read me this letter, 1254
**imitarie is nothing: So doth the Hound his maister, 1290
*I maruaile thy M.(aister) hath not eaten thee for a worde, for
thou 1779
*Remuneration I had of thy Maister, thou halfepennie 1809
* *Page.* Maister, let me take you a button hole lower. Do 2656
MAKE = 32*8
And make vs heires of all eternitie. 11
Make rich the ribbes, but bancrout quite the wits. 31
And make a darke nyght too of halfe the day: 49
Ber. Necessitie will make vs all forsworne 160
For he hath wit to make an ill shape good, 551
For youle proue periurde if you make me staie. 608
From reasons yeelding, your faire selfe should make 646
Make tender of to thy true worthines. 668
Prin. Your reason. | *Bo.* Why all his behauiours did make their
retire, 737
All sences to that sence did make their repaire, 744
* *Bra.* Warble child, make passionate my sense of hearing. | *Boy.*
Concolinel. 772
*without these, and make them men of note: do you 793
**A.* No Page, it is an epilogue or discourse to make plaine, 855
A Stand where you may make the fairest shoote. 984
Of one sore I an hundred make | by adding but one more l. 1225
If Loue make me forsworne, how shall I sweare to loue? 1267
My teares for glasses, and still make me weepe. 1371
Your eyes do make no couches in your teares. 1492
* *King.* What? | * *Ber.* That you three fooles, lackt me foole, to
make vp the | (messe. 1551
Where seuerall worthies make one dignitie, 1585
And therefore is she borne to make blacke fayre. 1610
Make heauen drowsie with the harmonie. 1696
ne inteligis domine, to make frantique lunatique? 1764
* *Pag.* Lende me your Horne to make one, and I will whip 1804
*What a ioyfull father wouldest thou make me? 1812
*Snake; that is the way to make an offence gracious, though 1871
* *Dull.* Ile make one in a daunce, or so: or I will play on 1884
Rosa. That was the way to make his god-head Wax: 1897
How I would make him fawne, and begge, and seeke, 1952
And make him proude to make me proude that iestes, 1956
Quee. Therefore I do it, and I make no doubt, 2043
To make theirs ours, and ours none but our owne. 2046
To make my Lady laugh, when shees disposd: 2405
Forestall our sport, to make vs thus vntrue? 2412
That oft in fielde with Targ and Shield did make my foe to sweat, 2500
Peda. What meane you sir? | *Boyet.* To make *Iudas* hang him
selfe. 2556
Suggested vs to make, therefore Ladies 2728
To those that make vs both faire Ladies you, 2732
To make a world-without-end bargaine in: 2749

MAKES = 11

A Phantasime a Monarcho, and one that makes sport | To the
Prince and his Booke-mates.   1080
If Sore be sore, then el to Sore, | makes fiftie sores o sorell: 1223
Studie his byas leaues, and makes his booke thine eyes.   1272
Bero. This is the lyuer veine, which makes flesh a deitie.   1407
King. What makes treason heere? | *Clow.* Nay it makes nothing
sir.   1531
Your wits makes wise thinges foolish when we greete   2301
Their forme confounded, makes most forme in myrth,   2463
Duma. Hee's a God or a Painter: for he makes faces.   2599
Our loue being yours, the errour that Loue makes   2729
Of him that makes it: then if sickly eares   2824
MAKEST = 1

Thou makest the triumpherie, the corner cap of societie,   1385
MAKETH = 1

O tis the Sunne that maketh all thinges shine.   1595
MAKING = 3

As Nature was in making Graces deare,   501
Making the bolde wagg by their prayses bolder.   2000
Quee. A speakes not like a man of God his making.   2471
MALADIES = 1

And abstinence ingenders maladies.   1645
MALE = *1

Clo. No egma, no riddle, no *lenuoy*, no salue, in thee male sir.   845
MALECONTENTS = 1

Liedge of all loyterers and malecontents: 949
MALLICHOLIE = *2

*loue, and it hath taught me to rime, and to be mallicholie: 1345
*and heere is part of my Rime, and heare my mallicholie.   1347
MALMSEY = 1

Methegline, Wort, and Malmsey; well runne dice: 2138
MAN = 30*20

Item, Yf any man be seene to talke with a woman within   139
For euery man with his affectes is borne,   162
A man in all the worldes new fashion planted,   175
A man of complements whom right and wrong   179
A man of fier new wordes, Fashions owne knight.   189
*Now sir for the manner, It is the manner of a man to speake   220
Clow. Such is the simplicitie of man to harken after the flesh   228
Clow. Be to me, and euerie man that dares not fight. | *Ferd.* No
wordes.   239
by thy sweete Graces Officer Anthonie Dull, *a man of*   266
Armado. Boy, What signe is it when a man of great spi-|rite
growes melancholy?   312
Arma. I confesse both, they are both the varnish of a com-|pleat
man.   351
Boy. Sampson Maister, he was a man of good carriage,   376
Ar. I do betray my selfe with blushing: Maide. | *Maide.* Man.   436
as an other man, & therfore I can be quiet. *Exit.*   468
Of all perfections that a man may owe,   497
Lor. Longauill is one. | *Princ.* Know you the man?   530
A man of soueraigne peerelesse he is esteemd: 536
Berowne they call him, but a merrier man,   558
*man after the olde painting, and keepe not too long in one   789
Boy. A man, if I liue (and this) by, in, and without, vpon the   809
a man buy for a remuneration?   912

MAN *cont.*

*was a man when King *Pippen* of Fraunce was a litle boy, as |	
touching the hit it.	1109
Thou canst not hit it my good man. *Exit.*	1115
Armatho ath toothen side, o a most daintie man,	1142
* *Naso* was the man. And why in deed *Naso*, but for smel-|ling	1288
A true man, or a theefe, that gallops so.	1525
That (like a rude and sauadge man of *Inde*.)	1571
Duma. I neuer knew man holde vile stuffe so deare.	1625
Then homeward euery man attach the hand	1726
* *Page.* Offerd by a childe to an old man: which is wit-old.	1798
* *Brag. Arts-man preambulat,* we will be singuled from the	1815
*a Souldier, a man of trauayle, that hath seene the worlde: but	1841
* *Peda. Via* good-man *Dull*, thou hast spoken no worde all | this	
while.	1880
And not a man of them shall haue the grace	2020
That some plaine man recount their purposes.	2074
King. Yet still she is the Moone, and I the Man.	2116
* *Mar.* Veale quoth the Dutch-man: is not veale a Calfe?	2159
Till this mad man shewed thee, and what art thou now?	2264
Some carry tale, some please-man, some sleight sainē:	2402
*am (as they say, but to parfect one man in one poore man) |	
Pompion the great sir.	2444
Quee. Doth this man serue God? | *Bero.* Why aske you?	2469
Quee. A speakes not like a man of God his making.	2471
*There ant shall please you a foolish mylde man, an	2533
*honest man; looke you, and soone dasht. He is a marueylous	2534
A man so breathed, that certaine he would fight; yea,	2608
Brag. The sweete War-man is dead and rotten,	2617
+When he breathed he was a man:	2618 +1
* *Clow.* I will not fight with a Pole like a Northren man;	2650
Proclaymes you for a man repleat with mockes,	2804

MANAGE *see* nuage
MANAGER = *1

*manager is in loue; yea he loueth. Assist me some extempo-|rall	484

MANER = 1

My Ladie (to the maner of the dayes) | In curtesie giues	
vndeseruing praise.	2292

MANIE = 7

Ber. And send you manie louers. | *Kath.* Amen, so you be none.	621
Rosa. It is not so. Aske them how manie inches	2086
Is in one mile? If they haue measured manie,	2087
And manie miles: the Princesse bids you tell,	2090
How manie inches doth fill vp one mile?	2091
Rosa. How manie weerie steps,	2094
Of manie weerie miles you haue ore gone,	2095

MANNER = 5*4

The grosser manner of these worldes delyghts:	33
The manner of it is, I was taken with the manner.	214
Bero. In what manner?	215
Clow. In manner and forme folowing sir all those three.	216
*I was seene with her in the Manner house, sitting with her	217
*which put togeather, is in manner and forme following.	219
*Now sir for the manner, It is the manner of a man to speake	220

MANOR *see* manner
MANS = 1*2

Bero. Ile lay my Head to any good mans Hat,	303

MANS *cont.*

    **Clow.* My sweete ounce of mans flesh, my in-conie Iew: 901

    **Bero.* I, if a'haue no more mans blood in his belly then wil |

    suppe a Flea.   2647

MANTUAN = *3

    *and so foorth. Ah good olde *Mantuan,* I may speake   1258

    **te vnde, que non te perreche.* Olde *Mantuan,* olde *Mantuan,*   1260

MANUS = 1

    Thus did he strangle Serpents in his Manus,   2544

MANY = 5

    In high borne wordes the worth of many a Knight: 183

    Boy. How many is one thrice tolde?   348

    Many can brooke the weather, that loue not the winde.   1188

    King. Say to her we haue measurd many miles,   2082

    Boy. They say that they haue measurd many a mile,   2084

MAR = 8*3

MARCAD = 3

MARCADE see also Marcad. = 1*1

    Enter a Messenger Mounsier Marcade.   2671

    **Quee.* Welcome *Marcade,* but that thou interrupptest our |

    merriment.   2673

MARG = 2

MARGENT = 2

    His faces owne margent did coate such amazes,   750

    Writ a both sides the leafe, margent and all,   1895

MARI = 3

MARIA see also Mar., Marg., Mari. = 3

    O sweete *Maria,* Empresse of my Loue,   1388

    You do not loue *Maria? Longauile,*   1470

    Longauill. What saies *Maria?* | *Mari.* At the tweluemonths ende,   2793

MARIA = 2*2

MARIE = 3

    Lady Ka. Two hot Sheepes marie. | *Bo.* And wherefore not

    Shipps?   720

    Ber. O what is a remuneration? | *Cost.* Marie sir, halfepennie

    farthing.   913

    Duma. I marie there, some flatterie for this euyll.   1635

MARK = 1*4

    **Bo.* A mark, O mark but that mark: a mark saies my Lady.   1121

    Let the mark haue a prick in't, to meate at, if it may be.   1123

MARKE = 4*1

    **Mar.* A marke marueilous wel shot, for they both did hit.   1119

    If knowledge be the marke, to know thee shall suffise.   1275

    Ber. Once more Ile marke how Loue can varrie Wit.   1436

    Pag. They do not marke me, and that bringes me out.   2069

    Ile marke no wordes that smothfast wooers say,   2788

MARKET = 1

and he ended the market.   876

MARKETS = 1

At Wakes and Wassels, meetings, markets, Faires.   2243

MARKING = 1

    Clo. I do confesse much of the hearing it, but little of the |

    marking of it.   281

MARKT = 1

And markt you both, and for you both did blush.   1475

MARR = 1

    King. Yf it marr nothing neither,   1533

MARRE = 1
Kath. Yole marre the light by taking it in snuffe: 1909
MARRIAGE = 1
1. *Lady.* I know him Maddame at a marriage feast,   532
MARRIANS = 1
And Marrians nose lookes red and raw: 2891
MARRIE = 2*4
Who deuis'd this penaltie? | *Long.* Marrie that did I.   134
Before I came: Marrie thus much I haue learnt,   578
Boy. Marrie sir, you must send the Asse vpon the Horse,   822
Clow. O marrie me to one Francis, I smell some *Lenuoy*,   887
Boy. My Lady goes to kill hornes, but if thou marrie,   1097
Clo. Marrie M.(aister) Scholemaster, he that is liklest to a
hoggs-|(head.   1249
MARRIED = 4
Mocks married men; for thus singes hee, | Cuckow.   2865
Cuckow, Cuckow: O word of feare, | Vnpleasing to a married
eare.   2867
Mockes married men, for thus singes he, | Cuckow.   2874
Vnpleasing to a married eare.   2877
MARS = *2
Braggart. The Armipotent Mars, *of Launces the almightie,* | *gaue*
Hector *a gift.*   2600
Brag. Peace. The Armipotent Mars, *of Launces the almighty,*   2606
MARUAILE = 1*1
Boy. And thats great maruaile, louing a light Wench.   427
*I maruaile thy M.(aister) hath not eaten thee for a worde, for
thou   1779
MARUEILOUS = 1*1
Mar. A marke marueilous wel shot, for they both did hit.   1119
Nath. Marueilous well for the pen.   1317
MARUEYLOUS = *1
*honest man; looke you, and soone dasht. He is a marueylous   2534
MASKE = 2
Ber. Now faire befall your maske.   619
Long. You haue a double tongue within your Maske,   2157
MASKERS = *1
Boy. The Trompet soundes, be maskt, the maskers come.   2049
MASKES = 1
For Reuels, Daunces, Maskes, and merrie houres,   1730
MASKT = 2*2
Boy. Most maculate thoughts Maister, are maskt vnder | such
colours.   396
For Ladies; we will euery one be maskt,   2019
Boy. The Trompet soundes, be maskt, the maskers come.   2049
Boy. Faire Ladies maskt, are Roses in their bud: 2218
MASTER = *1
Clo. Nay nothing M.(aster) *Moth*, but what they looke vppon.   465
MASTRED = 1
Not by might mastred, but by speciall grace.   163
MATCHLES = 1
Matchles *Nauar*, the plea of no lesse weight,   498
MATCHT = 1
Is a sharpe Wit matcht with too blunt a Will: 541
MATES = 1
A Phantasime a Monarcho, and one that makes sport | To the
Prince and his Booke-mates.   1080

MATTER = 4*1
*Bero. How low so euer the matter, I hope in God for high |
(words.   204
Clow. The matter is to me sir, as concerning Iaquenetta: 213
Arm. We will talke no more of this matter.   884
Clow. Till there be more matter in the shin.   885
Rosa. O vaine peticioner, begg a greater matter,   2106
MAY 1.9 24 66 *236 *308 *325 328 346 *419 497 515 606 667 669
707 *911 959 984 1014 *1060 *1111 1123 *1237 *1258 *1306 1446
1466 1600 1733 1736 1752 *1870 1904 2081 2099 2101 2165 2174
2267 2584 2625 2661 2663 = 32*11, 1
Loue, whose Month is euer May: 1439
MAYD = 1
MAYDEN = 1
And in our mayden counsaile rated them,   2737
MAYES = 1
Then wish a Snow in Mayes new fangled showes: 115
MAYNTEINED = *1
*This Ver, the Spring: The one maynteined by the Owle, | th'other
by the Cuckow.   2856
ME 1.20 54 59 74 85 125 164 169 201 213 239 *265 268 *366 *380
387 399 458 *484 591 592 *601 608 *614 664 673 714 724 734
*817 833 *849 *850 868 877 *887 893 919 987 991 1002 1098
*1183 *1189 *1241 *1254 *1255 *1265 1267 *1270 1285 1309
*1329 *1345 1368 1371 1452 1508 1526 1549 *1552 1587 *1763
*1804 *1812 *1843 1914 *1931 1943 1956 2025 2069 2109 *2147
2198 2204 2223 2237 2238 2268 *2271 2273 2300 2328 2329 2331
2341 2346 2350 2379 2382 2383 2385 2392 2395 2397 2419 *2447
2459 2573 *2590 2620 2634 *2651 *2656 *2659 2696 2748 2753
2765 2777 2783 2798 2801 2809 2842 = 91*33
MEADOWES = 1
Do paint the Meadowes with delight: 2863
MEALE = 1
And but one meale on euery day beside: 44
MEANE = 8*4
*Ber. Things hid & bard (you meane) from cammon sense.   62
*ground Which? which I meane I walkt vpon, it is ycliped Thy
Park.   248
*Then for the place Where? where I meane, I did incounter that
ob-| seene   250
Boy. How meane you sir, I prettie, and my saying apt?   330
Queene. Good L.(ord) Boyet, my beautie though but meane,   504
Meane time receiue such welcome at my hand,   666
*Arm. By my sweete soule, I meane, setting thee at libertie. 889
A meane most meanely, and in hushering.   2253
King. What meane you Madame: by my life my troth,   2388
Peda. What meane you sir? | Boyet. To make Iudas hang him
selfe.   2556
meane you? you will loose your reputation.   2658
Therefore if you my fauour meane to get,   2780
MEANELY = 1
A meane most meanely, and in hushering.   2253
MEANES = 2
He rather meanes to lodge you in the feelde,   579
The poore Deares blood, that my hart meanes no ill.   1010
MEANEST = 2
Brag. How meanest thou? brawling in French.   780

MEANEST *cont.*
  Brag. What meanest thou?   2630
MEANETIME *see* meane
MEANING = 1*2
  *Brag. The meaning prettie ingenius, is not Lead a mettal |
  heauie, dull, and slow?   826
  *Ros. Whats your darke meaning mouce, of this light word?   1905
  Ros. We neede more light to finde your meaning out.   1908
MEANT = 2
  Forr. Pardon me Madam, for I meant not so.   987
  That more for praise, then purpose meant to kill.   1004
MEASURABLE = *1
  *congruent, and measurable for the after noone: the worde is   1826
MEASURD = 2
  King. Say to her we haue measurd many miles,   2082
  Boy. They say that they haue measurd many a mile,   2084
MEASURDE = 1
  Boy. If to come hither, you haue measurde miles,   2089
MEASURE = 8*1
  And Iustice alwayes whirles in equall measure: 1735
  To treade a Measure with her on this grasse.   2083
  To tread a Measure with you on this grasse.   2085
  The measure then of one is easlie tolde.   2088
  Berow. Tell her we measure them by weerie steps. | *Boy.* She
  heares her selfe.   2092
  *King. Then in our measure, do but vouchsafe one change,   2108
  Curtsie sweete hartes, and so the Measure endes.   2124
  King. More measure of this measure be not nice.   2125
MEASURED = 1
  Is in one mile? If they haue measured manie,   2087
MEATE = 1
  Let the mark haue a prick in't, to meate at, if it may be.   1123
MEDITARANIUM = *1
  *Brag. Now by the sault waue of the meditaranium, a   1795
MEE *l.**257 *258 *259 *368 *370 *392 603 605 660 728 746 768
  *988 *1062 1278 *1314 *1340 *1341 1354 1379 1400 1405 1478
  1487 1489 1502 1514 1519 *1521 2024 = 18*13
MEEDE = *1
  *duetie prickes me on) *haue sent to thee, to receiue the meede of*
  pu-| nishment   265
MEEKELY = *1
  *Lon. To heare meekely sir, and to laugh moderatly, or | to
  forbeare both.   209
MEER = *1
  *Boy. He speakes the meer contrarie, crosses loue not him.   344
MEERE = 2
  Shee must lie heere on meere necessitie.   159
  I am forsworne on meere necessitie.   165
MEETE = 5
  Or studie where to meete some Mistris fine.   68
  And he and his compettitours in oth, | Were all addrest to meete
  you gentle Lady   576
  Do meete as at a faire in her faire cheeke,   1584
  Vpon the next occasion that we meete,   2035
  Bero. Thou greeuest my gall. | *Quee.* Gall, bitter, | *Bero.*
  Therefore meete.   2144

MEETINGS = 1
  At Wakes and Wassels, meetings, markets, Faires. 2243
MEHERCLE *see* hercle
MELANCHOLIE *see also* mallicholie = 2*1
  Ferd. So it is besedged with sable coloured melancholie, I did 242
  Most rude melancholie, Valour giues thee place. 838
  Kath. He made her melancholie, sad, and heauie, 1901
MELANCHOLY = 1*1
  *Armado. Boy, What signe is it when a man of great spi-|rite
  growes melancholy? 312
  *Arm. How canst thou part sadnes and melancholy, my | tender
  Iuuenall? 318
MELL = 1
  Pell, mell, downe with them: but be first aduisd, 1719
MELLOWING = *1
  *and deliuered vpon the mellowing of occasion: But the 1234
MEMBER = 2
  Boyet. Here comes a member of the common wealth. 1017
  *Daughters profite very greatly vnder you: you are a good |
  member of the common wealth. 1239
MEMORIE = 2*1
  Quee. Els your memorie is bad, going ore it erewhile. 1078
  *the ventricle of Memorie, nourisht in the wombe of prima-|ter, 1233
  And quite diuorce his memorie from his part. 2042
MEN = 15*7
  *most grase, Birdes best peck, and Men sit downe to that
  nourishment* 246
  men haue bin in loue? | *Boy. Hercules* Maister. 371
  *name more; and sweete my childe let them be men of good |
  repute and carriage. 374
  *men. Adue Valoure, rust Rapier, be still Drum, for your 483
  *without these, and make them men of note: do you 793
  note men that most are affected to these. 794
  Some men must loue my Ladie, and some Ione. 971
  Dul. You two are book-men, Can you tel me by your wit, 1189
  With men like men of inconstancie. 1518
  Haue at you then affections men at armes, 1640
  For Wisedomes sake, a worde that all men loue: 1708
  Or for Loues sake, a worde that loues all men. 1709
  Or Womens sake, by whom we Men are Men. 1711
  Light Wenches may proue plagues to men forsworne, 1736
  Brag. Men of peace well incontred. | *Ped.* Most millitarie sir
  salutation. 1774
  Curat. Where will you finde men worthie enough to pre-|sent
  them? 1857
  Nor God nor I delights in periurd men. 2272
  *that the two Learned men haue compiled, in prayse of the 2849
  Mocks married men; for thus singes hee, | Cuckow. 2865
  Mockes married men, for thus singes he, | Cuckow. 2874
MEND = 1
  Where faire is not, praise cannot mend the brow. 992
MENDE = 1
  Mende him who can, the Ladies call him sweete. 2254
MENS = 3
  Clow. Of other mens secrets I beseech you. 241
  Or for Mens sake, the authour of these Women: 1710
  For vertues office neuer breakes mens troth. 2276

MERCIE = 3
But come, the Bow: Now Mercie goes to kill,   999
Write *Lord haue mercie on vs*, on those three,   2352
That lie within the mercie of your wit: 2807
MERCURIE = *1
*The wordes of Mercurie, are harsh after the | songes of Apollo.   2897
MERELY = 1
Boyet. Full merely hath this braue nuage, this carreere | bin run.   2421
MEREMENT = 1
They do it but in mockerie merement,   2031
MERIMENT = 1
Knowing aforehand of our meriment,   2400
MERRIE = 6*1
Prin. Some merrie mocking Lord belike, ist so?   544
Lady Maria. That last is *Berowne*, the merrie madcap L.(ord)   715
For Reuels, Daunces, Maskes, and merrie houres,   1730
Duma. Though my mockes come home by me, I will | now be
merrie.   2590
And merrie Larkes are Ploughmens Clocks: 2870
Tu-whit to-who. | A merrie note,   2885
Tu-whit to-who. | A merrie note,   2894
MERRIER = 1
Berowne they call him, but a merrier man,   558
MERRILIE = 1
Holding a trencher, iesting merrilie?   2416
MERRIMENT = 2
Quee. Welcome *Marcade*, but that thou interrupptest our |
merriment.   2673
In their owne fashyon like a merriment.   2742
MERRINES = 1
Bero. Well sir, be it as the stile shall giue vs cause to clime | in
the merrines.   211
MERRIT = 1
Quee. See see, my beautie wilbe sau'd by merrit.   996
MERRY = *1
Clo. Well, if euer I do see the merry dayes of desolation   462
MERY = *1
*And so she died: had she bin Light like you, of such a mery   1902
MESSAGE = *1
Boy. A message well simpathisd, a Horse to be embassa-|doure
for an Asse.   819
MESSE = 2
King. What? | *Ber*. That you three fooles, lackt me foole, to
make vp the | (messe.   1551
A messe of *Russians* left vs but of late.   2287
MESSENGER = 1
Enter a Messenger Mounsier Marcade.   2671
MET = 2
Ber. O my good knaue *Costard*, exceedingly well met.   910
Haue we not been, and therefore met your Loues,   2741
METHEGLINE = 1
Methegline, Wort, and Malmsey; well runne dice: 2138
METHINKES *see* thinkes, thinks
METHOUGHT *see* thought
METTAL = *1
Brag. The meaning prettie ingenius, is not Lead a mettal |
heauie, dull, and slow?   826

MI = *1
*Who vnderstandeth thee not, loues thee not, vt re sol la mi fa: 1261
MIGHT l.*1047 1447 1592 1903 1947 1984 2411 2837 = 7*1, 3
  Not by might mastred, but by speciall grace.   163
  Of his almightie dreadfull little might.   969
  By East, West, North, and South, I spred my conquering might: 2514
MIGHTIE = *1
  *example my digression by some mightie presedent. Boy,   420
MILDE *see* mylde = 1
  And plant in Tyrants milde humilitie.   1700
MILE *see also* myle = 5
  The Letter is too long by halfe a mile.   1944
  Boy. They say that they haue measurd many a mile,   2084
  Is in one mile? If they haue measured manie,   2087
  How manie inches doth fill vp one mile?   2091
  Are numbred in the trauaile of one Mile?   2096
MILES = 4
  King. Say to her we haue measurd many miles,   2082
  Boy. If to come hither, you haue measurde miles,   2089
  And manie miles: the Princesse bids you tell,   2090
  Of manie weerie miles you haue ore gone,   2095
MILKE = 2
  Quee. Honie, and Milke, and Suger: there is three.   2136
  And Milke coms frozen home in paile: 2882
MILL *see* myll
MILLITARIE = 1
  Brag. Men of peace well incontred. | *Ped.* Most millitarie sir
  salutation.   1774
MIND = *1
  *to *Fortuna delaguar,* I wish you the peace of mind most royall |
  cupplement. *Exit.*   2475
MINDE = 4*1
  The minde shall banquet, though the body pine,   29
  Quee. Who ere a was, a showd a mounting minde.   978
  But *omne bene* say I, being of an olde Fathers minde,   1187
  Henceefoorth my wooing minde shalbe exprest   2344
  *are Worthies a comming will speake their minde in some | other
  sort. *Exit Curat.*   2537
MINDES = 1
  Rosal. What would these strangers? | Know their mindes *Boyet.* 2071
MINE l.510 588 *897 *1031 1088 *1319 1364 1404 1428 1429 1430
  1982 2206 2311 2376 2379 *2443 *2448 *2680 2774 2775
  2799 = 16*6
MINNIME = 1
  Boy. Minnime honest Maister, or rather Maister no.   828
MINORITIE = 1*1
  *in minoritie: his enter and exit shalbe strangling a Snake;   1867
  Quoniam, *he seemeth in minoritie,*   2545
MINOW = *1
  did I see that low spirited Swaine, that base Minow of thy myrth, 255
MINSTRELS = 1
  Tush, none but Minstrels like of Sonnetting.   1495
MINSTRELSIE = 1
  And I will vse him for my Minstrelsie.   187
MINT = 2
  That hath a mint of phrases in his braine: 176
  I am that Flower. | *Dum.* That Mint. | *Long.* That Cullambine.   2610

MINUTE = 1
King. Now at the latest minute of the houre, | Graunt vs your
loues.   2746
MINUTES = 1
Or grone for Ione? or spende a minutes time,   1520
MIRE = 1
Kath. Not till it leaue the rider in the mire.   616
MIRTH *see also* myrth = 2
Within the limit of becomming mirth,   559
Mirth cannot moue a soule in agonie.   2818
MIRTH-MOOUING = 1
The other turnes to a mirth-moouing iest,   563
MISBECOMBD = 1
Haue misbecombd our othes and grauities.   2726
MISCARRIE = 1
hang me by the necke, if horns that yeere miscarrie. | Finely put
on.   1098
MISCARRIED = *1
*of progression, hath miscarried. Trip and goe my sweete,   1305
MISDOUBTS = 1
Our person misdoubts it: twas treason he said.   1536
MISPRISON = 1
Would let her out in Sawcers, sweete misprison.   1434
MISSE = *1
Pedan. You finde not the apostraphas, and so misse the   1284
MISTAKEN = *1
Quee. Thou hast mistaken his letter. Come Lords away.   1090
MISTOOKE = 2
This letter is mistooke: it importeth none heere.   1036
To Loues mistooke, and so be mockt withall.   2034
MISTRES = 5*1
And your waste Mistres were as slender as my wit,   1025
My Loue (her Mistres) is a gracious Moone,   1579
Of his faire Mistres, in the after noone   1727
Vnto his seuerall Mistres: which they'le know   2016
Berow. White handed Mistres, one sweet word with thee.   2135
Berow. Studdies my Ladie? Mistres looke on me,   2798
MISTRESSES = 3
When Mistresses from common sense are hid.   69
Ber. Your Mistresses dare neuer come in raine,   1619
Boyet. Madame, and prettie mistresses giue eare.   2207
MISTRIS = 1
Or studie where to meete some Mistris fine.   68
MOCK = *1
King. We were descried, theyle mock vs now dounright.   2318
MOCKE = 4
Quee. We are wise girles to mocke our Louers so.   1948
And mocke for mocke is onely my intent.   2032
Lets mocke them still as well knowne as disguysde: 2224
MOCKER = *1
Ber. Well said old mocker, I must needes be friendes with |
(thee.   2495
MOCKERIE = 1
They do it but in mockerie merement,   2031
MOCKES = 2*1
Duma. Though my mockes come home by me, I will | now be
merrie.   2590

MOCKES   *cont.*
Proclaymes you for a man repleat with mockes,   2804
Mockes married men, for thus singes he, | Cuckow.   2874
MOCKING = 4
   Prin. Some merrie mocking Lord belike, ist so?   544
   Ros. They are worse fooles to purchase mocking so.   1949
So shall we stay mocking entended game,   2047
   Boyet. The tongues of mocking Wenches are as keene | As is the
Rasors edge inuisible: 2172
MOCKS = 1*1
   Lon. Looke how you butt your selfe in these sharpe mocks, 2166
Mocks married men; for thus singes hee, | Cuckow.   2865
MOCKT = 1*1
  To Loues mistooke, and so be mockt withall.   2034
  *And they wel mockt depart away with shame. *Sound Trom.*   2048
MODERATLY = *1
   Lon. To heare meekely sir, and to laugh moderatly, or | to
forbeare both.   209
MONARCH = 1
   Brag. That is al one my faire sweete honie monarch,   2472
MONARCHO = 1
A Phantasime a Monarcho, and one that makes sport | To the
Prince and his Booke-mates.   1080
MONEY = 1
And haue the money by our father lent,   643
MONGER = *1
   Lad. Thou art an old Loue-monger, & speakest skilfully. 758
MONIES = 1
Although not valued to the monies worth.   632
MONS = 1
on the top of the Mountaine? | *Peda.* Or *Mons* the hill.   1817
MONSIER = 1
   Clow. I haue a Letter from Monsier *Berowne,* | to one Ladie
Rosaline.   1029
MONSTER = *1
   Holo. Twice sodd simplicitie, bis coctus, O thou monster 1172
MONTH = 1*4
   Clo. I had rather pray a month with Mutton & Porridge.   297
  *What was a month old at *Cains* birth, that's not fiue weeks | old
as yet?   1190
   Holo. The Moone was a month old when *Adam* was no | (more. 1196
  *the Moone is neuer but a month olde: and I say beside   1205
Loue, whose Month is euer May: 1439
MONTHS = *1
   Clow. Fellow *Hector,* she is gone; she is two months on | her
way.   2628
MOONE = 7*3
   Dul. What is *dictima?* | *Nath.* A title to *Phebe,* to *Luna,* to the
Moone.   1194
   Holo. The Moone was a month old when *Adam* was no | (more. 1196
  *the Moone is neuer but a month olde: and I say beside   1205
Nor shines the siluer Moone one halfe so bright,   1362
My Loue (her Mistres) is a gracious Moone,   1579
   Rosa. My face is but a Moone, and clouded too.   2102
Vouchsafe bright Moone, and these thy Starrs to shine,   2104
Not yet no daunce: thus change I like the Moone.   2111
   Ro. You tooke the moone at ful, but now shee's changed? 2114

MOONE cont.

King. Yet still she is the Moone, and I the Man. 2116

MOONESHINE = 1

Thou now requests but Mooneshine in the water. 2107

MOORES = 1

Enter Black-moores with musicke, the Boy with a | speach, and the
rest of the Lordes disguysed. 2051

MOOUED = *1

Bero. **Pompey** is mooued more Ates more Atees stir them, | or
stir them on. 2644

MOOUING = 1

The other turnes to a mirth-moouing iest, 563

MORE = 37*10

Haue no more profite of their shyning nights, 95
At Christmas I no more desire a Rose, 114
And though I haue for barbarisme spoke more 121
Ther's villanie abrod, this letter will tell you more. 200
**more sweete vnderstanding a Woman: him, I (as my euer esteemed* 264
Arm. It doth amount to one more then two. 355
**Arm.* Most sweete *Hercules*: more authoritie deare Boy, 373
*name more; and sweete my childe let them be men of good |
repute and carriage. 374
**Clo.* I am more bound to you then your fellowes, for they | are
but lightly rewarded. 454
A hundred thousand more, in suretie of the which, 630
**Boy.* And three times as much more, and yet nothing | at all. 815
**Pag.* A good *Lenuoy*, ending in the Goose: woulde you | desire
more? 863
Arm. We will talke no more of this matter. 884
Clow. Till there be more matter in the shin. 885
Faire payment for foule wordes, is more then dew. 994
That more for praise, then purpose meant to kill. 1004
*thou art louelie: more fairer then faire, beautifull then
beau-|tious, 1043
*and feeling, are for those partes that doe fructifie in vs | more
then he. 1181
**Holo.* The Moone was a month old when *Adam* was no | (more. 1196
Of one sore I an hundred make | by adding but one more l. 1225
Berow. Now in thy likenesse, one more foole appeare. 1378
More Sacks to the myll. O heauens I haue my wysh, 1415
Dum. Once more Ile reade the Ode that I haue writ. 1435
Ber. Once more Ile marke how Loue can varrie Wit. 1436
This will I send, and something els more plaine. 1458
O dismisse this audience, and I shall tell you more. 1556
Duma. Some salue for periurie. | *Ber.* O tis more then neede. 1638
Loues feeling is more soft and sensible, 1688
Ros. We neede more light to finde your meaning out. 1908
King. More measure of this measure be not nice. 2125
Rosa. We can affoord no more at such a price. 2126
King. If you denie to daunce, lets holde more chat. 2132
Ile play no more with you. 2141
**Rosa.* Not one word more my Maides, break off, break off. 2178
And I will wish thee neuer more to daunce, 2332
Nor neuer more in Russian habite waite. 2333
King. That more then all the world, I did respect her. 2373
Aboue this Worlde: adding thereto more ouer, 2384
Now to our periurie, to add more terror, 2409

MORE *cont.*
  Peda. Iudas I am. | *Duma.* The more shame for you *Iudas.*   2554
  Long. His Legge is too bigge for *Hectors.* | *Duman.* More Calfe
  certaine.   2595
  *Bero. Pompey is mooued more Ates more Atees stir them, | or
  stir them on.   2644
  *Bero. I, if a'haue no more mans blood in his belly then wil |
  suppe a Flea.   2647
  But more deuout then this our respectes,   2740
  Dum. Our letters madame, shewed much more then iest.   2743
  King. If this, or more then this, I would denie,   2773
MOREOUER *see also* more = 1
  Quee. Did he not send you twaine? | *Kath.* Yes Madame: and
  moreouer,   1938
MORNE = 1
  From morne till night out of his Pauilion.   2609
MORNING = 1*1
  *Clow. I will come to your worship to morrow morning.   926
  To those fresh morning dropps vpon the Rose,   1359
MOROW = 1
  To morow shall we visite you againe.   674
MORRALL = 2*1
  +Ther's the morrall: Now the *lenuoy.*   856 +4
  + *Pag.* I will adde the *lenuoy,* say the morrall againe.   856 +5
  *Now will I begin your morrall, and do you follow with | my
  lenuoy.   857
MORROW = 2*1
  To morrow you shall haue a sight of them.   663
  *Clow. I will come to your worship to morrow morning.   926
  Iaquenetta. God giue you good morrow M.(aister) Person.   1246
MORTALL = 5*1
  *A domineering pedant ore the Boy, then whom no mor-|tall so
  magnificent.   943
  No thought can thinke, nor tongue of mortall tell.   1373
  Duma. By heauen the woonder in a mortall eye.   1419
  Turning mortall for thy loue.   1457
  ** Page. A holy parcell of the fayrest dames that euer turnd their |
  backes to mortall viewes.*   2055
  Page. That euer turnde their eyes to mortall viewes.   2059
MORTEFIED = 1
  Dumaine. My louing Lord, *Dumaine* is mortefied,   32
MOST = 35*18
  Bero. Why? all delightes are vaine, but that most vaine   77
  And when it hath the thing it hunteth most,   156
  Bero. Armado is a most illustrious wight,   188
  **commende the blacke oppressing humour to the most holsome
  phisicke*   243
  **most grase, Birdes best peck, and Men sit downe to that
  nourishment*   246
  ** & most propostrous euent that draweth fro(m) my snowhite pen
  the*   251
  Arm. A most fine Figure. | *Boy.* To proue you a Cypher.   361
  *Arm. Most sweete *Hercules:* more authoritie deare Boy,   373
  Arm. My loue is most immaculate white and red.   395
  *Boy. Most maculate thoughts Maister, are maskt vnder | such
  colours.   396
  *Ar. Sweet inuocation of a child, most pretty & pathetical.   401

MOST *cont.*

Lad. They say so most, that most his humors know.	545
Most power to do most harme, least knowing ill:	550
Lon. Nay my coller is ended. She is a most sweet Ladie. | *Exit*	
Longauil.	705
note men that most are affected to these.	794
Brag. A most acute Iuuenall, volable and free of grace,	836
Most rude melancholie, Valour giues thee place.	838
*a leuenpence-farthing better: most sweete gardon. I will	936
* *Boyet* | *reedes.* By heauen, that thou art faire, is most infallible:	1041
*heroicall Vassall. The magnanimous and most illustrate	1045
Clo. By my troth most plesant, how both did fit it.	1118
Clo. By my soule a Swaine, a most simple Clowne.	1137
O my troth most sweete iestes, most inconie vulgar wit,	1139
Armatho ath toothen side, o a most daintie man,	1142
*To see him kisse his hand, & how most sweetly a wil sweare:	1144
Ah heauens, it is most patheticall nit.	1147
* *Holo.* Most barbarous intimation: yet a kind of insinua-|tion,	1163
To the snow-white hand of the most bewtious Lady Rosaline.	1297
Peda. And certes the text most infallibly concludes it.	1328
Duma. O most deuine *Kate.*	1417
Berow. O most prophane coxcombe.	1418
These Wormes for louing, that art most in loue?	1491
Curat. A most singuler and choyce Epithat, | *Draw-out his*	
Table-booke.	1754
Brag. Men of peace well incontred. | *Ped.* Most millitarie sir	
salutation.	1774
* *Pag.* Ba most seely Sheepe, with a horne: you heare his |	
(learning.	1788
* *Bra.* Sir, it is the Kings most sweete pleasur & affection,	1821
* *Peda.* The *posterior* of the day, most generous sir, is liable,	1825
*import and most serious designes, and of great import in	1833
*assistants the Kinges commaund, and this most gallant	
il-|lustrate	1853
Peda. Most *Dull,* honest *Dull,* to our sport: away. *Exeunt.*	1886
Rosa. Come on then, weare the Fauours most in sight.	2028
A meane most meanely, and in hushering.	2253
Most honourablie doth vphold his word,	2387
Their forme confounded, makes most forme in myrth,	2463
*to *Fortuna delaguar,* I wish you the peace of mind most royall |	
cupplement. *Exit.*	2475
* *Be.* Your nose smels no in his most tender smelling knight.	2518
Boy. Most true, tis right: you were so *Alisander.*	2524
Duma. Most rare *Pompey.*	2639
Clow. Ile do it in my shyrt. | *Duma.* Most resolute *Pompey.*	2654
*But most esteemed greatnes, will you heare the Dialogue	2848

MOTH = 5*2

Enter Armado and Moth his page.	311
I am in loue too. Who was *Sampsons* loue my deare Moth?	381
* *Clo.* Nay nothing M.(aster) *Moth,* but what they looke vppon.	465
* *Clow.* Thou hast no feeling of it *Moth,* I will speake that |	
(*Lenuoy.*	880
*for the best ward of mine honour, is rewarding | my dependants.	
Moth, follow.	897
You found his Moth, the King your Moth did see:	1498

MOTHER = *1
  Lad. 3. Then was *Venus* like her mother, for her father is | but
grim.   762
MOTHERS = 2
  Boy. My fathers wit, and my mothers tongue assist me.   399
  Bo. Her mothers, I haue heard.   701
MOTION = 3*1
  As motion and long during action tyres   1657
  But with the motion of all elamentes,   1680
  Rosa. The musique playes, vouchsafe some motion to it,   2117
  Nor to the motion of a Schoole-boyes tongue: 2335
MOTIONS = *1
  *Ideas, aprehentions, motions, reuolutions. These are begot in   1232
MOUCE = *1
  Ros. Whats your darke meaning mouce, of this light word?   1905
MOUE = 2*3
  Long. I feare these stubborne lines lacke power to moue.   1387
  Long. It did moue him to passion, & therfore lets heare it.   1545
  Quee. No, to the death we will not moue a foot,   2038
  Berow. To moue wilde laughter in the throate of death?   2816
  Mirth cannot moue a soule in agonie.   2818
MOUING = 1
  As our best mouing faire soliciter: 520
MOUNSIER = 3*2
  Iag. I sir from one mounsier *Berowne*, one of the strange |
Queenes Lordes.   1294
  Brag. Mounsier, are you not lettred?   1784
  This is the Ape of Forme, Mounsier the nice,   2250
  Boyet. A light for Mounsier *Iudas*, it growes darke, he | may
stumble.   2583
  Enter a Messenger Mounsier Marcade.   2671
MOUNSIR = 1
  Dum. A gallant Lady *Mounsir*, fare you wel. *Exit*.   694
MOUNTAINE = 2
  on the top of the Mountaine? | *Peda*. Or *Mons* the hill.   1817
  Brag. At your sweete pleasure, for the Mountaine.   1819
MOUNTED = 1
  Arme Wenches arme, incounters mounted are,   1974
MOUNTING = 1
  Quee. Who ere a was, a showd a mounting minde.   978
MOURNES = 1
  It mournes, that painting vsurping haire   1608
MOURNING = 2
  And though the mourning brow of progenie   2702
  My wofull selfe vp in a mourning house, | Rayning the teares of
lamentation,   2768
MOUTH = 1
  I onelie haue made a mouth of his eie,   756
MUCH = 30*10
  So much deare Liedge, I haue already sworne,   38
  Too much to know, is to know nought but fame: 97
  *which is called Supper: So much for the time When. Now for the   247
  Clo. I do confesse much of the hearing it, but little of the |
marking of it.   281
  Boy. Then I am sure you know how much the grosse   353
  *thee in my rapier, as much as thou didst me in carying gates.   380
  *hard for *Hercules* Clubb, and therefore too much oddes for a   479

MUCH *cont.*

Then you much willing to be counted wise,	509
Haste, signifie so much while we attende,	524
And much too little of that good I saw,	554
Before I came: Marrie thus much I haue learnt,	578
Which we much rather had depart withall,	642
Prin. You do the King my father too much wrong,	649
This ciuill warre of wittes were much better vsed	730
Boy. And three times as much more, and yet nothing | at all.	815
Clow. Pray you sir, How much Carnation Ribbon may	911
Boy. I am much deceiued, but I remember the stile.	1077
Bo. I feare too much rubbing: good night my good owle.	1135
*concerne much: stay not thy complement, I forgiue thy | dewtie,	
adue.	1307
God amende vs, God amende, we are much out a th'way.	1409
You chide at him, offending twice as much.	1469
I would not haue him know so much by mee.	1487
All three of you, to be thus much ore'shot?	1497
King. No Diuel will fright thee then so much as shee.	1624
Her feete were much too daintie for such tread.	1628
Quee. Nothing but this: yes as much loue in Rime,	1893
Ros. Much in the letters, nothing in the praise.	1928
Duma. Please it you, as much in priuat, & ile bid adieu.	2152
So much I hate a breaking cause to be	2281
Vnseene, vnuisited, much to our shame.	2284
Much vpon this tis: and might not you	2411
Bero. How much is it?	2441
Brag. Annoynted, I implore so much expence of thy royal	2467
Clo. Tis not so much worth: but I hope I was perfect. I | made a	
litle fault in great.	2507
Quee. Speake braue *Hector*, we are much delighted.	2622
Is not by much so holdsome profitable,	2708
Hath much deformed vs, fashioning our humours	2715
Dum. Our letters madame, shewed much more then iest.	2743
No no my Lord, your Grace is periurde much,	2750
Then if I haue much loue, Ile giue you some.	2790

MULTITUDE = 1

of this day, which the rude multitude call the after-noone.	1823

MUMBLE = 1

Some mumble newes, some trencher Knight, some Dick	2403

MURTHERER = 1

That we must stand and play the murtherer in?	982

MUSCOUIE = 1

Sea sicke I thinke comming from *Muscouie.*	2325

MUSCOUITES = 2

Boy. They do, they do; and are appariled thus, | Like *Muscouites,*	
or *Russians,* as I gesse.	2012
Disguysd like *Muscouites* in shapeles geare:	2226

MUSICALL = 1

Subtil as *Sphinx,* as sweete and musicall,	1693

MUSICKE = 1

Enter Black-moores with musicke, the Boy with a | speach, and the	
rest of the Lordes disguysed.	2051

MUSIQUE = 3*1

On who the musique of his owne vaine tongue	177
Which not to anger bent, is musique, and sweete fier.	1281
Rosa. Play Musique then: nay you must do it soone.	2110

MUSIQUE *cont.*
   *Rosa. The musique playes, vouchsafe some motion to it,   2117
MUSKOUITS = 1
   Quee. Twentie adieus my frozen Muskouits.   2183
MUST = 18*9
   Ber. This Article my liedge your selfe must breake,   143
   Fer. We must of force dispence with this Decree,   158
   Shee must lie heere on meere necessitie.   159
   *safe, and you must suffer him to take no delight, nor no
   pe-|nance,   432
   *but a' must fast three dayes a weeke: for this Damsell   433
   *I must keepe her at the Parke, she is alowde for the Day |
   womand. Fare you well.   434
   Where now his knowledge must proue ignorance.   598
   Ber. You must not be so quicke.   613
   I must imploy him in a letter to my loue.   777
   *Brag. Fetch hither the Swaine, he must carrie me a letter.   817
   *Boy. Marrie sir, you must send the Asse vpon the Horse,   822
   By thy fauour sweete Welkin, I must sigh in thy face: 837
   Ber. O stay slaue, I must employ thee.   917
   Ber. Why villaine, thou must know first.   925
   Ber. It must be done this after noone,   927
   Some men must loue my Ladie, and some Ione.   971
   That we must stand and play the murtherer in?   982
   *Clo. Indeed a'must shoot nearer, or hele neare hit the clout.   1125
   Ber. I as some dayes, but then no Sunne must shine.   1426
   Therefore of all handes must we be forsworne.   1567
   *deede too: but let that passe, for I must tell thee it will   1834
   Thus must thou speake, and thus thy body beare.   1992
   Rosa. Play Musique then: nay you must do it soone.   2110
   The vertue of your eie must breake my oth.   2274
   *Ber. Well said old mocker, I must needes be friendes with |
   (thee.   2495
   *Long. I must rather giue it the raine: for it runnes against |
   Hector.   2614
   Rosal. You must be purged to, your sinnes are rackt.   2778
MUSTACHIE = *1
   *with my excrement, with my mustachie: but sweete hart   1837
MUSTER = 1
   Muster your Wits, stande in your owne defence,   1977
MUTE = 1
   No poynt (quoth I) my seruant, straight was mute.   2196
MUTENIE = 1
   Haue chose as vmpier of their mutenie.   180
MUTTON = *1
   *Clo. I had rather pray a month with Mutton & Porridge.   297
MY *see also* a'my *l.*21 32 54 71 *120 126 129 143 166 185 187 *195
   *224 *232 *244 *251 *264 294 300 303 *318 *320 330 331 335 341
   *365 *374 *380 381 395 399 *420 *424 426 436 *481 504 508 *528
   555 569 590 593 594 597 600 604 605 627 647 649 666 669 671 672
   677 *678 685 687 705 726 728 732 753 764 *772 777 *781 796 799
   839 *849 *850 858 883 *889 *892 898 *901 910 918 952 968 971
   981 985 993 996 1001 1003 1010 1025 *1063 1064 1084 1086 1088
   1095 *1097 1115 1118 *1121 1127 *1135 1137 1139 1168 *1237
   1263 1269 *1305 1311 *1320 1335 *1341 *1344 *1347 1361 1367
   1369 1371 1374 1388 1395 1399 *1402 1415 1427 1432 1448 1459
   1462 1489 1510 *1543 1550 1554 1579 1581 1582 1607 1626 1649

MY *cont.*
  1671 1797 *1811 *1829 *1836 *1837 *1859 1874 1920 1921 1926
  1932 1955 1958 1983 2024 2030 2032 2102 2144 2158 *2178 2183
  2195 2196 2203 2205 2239 2260 2267 2274 2277 2285 2289 2291
  2292 2296 2306 2309 *2321 2330 2336 2344 2347 2363 2385 2388
  2393 2396 2405 2413 *2455 2459 2465 2472 2500 *2503 *2509
  2514 2515 2558 *2590 *2619 2653 2654 2660 2676 2677 2678 2682
  2697 2710 2750 2752 2768 2770 2776 2777 2780 2783 2787 2789
  2795 2798 2799 2802 2833 = 189*53

MYLDE = *1
  *There ant shall please you a foolish mylde man, an   2533
MYLE = *1
  *Ber. Item, That no woman shall come within a myle of   128
MYLL = 1
  More Sacks to the myll. O heauens I haue my wysh,   1415
MYRTH = 2*2
  *did I see that low spirited Swaine, that base Minow of thy myrth,   255
  *and sodaine breaking out of myrth (as it were) I haue   1847
  Quee. Heere comes Boyet, and myrth is in his face.   1970
  Their forme confounded, makes most forme in myrth,   2463
MYSELFE see selfe
NA = 1
NAILE = 1
  And Dicke the Sheepheard blowes his naile: 2880
NAKED = 2
  Brag. The naked trueth of it is, I haue no Shirt.   2665
  To some forlorne and naked Hermytage,   2755
NAME = 16*2
  That giue a name to euery fixed Starre,   94
  And euery Godfather can giue a name.   98
  And to the strictest decrees Ile write my name.   126
  So to the Lawes at large I write my name,   166
  olde time, which we may name tough. | Arma. Prettie and apt.   328
  *name more; and sweete my childe let them be men of good |
  repute and carriage.   374
  And wrong the reputation of your name,   650
  Boyet. The heire of Alanson, Rosalin her name.   693
  Lon. Perchance light in the light. I desire her name?   697
  Bero. Whats her name in the capp? | Boy. Katherin by good happ.   709
  *Why? it is a fayrer name then French-Crowne.   906
  When tongues speake sweetely, then they name her name,   931
  Ber. One drunkard loues an other of the name.   1382
  Dum. It is Berownes writing, and heere is his name.   1547
  That he was faine to seale on Cupids name.   1896
  *Duman. Will you vouchsafe with me to change a word? | Maria.
  Name it.   2147
  Duma. For the latter ende of his name.   2579
NAMES = 1
  Your othes are past, and now subscribe your names: 23
NAPPING = 1
  To be ore-hard and taken napping so.   1467
NASO = *2
  *Naso was the man. And why in deed Naso, but for smel-|ling   1288
NAT = *1
NATH = 4*10
NATHANIEL see also Curat.Nath., Nat., Nath. = 3*1
  Enter Dull, Holofernes, the Pedant and Nathaniel.   1150

LOVE'S LABOUR'S LOST

NATHANIEL cont.

  Holo. Sir *Nathaniel*, haud credo. 1161
  **Holo.* Sir *Nathaniel*, will you heare an extemporall Epy-|taph 1207
*coloures. But to returne to the Verses, Did they please you | sir
Nathaniel? 1315
NATIUE = 2
  For still her cheekes possesse the same, | Which natiue she doth
owe 409
  For natiue blood is counted paynting now: 1612
NATURE = 2
  As Nature was in making Graces deare, 501
  Is of that nature, that to your hudge stoore, 2304
NAU = 5
NAUAR see also Na., Nau. = 10*1
  Enter Ferdinand K.(ing) of Nauar, Berowne, | *Longauill, and
Dumaine.* 2
  Nauar shall be the wonder of the worlde. 16
  *Nauar, *my soules earthes God, and bodies fostring patrone:* 232
  Matchles *Nauar*, the plea of no lesse weight, 498
  Doth noyse abroad *Nauar* hath made a Vow, 513
  Boyet. Nauar had notice of your faire approch, 575
  Enter *Nauar, Longauill, Dumaine, & Berowne.* 583
  Bo. Heere comes *Nauar.* 584
  Nauar. Faire Princesse, Welcome to the court of *Nauar.* 585
  On *Nauar* and his Bookmen, for heere tis abused. 731
  Deceaue me not now, *Nauar* is infected. 734
NAUAR = 1
NAUGHT *see* nought
NAY = 13*3
  Bero. By yea and nay sir, than I swore in iest. 58
  **Clo.* Nay nothing M.(aster) *Moth*, but what they looke vppon. 465
  Ber. Nay then will I be gon. 623
  Lon. Nay my coller is ended. She is a most sweet Ladie. | *Exit
Longauil.* 705
  *A verie Bedell to a humerous sigh, a Critick, nay a night-|watch
Constable, 941
  Nay to be periurde, which is worst of all: 960
  Quee. Nay, neuer paint me now, 991
  *Sir I do inuite you too, you shall not say me nay: *pauca verba.* 1329
  But are you not a shamed? nay, are you not 1496
  King. What makes treason heere? | *Clow.* Nay it makes nothing
sir. 1531
  Nay I haue Vearses too, I thanke *Berowne*, 1922
  Rosa. Play Musique then: nay you must do it soone. 2110
  Ber. Nay then two treyes, an if you grow so nice, 2137
  In honorable tearmes; nay he can sing 2252
  Quee. Nay my good Lord let me ore'rule you now. 2459
  And so adue sweete *Iude.* Nay, Why dost thou stay? 2578
NE *l.**1762 1764 1770 = 2*1
NEARE = 2*2
  **Ber.* The Spring is neare when greene geese are a bree-|(ding. 103
  neare. Finely put on in deede. 1103
  **Clo.* Indeed a'must shoot nearer, or hele neare hit the clout. 1125
  Ros. Youle neare be friendes with him, a kild your sister. 1900
NEARER = *1
  **Clo.* Indeed a'must shoot nearer, or hele neare hit the clout. 1125

172

NEBOUR = *1
  vocatur nebour; neigh abreuiated ne: this is abhominable,   1762
NECESSITIE = 3
  Shee must lie heere on meere necessitie.   159
  Ber. Necessitie will make vs all forsworne   160
  I am forsworne on meere necessitie.   165
NECKE = 2
  Breake the necke of the Waxe, and euery one giue eare.   1039
  hang me by the necke, if horns that yeere miscarrie. | Finely put
  on.   1098
NEEDE = 2
  Duma. Some salue for periurie. | *Ber*. O tis more then neede.   1638
  Ros. We neede more light to finde your meaning out.   1908
NEEDES = 2*2
  Needes not the painted florish of your prayse: 505
  Fie paynted Rethoricke, O shee needes it not,   1588
  Duma. Darke needes no Candles now, for darke is light.   1618
  Ber. Well said old mocker, I must needes be friendes with |
  (thee.   2495
NEEDFULL = 1
  Therefore to's seemeth it a needfull course,   516
NEEDLES = 1
  Kath. How needles was it then to aske the question?   612
NEEDS = *1
  Ber. A toy my Leedge, a toy: your grace needs not feare it.   1543
NEGLECT = 1
  That *Cupid* will impose for my neglect,   968
NEGLECTED = 1
  For your faire sakes, haue we neglected time.   2713
NEGLIGENT = 1
  Brag. Almost I had. | *Boy*. Negligent student, learne her by hart.   803
NEIGH = *1
  vocatur nebour; neigh abreuiated ne: this is abhominable,   1762
NEIGHBOUR = 1*2
  *not det: he clepeth a Calfe, Caufe: halfe, haufe: neighbour   1761
  I stole into a neighbour thicket by,   1986
  *good neighbour fayth, and a very good Bowler: but for   2535
NEITHER = 7*1
  Clo. This was no Damsel neither sir, she was a Virgin.   288
  were, it would neither serue for the writing, nor the tune.   417
  But say that he, or we, as neither haue   628
  *neither sauouring of Poetrie, wit, nor inuention.   1323
  King. Yf it marr nothing neither,   1533
  Dull. Nor vnderstoode none neither sir.   1882
  Berow. Neither of either: I remit both twaine.   2398
  Neither intitled in the others hart.   2772
NEMEAN = 1
  Thus dost thou heare the nemean Lion roare,   1068
NERE = 3
  Sweare me to this, and I will nere say no.   74
  Her faultes will nere be knowne: 404
  Nere to plucke thee from thy throne: 1449
NESTOR = 1
  And *Nestor* play at push-pin with the boyes,   1506
NEUER *see also* neare, nere = 23*2
  I neuer spent an houres talke withall.   560
  Ferd. I do protest I neuer heard of it: 653

NEUER *cont.*

I will neuer buy and sell out of this word.	907
And neuer going a right, being a Watch:	958
Quee. Nay, neuer paint me now,	991
*Nath. Sir he hath neuer fed of the dainties that are bred | in a booke.	1174
*the Moone is neuer but a month olde: and I say beside	1205
Ah neuer fayth could hold, yf not to beautie vowed.	1268
Did neuer Sonnet for her sake compile,	1471
Nor neuer lay his wreathed armes athwart	1472
Ber. Your Mistresses dare neuer come in raine,	1619
Duma. I neuer knew man holde vile stuffe so deare.	1625
Neuer durst Poet touch a pen to write,	1697
Marg. I, or I would these handes might neuer part.	1947
A better speach was neuer spoke before.	2002
Rosa. Your absence onely. | *King.* That can neuer be.	2128
In their owne shapes: for it can neuer be,	2209
For vertues office neuer breakes mens troth.	2276
And I will wish thee neuer more to daunce,	2332
Nor neuer more in Russian habite waite.	2333
O neuer will I trust to speaches pend,	2334
Nor neuer come in vizard to my friend,	2336
I neuer swore this Lady such an oth.	2390
A tweluemonth shall you spende and neuer rest,	2781
Of him that heares it, neuer in the tongue	2823

NEW = 5*1

Then wish a Snow in Mayes new fangled showes:	115
A man in all the worldes new fashion planted,	175
A man of fier new wordes, Fashions owne knight.	189
*for a new deuisde cursie. I thinke scorne to sigh, mee thinks	368
Beautie doth varnish Age, as if new borne,	1593
Out of a new sad-soule, that you vouchsafe,	2689

NEWES = 3*1

*Lad. 2. He is *Cupids* Graundfather, and learnes newes | of him.	760
Quee. Thy newes *Boyet?* | *Boy.* Prepare Maddame, prepare.	1972
Some mumble newes, some trencher Knight, some Dick	2403
Marcad. I am sorrie Madame for the newes I bring	2675

NEWLY = 1*1

*Ar. I will haue that subiect newly writ ore, that I may	419
As to reioyce at friendes but newly found.	2709

NEXT = 1*1

Vpon the next occasion that we meete,	2035
*of *Iaquenettaes*, and that a weares next his hart for a | Fauour.	2669

NICE = 4*1

*are humours, these betraie nice wenches that would be be-|traied	792
Weele not be nice, take handes, we will not daunce.	2121
King. More measure of this measure be not nice.	2125
Ber. Nay then two treyes, an if you grow so nice,	2137
This is the Ape of Forme, Mounsier the nice,	2250

NICKNAME = *1

*Que. You nickname vertue, vice you should haue spoke:	2275

NIGHT *see also* nyght = 4*1

*Bo. I feare too much rubbing: good night my good owle.	1135
The night of dew that on my cheekes downe flowes.	1361
O, but for my Loue, day would turne to night,	1582
The hue of dungions, and the Schoole of night:	1604
From morne till night out of his Pauilion.	2609

NIGHTLY = 2
Then nightly singes the staring Owle   2884
Then nightly singes the staring Owle,   2893
NIGHTS = 1
Haue no more profite of their shyning nights,   95
NIGHTWATCH = *1
*A verie Bedell to a humerous sigh, a Critick, nay a night-|watch
Constable,   941
NIMBLE = 2
Why vniuersall plodding poysons vp | The nimble spirites in the
arteries,   1655
nimble stiring spirit, she might a bin Grandam ere she died.   1903
NINE = 4*1
*Peda. Sir, you shall present before her the Nine Worthies,   1850
none so fit as to present the nine Worthies.   1855
Bero. And three times thrice is nine.   2431
we know: I hope sir three times thrice sir. | Bero. Is not nine.   2434
Bero. By Ioue, I all wayes tooke three threes for nine.   2438
NINTH = *1
*will be geuen to Aiax. He wilbe the ninth Worthie: a
Con-|querour,   2531
NIP = 1
Nip not the gaudie blossomes of your Loue: 2762
NIPT = 1
When Blood is nipt, and wayes be full,   2883
NIT = 1
Ah heauens, it is most patheticall nit.   1147
NO l.43 48 54 74 95 114 *120 *128 172 240 288 317 *432 460 *475
498 515 552 687 711 722 726 765 *781 *800 828 *845 *846 *855
*880 884 *905 *943 *988 995 1010 *1020 *1057 *1196 *1242 1366
1373 1404 1426 1492 1493 1581 1602 *1618 1624 1642 1732 1734
1737 *1838 *1880 1945 2038 2039 2043 2044 2045 2054 2111 2126
2141 2162 2164 2196 2357 2376 2427 2429 *2516 *2518 2561 2597
2605 *2647 2665 2750 2752 2788 2834 = 64*29
NOBLE = 1*1
*Brag. Sir, the King is a noble Gentleman, and my fami-|lier,   1829
Quee. God giue thee ioy of him: the Noble Lord   2386
NOES = 1
In russet yeas, and honest kersie noes.   2345
NOMINATE = *1
*apperteining to thy young dayes, which we may nominate |
tender.   325
NOMINATED = *1
*who is intituled, nominated, or called, Don Adriano de
Ar-|matho.   1746
NOMINATION = *1
*I will looke againe on the intellect of the letter, for the
no-|mination   1298
NON l.*1259 *1260 = *2
NONE = 11*2
*Clo. I was taken with none sir, I was taken with a Demsel.   285
It should none spare, that come within his power.   543
Ber. And send you manie louers. | Kath. Amen, so you be none.   621
Ber. Ladie I will commend you to my none hart.   677
This letter is mistooke: it importeth none heere.   1036
For none offende, where all alike do dote.   1463
Tush, none but Minstrels like of Sonnetting.   1495

NONE *cont.*

Els none at all in ought proues excellent.	1705
none so fit as to present the nine Worthies.	1855
Dull. Nor vnderstoode none neither sir.	1882
Quee. None are so surely caught, when they are catcht,	1959
To make theirs ours, and ours none but our owne.	2046
*Linnen: since when, Ile be sworne he wore none, but a dish-|cloute	2668

NOONE = 4*1

Clow. When would you haue it done sir? | *Ber.* O this after-noone.	920
Ber. It must be done this after noone,	927
Of his faire Mistres, in the after noone	1727
of this day, which the rude multitude call the after-noone.	1823
*congruent, and measurable for the after noone: the worde is	1826

NOR *l.*417 *432 *1323 1362 1373 1472 1581 1882 2039 2272 2333 2335 2336 2337 2362 = 14*2

NORMANDIE = 1

In *Normandie* saw I this *Longauill,*	535

NORTH = 2*1

*seest. But to the place Where? It standeth North North-east & by	253
By East, West, North, and South, I spred my conquering might:*	2514
Brag. By the North Pole I do challenge thee.	2649

NORTHREN = *1

Clow. I will not fight with a Pole like a Northren man;	2650

NORTH-EAST = *1

*seest. But to the place Where? It standeth North North-east & by	253

NOSE = 1*3

*loue sometime through: nose as if you snufft vp loue by	785
Boyet. Your Nose saies no, you are not: for it stands too | (right.	2516
Be. Your nose smels no in his most tender smelling knight.	2518
And Marrians nose lookes red and raw:	2891

NOT *l.*41 42 45 47 50 52 *60 71 73 90 96 163 185 234 239 *275 293 343 *344 408 *413 *416 458 *466 *480 *481 *482 505 507 512 *587 594 609 610 613 616 632 639 645 661 669 *703 707 716 721 725 734 742 757 *789 *826 853 923 977 987 989 992 1002 1011 1027 *1102 1114 1115 1162 *1170 *1176 *1178 1188 *1190 1198 1217 *1261 1268 1281 *1284 *1307 *1314 *1329 *1341 *1342 *1343 *1350 1358 1370 *1384 1391 1393 1396 1398 1405 1420 1430 1452 1470 1487 1494 1496 1514 *1543 1565 1566 1573 1577 1588 1601 1602 1622 1631 1634 1659 1668 1679 1691 *1761 1773 *1779 *1780 1784 *1816 *1863 *1864 *1878 1912 1913 1914 *1931 1933 1938 1945 1963 1965 1996 1997 2020 2038 2063 2067 2069 2086 2109 2111 *2112 2121 2125 2143 *2159 2164 2168 *2178 2189 2245 2258 2273 2280 2285 2291 2297 2298 2355 2358 2359 2361 2362 2367 2378 2411 2413 2432 2435 *2448 *2453 2458 2471 2484 2492 *2507 *2516 2550 2560 2582 2594 2618 2625 *2650 *2657 *2659 2661 2686 2695 2701 2706 2708 2710 2741 2745 2754 2760 2762 2787 2792 2810 2828 2835 2836 2843 = 168*49

NOTE = 5*3

*with turning vp your eylids, sigh a note and sing a note som-|time	783
*without these, and make them men of note: do you	793
note men that most are affected to these.	794
Would from my forehead wipe a periurde note:	1462
Mar. Follie in Fooles beares not so strong a note,	1965
Tu-whit to-who. | A merrie note,	2885
Tu-whit to-who. | A merrie note,	2894

NOTED = 2
   Ber. An amber colourd Rauen was well noted.   1422
   Saw sighes reeke from you, noted well your pashion.   1477
NOTHING *see also* thing = 13*6
   Duma. In reason nothing. | *Bero.* Something then in rime.   107
   **Clo.* Nay nothing M.(aster) *Moth*, but what they looke vppon.   465
   *therfore I will say nothing: I thanke God I haue as little
   pa-|tience   467
   Nothing becoms him ill that he would well.   538
   Prin. Why, will shall breake it will, and nothing els.   595
   **Boy.* And three times as much more, and yet nothing | at all.   815
   *lewe thereof, impose on thee nothing but this: Beare this   895
   *imitarie is nothing: So doth the Hound his maister,   1290
   *would not loue her; yes for her two eyes. Well, I do nothing   1343
   King. What makes treason heere? | *Clow.* Nay it makes nothing
   sir.   1531
   King. Yf it marr nothing neither,   1533
   Where nothing wantes, that want it selfe doth seeke.   1586
   Ber. O nothing so sure, and thereby all forsworne.   1632
   Rosa. Madame, came nothing els along with that?   1892
   Quee. Nothing but this: yes as much loue in Rime,   1893
   Ros. Much in the letters, nothing in the praise.   1928
   Berow. Nothing but peace, and gentle visitation.   2077
   Rosa. What would they, say they? | *Boy.* Nothing but peace, and
   gentle visitation.   2078
   Bero. We number nothing that we spend for you,   2097
NOTICE = 1*1
   **thy Lawes furie, and shall at the least of thy sweete notice, bring*   271
   Boyet. Nauar had notice of your faire approch,   575
NOUGHT = 1
   Too much to know, is to know nought but fame: 97
NOUI = *1
   **Ped. Noui hominum tanquam te,* His humour is loftie, his   1748
NOURISH = 1
   That shew, containe, and nourish all the worlde.   1704
NOURISHMENT = *1
   **most grase, Birdes best peck, and Men sit downe to that*
   nourishment   246
NOURISHT = *1
   *the ventricle of Memorie, nourisht in the wombe of prima-|ter,   1233
NOUUM = 1
   Abate throw at Nouum, and the whole world againe,   2487
NOW = 36*14
   Your othes are past, and now subscribe your names: 23
   So you to studie now it is too late,   117
   *Now sir for the manner, It is the manner of a man to speake   220
   **which is called Supper: So much for the time When. Now for the*   247
   Arma. True. | **Boy.* Why sir is this such a peece of studie? Now
   heere is   357
   *three ages since, but I thinke now tis not to be found: or if it   416
   Boyet. Now Maddame summon vp your dearest spirrits,   492
   Be now as prodigall of all Deare grace,   500
   But now to taske the tasker, good *Boyet,*   511
   Prin. Now, What admittance Lord?   574
   Where now his knowledge must proue ignorance.   598
   Ber. Now faire befall your maske.   619
   Ber. Now God saue thy life. | *Ros.* And yours from long liuing.   688

NOW *cont.*

Deceaue me not now, *Nauar* is infected.	734
+Ther's the morrall: Now the *lenuoy*.	856 +4
*Now will I begin your morrall, and do you follow with | my	
lenuoy.	857
Clown. True, true, and now you wilbe my purgation, | and let me	
loose.	892
Now will I looke to his remuneration.	902
Quee. Nay, neuer paint me now,	991
But come, the Bow: Now Mercie goes to kill,	999
As I for praise alone now seeke to spill	1009
Boyet. But she her selfe is hit lower: Haue I hit her now?	1106
*as the Pomwater, who now hangeth like a Iewel in the eare	1154
Some say a Sore, but not a sore, | till now made sore with	
shooting.	1217
Berow. Now in thy likenesse, one more foole appeare.	1378
Bero. Now step I foorth to whip hipocrisie.	1488
Kin. How now, What is in you? Why dost thou teare it?	1542
Duma. Now the number is euen.	1557
King. What zeale, what furie, hath inspirde thee now?	1578
For natiue blood is counted paynting now:	1612
Duma. Darke needes no Candles now, for darke is light.	1618
King. Then leaue this chat, and good *Berowne* now proue	1633
Now for not looking on a womans face,	1659
Long. Now to plaine dealing, Lay these glozes by,	1721
Brag. Now by the sault waue of the meditaranium, a	1795
*or pageant, or antique, or fierworke: Now vnderstanding	1845
*you may cry, Well done *Hercules*, now thou crusshest the	1870
Thou now requests but Mooneshine in the water.	2107
Ro. You tooke the moone at ful, but now shee's changed?	2114
Till this mad man shewed thee, and what art thou now?	2264
King. We came to visite you, and purpose now,	2269
Now by my maiden honour yet as pure, | As the vnsallied Lilly I	
protest,	2277
King. We were descried, theyle mock vs now dounright.	2318
Were not you here but euen now, disguysde? | *King.* Madame, I	
was.	2367
Now to our periurie, to add more terror,	2409
Quee. Nay my good Lord let me ore'rule you now.	2459
And now forward, for we haue put thee in countenance.	2572
Duma. Though my mockes come home by me, I will | now be	
merrie.	2590
King. Now at the latest minute of the houre, | Graunt vs your	
loues.	2746
And by this Virgin palme now kissing thine,	2766

NOYSE = 1

Doth noyse abroad *Nauar* hath made a Vow,	513

NUAGE = 1

Boyet. Full merely hath this braue nuage, this carreere | bin run.	2421

NUMBER = 2

Duma. Now the number is euen.	1557
Bero. We number nothing that we spend for you,	2097

NUMBERS = 3*1

Nath. Here are onely numbers ratefied, but for the ele-|gancie	1286
These numbers will I teare, and write in prose.	1389
Such fierie Numbers as the prompting eyes,	1673
The numbers true, and were the numbring too,	1923

NUMBRED = 1
Are numbred in the trauaile of one Mile?   2096
NUMBRING = 1
The numbers true, and were the numbring too,   1923
NUPTIALL = *1
*whose side? the Beggers. The catastrophe is a Nuptiall, on   1056
NUTMEGG = 1
Duma. A gift Nutmegg. | *Bero.* A Lemmon.   2602
NYGHT = 5
And then to sleepe but three houres in the nyght,   46
When I was wont to thinke no harme all nyght,   48
And make a darke nyght too of halfe the day: 49
Will they not (thinke you) hange them selues to nyght?   2189
Quee. Boyet prepare, I will away to nyght.   2685
O *l.*51 *259 261 317 *379 713 797 *846 *850 *887 *903 910 913 915
917 921 923 *935 *939 952 989 997 *1031 *1048 *1121 1139 1142
*1172 *1342 1372 1388 1390 1415 1417 1418 1427 1460 1478 1500
1502 1508 1556 1562 1582 1588 1595 1597 1599 1603 1607 1627
1629 1632 1636 1639 1669 1699 *1778 *1810 1914 1926 1933 1951
1971 2106 2156 2188 2283 2310 2334 2426 *2439 *2442 *2528
2786 2867 2876 = 60*18, 2
If Sore be sore, then el to Sore, | makes fiftie sores o sorell: 1223
Pag. The Sheepe, the other two concludes it o u.   1794
OAKES *see* Okes
OATEN *see* Oten
OATH *see also* oth, othe = 1
Tis deadlie sinne to keepe that oath my Lord,   600
OATHES *see* othes
OBAY = 1
Young blood doth not obay an olde decree.   1565
OBEDIENT = 1
Kisses the base ground with obedient breast.   1574
OBIECT = 2
For euery obiect that the one doth catch,   562
To euery varied obiect in his glaunce: 2723
OBIECTES = *1
*extrauagant spirit, full of formes, figures, shapes, obiectes,   1231
OBSCENLY = *1
*When it comes so smoothly off, so obscenly as it were, so fit.   1140
OBSCURE = 1*1
Some obscure presedence that hath tofore bin saine.   856
*and obscure vulgar; *videliset*, He came, see, and ouercame: 1049
OBSEENE = *1
Then for the place Where? where I meane, I did incounter that
ob-| seene   250
OBSERUANCES = 1
But there are other strickt obseruances: 40
OBSERUATION = 2
Bo. If my obseruation (which very seldome lyes   732
Boy. By my penne of obseruation. | *Brag.* But o but o.   796
OBSERUDE = 1
I heard your guyltie Rimes, obserude your fashion: 1476
OBSERUE = 1
And wayte the season, and obserue the times,   1953
OBTAINDE = 1
For my great sute, so easely obtainde.   2697

OCCASION = 2*1
His eye begets occasion for his wit,   561
*and deliuered vpon the mellowing of occasion: But the   1234
Vpon the next occasion that we meete,   2035
OD = 1
to od as it were, too peregrinat as I may call it.   1752
ODDES = 5*1
*hard for *Hercules* Clubb, and therefore too much oddes for a   479
+Were still at oddes being but three.   856 +3
+Were still at oddes, being but three.   856 +7
+And staied the oddes by adding foure.   856 +9
Were still at oddes, being but three.   860
Staying the oddes by adding foure.   862
ODE = 1
Dum. Once more Ile reade the Ode that I haue writ.   1435
ODORIFEROUS = *1
*out the odoriferous flowers of fancie? the ierkes of in-|uention   1289
OES = 1
O that your face were not so full of Oes.   1933
OF *see also* a, o = 308*130
OFF *l.**781 1096 *1140 1592 *2178 *2451 = 2*5
OFFENCE = *1
*Snake; that is the way to make an offence gracious, though   1871
OFFENCES = *1
**Ar.* Villaine, thou shalt fast for thy offences ere thou be |
pardoned.   449
OFFENDE = 1
For none offende, where all alike do dote.   1463
OFFENDED = *1
**Bo.* Good sir be not offended, She is an heire of *Falcon-|(bridge.*   703
OFFENDING = 1
You chide at him, offending twice as much.   1469
OFFER = 1
If this Austere insociable life, | Change not your offer made in
heate of blood.   2759
OFFERD = *1
**Page.* Offerd by a childe to an old man: which is wit-old.   1798
OFFICE = 1
For vertues office neuer breakes mens troth.   2276
OFFICER = *1
**by thy sweete Graces Officer* Anthonie Dull, *a man of*   266
OFFICERS = 1
For such a summe from speciall officers, | Of *Charles* his father.   658
OFFICES = 1
Aboue their functions and their offices.   1683
OFT = 2
That oft in fielde with Targ and Shield did make my foe to sweat,   2500
Rosa. Oft haue I heard of you my Lord *Berowne,*   2802
OFTEN = 1
And often at his very loose decides   2700
OH *see also* o *l.*1282 1814 = 2
OKES = *1
*Those thoughts to me were Okes, to thee like Osiers bowed   1270
OLD = 1*6
**Lad.* Thou art an old Loue-monger, & speakest skilfully.   758
*What was a month old at *Cains* birth, that's not fiue weeks | old
as yet?   1190

OLD *cont.*

   *Holo. The Moone was a month old when *Adam* was no | (more.   1196
   *Page. Offerd by a childe to an old man: which is wit-old.   1798
   *Ber. Well said old mocker, I must needes be friendes with |
   (thee.   2495

OLDE = 7*7

   olde time, which we may name tough. | *Arma*. Prettie and apt.   328
   *man after the olde painting, and keepe not too long in one   789
   *Rosa. Shall I come vpon thee with an olde saying, that   1108
   *Boy. So I may answere thee with one as olde that was a   1111
   But *omne bene* say I, being of an olde Fathers minde,   1187
   *the Moone is neuer but a month olde: and I say beside   1205
   *and so foorth. Ah good olde *Mantuan*, I may speake   1258
   *te vnde, que non te perreche. Olde *Mantuan*, olde *Mantuan*,   1260
   Berow. All hid, all hid, an olde infant play,   1412
   Young blood doth not obay an olde decree.   1565
   Of the olde rage: beare with me, I am sicke.   2350
   Long. The face of an olde Roman coyne, scarce seene.   2566
   Berow. Our wooing doth not ende like an olde Play: 2835

OMITTED = 1

   King. Away, away, no time shalbe omitted,   1732

OMNE = 1

   But *omne bene* say I, being of an olde Fathers minde,   1187

OMNES = 1

   Boy. You are too hard for mee. *Exeunt omnes.*   768

OMNIA = *1

   *Nath. Facile precor gellida, quando pecas omnia sub vmbra
   ru-| minat,   1257

ON *see also* a, com'on, one = 52*22, 1

   On who the musique of his owne vaine tongue   177

ONCE = 11*1

   I saw him at the Duke *Alansoes* once,   553
   Berowne. Did not I dance with you in *Brabant* once?   609
   Kather. Did not I dance with you in *Brabant* once? | *Ber*. I know
   you did.   610
   Dum. Once more Ile reade the Ode that I haue writ.   1435
   Ber. Once more Ile marke how Loue can varrie Wit.   1436
   Lets vs once loose our othes to finde our selues,   1712
   Not to beholde. | *Berow*. Once to beholde, rogue.   2063
   Page. Once to beholde with your Sunne beamed eyes,   2065
   Twice to your Visore, and halfe once to you.   2131
   *Quee. Peace peace, forbeare: your Oth once broke, you | force
   not to forsweare.   2377
   Tolde our intentes before: which once disclosd,   2406
   By being once falce, for euer to be true   2731

ONE *see also* i.d., on, toothen = 46*25

   And one day in a weeke to touch no foode: 43
   And but one meale on euery day beside: 44
   *welcome the sower Cup of prosperitie, affliccio(n) may one day   308
   *Ar. Why? sadnes is one & the selfe same thing deare imp.   315
   Boy. How many is one thrice tolde?   348
   Arm. It doth amount to one more then two.   355
   *Boy. Of all the foure, or the three, or the two, or one of | the
   foure.   385
   Arm. Is that one of the foure complexions?   389
   Lor. Longauill is one. | *Princ*. Know you the man?   530
   For euery obiect that the one doth catch,   562

ONE *cont.*

That euery one her owne hath garnished,	570
Like one that comes heere to besiedge his Court,	580
Being but the one halfe of, of an intire summe,	626
One part of *Aquitaine* is bound to vs,	631
But that one halfe which is vnsatisfied,	634
One paiment of a hundred thousand Crownes,	640
Bo. She hath but one for her selfe, to desire that were a │ (shame.	698
And you giue him for my sake but one louing kisse.	753
*man after the olde painting, and keepe not too long in one	789
Clow. O marrie me to one Francis, I smell some *Lenuoy,*	887
Do one thing for me that I shall intreate.	919
I and by heauen, one that will do the deede,	964
One a these Maides girdles for your waste should be fit.	1026
Clow. I haue a Letter from Monsier *Berowne,* │ to one Ladie *Rosaline.*	1029
Breake the necke of the Waxe, and euery one giue eare.	1039
*He came, one; see, two; ouercame, three. Who came? the	1050
*whose side? the Kinges: no, on both in one, or one in both.	1057
A Phantasime a Monarcho, and one that makes sport │ To the Prince and his Booke-mates.	1080
Boy. So I may answere thee with one as olde that was a	1111
Of one sore I an hundred make │ by adding but one more l.	1225
Nath. Maister Person, *quasi* Person? And if one shoulde	1247
be perst, Which is the one?	1248
Iag. I sir from one mounsier *Berowne,* one of the strange │ Queenes Lordes.	1294
Ped. Sir *Holofernes,* this *Berowne* is one of the Votaries	1302
*Well, she hath one a'my Sonnets already, the Clowne bore	1348
*care a pin, if the other three were in. Heere comes one with	1351
Nor shines the siluer Moone one halfe so bright,	1362
Berow. Now in thy likenesse, one more foole appeare.	1378
Ber. One drunkard loues an other of the name.	1382
Ay mee sayes one! O *loue* the other cryes!	1478
One her haires were Golde, Christal the others eyes.	1479
Where seuerall worthies make one dignitie,	1585
Pag. Lende me your Horne to make one, and I will whip	1804
Clow. And I had but one peny in the world thou shouldst	1807
Dull. Ile make one in a daunce, or so: or I will play on	1884
One rubbd his elbow thus, and fleerd, and swore,	2001
And euery one his Loue-feat will aduance,	2015
For Ladies; we will euery one be maskt,	2019
Is in one mile? If they haue measured manie,	2087
The measure then of one is easlie tolde.	2088
How manie inches doth fill vp one mile?	2091
Are numbred in the trauaile of one Mile?	2096
King. Then in our measure, do but vouchsafe one change,	2108
Berow. White handed Mistres, one sweet word with thee.	2135
Ber. One word in secret. │ *Quee.* Let it not be sweete.	2142
Long. One word in priuate with you ere I die.	2170
Rosa. Not one word more my Maides, break off, break off.	2178
King. That she vouchsafe me audience for one word.	2238
This is the floure that smyles on euery one.	2256
They did not blesse vs with one happie word.	2297
For euerie one pursents three.	2430
*am (as they say, but to parfect one man in one poore man) │ *Pompion* the great sir.	2444

ONE *cont.*
   Bero. Art thou one of the Worthies?   2446
   To haue one show worse then the Kings and his company.   2456
   Brag. That is al one my faire sweete honie monarch,   2472
   Cannot picke out fiue such, take each one in his vaine.   2488
   *This *Ver*, the Spring: The one maynteined by the Owle, | th'other
   by the Cuckow.   2856
ONELIE = 1
   I onelie haue made a mouth of his eie,   756
ONELY = 7*1
   I onely swore to study with your grace,   55
   The onely soyle of his fayre vertues glose,   539
   Onely for praise sake, when they striue to be | Lords ore their
   Lordes?   1012
   Quee. Onely for praise, and praise we may afford,   1014
   Nath. Here are onely numbers ratefied, but for the ele-|gancie   1286
   And mocke for mocke is onely my intent.   2032
   King. Why take we handes then? | *Rosa.* Onely to part friendes.   2122
   Rosa. Your absence onely. | *King.* That can neuer be.   2128
ONLY = 1*2
   To feele only looking on fairest of faire: 745
   *His intellect is not replenished, he is only an annimall, only   1178
OPINION = *1
   *learned without opinion, and strange without heresie: I did   1744
OPNING = 1
   At the first opning of the gorgious East,   1572
OPPOSED = 1
   Euen to the opposed ende of our ententes.   2716
OPPOSITION = 1
   The liberall opposition of our spirites,   2691
OPPRESSING = *1
   *commende the blacke oppressing humour to the most holsome
   phisicke   243
OR *l.*68 70 150 208 *209 *252 *263 331 *385 407 *416 628 655 711
   712 *788 828 *855 *1057 *1125 *1165 *1167 *1183 1221 *1262
   *1304 *1321 1520 1525 1623 1649 1671 1707 1709 1710 1711 1713
   *1746 1792 1818 *1844 *1845 1861 *1884 1947 1978 2013 2190
   2220 2347 2385 2397 2427 2599 2645 2690 2773 = 42*25
ORACLE = 1
   Bero. As we would heare an Oracle.   227
ORE = 10*3
   Clymbe ore the house to vnlocke the little gate.   118
   My Lord *Berowne*, see him deliuered ore,   300
   Ar. I will haue that subiect newly writ ore, that I may   419
   *smelling loue with your hat penthouse like one the shop of   786
   *A domineering pedant ore the Boy, then whom no mor-|tall so
   magnificent.   943
   Ore Saterday we will returne to Fraunce.   980
   Onely for praise sake, when they striue to be | Lords ore their
   Lordes?   1012
   Quee. Els your memorie is bad, going ore it erewhile.   1078
   And wretched fooles secrets heedfully ore ey.   1414
   So perttaunt like would I ore'sway his state,   1957
   Of manie weerie miles you haue ore gone,   2095
   Kath. Lord *Longauill* said I came ore his hart: 2197
   Quee. Whip to our Tents as Roes runs ore land. *Exeunt.*   2232

OREPARTED = *1
*Alisander, alas you see how tis a little oreparted, but there   2536
ORERULE = 1
Quee. Nay my good Lord let me ore'rule you now.   2459
ORESHOT = 1
All three of you, to be thus much ore'shot?   1497
ORETHROWNE = 2
Theres no such sport, as sport by sport orethrowne: 2044
Theres no such sport by sport, as sport orethrowne: 2045
ORE-HARD = 1
To be ore-hard and taken napping so.   1467
ORNAMENTS = 1
With such bedecking ornaments of praise.   571
ORTAGRIPHIE = *1
*such rackers of ortagriphie, as to speake dout fine, when he   1759
OSIERS = *1
*Those thoughts to me were Okes, to thee like Osiers bowed   1270
OSTENTARE = *1
*replication, or rather ostentare, to show as it were his inclina-|tion   1165
OSTENTATION = 1*1
*(sweete chuck) with some delightfull ostentation, or show,   1844
Haue blowne me full of maggot ostentation.   2341
OTEN = 1
When Shepheards pipe on Oten Strawes,   2869
OTH = 12*1
Or hauing sworne too hard a keeping oth,   70
I am the last that will last keepe his oth.   171
And he and his compettitours in oth, | Were all addrest to meete you gentle Lady   576
Then seeke a dispensation for his oth: 581
Nau. Heare me deare Lady, I haue sworne an oth,   592
To loose an oth, to winn a Parradise?   1406
And Ioue for your Loue would infringe an oth.   1481
O who can giue an oth? Where is a booke?   1599
The vertue of your eie must breake my oth.   2274
*Quee. Peace peace, forbeare: your Oth once broke, you | force not to forsweare.   2377
King. Despise me when I breake this Oth of mine.   2379
I neuer swore this Lady such an oth.   2390
Your oth I will not trust, but goe with speede   2754
OTHE = 1
Ferd. Your othe is past, to passe away from these.   53
OTHER see also atother = 16*3
But there are other strickt obseruances: 40
Suggestions are to other as to me: 169
Clow. Of other mens secrets I beseech you.   241
Which each to other hath so strongly sworne.   302
as an other man, & therfore I can be quiet. Exit.   468
3. Lad. An other of these Studentes at that time,   556
The other turnes to a mirth-moouing iest,   563
Where that and other specialties are bound: 662
Pag. Do the wise thinke them other, is not lenuoy a salue?   853
*Boy. And I cannot, cannot, cannot: and I cannot, an other | (can,   1116
*care a pin, if the other three were in. Heere comes one with   1351
Ber. One drunkard loues an other of the name.   1382

OTHER *cont.*

Ay mee sayes one! O *Ioue* the other cryes!	1478
Other slow Artes intirely keepe the braine:	1675
Pag. The Sheepe, the other two concludes it o u.	1794
*curtesie. I beseech thee apparrell thy head: and among other	1832
*first shew thriue, these foure will change habites, and present |	
the other fiue.	2481
*are Worthies a comming will speake their minde in some | other	
sort. *Exit Curat.*	2537
*This *Ver*, the Spring: The one maynteined by the Owle, | th'other	
by the Cuckow.	2856

OTHERS = 3

Saue base aucthoritie from others Bookes.	92
One her haires were Golde, Christal the others eyes.	1479
Neither intitled in the others hart.	2772

OTHES = 8

Your othes are past, and now subscribe your names:	23
Subscribe to your deepe othes, and keepe it to.	27
These othes and lawes will proue an idle scorne. | Surra, Come	
on.	304
Lets vs once loose our othes to finde our selues,	1712
Or els we loose our selues, to keepe our othes:	1713
Of heauenly Othes vowed with integritie.	2282
Plaide fouleplay with our othes: your beautie Ladies	2714
Haue misbecombd our othes and grauities.	2726

OUER *see also* ore = 7

Berowne. I can but say their protestation ouer,	37
Fell ouer the threshold, and broke my shin.	883
King. Berowne reade it ouer. *He reades the letter.*	1537
The streete should see as she walkt ouer head.	1630
And ouer hard, what you shall ouer heare:	1987
Aboue this Worlde: adding thereto more ouer,	2384

OUERBOLDLY = 1

If ouerboldly we haue borne our selues,	2692

OUERCAME = *3

*and obscure vulgar; *videliset*, He came, see, and ouercame:	1049
*He came, one; see, two; ouercame, three. Who came? the	1050
*Begger. Who ouercame he? the Begger. The conclusion is	1054

OUERCOME = *1

*King. Why did he come? to see. Why did he see? to ouer-|come.	1051

OUERGLAUNCE = 1

Nath. I will ouerglaunce the superscript.	1296

OUERHEARD *see* hard

OUERHEARE *see* heare

OUERSHOT = 1

Ber. So Studie euermore is ouershot,	153

OUERTHROWNE = *1

Clow. O sir, you haue ouerthrowne *Alisander* the Conque-|rour:	2528

OUER-VIEW = 1

Are we betrayed thus to thy ouer-view?	1513

OUGHT = 2

Els none at all in ought proues excellent.	1705
You will do ought, this shall you do for me:	2753

OUIDDIUS = *1

*facilitie, and golden cadence of poesie *caret*: *Ouiddius*	1287

OUNCE = *1

Clow. My sweete ounce of mans flesh, my in-conie Iew:	901

OUR *l.*6 15 17 76 173 182 190 *263 520 593 635 643 754 767 979
*1331 1536 1634 1664 1665 1666 1667 1668 1670 1712 1713 1737
*1852 1886 1948 2046 2073 2098 2105 *2108 2118 2230 2232 2270
2284 2358 *2364 2400 2406 2409 2412 2417 2465 *2673 2691 2692
2714 2715 2716 2726 2729 2730 2737 2740 2743 2744 2771 2835
2837 2851 = 63*6
OURS = 2
To make theirs ours, and ours none but our owne.   2046
OURSELFE *see* selfe
OURSELUES *see* selues
OUT *see also* Draw-out *l.*119 599 *806 *812 856 +8 861 882 907 957
1005 1124 1127 *1289 1409 1434 1672 1755 *1756 *1847 1908
1994 2061 2062 2069 *2185 2191 2194 2261 2327 2417 2488 *2529
2560 2573 2609 2689 = 29*8, 1
Out | Boy. True, out in deede.   2060
OUTFASTE = 1
Peda. But you haue outfaste them all.   2575
OUTSWEARE = *1
*I should outsweare *Cupid.* Comfort mee Boy, what great   370
OUTWARD = 1
When for Fames sake, for praise an outward part,   1007
OUTWEARE = 1
Till painefull studie shall outweare three yeeres,   514
OWE = 2
For still her cheekes possesse the same, | Which natiue she doth
owe   409
Of all perfections that a man may owe,   497
OWLE = 2*3
Bo. I feare too much rubbing: good night my good owle.   1135
*Owle and the Cuckow? it should haue followed in the   2850
*This *Ver*, the Spring: The one maynteined by the Owle, | th'other
by the Cuckow.   2856
Then nightly singes the staring Owle   2884
Then nightly singes the staring Owle,   2893
OWNE *see also* none = 16*6
That warre agaynst your owne affections,   13
That his owne hand may strike his honour downe,   24
On who the musique of his owne vaine tongue   177
A man of fier new wordes, Fashions owne knight.   189
Constab. Which is the Dukes owne person?   193
Const. I my selfe reprehend his owne person, for I am his   195
*graces Farborough: But I would see his owne person | in flesh
and blood. | *Ber.* This is he.   196
That euery one her owne hath garnished,   570
Your owne good thoughtes excuse me, and farewell.   673
Na. Thy owne wish wish I thee in euery place. *Exit.*   676
*Who tendring their owne worth from where they were | (glast,   748
His faces owne margent did coate such amazes,   750
And Wits owne grace to grace a learned Foole.   1962
Muster your Wits, stande in your owne defence,   1977
To make theirs ours, and ours none but our owne.   2046
In their owne shapes: for it can neuer be,   2209
If they returne in their owne shapes to woe?   2222
*will shew wher-vntill it doth amount: for mine owne part, I   2443
*the great: for mine owne part I know not the degree of the   2448
Brag. For mine owne part I breath free breath: I haue   2680
In their owne fashyon like a merriment.   2742

OWNE *cont.*
  Deaft with the clamours of their owne deare grones,   2825
OXE = 1
  Take all and weane it, it may proue an Oxe.   2165
PACKET = 1
  Boyet. So please your Grace, the packet is not come,   661
PAG = 8*5
PAGE see also Pag. = 7*2
  Enter Armado and Moth his page.   311
  Enter *Page* and *Clowne.*   840
  **A.* No Page, it is an epilogue or discourse to make plaine,   855
  And his Page atother side, that handfull of wit,   1146
  or ioynt) shall passe *Pompey* the great, the Page *Hercules.*   1861
  Their Heralde is a prettie knauish Page: 1989
  That put *Armathoes* Page out of his part.   2261
  You put our Page out: goe, you are aloude.   2417
  *parish Curate *Alexander, Armadoes* Page *Hercules,* the Pe-|dant   2479
PAGE = 6*5
PAGEANT = *1
  *or pageant, or antique, or fierworke: Now vnderstanding   1845
PAIDE = 1
  Of that which hath so faithfully been paide.   652
PAILE = 1
  And Milke coms frozen home in paile: 2882
PAIMENT = 1
  One paiment of a hundred thousand Crownes,   640
PAINE = 2
  That shall expresse my trueloues fasting paine.   1459
  And gentle *Longauill,* where lies thy paine?   1509
PAINED = 1
  To enforce the pained impotent to smile.   2815
PAINEFULL = 1
  Till painefull studie shall outweare three yeeres,   514
PAINT = 2
  Quee. Nay, neuer paint me now,   991
  Do paint the Meadowes with delight: 2863
PAINTED = 1*1
  Needes not the painted florish of your prayse: 505
  *you will be scrapt out of the painted cloth for this.   2529
PAINTER = 1
  Duma. Hee's a God or a Painter: for he makes faces.   2599
PAINTES = 1
  Paintes it selfe blacke, to imitate her brow.   1614
PAINTING = 1*1
  *man after the olde painting, and keepe not too long in one   789
  It mournes, that painting vsurping haire   1608
PALE = 3
  And feares by pale white showne: 406
  You may looke pale, but I should blush I know,   1466
  **Rosa.* Helpe holde his browes, heele sound: why looke | you
  pale?   2323
PALME = 1
  And by this Virgin palme now kissing thine,   2766
PAPER = 5*2
  Giue me the paper, let me reade the same,   125
  *He hath not eate paper as it were: he hath not drunke inck.   1176
  *deliuer this Paper into the royall hand of the King, it may   1306

PAPER *cont.*
Enter Berowne with a paper in his hand, alone.	1333
a paper, God giue him grace to grone.	1352
How shall she know my griefes? Ile drop the paper.	1374
As would be crambd vp in a sheete of paper	1894

PAPERS = 1
Berow. Why he comes in like a periure, wearing papers.	1380

PAPP = 1
him with thy Birdbolt vnder the left papp: in fayth secrets.	1356

PARADOX = 1
King. O paradox, Blacke is the badge of Hell,	1603

PARCELL = *1
Page. A holy parcell of the fayrest dames that euer turnd their | backes to mortall viewes.	2055

PARDON = 4*4
*And sin to breake it: but pardon me, I am too sodaine bold,	601
Forr. Pardon me Madam, for I meant not so.	987
*Vnder pardon sir, What are the contentes? or rather as *Hor-|race*	1262
Celestiall as thou art, Oh pardon loue this wrong,	1282
Ah good my Leidge, I pray thee pardon mee.	1489
Brag. Pardon sir, error: He is not quantitie enough for	1863
Quee. Pardon me sir, this Iewell did she weare,	2395
Brag. Gentlemen and Souldiers, pardon me, I will not | combat in my shyrt.	2659

PARDONE = *1
*smyling: O pardone me my starres, doth the incon-|siderate	850

PARDONED = 1
Ar. Villaine, thou shalt fast for thy offences ere thou be | pardoned.	449

PARENTES = *1
*the parentes of the foresaid childe or pupill, vndertake your	1321

PARFECT = *1
*am (as they say, but to parfect one man in one poore man) | *Pompion* the great sir.	2444

PARISH = *1
*parish Curate *Alexander, Armadoes* Page *Hercules,* the Pe-|dant	2479

PARISHIONERS = *1
Holo. Sir, I prayse the L.(ord) for you, and so may my parishi-|oners,	1237

PARK = *1
ground Which? which I meane I walkt vpon, it is ycliped Thy Park.	248

PARKE = 2*3
*vppon the Forme, and taken following her into the Parke:	218
*I do loue, that Countrey girle that I tooke in the Parke	421
*I must keepe her at the Parke, she is alowde for the Day | womand. Fare you well.	434
The Princesse comes to hunt here in the Parke,	929
Ber. First from the Parke let vs conduct them thither,	1725

PARLEE = 2
To parlee with the sole inheritoure	496
Their purpose is to parlee, to court, and daunce,	2014

PARRADISE = 2
To loose an oth, to winn a Parradise?	1406
You would for Parradise breake Fayth and troth,	1480

PARRATORS = 1
  Sole Emperator and great generall | Of trotting Parrators (O my
  litle hart.)   951
PARSON = *1
  *Iaque. Good M.(aister) Parson be so good as read me this letter,   1254
PARSONS = 1
  And coffing drownes the Parsons saw;   2889
PART = 9*5
  *Arm. How canst thou part sadnes and melancholy, my | tender
  Iuuenall?   318
  One part of Aquitaine is bound to vs,   631
  When for Fames sake, for praise an outward part,   1007
  thy picture, and my hart on thy euerie part.   1064
  *and heere is part of my Rime, and heare my mallicholie.   1347
  Marg. I, or I would these handes might neuer part.   1947
  And quite diuorce his memorie from his part.   2042
  King. Why take we handes then? | Rosa. Onely to part friendes.   2122
  Long. Let's part the word? | Mar. No, Ile not be your halfe: 2163
  That put Armathoes Page out of his part.   2261
  *will shew wher-vntill it doth amount: for mine owne part, I   2443
  *the great: for mine owne part I know not the degree of the   2448
  *Brag. For mine owne part I breath free breath: I haue   2680
  If this thou do deny, let our handes part,   2771
PARTES = 2*2
  *sensible in the duller partes: and such barren plantes are   1179
  *and feeling, are for those partes that doe fructifie in vs | more
  then he.   1181
  Which is to mee some prayse, that I thy partes admire,   1278
  King. The extreame partes of time extreamly formes,   2698
PARTIE = 3
  of the partie written to the person written vnto.   1299
  The partie is gone.   2627
  Which partie coted presence of loose loue   2724
PARTIES = *1
  *Clow. O Lord sir, the parties themselues, the actors sir   2442
PARTST = 1
  Ber. Welcome pure wit, thou partst a faire fray.   2425
PASHION = 1
  Saw sighes reeke from you, noted well your pashion.   1477
PASHIONS = 1
  To checke their follie pashions solembe teares.   2010
PASSADO = *1
  *my turne: Passado he respects not, the Duella he regards   481
PASSAGE = 1
  All vnseene, can passage finde: 1443
PASSE = 2*4
  Ferd. Your othe is past, to passe away from these.   53
  *betweene vs, let it passe. I do beseech thee remember thy   1831
  *deede too: but let that passe, for I must tell thee it will   1834
  *let that passe. By the world I recount no fable, some certaine   1838
  *let that passe; the very all of all is: but sweet hart, I do implore 1842
  or ioynt) shall passe Pompey the great, the Page Hercules.   1861
PASSES = 1
  She passes prayse, then prayse too short doth blot.   1590
PASSING = 1
  Spied a blossome passing faire,   1440

189

PASSION = 1*1
with, o with, but with this I passion to say wherewith: | *Clo.* With a
Wench. 261
**Long.* It did moue him to passion, & therfore lets heare it. 1545
PASSIONATE = *1
**Bra.* Warble child, make passionate my sense of hearing. | *Boy.*
Concolinel. 772
PAST = 6
Your othes are past, and now subscribe your names: 23
Ferd. Your othe is past, to passe away from these. 53
Ar. I say sing. | *Boy.* Forbeare till this companie be past. 428
Did poynt you to buy them along as you past. 749
Ros. Great reason: for past care, is still past cure. 1915
PASTIME = 1
We will with some strange pastime solace them: 1728
PASTIMES = 1
We haue had pastimes here and pleasant game, 2286
PASTURE = 1*1
**La.* You Sheepe and I pasture: shall that finish the iest? 723
Bo. So you graunt pasture for me. | *Lad.* Not so gentle Beast. 724
PATCH = *1
*So were there a patch set on Learning, to see him in a schole. 1185
PATES = 1
Fat paunches haue leane pates: and daynty bits 30
PATHETICAL = *1
**Ar.* Sweet inuocation of a child, most pretty & pathetical. 401
PATHETICALL = 1
Ah heauens, it is most patheticall nit. 1147
PATIENCE = 2*2
**Lon.* A high hope for a low heauen. God grant vs patience 206
*therfore I will say nothing: I thanke God I haue as little
pa-|tience 467
O mee, with what strickt patience haue I sat, 1502
Long. Ile stay with patience, but the time is long. 2796
PATRONE = *1
*Nauar, *my soules earthes God, and bodies fostring patrone:* 232
PAUCA = *2
*put it to them. But *Vir sapis qui pauca loquitur,* a soule Femi-
|nine saluteth vs. 1243
*Sir I do inuite you too, you shall not say me nay: *pauca verba.* 1329
PAUED = 1
Ber O if the streetes were paued with thine eyes, 1627
PAUILION = 2*1
Prin. Come, to our Pauilion, *Boyet* is disposde. 754
*to congratulate the Princesse at her Pauilion, in the *posteriors* 1822
From morne till night out of his Pauilion. 2609
PAUNCHES = 1
Fat paunches haue leane pates: and daynty bits 30
PAY = 1
Pay him the due of honie-tonged *Boyet.* 2259
PAYMENT = 2
The payment of a hundred thousand Crownes, 625
Faire payment for foule wordes, is more then dew. 994
PAYNE = 3
Which with payne purchas'd, doth inherite payne, 78
Ber. Lets see the penaltie. On payne of loosing her tung. 132

PAYNEFULLY = 1
As paynefully to poare vpon a Booke,   79
PAYNTED = 1
Fie paynted Rethoricke, O shee needes it not,   1588
PAYNTING = 1
For natiue blood is counted paynting now: 1612
PEACE = 9*4
*Cost. It may be so: but if he say it is so, he is in telling true: |
but so. | Ferd. Peace.   236
The treason and you goe in peace away togeather.   1534
Brag. Men of peace well incontred. | Ped. Most millitarie sir
salutation.   1774
Page. Peace, the peale begins.   1783
Against your Peace Loue doth approch, disguysd: 1975
Berow. Nothing but peace, and gentle visitation.   2077
Rosa. What would they, say they? | Boy. Nothing but peace, and
gentle visitation.   2078
Bero. Peace, for I will not haue to doe with you.   2361
*Quee. Peace peace, forbeare: your Oth once broke, you | force
not to forsweare.   2377
Bero. Loe, he is tilting straight. Peace, I haue don.   2423
*to Fortuna delaguar, I wish you the peace of mind most royall |
cupplement. Exit.   2475
*Brag. Peace. The Armipotent Mars, of Launces the almighty,   2606
PEALE = 1
Page. Peace, the peale begins.   1783
PEARCE = *1
*Bero. Honest plaine words, best pearce the eare of griefe,   2711
PEARLE = 2*1
*in a turph of Earth, Fier enough for a Flint, Pearle enough   1252
Marg. This, and these Pearle, to me sent Longauile.   1943
What? will you haue me, or your Pearle againe?   2397
PEARST = 1
The prayfull Princesse pearst and prickt | a prettie pleasing
Pricket,   1215
PEASE = 1
Berow. This fellow peckes vp Wit as Pidgions Pease,   2240
PECAS = *1
*Nath. Facile precor gellida, quando pecas omnia sub vmbra
ru- | minat,   1257
PECK = *1
*most grase, Birdes best peck, and Men sit downe to that
nourishment   246
PECKES = 1
Berow. This fellow peckes vp Wit as Pidgions Pease,   2240
PED = 2*4
PEDA = 19*9
PEDAN = 5*1
PEDANT see also Ped., Peda., Pedan. = 3*3
*A domineering pedant ore the Boy, then whom no mor- | tall so
magnificent.   943
Enter Dull, Holofernes, the Pedant and Nathaniel.   1150
Enter the Pedant, the Curat, and Dull.   1739
*parish Curate Alexander, Armadoes Page Hercules, the Pe- | dant   2479
*Bero. The Pedant, the Bragart, the Hedge-Priest, the | Foole,
and the Boy,   2485
Enter Pedant for Iudas, and the Boy for Hercules.   2540

PEDANT = 1
PEDANTICALL = 1
  Figures pedanticall, these sommer flies,   2340
PEDLER = 1
  He is Witts Pedler, and retales his wares: 2242
PEECE = *1
  Arma. True. | *Boy.* Why sir is this such a peece of studie? Now
heere is   357
PEECES = 1
  Cut me to peeces with thy keene conceit.   2331
PEEPING = 1
  To the court of his eye, peeping thorough desier.   739
PEERELESSE = 1
  A man of soueraigne peerelesse he is esteemd: 536
PELL = 1
  Pell, mell, downe with them: but be first aduisd,   1719
PEN = 2*2
  & most propostrous euent that draweth fro(m) my snowhite pen
  the   251
  *Wit, write Pen, for I am for whole volumes in folio. *Exit.* 486
  Nath. Marueilous well for the pen.   1317
  Neuer durst Poet touch a pen to write,   1697
PENALTIE = 3
  Ber. Lets see the penaltie. On payne of loosing her tung. 132
  Who deuis'd this penaltie? | *Long.* Marrie that did I.   134
  Bero. Sweete Lord and why? | *Long.* To fright them hence with
that dread penaltie.   136
PENANCE = *1
  *safe, and you must suffer him to take no delight, nor no
pe-|nance,   432
PEND = 2
  Nor to their perid speach render we no grace: 2039
  O neuer will trust to speaches pend,   2334
PENDE = 1
  Their shallow showes, and Prologue vildly pende. 2228
PENNANCE = 2
  And bide the pennance of each three yeeres day.   124
  I goe Woolward for pennance.   2666
PENNE = 1
  Boy. By my penne of obseruation. | *Brag.* But o but o. 796
PENNIE *see also* i.d. = *1
  Bero. My hat to a halfe-pennie, *Pompey* prooues the best |
Worthie.   2509
PENNY-WORTH = 1
  Sir, your penny-worth is good, and your Goose be fat. 866
PENSALLS = *1
  Ros. Ware pensalls, How? Let me not die your debtor, 1931
PENT = 1
  Clo. Let me not be pent vp sir, I will fast being loose. 458
PENTHOUSE = *1
  *smelling loue with your hat penthouse like ore the shop of 786
PENY = *1
  Clow. And I had but one peny in the world thou shouldst 1807
PEOPLE = 2
  Or Pricket-sore, or els Sorell, | the people fall a hooting. 1221
  But seeke the weery beddes of people sicke.   2782

PERCHANCE = 1
    Lon. Perchance light in the light. I desire her name?   697
PEREGRINAT = 1
    to od as it were, too peregrinat as I may call it.   1752
PEREMPTORIE = *1
    *discourse peremptorie: his tongue fyled, his eye ambitious,   1749
PERFECT *see also* parfect = *1
    Clo. Tis not so much worth: but I hope I was perfect. I | made a
litle fault in great.   2507
PERFECTIONS = 1
    Of all perfections that a man may owe,   497
PERFECTNES = 1
    Ber. Is this your perfectnes? begon you rogue.   2070
PERGE = *2
    Nath. Perge, good M.(aister) *Holofernes perge*, so it shall please |
you to abrogate squirilitie.   1211
PERHAPS = 2
    loue perhaps, a hacknie: But haue you forgot your Loue?   801
    And trow you what he calde me? | *Quee.* Qualme perhaps.   2198
PERIGORT = 1
    Betweene L.(ord) *Perigort* and the bewtious heire | Of *Iaques
Fauconbridge* solemnized.   533
PERISH = 1
    When great thinges labouring perish in their byrth.   2464
PERIURD = 2
    Long. Am I the first that haue been periurd so?   1383
    Nor God nor I delights in periurd men.   2272
PERIURDE = 5
    For youle proue periurde if you make me staie.   608
    Nay to be periurde, which is worst of all: 960
    Would from my forehead wipe a periurde note: 1462
    Youle not be periurde, tis a hatefull thing: 1494
    No nò my Lord, your Grace is periurde much,   2750
PERIURE = 1
    Berow. Why he comes in like a periure, wearing papers.   1380
PERIURIE = 4*1
    Perswade my hart to this false periurie?   1395
    Duma. Some salue for periurie. | *Ber.* O tis more then neede.   1638
    Bero. Thus pooure the Starres downe plagues for periurie.   2326
    Now to our periurie, to add more terror,   2409
    You are attaint with faultes and periurie: 2779
PERNICIOUS = *1
    *King *Cophetua* set eie vpon the pernicious and indubitate   1046
PEROMPTORIE = 1
    What peromptorie Eagle-sighted eye   1575
PERPLEXITIE = 1
    Quee. Auaunt perplexitie, What shall we do,   2221
PERRECHE = *1
    te vnde, que non te perreche. Olde *Mantuan*, olde *Mantuan*,   1260
PERSING = *1
    Nath. Of persing a Hogshead, a good luster of conceit   1251
PERSON = 4*5
    Constab. Which is the Dukes owne person?   193
    Const. I my selfe reprehend his owne person, for I am his   195
    *graces Farborough: But I would see his owne person | in flesh
and blood. | *Ber.* This is he.   196

PERSON *cont.*
  *Enfreedoming thy person: thou wert emured, restrained, |
  captiuated, bound. 890
  Iaquenetta. God giue you good morrow M.(aister) Person. 1246
  * *Nath.* Maister Person, *quasi* Person? And if one shoulde 1247
  of the partie written to the person written vnto. 1299
  Our person misdoubts it: twas treason he said. 1536
PERSONALL = 1
  Importuous personall conference with his grace. 523
PERST = 1
  be perst, Which is the one? 1248
PERSWADE = 1
  Perswade my hart to this false periurie? 1395
PERT = 1
  This pert *Berowne* was out of countnance quite. 2191
PERTTAUNT = 1
  So perttaunt like would I ore'sway his state, 1957
PETICIONER = 1
  Rosa. O vaine peticioner, begg a greater matter, 2106
PHANATTICALL = *1
  *then the staple of his argument. I abhorre such phanatticall 1757
PHANTASIME = 1
  A Phantasime a Monarcho, and one that makes sport | To the
  Prince and his Booke-mates. 1080
PHANTASIMS = *1
  *phantasims, such insociable and poynt deuise companions, 1758
PHEBE = 1
  Dul. What is *dictima*? | *Nath.* A title to *Phebe*, to *Luna*, to the
  Moone. 1194
PHILOSOPHIE = 1
  With all these lyuing in Philosophie. 36
PHISICKE = 1*1
  * *commende the blacke oppressing humour to the most holsome
  phisicke* 243
  Ber. Would that do it good? | *Ros.* My Phisicke saies I. 684
PHRASES = 2
  That hath a mint of phrases in his braine: 176
  Taffata phrases, silken tearmes precise, 2338
PICKE = 1
  Cannot picke out fiue such, take each one in his vaine. 2488
PICKED = *1
  *& thrasonicall. He is too picked, to spruce, too affected, 1751
PICK-PURSES = 1
  Are pick-purses in Loue, and we deserue to die. 1555
PICTURE = 2
  thy picture, and my hart on thy euerie part. 1064
  O he hath drawen my picture in his letter. | *Quee.* Any thing like? 1926
PIDGIN-EGGE = *1
  *purse of wit, thou Pidgin-egge of discretion. O and the 1810
PIDGIONS = 1
  Berow. This fellow peckes vp Wit as Pidgions Pease, 2240
PIECE *see* peece
PIECES *see* peeces
PIED = 1
  The Song. | When Dasies pied, and Violets blew, 2859
PIERCE *see* pearce

PIERCING *see* persing
PIERCT *see* pearst, perst
PILDE = 1
    Three pilde Hiberboles, spruce affection: 2339
PIN = 1*1
    *care a pin, if the other three were in. Heere comes one with   1351
    And *Nestor* play at push-pin with the boyes,   1506
PINE = 2
    The minde shall banquet, though the body pine,   29
    To loue, to wealth, to pompe, I pine and die,   35
PINS = 1
    This Gallant pins the Wenches on his sleeue.   2246
PIPE = 1
    When Shepheards pipe on Oten Strawes,   2869
PIPPEN = *1
    *was a man when King *Pippen* of Fraunce was a litle boy, as |
    touching the hit it.   1109
PITCH *see also* pytch = 1
    With two pitch balles stucke in her face for eyes.   963
PITCHT = *1
    *They haue pitcht a Toyle, I am toyling in a pytch, pytch   1336
PITTIE = 1*1
    Not wounding, pittie would not let me doote.   1002
    Clow. O Lord sir, it were pittie you should get your liuing | by
    reckning sir.   2439
PLACCATS = 1
    Dread Prince of Placcats, King of Codpeeces.   950
PLACE = 3*2
    Duma. How followes that? | *Ber.* Fit in his place and tyme. 105
    Then for the place Where? where I meane, I did incounter that
    ob-| seene   250
    seest. But to the place Where? It standeth North North-east & by
    Na. Thy owne wish wish I thee in euery place. *Exit.*   676
    Most rude melancholie, Valour giues thee place.   838
PLAGUE = 2
    To pray for her, go to: it is a plague   967
    They haue the Plague, and caught it of your eyes,   2354
PLAGUES = 1*1
    Light Wenches may proue plagues to men forsworne,   1736
    Bero. Thus pooure the Starres downe plagues for periurie. 2326
PLAIDE = 1
    Plaide fouleplay with our othes: your beautie Ladies   2714
PLAINE = 8*3
    *O sir, Plantan, a plaine Plantan: no *lenuoy*, no *lenuoy*, no Salue |
    sir, but a Plantan.   846
    A. No Page, it is an epilogue or discourse to make plaine, 855
    This will I send, and something els more plaine.   1458
    King. Twere good yours did: for sir to tell you plaine,   1621
    Long. Now to plaine dealing, Lay these glozes by,   1721
    That some plaine man recount their purposes.   2074
    Ros. Well, better wits haue worne plaine statute Caps,   2202
    Rosal. By heauen you did; and to confirme it plaine,   2391
    My Scutchion plaine declares that I am Alisander.   2515
    Dum. Iudas Machabeus *clipt, is plaine* Iudas.   2552
    Bero. Honest plaine words, best pearce the eare of griefe, 2711
PLANT = 1
    And plant in Tyrants milde humilitie.   1700

PLANTAN = 1*3
  *O sir, Plantan, a plaine Plantan: no *lenuoy*, no *lenuoy*, no Salue |
  sir, but a Plantan.   846
  Clow. True, and I for a Plantan, thus came your argument | (in,   873
PLANTED = 1
  A man in all the worldes new fashion planted,   175
PLANTES = *1
  *sensible in the duller partes: and such barren plantes are   1179
PLAY = 10*2
  That aged eares play treuant at his tales,   566
  That we must stand and play the murtherer in?   982
  And he from forrage will incline to play.   1071
  Berow. All hid, all hid, an olde infant play,   1412
  And *Nestor* play at push-pin with the boyes,   1506
  Brag. For the rest of the Worthies? | *Peda.* I will play three my
  selfe.   1873
  Dull. Ile make one in a daunce, or so: or I will play on   1884
  Rosa. Play Musique then: nay you must do it soone.   2110
  Ile play no more with you.   2141
  Clow. Faith vnlesse you play the honest *Troyan*, the poore   2631
  Berow. Our wooing doth not ende like an olde Play: 2835
  Berow. That's too long for a Play.   2840
PLAYED = 1
  Quee. Well bandied both, a set of Wit well played.   1916
PLAYES = 1*1
  Rosa. The musique playes, vouchsafe some motion to it,   2117
  That when he playes at Tables chides the Dice   2251
PLAYING = 1
  Playing in the wanton aire: 1441
PLEA = 1
  Matchles *Nauar*, the plea of no lesse weight,   498
PLEASANT = 2*1
  *haue been sharpe & sententious: pleasant without scurillitie,   1742
  We haue had pastimes here and pleasant game,   2286
  At courtshyp pleasant iest and courtecie,   2738
PLEASD = 1
  Rosa. In priuat then. | *King.* I am best pleasd with that.   2133
PLEASE = 7*6
  Berow. Let me say no my liedge, and yf you please,   54
  Studie me how to please the eye in deede,   85
  Antho. Me ant shall please you? I am *Anthony Dull.*   268
  Boyet. So please your Grace, the packet is not come,   661
  Nath. Perge, good M.(aister) *Holofernes perge*, so it shall please |
  you to abrogate squirilitie.   1211
  *coloures. But to returne to the Verses, Did they please you | sir
  Nathaniel?   1315
  *mine, where if (before repast) it shall please you to gratifie   1319
  *please his Grace (by the worlde) sometime to leane vpon   1835
  Duma. Please it you, as much in priuat, & ile bid adieu.   2152
  Boyet. Gone to her Tent. Please it your Maiestie com-|maunde   2236
  And vtters it againe when God dooth please.   2241
  *There ant shall please you a foolish mylde man, an   2533
  And therewithall to winne me, yf you please,   2809
PLEASED = *2
  *heauens were so pleased, that thou wart but my Ba-|stard;   1811
  Clow. It pleased them to thinke me worthie of *Pompey*   2447

PLEASES = 1
That sport best pleases, that doth best know how: 2460
PLEASETH = *1
*special honours it pleaseth his greatnes to impart to *Armado*   1839
PLEASE-MAN = 1
Some carry tale, some please-man, some sleight saine: 2402
PLEASING = 1
The prayfull Princesse pearst and prickt | a prettie pleasing
Pricket,   1215
PLEASUR = *1
Bra. Sir, it is the Kings most sweete pleasur & affection,   1821
PLEASURE = 2*1
Constab. Sir, the Dukes pleasure is that you keepe *Costard*   431
To know his pleasure, and in that behalfe   518
Brag. At your sweete pleasure, for the Mountaine.   1819
PLEASURES = *1
*Where all those pleasures liue, that Art would comprehend.   1273
PLEASURS = 1
Remote from all the pleasurs of the world: 2756
PLENTIFULLY = 1
Yf Fayrings come thus plentifully in.   1889
PLESANT = 1
Clo. By my troth most plesant, how both did fit it.   1118
PLIGHTED = 1
Quee. And quicke *Berowne* hath plighted Fayth to me.   2204
PLODDERS = 1
Small haue continuall plodders euer wonne,   91
PLODDING = 1
Why vniuersall plodding poysons vp | The nimble spirites in the
arteries,   1655
PLOUGH = 1
To holde the Plough for her sweete loue three yeere.   2847
PLOUGHMENS = 1
And merrie Larkes are Ploughmens Clocks: 2870
PLUCK = 1
Youth so apt to pluck a sweete.   1451
PLUCKE = 1
Nere to plucke thee from thy throne: 1449
PLUME = *1
Quee. What plume of fethers is he that indited this letter?   1074
POARE = 2
As paynefully to poare vpon a Booke,   79
Can you still dreame and poare and thereon looke.   1648
POCKET = *1
*like a Rabbet on a spit, or your handes in your pocket like a   788
POESIE = *1
*facilitie, and golden cadence of poesie *caret*: *Ouiddius*   1287
POET = 1
Neuer durst Poet touch a pen to write,   1697
POETRIE = *1
*neither sauouring of Poetrie, wit, nor inuention.   1323
POLAX = *1
*Your Lion that holdes his Polax sitting on a close stoole,   2530
POLE = 1*1
Brag. By the North Pole I do challenge thee.   2649
Clow. I will not fight with a Pole like a Northren man;   2650

197

POLICIE = *1
*Bero. We are shame proofe my Lord: & tis some policie   2455
POLUSION = *1
*Dul. And I say the polusion holdes in the Exchange: for   1204
POMPE = 1
To loue, to wealth, to pompe, I pine and die,   35
POMPEY = 16*7
or ioynt) shall passe *Pompey* the great, the Page *Hercules.*   1861
*Clow. It pleased them to thinke me worthie of *Pompey*   2447
*He presents *Hector* of *Troy*, the Swaine *Pompey* the great, the   2478
Enter Pompey.   2490
Clowne. I *Pompey* am. | Bero. You lie, you are not he.   2491
Clow. I *Pompey* am, | Boyet. With Libbards head on knee.   2493
Clow. I *Pompey* am, *Pompey* surnamde the bigge. | Duma. The
great.   2497
Clow. It is great sir, Pompey *surnamd the great.*   2499
If your Ladishyp would say thankes Pompey, I had done.   2505
Lady. Great thankes great *Pompey.*   2506
*Bero. My hat to a halfe-pennie, *Pompey* prooues the best |
Worthie.   2509
Bero. Pompey the great. | Clow. Your seruant and *Costard.*   2525
Quee. Stand aside good *Pompey.*   2539
quicke by him, and hangd for *Pompey* that is dead by him.   2637
Duma. Most rare *Pompey.*   2639
Boyet. Renowned *Pompey.*   2640
*Bero. Greater then great, great, great, great *Pompey*: Pom-|pey
the hudge.   2641
*Bero. *Pompey* is mooued more Ates more Atees stir them, | or
stir them on.   2644
Clow. Ile do it in my shyrt. | Duma. Most resolute *Pompey.*   2654
*you not see, *Pompey* is vncasing for the Combat: What   2657
Duma. You may not deny it, *Pompey* hath made the chal-|(lenge.   2661
POMPION = 1
*am (as they say, but to parfect one man in one poore man) |
Pompion the great sir.   2444
POMWATER = *1
*as the Pomwater, who now hangeth like a Iewel in the eare   1154
POORE = 5*3
The poore Deares blood, that my hart meanes no ill.   1010
But if thou striue (poore soule) what art thou then?   1072
*my poore shoulder, and with his royall finger thus dallie   1836
Quee. O pouertie in wit, Kingly poore flout.   2188
Wise thinges seeme foolish, and rich thinges but poore.   2305
*am (as they say, but to parfect one man in one poore man) |
Pompion the great sir.   2444
Quee. Alas poore *Machabeus*, how hath he bin bayted.   2585
*Clow. Faith vnlesse you play the honest *Troyan*, the poore   2631
POOURE = *1
*Bero. Thus pooure the Starres downe plagues for periurie.   2326
PORRIDGE = *1
*Clo. I had rather pray a month with Mutton & Porridge.   297
PORTER = 1
like a Porter: and he was in loue.   378
POSSESSE = 2
For still her cheekes possesse the same, | Which natiue she doth
owe   409

POSSESSE *cont.*
  Ber. O, I am yours and all that I possesse. | *Rosa.* All the foole
  mine.   2310
POSSIBLE = 1
  shame as the rest of the Court can possible deuise.   141
POST = 1
  Ber. I post from Loue, good Louer let me go.   1526
POSTERIOR = *2
  * *Peda.* The *posterior* of the day, most generous sir, is liable,   1825
  *some show in the posterior of this day, to be rended by our   1852
POSTERIORS = *1
  *to congratulate the Princesse at her Pauilion, in the *posteriors*   1822
POT = 2
  While greasie Ione doth keele the pot.   2887
  While greasie Ione doth keele the pot.   2896
POTENTATES = 1
  Brag. Dost thou infamonize me among potentates: 2634
POUERTIE = 2
  Quee. O pouertie in wit, Kingly poore flout.   2188
  Bero. I am a foole, and full of pouertie.   2307
POWER = 7*1
  Whose edge hath power to cut whose will still wils,   542
  It should none spare, that come within his power.   543
  Most power to do most harme, least knowing ill: 550
  * *Long.* I feare these stubborne lines lacke power to moue.   1387
  Courses as swift as thought in euery power,   1681
  And giues to euery power a double power,   1682
  Since all the power thereof it doth apply,   1967
POWERS = 1
  To flatter vp these powers of mine with rest,   2774
POXE = 1
  Quee. A Poxe of that iest, and I beshrow all Shrowes,   1934
POYNT = 3*1
  Ber. Will you prickt with your eye. | *Ros. No poynt,* with my
  knife.   686
  Did poynt you to buy them along as you past.   749
  *phantasims, such insociable and poynt deuise companions,   1758
  No poynt (quoth I) my seruant, straight was mute.   2196
POYSONS = 1
  Why vniuersall plodding poysons vp | The nimble spirites in the
  arteries,   1655
PRACTISE = 1
  And goe we Lordes to put in practise that,   301
PRACTIZERS = 1
  And therefore finding barraine practizers,   1676
PRAISE = 15*1
  Boy. Speake you this in my praise Maister?   335
  Arma. In thy condigne praise.   336
  Boy. I will praise an Eele with the same praise.   337
  With such bedecking ornaments of praise.   571
  * *Quee.* What, what? First praise mee, and againe say no.   988
  Where faire is not, praise cannot mend the brow.   992
  A giuing hand, though fowle, shall haue faire praise.   998
  That more for praise, then purpose meant to kill.   1004
  When for Fames sake, for praise an outward part,   1007
  As I for praise alone now seeke to spill   1009

PRAISE *cont.*

Onely for praise sake, when they striue to be | Lords ore their
Lordes?   1012
Quee. Onely for praise, and praise we may afford,   1014
Ros. Much in the letters, nothing in the praise.   1928
My Ladie (to the maner of the dayes) | In curtesie giues
vndeseruing praise.   2292

PRAY = 7*4

Clo. I had rather pray a month with Mutton & Porridge.   297
Ros. Pray you, do my commendations, I would be glad | to see
it.   678
Dum. Sir, I pray you a word, What Ladie is that same?   692
Lon. Pray you sir, Whose daughter?   700
Clow. Pray you sir, How much Carnation Ribbon may   911
To pray for her, go to: it is a plague   967
Well, I will loue, write, sigh, pray, shue, grone,   970
Clo. God dig-you-den al, pray you which is the head lady?   1018
Gainst thee thou Lambe, that standest as his pray: 1069
Ah good my Leidge, I pray thee pardon mee.   1489
Rosa. Sans, sans, I pray you.   2348

PRAYFULL = 1

The prayfull Princesse pearst and prickt | a prettie pleasing
Pricket,   1215

PRAYSE = 7*4

Needes not the painted florish of your prayse: 505
In spending your Wit in the prayse of mine.   510
Holo. Sir, I prayse the L.(ord) for you, and so may my
parishi- | oners,   1237
Which is to mee some prayse, that I thy partes admire,   1278
That singes heauens prayse, with such an earthly tong.   1283
*In pruning mee when shall you heare that I will prayse a   1521
To thinges of sale, a sellers prayse belonges: 1589
She passes prayse, then prayse too short doth blot.   1590
Curat. I prayse God for you sir, your reasons at Dinner   1741
*that the two Learned men haue compiled, in prayse of the   2849

PRAYSES = 1

Making the bolde wagg by their prayses bolder.   2000

PREAMBULAT = *1

Brag. Arts-man preambulat, we will be singuled from the   1815

PRECIOUS = 3

Your selfe, helde precious in the worldes esteeme,   495
It addes a precious seeing to the eye: 1684
As precious ey-sight, and did value me   2383

PRECISE = 1

Taffata phrases, silken tearmes precise,   2338

PRECISELY = 1

Arm. Tell me precisely of what complexion? | *Boy.* Of the sea-
water Greene sir.   387

PRECOR = *1

Nath. Facile precor gellida, quando pecas omnia sub vmbra
ru- | minat,   1257

PREPARE = 5

Quee. Thy newes *Boyet*? | *Boy.* Prepare Maddame, prepare.   1972
Bero. Goe bid them prepare. (*Exit.*   2450
Quee. Boyet prepare, I will away to nyght.   2685
Quee. Prepare I say: I thanke you gracious Lords   2687

PRESCIAN = *1
   Curat. Laus deo, bene intelligo. | * *Peda. Bome boon for boon
   prescian*, a litle scratcht, twil serue.   ·   1766
PRESEDENCE = 1
   Some obscure presedence that hath tofore bin saine.   856
PRESEDENT = *1
   *example my digression by some mightie presedent. Boy,   420
PRESENCE = 3
   Presence maiesticall would put him out: 1994
   King. Heere is like to be a good presence of Worthies: 2477
   Which partie coted presence of loose loue   2724
PRESENT = 3*5
   Thendeuour of this present breath may buy: 9
   King. What present hast thou there? | *Clow.* Some certaine
   treason.   1529
   *secrecie, that the King would haue me present the Princesse   1843
   * *Peda.* Sir, you shall present before her the Nine Worthies,   1850
   none so fit as to present the nine Worthies.   .   1855
   * *Curat.* Where will you finde men worthie enough to pre-|sent
   them?   1857
   * *Peda.* Shall I haue audience? He shall present *Hercules*   1866
   *first shew thriue, these foure will change habites, and present |
   the other fiue.   2481
PRESENTED = 2
   Should be presented at our Tent to vs.   2230
   Peda. Great Hercules *is presented by this Impe,*   2541
PRESENTES = 1
   Dies in the zeale of that which it presentes: 2462
PRESENTS *see also* pursents = *1
   *He presents *Hector* of *Troy*, the Swaine *Pompey* the great, the   2478
PRETIA *see* perreche
PRETTIE = 9*1
   olde time, which we may name tough. | *Arma.* Prettie and apt.   328
   Boy. How meane you sir, I prettie, and my saying apt?   330
   or I apt, and my saying prettie?   331
   Arma. Thou prettie because little.   332
   Boy. Little prettie, because little: wherefore apt.   333
   * *Brag.* The meaning prettie ingenius, is not Lead a mettal |
   heauie, dull, and slow?   826
   The prayfull Princesse pearst and prickt | a prettie pleasing
   Pricket,   1215
   for a Swine: tis prettie, it is well.   1253
   Their Heralde is a prettie knauish Page: 1989
   Boyet. Madame, and prettie mistresses giue eare.   2207
PRETTY = *1
   * *Ar.* Sweet inuocation of a child, most pretty & pathetical.   401
PREY *see* pray
PRI = *1
PRICE = 1*1
   *Three-farthings remuneration, What's the price of this yncle?   904
   Rosa. We can affoord no more at such a price.   2126
PRICK = 1
   Let the mark haue a prick in't, to meate at, if it may be.   1123
PRICKES = *1
   duetie prickes me on) *haue sent to thee, to receiue the meede of
   pu-| nishment*   265

PRICKET = 4*1
   Dul. Twas not a *haud credo*, twas a Pricket. 1162
   *Dul. I said the Deare was not a *haud credo*, twas a Pricket. 1170
   that, twas a Pricket that the Princesse kild. 1206
   cald the Deare: the Princesse kild a Pricket. 1209
   The prayfull Princesse pearst and prickt | a prettie pleasing
   Pricket, 1215
PRICKET-SORE = 1
   Or Pricket-sore, or els Sorell, | the people fall a hooting. 1221
PRICKS = *1
   *Cl. Shes to hard for you at pricks, sir challeng her to bowle 1133
PRICKT = 2
   Ber. Will you prickt with your eye. | *Ros. No poynt,* with my
   knife. 686
   The prayfull Princesse pearst and prickt | a prettie pleasing
   Pricket, 1215
PRIDE = 4
   Prince. All pride is willing pride, and yours is so: 527
   Proud with his forme, in his eye pride expressed. 741
   O short liu'd pride. Not faire? alacke for woe | *For.* Yes Madam
   faire. 989
PRIEST = *1
   *Bero. The Pedant, the Bragart, the Hedge-Priest, the | Foole,
   and the Boy, 2485
PRIMATER = *1
   **the ventricle of Memorie, nourisht in the wombe of prima-|ter, 1233
PRIN = 15*1
PRINC = 2
PRINCE see also Pri., Prin., Princ. = 4
   Prince. All pride is willing pride, and yours is so: 527
   As Iewels in Christall for some Prince to buy. 747
   Dread Prince of Placcats, King of Codpeeces. 950
   A Phantasime a Monarcho, and one that makes sport | To the
   Prince and his Booke-mates. 1080
PRINCELY = 1
   Submissiue fall his princely feete before, 1070
PRINCES = 1
   Boyet. What would you with the Princes? 2076
PRINCESSE = 14*3
   Or vainely comes th'admired Princesse hither. 150
   Enter the Princesse of Fraunce, with three | attending Ladies and
   three Lordes. 490
   Nauar. Faire Princesse, Welcome to the court of *Nauar.* 585
   Deare Princesse were not his requestes so farr 645
   You may not come (faire Princesse) within my gates, 669
   The Princesse comes to hunt here in the Parke, 929
   Enter the Princesse, a Forrester, her Ladyes, | and her Lordes. 973
   that, twas a Pricket that the Princesse kild. 1206
   cald the Deare: the Princesse kild a Pricket. 1209
   The prayfull Princesse pearst and prickt | a prettie pleasing
   Pricket, 1215
   There is no certaine Princesse that appeares. 1493
   *to congratulate the Princesse at her Pauilion, in the *posteriors* 1822
   *secrecie, that the King would haue me present the Princesse 1843
   *and learned Gentleman, before the Princesse: I say 1854
   And manie miles: the Princesse bids you tell, 2090
   King. Faire sir, God saue you: Wher's the Princesse? 2235

PRINCESSE *cont.*

King. My faith and this, the Princesse I did giue,	2393

PRINT = 2

His hart like an Agot with your print impressed, | 740
do it sir in print: gardon remuneration. | *Exit.* | 937

PRISE = *1

King. Prise you your selues: What buyes your company? | 2127

PRISON = 1

Boy. No sir, that were fast and loose: thou shalt to prison. | 460

PRISONER = *1

*Desire prisoner, and ransome him to anie French Courtier | 367

PRISONERS = *1

*It is not for prisoners to be too silent in their wordes, and | 466

PRIUAT = 2

Rosa. In priuat then. | *King.* I am best pleasd with that. | 2133
Duma. Please it you, as much in priuat, & ile bid adieu. | 2152

PRIUATE = 1

Long. One word in priuate with you ere I die. | 2170

PRIUILEDGE = *1

*the table with a Grace, I will on my priuiledge I haue with | 1320

PROCEED = *2

Be. Shot by heauen, proceed sweet *Cupid*, thou hast thumpt | 1355
Qu. The conqueror is dismaid: proceed good *Alexander.* | 2520

PROCEEDE = 1

Long. O some authoritie how to proceede, | 1636

PROCEEDED = 1

Dum. Proceeded well, to stop all good proceeding. | 100

PROCEEDING = 1

Dum. Proceeded well, to stop all good proceeding. | 100

PROCESSE = 1

That, which long processe could not arbitrate. | 2701

PROCLAIMED = 2

Fer. Well, it was proclaimed Damsel. | 287
Ber. It is so varried to, for it was proclaimed Virgin. | 290

PROCLAMATION = 1

Fer. Did you heare the Proclamation? | 280

PROCLAYMED = 1*2

my Court. Hath this bin proclaymed? | 129
*thy established proclaymed Edict and continent Cannon: Which | 260
Fer. It was proclaymed a yeeres imprisonment to be ta-|ken with
a Wench. | 283

PROCLAYMES = 1

Proclaymes you for a man repleat with mockes, | 2804

PRODIGALL = 2

Be now as prodigall of all Deare grace, | 500
And spend his prodigall wittes in booteles rimes, | 1954

PRODIGALLY = 1

And prodigally gaue them all to you. | 503

PRODUCE = 1

Boyet you can produce acquittances, | 657

PROFITABLE = 1

Is not by much so holdsome profitable, | 2708

PROFITE = 1*1

Haue no more profite of their shyning nights, | 95
*Daughters profite very greatly vnder you: you are a good |
member of the common wealth. | 1239

PROFOUND = 2
And profound *Sallomon* to tune a Iigge. 1505
A hudge translation of hipocrisie, | Vildly compyled, profound
· simplicitie. 1941
PROFUND = 1
With such a zelous laughter so profund, 2008
PROGENIE = 1
And though the mourning brow of progenie 2702
PROGRESSION = *1
*of progression, hath miscarried. Trip and goe my sweete, 1305
PROLOGUE = 1
Their shallow showes, and Prologue vildly pende. 2228
PROMETHEAN = 2
From whence doth spring the true *Promethean* fire. 1654
They sparcle still the right promethean fier, 1702
PROMISED = *1
Ar. I haue promised to studie three yeeres with the duke. 345
PROMPTING = 1
Such fierie Numbers as the prompting eyes, 1673
PRONOUNCE = *2
Fer. Sir I will pronounce your sentence: You shall fast a | weeke
with Branne and Water. 295
*should say doubt; det, when he shold pronounce debt; debt, 1760
PROOFE = *1
Bero. We are shame proofe my Lord: & tis some policie 2455
PROOUED = *1
*as *Aiax*, it kills Sheepe, it kills mee, I a Sheepe well prooued 1340
PROOUES = *1
Bero. My hat to a halfe-pennie, *Pompey* prooues the best |
Worthie. 2509
PROPHANE = 1*1
*thy replie, I prophane my lippes on thy foote, my eyes on 1063
Berow. O most prophane coxcombe. 1418
PROPOSTROUS = *1
*& most propostrous euent that draweth fro(m) my snowhite pen
the* 251
PROSE = 1
These numbers will I teare, and write in prose. 1389
PROSPERITIE = 1*1
*welcome the sower Cup of prosperitie, affliccio(n) may one day 308
A iestes prosperitie lies in the eare, 2822
PROTEST = 5
But I protest I loue to heare him lie, 186
Ferd. I do protest I neuer heard of it: 653
Now by my maiden honour yet as pure, | As the vnsallied Lilly I
protest, 2277
I do forsweare them, and I here protest, 2342
For I protest, the Schoolemaister is exceeding fantasticall, 2473
PROTESTATION = 1
Berowne. I can but say their protestation ouer, 37
PROUD = 3
Boy. Proud of imployment, willingly I go. *Exit Boy.* 526
Proud with his forme, in his eye pride expressed. 741
Bero. A kissing traytour. How art thou proud *Iudas*? 2553
PROUDE = 4
Bero. Well, say I am, why should proude Sommer boast, 111
I am lesse proude to heare you tell my worth, 508

PROUDE *cont.*
And make him proude to make me proude that iestes,   1956
PROUE = 15*2
These othes and lawes will proue an idle scorne. | Surra, Come
on.   304
Arm. A most fine Figure. | *Boy.* To proue you a Cypher.   361
Where now his knowledge must proue ignorance.   598
For youle proue periurde if you make me staie.   608
And if you proue it, Ile repay it backe, | Or yeelde vp *Aquitaine.* 654
Boy. And out of hart Maister: all those three I will | proue.   806
Brag. What wilt thou proue?   808
Though to my selfe forsworne, to thee Ile faythfull proue.   1269
bien venuto, where I will proue those Verses to be very
vn-|learned,   1322
A Woman I forswore, but I will proue,   1397
Ber. Ile proue her faire, or talke till doomse-day heere.   1623
King. Then leaue this chat, and good *Berowne* now proue   1633
Or keeping what is sworne, you will proue fooles,   1707
Light Wenches may proue plagues to men forsworne,   1736
To proue by Wit, worth in simplicitie.   1968
Take all and weane it, it may proue an Oxe.   2165
Is likewise yours: we to our selues proue false,   2730
PROUED = *1
*foole: Well proued wit. By the Lord this Loue is as madd   1339
PROUES = 3
Loues tongue proues daintie, *Bachus* grosse in taste,   1690
Els none at all in ought proues excellent.   1705
Rosa. This proues you wise and rich: for in my eie.   2306
PROUOKE = 1
King. Rebuke me not for that which you prouoke: 2273
PROUOKES = *1
*my spleene, the heauing of my lunges prouokes me to
redi-|culous   849
PRUNING = *1
*In pruning mee when shall you heare that I will prayse a   1521
PUBLIQUE = *1
*the tearme of three yeeres, he shall indure such publique   140
PUERICIA = 1
Peda. Ba, *puericia* with a horne added.   1787
PUFT = *1
Boye. Tapers they are with your sweete breaths puft out.   2185
PUMMEL = 1
Boyet. The pummel of *Caesars* Fauchion.   2567
PUNISHED = 1
Ar. Thou shalt be heauely punished.   453
PUNISHMENT = 1*1
*duetie prickes me on) haue sent to thee, to receiue the meede of
pu-|nishment   265
Vowes for thee broke deserue not punishment.   1396
PUPILL = *2
Peda. I do dine to day at the fathers of a certaine pupill of   1318
*the parentes of the foresaid childe or pupill, vndertake your   1321
PURBLIND = 1
This wimpled whyning purblind wayward Boy,   945
PURCHASD = 1
Which with payne purchas'd, doth inherite payne,   78

PURCHASE = 1
Ros. They are worse fooles to purchase mocking so.   1949
PURCHASED = 1
Brag. How hast thou purchased this experience?   795
PURE = 5
A greene Goose, a Goddesse, pure pure ydolatarie.   1408
Bero. By heauen, all drie beaten with pure scoffe.   2180
Now by my maiden honour yet as pure, | As the vnsallied Lilly I protest,   2277
Ber. Welcome pure wit, thou partst a faire fray.   2425
PURGATION = *1
*Clown. True, true, and now you wilbe my purgation, | and let me loose.   892
PURGED = 1
Rosal. You must be purged to, your sinnes are rackt.   2778
PURIFIES = 1
Thus purifies it selfe and turns to grace.   2734
PURPOSD = 1
From what it purposd, since to wayle friendes lost,   2707
PURPOSE = 6
Vouchsafe to read the purpose of my comming,   604
That more for praise, then purpose meant to kill.   1004
and I will haue an Apologie for that purpose.   1868
Their purpose is to parlee, to court, and daunce,   2014
King. We came to visite you, and purpose now,   2269
All causes to the purpose of his speede: 2699
PURPOSED = 1
When lo to interrupt my purposed rest,   1983
PURPOSES = 1
That some plaine man recount their purposes.   2074
PURPOSETH = 1
But that it seemes he little purposeth: 637
PURSE = *1
*purse of wit, thou Pidgin-egge of discretion. O and the   1810
PURSENTS = 1
For euerie one pursents three.   2430
PURSES = 1
Are pick-purses in Loue, and we deserue to die.   1555
PUSH-PIN = 1
And *Nestor* play at push-pin with the boyes,   1506
PUT = 14*5
*which put togeather, is in manner and forme following.   219
And goe we Lordes to put in practise that,   301
*put yeeres to the worde three, and studie three yeeres in two   359
Here sweete, put vp this, twilbe thine annother day.   1091
Rosa. Why she that beares the Bow. Finely put off.   1096
hang me by the necke, if horns that yeere miscarrie. | Finely put on.   1098
neare. Finely put on in deede.   1103
Lord, Lord, how the Ladies and I haue put him downe.   1138
The Dogges did yell, put ell to Sore, | then Sorell iumps from thicket: 1219
*put it to them. But *Vir sapis qui pauca loquitur*, a soule Femi- |nine saluteth vs.   1243
*Ber. I could put thee in comfort, not by two that I know,   1384
Presence maiesticall would put him out: 1994
That put *Armathoes* Page out of his part.   2261

PUT *cont.*

    You put our Page out: goe, you are aloude.   2417
    *Too too vaine, too too vaine: but we will put it (as they say)   2474
    Pedan. I will not be put out of countenance. | *Bero.* Because thou
    hast no face.   2560
    And now forward, for we haue put thee in countenance.   2572
    Peda. You haue put me out of countenance.   2573
    Put on by vs, if in your heauenly eyes,   2725
PYTCH = *2
    *They haue pitcht a Toyle, I am toyling in a pytch, pytch   1336
QU = *1
QUALME = 1
    And trow you what he calde me? | *Quee.* Qualme perhaps.   2198
QUANDO = *1
    **Nath.* Facile precor gellida, quando pecas omnia sub vmbra
    ru- | minat,   1257
QUANTITIE = *1
    **Brag.* Pardon sir, error: He is not quantitie enough for   1863
QUARI = 1
    Brag. Chirra. | *Peda. Quari* Chirra, not Sirra?   1772
QUASI = *1
    **Nath.* Maister Person, *quasi* Person? And if one shoulde   1247
QUE *l.**1259 *1260 = *2
QUE = *3
QUEE = 68*8
QUEEN = 2
    Queen. I sweete my Lord, and so I take my leaue.   2833
    Queen. Was not that *Hector?* | *Duma.* The worthie Knight of
    Troy.   2843
QUEENE see also *Qu., Que., Quee.* = 2*1
    Then *Aquitaine* a Dowrie for a Queene.   499
    *woman when queene *Guinouer* of Brittaine was a litle wench | as
    toching the hit it.   1112
    O Queene of queenes, how farre doost thou excell,   1372
QUEENE = 1
QUEENES = 2*1
    **Iag.* I sir from one mounsier *Berowne*, one of the strange |
    Queenes Lordes.   1294
    *of the stranger Queenes: which accidentally, or by the way   1304
    O Queene of queenes, how farre doost thou excell,   1372
QUESTION = 3
    Kath. How needles was it then to aske the question?   612
    And out of question so it is sometimes: 1005
    Peda. I do *sans question.*   1820
QUESTIONS = *1
    **Kath.* Tis long of you that spur me with such questions.   614
QUI = *1
    *put it to them. But *Vir sapis qui pauca loquitur,* a soule Femi-
    | nine saluteth vs.   1243
QUICKE = 7*4
    But is there no quicke recreation graunted?   172
    Arma. And therfore apt, because quicke.   334
    Boy. That an Eele is quicke.   339
    **Arma.* I do say thou art quicke in answeres. Thou heatst | my
    blood.   340
    On serious busines crauing quicke dispatch,   522

QUICKE *cont.*

 Ber. You must not be so quicke.   613
 *sweete tutch, a quicke venewe of wit, snip snap, quicke and   1796
 Quee. And quicke *Berowne* hath plighted Fayth to me.   2204
 *wench is cast away: shee's quicke, the childe bragges in her |
 bellie already: tis yours.   2632
 quicke by him, and hangd for *Pompey* that is dead by him. 2637
QUICKLY = 2
 Mari. O for your reason, quickly sir, I long?   2156
 ende of our shew. | *King.* Call them foorth quickly, we will do so. 2851
QUID = 1
 Pedant. Satis quid sufficit.   1740
QUIET = 1
 as an other man, & therfore I can be quiet. *Exit.*   468
QUILLETS = 1
 Some tricks, some quillets, how to cheate the diuell.   1637
QUIS = 3
 Curat. Vides ne quis venit? | *Peda. Video, et gaudio.*   1770
 Peda. Quis quis thou Consonant?   1790
QUIT = 1
 Ferd. These be the stopps that hinder studie quit,   75
QUITE *see also* quit = 5*1
 Make rich the ribbes, but bancrout quite the wits.   31
 Ferd. What say you Lordes? why, this was quite forgot.   151
 And younger hearinges are quite rauished.   567
 And quite diuorce his memorie from his part.   2042
 This pert *Berowne* was out of countnance quite.   2191
 Thrust thy sharpe wit quite through my ignorance,   2330
QUONDAM = *1
 *conuerse this quondam day with a companion of the kings, 1745
QUONIAM = 1
 Quoniam, *he seemeth in minoritie,*   2545
QUOTH = 3*2
 Ayre (quoth he) thy cheekes may blow,   1446
 Ber. Did they quoth you? Who sees the heauenly *Rosaline,* 1570
 For quoth the King, an Angell shalt thou see: 1995
 Mar. Veale quoth the Dutch-man: is not veale a Calfe?   2159
 No poynt (quoth I) my seruant, straight was mute.   2196
RABBET = *1
 *like a Rabbet on a spit, or your handes in your pocket like a 788
RACKERS = *1
 *such rackers of ortagriphie, as to speake dout fine, when he 1759
RACKT = 1
 Rosal. You must be purged to, your sinnes are rackt.   2778
RAGE = 2
 Foode for his rage, repasture for his den.   1073
 Of the olde rage: beare with me, I am sicke.   2350
RAGGS = *1
 *thy loue? I will. What, shalt thou exchange for raggs   1061
RAIGNES = 1
 Raignes in my blood, and will remembred be.   1432
RAINE = 2*1
 Ber. Your Mistresses dare neuer come in raine,   1619
 Brag. Sweete Lord *Longauill* raine thy tongue.   2613
 Long. I must rather giue it the raine: for it runnes against |
 Hector.   2614

RANSOME = *1
    *Desire prisoner, and ransome him to anie French Courtier   367
RAPIER = *3
    *thee in my rapier, as much as thou didst me in carying gates.   380
    *Spaniards Rapier: The first and second cause will not serue   480
    *men. Adue Valoure, rust Rapier, be still Drum, for your   483
RARE = 2
    Nath. A rare talent.   1227
    Duma. Most rare *Pompey.*   2639
RASORS = 1
    Boyet. The tongues of mocking Wenches are as keene | As is the
    Rasors edge inuisible: 2172
RATED = 1
    And in our mayden counsaile rated them,   2737
RATEFIED = *1
    Nath. Here are onely numbers ratefied, but for the ele-|gancie   1286
RATHER = 3*5
    Clo. I had rather pray a month with Mutton & Porridge.   297
    He rather meanes to lodge you in the feelde,   579
    Which we much rather had depart withall,   642
    Boy. Minnime honest Maister, or rather Maister no.   828
    *replication, or rather *ostentare*, to show as it were his
    inclina-|tion   1165
    *vntrained, or rather vnlettered, or ratherest vnconfirmed
    fa-|shion,   1167
    *Vnder pardon sir, What are the contentes? or rather as *Hor-|race*   1262
    Long. I must rather giue it the raine: for it runnes against |
    Hector.   2614
RATHEREST = *1
    *vntrained, or rather vnlettered, or ratherest vnconfirmed
    fa-|shion,   1167
RATIONAL = 1
    with the rational hinde *Costard*: she deserues well.   422
RAUEN = 1
    Ber. An amber colourd Rauen was well noted.   1422
RAUGHT *see* rought
RAUISH = 3
    Doth rauish like inchaunting harmonie: 178
    Should rauish dooters with a false aspect: 1609
    O then his lines would rauish sauage eares,   1699
RAUISHED = 1
    And younger hearinges are quite rauished.   567
RAW = 1
    And Marrians nose lookes red and raw: 2891
RAYNING = 1
    My wofull selfe vp in a mourning house, | Rayning the teares of
    lamentation,   2768
RAYSE = 1
    As thy eye beames, when their fresh rayse haue smot.   1360
RE = *1
    *Who vnderstandeth thee not, loues thee not, *vt re sol la mi fa*:   1261
READ = 5*1
    Ferd. How well hees read to reason against reading.   99
    Boy. As I haue read sir, and the best of them too.   390
    Vouchsafe to read the purpose of my comming,   604
    Iaque. Good M.(aister) Parson be so good as read me this letter,   1254
    I beseech you read it.   1256

READ *cont.*
Iaque. I beseech your Grace let this Letter be read,   1535
READE = 4
Giue me the paper, let me reade the same,   125
Quee. We will reade it, I sweare.   1038
Dum. Once more Ile reade the Ode that I haue writ.   1435
King. Berowne reade it ouer. *He reades the letter.*   1537
READES = 3
Long. This same shall go. *He reades the Sonnet.*   1392
Dumaine reades his Sonnet.   1437
King. Berowne reade it ouer. *He reades the letter.*   1537
READING = 2
Ferd. How well hees read to reason against reading.   99
What *Longauill*, and reading: listen eare.   1377
REAPT = 1
Ber. Alone alone sowed Cockell, reapt no Corne,   1734
REASON = 10*1
Ferd. How well hees read to reason against reading.   99
Duma. In reason nothing. | *Bero.* Something then in rime.   107
reason for it. He surely affected her for her wit.   393
*A dangerous rime maister against the reason of white & red.   411
A yeelding gainst some reason in my brest,   647
All liberall reason I will yeelde vnto.   665
Prin. Your reason. | *Bo.* Why all his behauiours did make their
retire,   737
Ros. Great reason: for past care, is still past cure.   1915
Long. I know the reason (Lady) why you aske.   2155
Mari. O for your reason, quickly sir, I long?   2156
Bero. What reason haue you fort.   2664
REASONS = 1*1
From reasons yeelding, your faire selfe should make   646
Curat. I prayse God for you sir, your reasons at Dinner   1741
REBUKE = 1
King. Rebuke me not for that which you prouoke: 2273
RECEIT = 1
In so vnseeming to confesse receit,   651
RECEIUD = 2
Receiud that summe, yet there remaines vnpaide   629
Quee. We haue receiud your Letters, full of Loue: 2735
RECEIUDE = 1
But here without you shalbe so receiude,   670
RECEIUE = 1*1
duetie prickes me on) haue sent to thee, to receiue the meede of
pu- | nishment   265
Meane time receiue such welcome at my hand,   666
RECKNING = 1*1
Arm. I am ill at reckning, it fitteth the spirit of a Tapster.   349
Clow. O Lord sir, it were pittie you should get your liuing | by
reckning sir.   2439
RECKONING = 1
Haue brought about the annuall reckoning.   2758
RECOMPENCE = 1
Ferd. I, that is studies god-like recompence.   63
RECORDED = 1
That are recorded in this sedule here.   22
RECOUNT = 1*1
*let that passe. By the world I recount no fable, some certaine   1838

RECOUNT *cont.*
That some plaine man recount their purposes.   2074
RECREATION = 1*1
But is there no quicke recreation graunted?   172
*Away, the gentles are at their game, and we will to our re-
|creation. *Exeunt.*   1331
RED = 4*1
Arm. My loue is most immaculate white and red.   395
Boy. Yf she be made of white and red,   403
*A dangerous rime maister against the reason of white & red.   411
My red Dominicall, my golden letter,   1932
And Marrians nose lookes red and raw: 2891
REDD = 1
And therefore redd that would auoyde disprayse,   1613
REDICULOUS = 3*2
*my spleene, the heauing of my lunges prouokes me to
redi-|culous   849
*his gate maiesticall, and his generall behauiour vaine,
redicu-|lous,   1750
That in this spleene rediculous appeares,   2009
And their rough carriage so rediculous,   2229
And what in vs hath seemed rediculous: 2717
REEDES = 1
Boyet | reedes.* By heauen, that thou art faire, is most infallible: 1041
REEKE = 1
Saw sighes reeke from you, noted well your pashion.   1477
REFINED = 1
With a refined trauailer of Spaine,   174
REFORMATION = 1
And I shall finde you emptie of that fault, | Right ioyfull of your
reformation.   2829
REGARDS = *1
*my turne: *Passado* he respects not, the *Duella* he regards   481
REGENT = 1
Regent of Loue-rimes, Lord of folded armes,   947
REGISTRED = 1
Liue registred vpon our brazen Tombes,   6
REIECT = *1
Quee. When she shall challenge this, you wil reiect her.   2374
REIGNES *see* raignes
REINE *see* raine
REIOICETH = 1
home, it reioiceth my intellect, true wit.   1797
REIOYCE = 1
As to reioyce at friendes but newly found.   2709
RELATE = 1
For interim to our studies shall relate,   182
RELIGION = 1
It is Religion to be thus forsworne.   1714
RELIGIOUSLY = *1
Holo. Sir you haue done this in the feare of God verie
reli-|giously: 1312
REMAINES = 1
Receiud that summe, yet there remaines vnpaide   629
REMEMBER = 1*2
*that shallow vassall (*Clown.* Still mee.) *which as I remember,* 258
Boy. I am much deceiued, but I remember the stile.   1077

211

REMEMBER *cont.*
   *betweene vs, let it passe. I do beseech thee remember thy   1831
REMEMBRAUNCE = 1
   For the remembraunce of my Fathers death.   2770
REMEMBRED = 1
   Raignes in my blood, and will remembred be.   1432
REMIT = 1
   Berow. Neither of either: I remit both twaine.   2398
REMOOUED = 1
   (Those cloudes remooued) vpon our waterie eyne.   2105
REMOTE = 1
   Remote from all the pleasurs of the world: 2756
REMOUES = 1
   Woo contrarie, deceyued by these remoues.   2027
REMUNERATION = 4*7
   *significant to the countrey Maide *Iaquenetta*: there is
   remu-|neration,   896
   Now will I looke to his remuneration.   902
   *Remuneration, O that's the latine word for three-farthings: 903
   *Three-farthings remuneration, What's the price of this yncle?   904
   *i.d. no, Ile giue you a remuneration: Why? it carries it
   re-|muneration: 905
   a man buy for a remuneration?   912
   Ber. O what is a remuneration?| *Cost.* Marie sir, halfepennie
   farthing.   913
   Clow. Gardon, O sweete gardon, better then remuneratio(n).   935
   do it sir in print: gardon remuneration. | *Exit.*   937
   *Remuneration I had of thy Maister, thou halfepennie   1809
RENDED = *1
   *some show in the posterior of this day, to be rended by our   1852
RENDER = 1
   Nor to their pend speach render we no grace: 2039
RENOWNED = 1
   Boyet. Renowned *Pompey.*   2640
RENT = *1
   King. What, did these rent lines shew some loue of thine?   1568
REPAIDE = 1
   For here he doth demaund to haue repaide,   638
REPAIRE = 2
   All sences to that sence did make their repaire,   744
   Therefore change Fauours, and when they repaire,   2214
REPAIRING = 1
   Still a repairing: euer out of frame,   957
REPAST = *1
   *mine, where if (before repast) it shall please you to gratifie   1319
REPASTURE = 1
   Foode for his rage, repasture for his den.   1073
REPAY = 1
   And if you proue it, Ile repay it backe, | Or yeelde vp *Aquitaine.*   654
REPEATE = 1*1
   * *Pag.* The last of the fiue Vowels if You repeate them, | or the fift
   if I.   1791
   Peda. I will repeate them: a e I.   1793
REPLEAT = 1
   Proclaymes you for a man repleat with mockes,   2804
REPLENISHED = *1
   *His intellect is not replenished, he is only an annimall, only   1178

REPLICATION = *1
  *replication, or rather *ostentare*, to show as it were his
  inclina-|tion 1165
REPLIE = *1
  *thy replie, I prophane my lippes on thy foote, my eyes on 1063
REPLYDE = 1
  The Boy replyde, An Angell is not euill: 1997
REPORT = 1
  Is my report to his great worthines. 555
REPREHEND = *1
  *Const. I my selfe reprehend his owne person, for I am his 195
REPROBATE = *1
  *deliuer me from the reprobate thought of it, I would take 366
REPROUE = 1
  Good hart, What grace hast thou thus to reproue 1490
REPUT = 1
  good reput, carriage bearing, and estimation. 267
REPUTATION = 2
  And wrong the reputation of your name, 650
  meane you? you will loose your reputation. 2658
REPUTE = 1
  *name more; and sweete my childe let them be men of good |
  repute and carriage. 374
REPUTES = 1
  He reputes me a Cannon, and the Bullet thats hee: 833
REQUESTES = 1
  Deare Princesse were not his requestes so farr 645
REQUESTS = 1
  Thou now requests but Mooneshine in the water. 2107
RESCEWES = 1
  Fer. How well this yeelding rescewes thee from shame. 127
RESEMBLING = 1
  Ber. Diuels soonest tempt resembling spirites of light. 1606
RESOLUE = 2
  And sodainelie resolue mee in my suite. 605
  Shall we resolue to woe these gyrles of Fraunce? 1722
RESOLUED = 1
  Longauill. I am resolued, tis but a three yeeres fast: 28
RESOLUTE = 1
  Clow. Ile do it in my shyrt. | *Duma.* Most resolute *Pompey.* 2654
RESPECT = 2
  King. That more then all the world, I did respect her. 2373
  King. Hector was but a *Troyan* in respect of this. 2592
RESPECTES = 1
  But more deuout then this our respectes, 2740
RESPECTS = *1
  *my turne: *Passado* he respects not, the *Duella* he regards 481
REST = 9*1
  Longa. You swore to that *Berowne*, and to the rest. 57
  shame as the rest of the Court can possible deuise. 141
  Who are the rest? 547
  Que. Thou shalt know her fellow by the rest that haue no |
  (heads. 1020
  Brag. For the rest of the Worthies? | *Peda.* I will play three my
  selfe. 1873
  When lo to interrupt my purposed rest, 1983

REST *cont.*
   Enter Black-moores with musicke, the Boy with a | speach, and the
   rest of the Lordes disguysed.   2051
   Enter the King and the rest.   2234
   To flatter vp these powers of mine with rest,   2774
   A tweluemonth shall you spende and neuer rest,   2781
RESTORE = 1
   If then the King your father will restore,   633
RESTRAINED = *1
   *Enfreedoming thy person: thou wert emured, restrained, |
   captiuated, bound.   890
RETALES = 1
   He is Witts Pedler, and retales his wares: 2242
RETHORICKE = 2
   By the hartes still rethoricke, disclosed with eyes.   733
   Fie paynted Rethoricke, O shee needes it not,   1588
RETHORIQUE = 1
   Did not the heauenly Rethorique of thine eye,   1393
RETIRE = 1
   Prin. Your reason. | *Bo.* Why all his behauiours did make their
   retire,   737
RETURND = 1
   My Herald is returnd.   839
RETURNE = 3*1
   Ore Saterday we will returne to Fraunce.   980
   *coloures. But to returne to the Verses, Did they please you | sir
   Nathaniel?*   1315
   Quee. Will they returne? | *Boy.* They will they will, God knowes,   2211
   If they returne in their owne shapes to woe?   2222
REUELS = 1
   For Reuels, Daunces, Maskes, and merrie houres,   1730
REUERENT = *1
   Nat. Very reuerent sport truly, and done in the testimonie | of a
   good conscience.   1151
REUOLT = 1
   As grauities reuolt to wantons be.   1964
REUOLUTIONS = *1
   *Ideas, aprehentions, motions, reuolutions. These are begot in   1232
REWARDED = 1
   Clo. I am more bound to you then your fellowes, for they | are
   but lightly rewarded.   454
REWARDING = *1
   *for the best ward of mine honour, is rewarding | my dependants.
   Moth,* follow.   897
RHETORIKE = 1
   Brag. Sweete smoke of Rhetorike,   832
RHYME *see* rime
RHYMES *see* rimes
RIBBES = 1
   Make rich the ribbes, but bancrout quite the wits.   31
RIBBON = *1
   Clow. Pray you sir, How much Carnation Ribbon may   911
RICH = 7
   Make rich the ribbes, but bancrout quite the wits.   31
   Quee. Sweete hartes we shalbe rich ere we depart,   1888
   Berow. Beauties no richer then rich Taffata.   2054
   Our duetie is so rich, so infinite,   2098

RICH *cont.*

Wise thinges seeme foolish, and rich thinges but poore.	2305
Rosa. This proues you wise and rich: for in my eie.	2306
In your rich wisedome to excuse, or hide,	2690

RICHER = 1

Berow. Beauties no richer then rich Taffata.	2054

RICHEST = 1

Page. All haile, the richest Beauties on the earth.	2053

RIDDLE = *2

Ar. Some enigma, some riddle, come, thy *Lenuoy* begin.	843
Clo. No egma, no riddle, no *lenuoy*, no salue, in thee male sir.	845

RIDER = 1*1

Kath. Not till it leaue the rider in the mire.	616
*the Ape his keeper, the tyred Horse his rider: But *Damosella*	1291

RIDEST = 1

So ridest thou triumphing in my wo.	1367

RIDICULOUS *see* rediculous

RIGHT = 11

A man of complements whom right and wrong	179
Clow. As it shall follow in my correction, and God defend | the right.	224
We will giue vp our right in *Aquitaine,*	635
And neuer going a right, being a Watch:	958
But being watcht, that it may still go right.	959
They sparcle still the right promethean fier,	1702
Bero. A right description of our sport my Lord.	2465
Boyet. Your Nose saies no, you are not: for it stands too | (right.	2516
Boy. Most true, tis right: you were so *Alisander.*	2524
and I will right my selfe like a Souldier. *Exeunt Worthys*	2682
And I shall finde you emptie of that fault, | Right ioyfull of your reformation.	2829

RIGHTLY = *1

*Begger *Zenelophon*: and he it was that might rightly say,	1047

RIME = 4*4

Duma. In reason nothing. | *Bero.* Something then in rime.	107
*A dangerous rime maister against the reason of white & red.	411
*God of Rime, for I am sure I shall turne Sonnet. Deuise	485
*loue, and it hath taught me to rime, and to be mallicholie:	1345
*and heere is part of my Rime, and heare my mallicholie.	1347
When shall you see mee write a thing in rime?	1519
Quee. Nothing but this: yes as much loue in Rime,	1893
Nor woo in rime like a blind harpers songue.	2337

RIMES = 4

Regent of Loue-rimes, Lord of folded armes,	947
Ber. O Rimes are gardes on wanton *Cupids* hose, | Disfigure not his Shop.	1390
I heard your guyltie Rimes, obserude your fashion:	1476
And spend his prodigall wittes in booteles rimes,	1954

RING = 1

Bero. A deaths face in a Ring.	2565

RIPE = 1*1

Ped. The Deare was (as you know) sanguis in blood, ripe	1153
The King was weeping ripe for a good word.	2193

RISING = 1

Against the steepe vp rising of the hill?	976

RO = *1

ROABES = *1
*roabes, for tittles tytles, for thy selfe, mee. Thus expecting   1062
ROARE = 1
Thus dost thou heare the nemean Lion roare,   1068
ROASTED = 1
When roasted Crabbs hisse in the bowle,   2892
ROES = 1
Quee. Whip to our Tents as Roes runs ore land. *Exeunt.*   2232
ROGUE = 2
Not to beholde. | *Berow.* Once to beholde, rogue.   2063
Ber. Is this your perfectnes? begon you rogue.   2070
ROMAN = 1
Long. The face of an olde Roman coyne, scarce seene.   2566
ROME = *1
Boy. True, and it was inioyned him in *Rome* for want of   2667
ROOFE = *1
*not yet: the roofe of this Court is too high to be yours, and   587
ROOKES = 1
When Turtles tread and Rookes and Dawes,   2871
ROOME = 1
Duma. Roome for the incensed Worthies.   2653
ROS = 16*3
ROSA = 34*6
ROSAL = 4
ROSALIN = 1
Boyet. The heire of *Alanson, Rosalin* her name.   693
ROSALINE see also Ro., Ros., Rosa., Rosal. = 8*1
And *Rosaline* they call her, aske for her: 932
Clow. I haue a Letter from Monsier *Berowne,* | to one Ladie
Rosaline.   1029
To a Ladie of France, that he calde *Rosaline.*   1089
To the snow-white hand of the most bewtious Lady Rosaline.   1297
Ber. Did they quoth you? Who sees the heauenly *Rosaline,*   1570
But *Rosaline,* you haue a Fauour too?   1917
Holde *Rosaline,* this Fauour thou shalt weare,   2022
So shall *Berowne* take me for *Rosaline.*   2025
Quee. I will, and therefore keepe it. *Rosaline,*   2380
ROSE = 2
At Christmas I no more desire a Rose,   114
To those fresh morning dropps vpon the Rose,   1359
ROSES = 3
Blow like sweete Roses, in this sommer aire.   2215
Boy. Faire Ladies maskt, are Roses in their bud: 2218
Are Angels varling cloudes, or Roses blowne.   2220
ROTTEN = 1
Brag. The sweete War-man is dead and rotten,   2617
ROUGH = 1
And their rough carriage so rediculous,   2229
ROUGHT = 1
And rought not to fiue-weeks when he came to fiuescore.   1198
ROULE = 1
Varying in subiectes as the eye doth roule,   2722
ROYAL = *1
Brag. Annoynted, I implore so much expence of thy royal   2467
ROYALL = 1*3
*deliuer this Paper into the royall hand of the King, it may   1306
*my poore shoulder, and with his royall finger thus dallie   1836

ROYALL *cont.*
*to *Fortuna delaguar*, I wish you the peace of mind most royall |
cupplement. *Exit.*   2475
Brag. I will kisse thy royall finger, and take leaue.   2845
ROYALTIE = *1
*But I will forward with my deuice; sweete royaltie bestow | on
me the sence of hearing.   2619
RUBBD = 1
One rubbd his elbow thus, and fleerd, and swore,   2001
RUBBING = *1
Bo. I feare too much rubbing: good night my good owle.   1135
RUDE = 3*1
Most rude melancholie, Valour giues thee place.   838
That (like a rude and sauadge man of *Inde*.)   1571
of this day, which the rude multitude call the after-noone.   1823
King. Teach vs sweet Madame, for our rude transgression | Some
faire excuse.   2364
RUMINAT = *1
*Nath. Facile precor gellida, quando pecas omnia sub vmbra
ru-|minat,*   1257
RUN = 1*1
Boyet. Full merely hath this braue nuage, this carreere | bin run. 2421
*and a feard to speake? Run away for shame *Ali-|sander.*   2532
RUNNE = 1
Methegline, Wort, and Malmsey; well runne dice: 2138
RUNNES = *1
Long. I must rather giue it the raine: for it runnes against |
Hector.   2614
RUNNING = 1
I *Costard* running out, that was safely within,   882
RUNS = 1
Quee. Whip to our Tents as Roes runs ore land. *Exeunt.*   2232
RUSSET = 1
In russet yeas, and honest kersie noes.   2345
RUSSIAN = 3
In *Russian* habite: heere they stayed an houre,   2295
Nor neuer more in Russian habite waite.   2333
What did the *Russian* whisper in your eare?   2381
RUSSIANS = 3
Boy. They do, they do; and are appariled thus, | Like *Muscouites*,
or *Russians*, as I gesse.   2012
A messe of *Russians* left vs but of late.   2287
King. How Madame? *Russians*? | *Quee.* I in trueth My Lord.   2288
RUST = *1
*men. Adue Valoure, rust Rapier, be still Drum, for your   483
SABLE = *1
Ferd. So it is besedged with sable coloured melancholie, I did   242
SACKS = 1
More Sacks to the myll. O heauens I haue my wysh,   1415
SAD = 1*1
Kath. He made her melancholie, sad, and heauie,   1901
Quee. Amazde my Lord? Why lookes your highnes sad?   2321
SADD = 1
Boy. A great signe sir that he will looke sadd.   314
SADNES = *2
Ar. Why? sadnes is one & the selfe same thing deare imp.   315

SADNES *cont.*
Arm. How canst thou part sadnes and melancholy, my | tender
Iuuenall?   318
SAD-SOULE = 1
Out of a new sad-soule, that you vouchsafe,   2689
SAFE = *1
*safe, and you must suffer him to take no delight, nor no
pe-|nance,   432
SAFELY = 1
I *Costard* running out, that was safely within,   882
SAID = 2*2
Dul. I said the Deare was not a *haud credo*, twas a Pricket.   1170
Our person misdoubts it: twas treason he said.   1536
Kath. Lord *Longauill* said I came ore his hart: 2197
Ber. Well said old mocker, I must needes be friendes with |
(thee.   2495
SAIES = 3*2
Ber. Would that do it good? | *Ros.* My Phisicke saies I.   684
Bo. A mark, O mark but that mark: a mark saies my Lady.   1121
Boy. She saies you haue it, and you may be gon.   2081
Boyet. Your Nose saies no, you are not: for it stands too | (right. 2516
Longauill. What saies *Maria*? | *Mari.* At the tweluemonths ende, 2793
SAIEST = 1
Brag. Ha ha, What saiest thou?   821
SAINE = 2
Some obscure presedence that hath tofore bin saine.   856
Some carry tale, some please-man, some sleight saine: 2402
SAINT = 4
King. Saint *Cupid* then and Souldiers to the fielde.   1717
Quee. Saint *Dennis* to S.(aint) *Cupid*: What are they,   1979
Bero. Saint *Georges* halfe cheeke in a Brooch.   2569
SAITH = 1*1
and as a certaine Father saith   1313
Nath. And thanke you to: for societie (saith the text) | is the
happines of life.   1326
SAKE = 8
And you giue him for my sake but one louing kisse.   753
When for Fames sake, for praise an outward part,   1007
Onely for praise sake, when they striue to be | Lords ore their
Lordes?   1012
Did neuer Sonnet for her sake compile,   1471
For Wisedomes sake, a worde that all men loue: 1708
Or for Loues sake, a worde that loues all men.   1709
Or for Mens sake, the authour of these Women: 1710
Or Womens sake, by whom we Men are Men.   1711
SAKES = 1
For your faire sakes, haue we neglected time.   2713
SALE = 2
Not vttred by base sale of chapmens tongues: 507
To thinges of sale, a sellers prayse belonges: 1589
SALLOMON = 1
And profound *Sallomon* to tune a Iigge.   1505
SALOMON = *1
*and he had an excellent strength: Yet was *Salomon* so   476
SALUE = 4*2
Clo. No egma, no riddle, no *lenuoy*, no salue, in thee male sir. 845

SALUE *cont.*
  *O sir, Plantan, a plaine Plantan: no *lenuoy*, no *lenuoy*, no Salue |
sir, but a Plantan. 846
  take *salue* for *lenuoy*, and the word *lenuoy* for a *salue?* 851
  Pag. Do the wise thinke them other, is not *lenuoy* a *salue?* 853
  Duma. Some salue for periurie. | *Ber.* O tis more then neede. 1638
SALUTATION = 1
  Brag. Men of peace well incontred. | *Ped.* Most millitarie sir
salutation. 1774
SALUTETH = 1
  *put it to them. But *Vir sapis qui pauca loquitur*, a soule Femi-
|nine saluteth vs. 1243
SAME = 6*1
  Giue me the paper, let me reade the same, 125
  * *Ar.* Why? sadnes is one & the selfe same thing deare imp. 315
  Boy. I will praise an Eele with the same praise. 337
  For still her cheekes possesse the same, | Which natiue she doth
owe 409
  Dum. Sir, I pray you a word, What Ladie is that same? 692
  Long. This same shall go. *He reades the Sonnet.* 1392
  That same *Berowne* ile torture ere I go. 1950
SAMPSON = *5
  * *Boy.* *Sampson* Maister, he was a man of good carriage, 376
  * *Arm.* O wel knit *Sampson*, strong ioynted *Sampson*; I do excel 379
  *haue a loue of that colour, mee thinkes *Sampson* had small 392
  *There is no euill angel but Loue, yet was *Sampson* so temp-|ted, 475
SAMPSONS = 1
  I am in loue too. Who was *Sampsons* loue my deare Moth? 381
SANCE = 1
  My loue to thee is sound, *sance* cracke or flaw. 2347
SANGUIS = *1
  * *Ped.* The Deare was (as you know) sanguis in blood, ripe 1153
SANS = 3
  Peda. I do *sans question.* 1820
  Rosa. Sans, sans, I pray you. 2348
SAPIS = *1
  *put it to them. But *Vir sapis qui pauca loquitur*, a soule Femi-
|nine saluteth vs. 1243
SAT = 1
  O mee, with what strickt patience haue I sat, 1502
SATERDAY = 1
  Ore Saterday we will returne to Fraunce. 980
SATIS = 1
  Pedant. Satis quid sufficit. 1740
SATISFIE = 1
  Ferd. Satisfie mee so. 660
SATISFIED = 1
  And go well satisfied to France againe. 648
SAUADGE = 1
  That (like a rude and sauadge man of *Inde.*) 1571
SAUAGE = 1
  O then his lines would rauish sauage eares, 1699
SAUAGES = 1
  That we (like sauages) may worship it. 2101
SAUD = 1
  Quee. See see, my beautie wilbe sau'd by merrit. 996

SAUE = 6

Saue base aucthoritie from others Bookes.	92
Ber. Now God saue thy life. | *Ros.* And yours from long liuing.	688
Thus will I saue my Credite in the shoote,	1001
Mayd. Good *Costard* go with me: sir God saue your life.	1309
King. Faire sir, God saue you: Wher's the Princesse?	2235
Marcad. God saue you Madame.	2672

SAULT = *1

Brag. Now by the sault waue of the meditaranium, a	1795

SAUOURING = *1

*neither sauouring of Poetrie, wit, nor inuention.	1323

SAW = 7*2

In *Normandie* saw I this *Longauill,*	535
I saw him at the Duke *Alansoes* once,	553
And much too little of that good I saw,	554
Boyet. A woman sometimes, and you saw her in the light.	696
That all eyes saw his eyes inchaunted with gazes.	751
*To whom came he? to the Begger. What saw he? the	1053
Saw sighes reeke from you, noted well your pashion.	1477
Before I saw you: and the worldes large tongue	2803
And coffing drownes the Parsons saw;	2889

SAWCERS = 1

Would let her out in Sawcers, sweete misprison.	1434

SAWCIE = 1

That will not be deepe searcht with sawcie lookes:	90

SAY = 28*19

Berowne. I can but say their protestation ouer,	37
Berow. Let me say no my liedge, and yf you please,	54
Sweare me to this, and I will nere say no.	74
Bero. Well, say I am, why should proude Sommer boast,	111
Then for that Angell knowledge you can say,	122
Ferd. What say you Lordes? why, this was quite forgot.	151
Cost. It may be so: but if he say it is so, he is in telling true: | but so. | *Ferd.* Peace.	236
with, o with, but with this I passion to say wherewith: | *Clo.* With a Wench.	261
Fer. I the best, for the worst. But sirra, What say you to this?	277
Arma. I do say thou art quicke in answeres. Thou heatst | my blood.	340
Ar. I say sing. | *Boy.* Forbeare till this companie be past.	428
Ar. I loue thee. | *Ma.* So I heard you say.	444
*therfore I will say nothing: I thanke God I haue as little pa-|tience	467
Lad. They say so most, that most his humors know.	545
But say that he, or we, as neither haue	628
Brag. I say Lead is slow.	829
Boy. You are too swift sir to say so.	830
+ *Pag.* I will adde the *lenuoy,* say the morrall againe.	856 +5
Quee. What, what? First praise mee, and againe say no.	988
*Begger *Zenelophon*: and he it was that might rightly say,	1047
But *omne bene* say I, being of an olde Fathers minde,	1187
Holo. God comfort thy capacitie, I say th'allusion holdes | in the Exchange.	1202
Dul. And I say the polusion holdes in the Exchange: for	1204
*the Moone is neuer but a month olde: and I say beside	1205
Some say a Sore, but not a sore, | till now made sore with shooting.	1217

SAY *cont.*

*Sir I do inuite you too, you shall not say me nay: *pauca verba.*	1329
*sorrow; for so they say the foole sayd, and so say I, and I the	1338
Ber. Stoope I say, her shoulder is with child.	1424
What will *Berowne* say when that he shall heare	1482
Say, Can you fast? your stomacks are too young:	1644
*should say doubt; det, when he shold pronounce debt; debt,	1760
*Go to, thou hast it *ad dungil* at the fingers ends, as they say.	1813
*and learned Gentleman, before the Princesse: I say	1854
That charge their breath against vs? Say scout say.	1980
Rosa. What would they, say they?	*Boy.* Nothing but peace, and	
gentle visitation.	2078
King. Say to her we haue measurd many miles,	2082
Boy. They say that they haue measurd many a mile,	2084
Mar. Say you so? Faire Lord, take that for your faire Lady	2150
*am (as they say, but to parfect one man in one poore man)		
Pompion the great sir.	2444
King. I say they shall not come.	2458
*Too too vaine, too too vaine: but we will put it (as they say)	2474
If your Ladishyp would say thankes Pompey, *I had done.*	2505
Quee. Prepare I say: I thanke you gracious Lords	2687
Duma. O shall I say, I thanke you gentle Wife?	2786
Ile marke no wordes that smothfast wooers say,	2788

SAYD = *1

*sorrow; for so they say the foole sayd, and so say I, and I the	1338

SAYES = 2

sayes in his, What my soule verses.	1263
Ay mee sayes one! O *Ioue* the other cryes!	1478

SAYING = 3*1

Boy. How meane you sir, I prettie, and my saying apt?	330
or I apt, and my saying prettie?	331
Boy. By saying that a *Costard* was broken in a shin.	871
Rosa. Shall I come vpon thee with an olde saying, that	1108

SAYLE = *1

Kin. The Ship is vnder sayle, and heere she coms amaine.	2489

SCAENE = 2

O what a Scaene of foolrie haue I seene,	1500
Ber. Worthies away, the Scaene begins to cloude.	2679

SCARCE = 3

Shee (an attending Starre) scarce seene a light.	1580
Scarce shew a haruest of their heauie toyle.	1677
Long. The face of an olde Roman coyne, scarce seene.	2566

SCHEDULE *see* sedule

SCHOLE = *1

*So were there a patch set on Learning, to see him in a schole.	1185

SCHOLEMASTER = *1

Clo. Marrie M.(aister) Scholemaster, he that is liklest to a	
hoggs-	(head.	1249

SCHOLLER = *1

*sweetly varried like a scholler at the least: but sir I assure ye	1159

SCHOLLERS = 1

My fellow Schollers, and to keepe those statutes	21

SCHOOLE = 2

The hue of dungions, and the Schoole of night:	1604
Hath Wisedomes warrant, and the helpe of Schoole,	1961

SCHOOLEMAISTER = 1

For I protest, the Schoolemaister is exceeding fantasticall,	2473

LOVE'S LABOUR'S LOST

SCHOOLE-BOYES = 1
Nor to the motion of a Schoole-boyes tongue: 2335
SCOFFE = 1
Bero. By heauen, all drie beaten with pure scoffe. 2180
SCORE = 1
A witherd Hermite fiue score winters worne, 1591
SCORNE = 3*1
These othes and lawes will proue an idle scorne. | Surra, Come
on. 304
*for a new deuisde cursie. I thinke scorne to sigh, mee thinks 368
How will he scorne, how will he spende his wit? 1484
Bruse me with scorne, confound me with a flout. 2329
SCORNES = 1
Will heare your idle scornes; continue then, 2826
SCOUT = 1
That charge their breath against vs? Say scout say. 1980
SCRAPS = 1
**Boy.* They haue been at a great feast of Languages, and | stolne
the scraps. 1776
SCRAPT = *1
*you will be scrapt out of the painted cloth for this. 2529
SCRATCHT = *1
Curat. Laus deo, bene intelligo. | * Peda. Bome boon for boon
prescian, a litle scratcht, twil serue. 1766
SCURILLITIE *see also* squirilitie = *1
*haue been sharpe & sententious: pleasant without scurillitie, 1742
SCUTCHION = 1
My Scutchion plaine declares that I am Alisander. 2515
SCYTHES *see* sythes
SEA = 2
The Sea will ebb and flow, heauen shew his face: 1564
Sea sicke I thinke comming from *Muscouie.* 2325
SEALD-VP = 1
This seald-vp counsaile. Ther's thy guerdon: goe. 934
SEALE = 1
That he was faine to seale on *Cupids* name. 1896
SEARCHT = 1
That will not be deepe searcht with sawcie lookes: 90
SEASON = 2
But like of each thing that in season growes. 116
And wayte the season, and obserue the times, 1953
SEA-WATER = 1
Arm. Tell me precisely of what complexion? | *Boy.* Of the sea-
water Greene sir. 387
SECOND = *1
*Spaniards Rapier: The first and second cause will not serue 480
SECRECIE = *1
*secrecie, that the King would haue me present the Princesse 1843
SECRET = 1
Ber. One word in secret. | *Quee.* Let it not be sweete. 2142
SECRETS = 3
Clow. Of other mens secrets I beseech you. 241
him with thy Birdbolt vnder the left papp: in fayth secrets. 1356
And wretched fooles secrets heedfully ore ey. 1414
SEDUCED = *1
*seduced, and he had a very good wit. *Cupids* Butshaft is too 478

222

SEDULE = 1
That are recorded in this sedule here. 22
SEE = 30*11
As not to see a woman in that terme, 41
Not to see Ladyes, study, fast, not sleepe. 52
Ber. Lets see the penaltie. On payne of loosing her tung. 132
*graces Farborough: But I would see his owne person | in flesh
and blood. | *Ber.* This is he. 196
did I see that low spirited Swaine, that base Minow of thy myrth, 255
My Lord *Berowne,* see him deliuered ore, 300
**Clo.* Well, if euer I do see the merry dayes of desolation 462
that I haue seene, some shall see. 463
Boy. What shall some see? 464
**Ros.* Pray you, do my commendations, I would be glad | to see
it. 678
His tongue all impacient to speake and not see, 742
Boy. What then, do you see?| *Lad.* I, our way to be gone. 766
Let me see a fat *Lenuoy,* I thats a fat Goose. 868
And to her white hand see thou do commend 933
Quee. See see, my beautie wilbe sau'd by merrit. 996
*and obscure vulgar; *videliset,* He came, see, and ouercame: 1049
*He came, one; see, two; ouercame, three. Who came? the 1050
*King. Why did he come? to see. Why did he see? to ouer-|come. 1051
To see him walke before a Lady, and to beare her Fann. 1143
*To see him kisse his hand, & how most sweetly a wil sweare: 1144
*So were there a patch set on Learning, to see him in a schole. 1185
For all the wealth that euer I did see, 1486
You found his Moth, the King your Moth did see: 1498
To see a King transformed to a Gnat. 1503
To see great *Hercules* whipping a Gigge, 1504
When shall you see mee write a thing in rime? 1519
Long. Looke, heer's thy loue, my foote and her face see. 1626
The streete should see as she walkt ouer head. 1630
To fast, to study, and to see no woman: 1642
Then when our selues we see in Ladies eyes, | With our selues. 1666
Do we not likewise see our learning there? 1668
For quoth the King, an Angell shalt thou see: 1995
Despight of sute, to see a Ladies face. 2021
Bero. See where it comes. Behauiour what wert thou? 2263
Ile leaue it by degrees; soft, let vs see, 2351
For the Lords tokens on you do I see. 2356
I see the tricke ant: here was a consent, 2399
**Alisander,* alas you see how tis a little oreparted, but there 2536
*you not see, *Pompey* is vncasing for the Combat: What 2657
SEEING = 2
It addes a precious seeing to the eye: 1684
With eies best seeing, heauens fierie eie: 2302
SEEKE = 8
To seeke the lyght of trueth, while trueth the whyle 80
Then seeke a dispensation for his oth: 581
What? I loue, I sue, I seeke a wife, 955
As I for praise alone now seeke to spill 1009
Where nothing wantes, that want it selfe doth seeke. 1586
How I would make him fawne, and begge, and seeke, 1952
Berow. Our states are forfait, seeke not to vndoo vs. 2358
But seeke the weery beddes of people sicke. 2782

SEEKING = 1
Light seeking light, doth light of light beguyle: 82
SEELY = *1
  *Pag. Ba most seely Sheepe, with a horne: you heare his |
  (learning.   1788
SEEME = 2
But I beleeue although I seeme so loth,   170
Wise thinges seeme foolish, and rich thinges but poore.   2305
SEEMED = 1
And what in vs hath seemed rediculous: 2717
SEEMES = 1
But that it seemes he little purposeth: 637
SEEMETH = 3
Therefore to's seemeth it a needfull course,   516
Seemeth their conference, their conceites haue winges,   2176
Quoniam, *he seemeth in minoritie,*   2545
SEENE = 6*4
And not be seene to wincke of all the day.   47
*Item, Yf any man be seene to talke with a woman within   139
*I was seene with her in the Manner house, sitting with her   217
that I haue seene, some shall see.   463
O what a Scaene of foolrie haue I seene,   1500
Shee (an attending Starre) scarce seene a light.   1580
*a Souldier, a man of trauayle, that hath seene the worlde: but   1841
Cutting a smaller haire then may be seene,   2174
*Long. The face of an olde Roman coyne, scarce seene.   2566
*seene the day of wrong through the litle hole of discretion,   2681
SEES = 1*1
All ignorant that soule, that sees thee without wonder.   1277
*Ber. Did they quoth you? Who sees the heauenly Rosaline,   1570
SEEST = *1
*seest. But to the place Where? It standeth North North-east & by   253
SELDOME = 1
Bo. If my obseruation (which very seldome lyes   732
SELFE = 22*12
Ber. This Article my liedge your selfe must breake,   143
The French kinges daughter with your selfe to speake: 145
*Const. I my selfe reprehend his owne person, for I am his   195
*selfe to walke: the time When? about the sixt houre, When
Beastes   245
*Ar. Why? sadnes is one & the selfe same thing deare imp.   315
Ar. I do betray my selfe with blushing: Maide. | Maide. Man.   436
Your selfe, helde precious in the worldes esteeme,   495
From reasons yeelding, your faire selfe should make   646
As you shall deeme your selfe lodgd in my hart.   671
*Bo. She hath but one for her selfe, to desire that were a | (shame.   698
*true that thou art beautious, trueth it selfe that   1042
*truer then trueth it selfe: haue comiseration on thy   1044
*roabes, for tittles tytles, for thy selfe, mee. Thus expecting   1062
*Rosa. If we choose by the hornes, your selfe come not   1102
Boyet. But she her selfe is hit lower: Haue I hit her now?   1106
Though to my selfe forsworne, to thee Ile faythfull proue.   1269
I am coursing my selfe.   1335
But do not loue thy selfe, then thou will keepe   1370
Where nothing wantes, that want it selfe doth seeke.   1586
Paintes it selfe blacke, to imitate her brow.   1614
Learning is but an adiunct to our selfe,   1664

SELFE *cont.*
For Charitie it selfe fulfilles the Law: 1745
*that the Curate and your sweete selfe, are good at such
erup-|tions,   1846
* *Peda. Iosua*, your selfe, my selfe, and this gallant Gentle-|man   1859
Brag. For the rest of the Worthies?| *Peda.* I will play three my
selfe.   1873
Berow. Tell her we measure them by weerie steps. | *Boy.* She
heares her selfe.   2092
* *Lon.* Looke how you butt your selfe in these sharpe mocks,   2166
Quee. Berowne did sweare him selfe out of all suite.   2194
Peda. What meane you sir?| *Boyet.* To make *Iudas* hang him
selfe.   2556
and I will right my selfe like a Souldier. *Exeunt Worthys*   2682
And euen that falshood in it selfe a sinne,   2733
Thus purifies it selfe and turns to grace.   2734
My wofull selfe vp in a mourning house, | Rayning the teares of
lamentation,   2768
SELFE-SOUERAIGNTIE = 1
Boy. Do not curst wiues hold that selfe-soueraigntie   1011
SELL = 3
To sell a bargaine well is as cunning as fast and loose: 867
I will neuer buy and sell out of this word.   907
And we that sell by grosse, the Lord doth know,   2244
SELLERS = 1
To thinges of sale, a sellers prayse belonges: 1589
SELUES = 8*1
Then when our selues we see in Ladies eyes, | With our selues.   1666
Lets vs once loose our othes to finde our selues,   1712
Or els we loose our selues, to keepe our othes: 1713
* *King.* Prise you your selues: What buyes your company?   2127
Will they not (thinke you) hange them selues to nyght?   2189
Bero. Speake for your selues, my wit is at an ende.   2363
If ouerboldly we haue borne our selues,   2692
Is likewise yours: we to our selues proue false,   2730
SENCE = 4
All sences to that sence did make their repaire,   744
Aboue the sence of sence so sensible,   2175
*But I will forward with my deuice; sweete royaltie bestow | on
me the sence of hearing.   2619
SENCES = 1
All sences to that sence did make their repaire,   744
SENCIBLY = 1
Pag. I will tell you sencibly.   879
SEND = 4*1
Ber. And send you manie louers. | *Kath.* Amen, so you be none.   621
* *Boy.* Marrie sir, you must send the Asse vpon the Horse,   822
Long. By whom shall I send this (companie?) Stay.   1411
This will I send, and something els more plaine.   1458
Quee. Did he not send you twaine?| *Kath.* Yes Madame: and
moreouer,   1938
SENDES = 2
Consider who the King your father sendes: 493
To whom he sendes, and whats his Embassie.   494
SENSE = 1*2
* *Ber.* Things hid & bard (you meane) from cammon sense.   62
When Mistresses from common sense are hid.   69

SENSE *cont.*
  *Bra. Warble child, make passionate my sense of hearing. | *Boy.*
  Concolinel.   772
SENSES = 1
  Mee thought all his senses were lokt in his eye,   746
SENSIBLE = 2*1
  *sensible in the duller partes: and such barren plantes are   1179
  Loues feeling is more soft and sensible,   1688
  Aboue the sence of sence so sensible,   2175
SENT = 3*3
  *duetie prickes me on) *haue sent to thee, to receiue the meede of*
  pu-| *nishment*   265
  *it was geuen me by *Costard*, and sent me from *Don Armatho*:   1255
  *it, the Foole sent it, and the Lady hath it: sweete Clowne,   1349
  Who sent it? and what is it?   1918
  But *Katherine* what was sent to you | From faire *Dumaine*?   1935
  Marg. This, and these Pearle, to me sent *Longauile*.   1943
SENTENCE = *1
  * Fer. Sir I will pronounce your sentence: You shall fast a | weeke
  with Branne and Water.   295
SENTENTIOUS = *1
  *haue been sharpe & sententious: pleasant without scurillitie,   1742
SEQUELL = 1
  Pag. Like the sequell I. Signeur *Costard* adew. *Exit.*   899
SEQUENT = *1
  *with the King, and here he hath framed a letter to a sequent   1303
SERIOUS = 1*1
  On serious busines crauing quicke dispatch,   522
  *important and most serious designes, and of great import in   1833
SERPENTS = 1
  Thus did he strangle Serpents in his Manus,   2544
SERUANT = 2
  No poynt (quoth I) my seruant, straight was mute.   2196
  Bero. Pompey the great. | *Clow.* Your seruant and *Costard.*   2525
SERUE = 6*2
  Fer. This Maide will not serue your turne sir.   293
  Clo. This Maide will serue my turne sir.   294
  were, it would neither serue for the writing, nor the tune.   417
  *Spaniards Rapier: The first and second cause will not serue   480
  Breake vp this Capon. | *Boyet* I am bound to serue.   1034
  Curat. Laus deo, bene intelligo. | ** Peda. Bome boon for boon*
  prescian, a litle scratcht, twil serue.   1766
  Quee. Doth this man serue God? | *Bero.* Why aske you?   2469
  Duma. Ile serue thee true and faythfully till then.   2791
SERUICE = 5
  And shape his seruice wholly to my deuice,   1955
  Mar. Dumaine was at my seruice, and his sword,   2195
  Kath. And *Longauill* was for my seruice borne.   2205
  me any seruice to her thither,   2237
  Impose some seruice on me for thy Loue.   2801
SET = 1*5
  * Arm. I giue thee thy libertie, set thee from durance, and in   894
  *King *Cophetua* set eie vpon the pernicious and indubitate   1046
  *set before vs, that we thankful should be: which we taste,   1180
  *So were there a patch set on Learning, to see him in a schole.   1185
  *that defiles; defile, a foule worde: Well, set thee downe   1337
  Quee. Well bandied both, a set of Wit well played.   1916

SETTING = *1
*Arm. By my sweete soule, I meane, setting thee at libertie.   889
SEUENTH = 1
Quee. Seuenth sweete adue, since you can cogg,   2140
SEUER = 1
And who can seuer Loue from Charitie.   1716
SEUERALL = 5
My lippes are no Common, though seuerall they be.   726
Where seuerall worthies make one dignitie,   1585
Vnto his seuerall Mistres: which they'le know   2016
By Fauours seuerall, which they did bestow.   2017
Their seuerall counsailes they vnboosome shall,   2033
SHADE = 3
Sweete leaues shade follie. Who is he comes heere?   1375
Boy. Vnder the coole shade of a Siccamore,   1981
Toward that shade I might beholde addrest,   1984
SHAKE = 1
Might shake off fiftie, looking in her eye: 1592
SHAL l.*1241 = *1
SHALBE = 10*1
Our Court shalbe a lytlle Achademe,   17
Who dazling so, that eye shalbe his heed,   87
Lon. Costard the swaine and he, shalbe our sport,   190
Nau. You shalbe welcome Madame to my Court.   590
But here without you shalbe so receiude,   670
King. Away, away, no time shalbe omitted,   1732
*in minoritie: his enter and exit shalbe strangling a Snake;   1867
Quee. Sweete hartes we shalbe rich ere we depart,   1888
Quee. And will they so? the Gallants shalbe taskt: 2018
Hencefoorth my wooing minde shalbe exprest   2344
Die when you will, a Smocke shalbe your shroude.   2418
SHALL l.10 15 16 29 *128 *140 164 182 *211 *224 268 *271 *295
   299 408 *451 463 464 *472 *485 514 595 663 664 671 674 *723
   919 924 979 998 *1059 *1060 1094 *1108 *1211 1267 1275 *1319
   *1329 1374 1392 1411 1459 1482 1519 *1521 1556 1722 *1850
   1861 *1866 1876 1987 2020 2025 2026 2033 2037 2047 2221 *2271
   2362 *2374 2427 2458 *2533 *2636 2753 2781 2786 2811 2813
   2829 = 51*25
SHALLOW = 2*1
*that shallow vassall (Clown. Still mee.) which as I remember,   258
Their shallow showes, and Prologue vildly pende.   2228
Which shallow laughing hearers giue to fooles,   2821
SHALT l.*449 453 460 *1020 *1061 1995 2022 2635 = 5*3
SHAME = 8*4
Fer. How well this yeelding rescewes thee from shame.   127
shame as the rest of the Court can possible deuise.   141
Standes in attainder of eternall shame.   168
*Bo. She hath but one for her selfe, to desire that were a | (shame.   698
Long. In loue I hope, sweete fellowship in shame.   1381
*Berow. Ah you whoreson loggerhead, you were borne to | do me
shame.   1548
*And they wel mockt depart away with shame. Sound Trom.   2048
Vnseene, vnuisited, much to our shame.   2284
*King. Berowne, they will shame vs: let them not approch.   2453
*Bero. We are shame proofe my Lord: & tis some policie   2455
*and a feard to speake? Run away for shame Ali-| sander.   2532
Peda. Iudas I am. | Duma. The more shame for you Iudas.   2554

SHAMED = 1
But are you not a shamed? nay, are you not   1496
SHAPE = 5
For he hath wit to make an ill shape good,   551
And shape to win grace though he had no wit.   552
The shape of Loues Tiburne, that hanges vp Simplicitie.   1386
Such as the shortnesse of the time can shape,   1729
And shape his seruice wholly to my deuice,   1955
SHAPELES = 1
Disguysd like *Muscouites* in shapeles geare: 2226
SHAPES = 3*1
*extrauagant spirit, full of formes, figures, shapes, obiectes,   1231
In their owne shapes: for it can neuer be,   2209
If they returne in their owne shapes to woe?   2222
Full of straying shapes, of habites and of formes: 2721
SHARPE = 2*2
Is a sharpe Wit matcht with too blunt a Will: 541
*haue been sharpe & sententious: pleasant without scurillitie,   1742
*Lon. Looke how you butt your selfe in these sharpe mocks,   2166
Thrust thy sharpe wit quite through my ignorance,   2330
SHE = 27*12
SHEE *l.*159 1431 1580 1588 1624 1998 2408 = 7
SHEEPE = 2*4
No Sheepe (sweete Lambe) vnlesse we feede on your lippes.   722
*La. You Sheepe and I pasture: shall that finish the iest?   723
*as *Aiax*, it kills Sheepe, it kills mee, I a Sheepe well prooued   1340
*Pag. Ba most seely Sheepe, with a horne: you heare his |
(learning.   1788
Pag. The Sheepe, the other two concludes it o u.   1794
SHEEPES = 1
Lady Ka. Two hot Sheepes marie. | *Bo.* And wherefore not
Shipps?   720
SHEEPHEARD = 1
And Dicke the Sheepheard blowes his naile: 2880
SHEES = 1*2
*Ro. You tooke the moone at ful, but now shee's changed?   2114
To make my Lady laugh, when shees disposd: 2405
*wench is cast away: shee's quicke, the childe bragges in her |
bellie already: tis yours.   2632
SHEETE *see also* asheete = 1
As would be crambd vp in a sheete of paper   1894
SHEPHEARDS = 1
When Shepheards pipe on Oten Strawes,   2869
SHES = *1
*Cl. Shes to hard for you at pricks, sir challeng her to bowle   1133
SHEW = 9*3
If wounding then it was to shew my skill,   1003
The Sea will ebb and flow, heauen shew his face: 1564
*King. What, did these rent lines shew some loue of thine?   1568
Scarce shew a haruest of their heauie toyle.   1677
That shew, containe, and nourish all the worlde.   1704
Vouchsafe to shew the sunshine of your face,   2100
Or euer but in vizards shew their faces.   2190
To shew his teeth as white as Whales bone,   2257
*will shew wher-vntill it doth amount: for mine owne part, I   2443
*first shew thriue, these foure will change habites, and present |
the other fiue.   2481

SHEW *cont.*
  Bero. There is fiue in the first shew. 2483
  ende of our shew. | *King.* Call them foorth quickly, we will do so. 2851
SHEWED = 3
  Till this mad man shewed thee, and what art thou now? 2264
  That hid the worse, and shewed the better face. 2317
  Dum. Our letters madame, shewed much more then iest. 2743
SHIELD = 1
  That oft in fielde with Targ and Shield did make my foe to sweat, 2500
SHIN = 4*1
  *Pag. A wonder Maister, Heers a *Costard* broken in a shin. 841
  Boy. By saying that a *Costard* was broken in a shin. 871
  Ar. But tel me, How was there a *Costard* broken in a shin? 877
  Fell ouer the threshold, and broke my shin. 883
  Clow. Till there be more matter in the shin. 885
SHINE = 3*1
  *Then thou faire Sunne, which on my earth doost shine, 1402
  Ber. I as some dayes, but then no Sunne must shine. 1426
  O tis the Sunne that maketh all thinges shine. 1595
  Vouchsafe bright Moone, and these thy Starrs to shine, 2104
SHINES = 1
  Nor shines the siluer Moone one halfe so bright, 1362
SHINST = 1
  Thou shinst in euerie teare that I do weepe, 1365
SHIP = *1
  *Kin. The Ship is vnder sayle, and heere she coms amaine. 2489
SHIPPS = 1
  Lady Ka. Two hot Sheepes marie. | *Bo.* And wherefore not
  Shipps? 720
SHIRT = 1
  Brag. The naked trueth of it is, I haue no Shirt. 2665
SHOLD *l.**1760 = *1
SHOO = *1
  *shoo (which is baser) guided by her foote (which is basest) 471
SHOOT = 1*1
  *Clo. Indeed a'must shoot nearer, or hele neare hit the clout. 1125
  Sowla, sowla. *Exeunt.* Shoot within. 1148
SHOOTE = 5
  I shoote thee at the Swaine. 834
  A Stand where you may make the fairest shoote. 984
  Quee. I thanke my Beautie, I am faire that shoote, 985
  And thereupon thou speakst the fairest shoote. 986
  Thus will I saue my Credite in the shoote, 1001
SHOOTER = 3
  Boy. Who is the shooter? Who is the shooter? 1093
  Rosa. Well then I am the shooter. | *Boy.* And who is your Deare? 1100
SHOOTING = 2
  And shooting well, is then accounted ill: 1000
  Some say a Sore, but not a sore, | till now made sore with
  shooting. 1217
SHOP = 1*1
  *smelling loue with your hat penthouse like ore the shop of 786
  Ber. O Rimes are gardes on wanton *Cupids* hose, | Disfigure not
  his Shop. 1390
SHORT = 8
  And so to studie three yeeres is but short. 191
  Prin. Such short liued wits do wither as they grow. 546

SHORT *cont.*
    Brag. The way is but short, away. | *Boy.* As swift as Lead sir.   824
    O short liu'd pride. Not faire? alacke for woe | *For.* Yes Madam
    faire.   989
    She passes prayse, then prayse too short doth blot.   1590
    The Chaine were longer, and the Letter short.   1946
    Excuse me so comming too short of thankes,   2696
    Quee. A time me thinkes too short,   2748
SHORTNESSE = 1
    Such as the shortnesse of the time can shape,   1729
SHOT = *2
    Mar. A marke marueilous wel shot, for they both did hit.   1119
    Be. Shot by heauen, proceed sweet *Cupid*, thou hast thumpt   1355
SHOULD *l.**60 111 113 155 *370 543 618 646 1026 *1180 1466 1609
    1620 1630 *1760 1958 1998 2119 2230 *2275 2279 *2439
    *2850 = 16*7
SHOULDE *l.**1247 = *1
SHOULDER = 2*1
    Ber. Stoope I say, her shoulder is with child.   1424
    *my poore shoulder, and with his royall finger thus dallie   1836
    With that all laught, and clapt him on the shoulder,   1999
SHOULDST *l.*1085 *1807 = 1*1
SHOW *see also* shew = 3*3
    *replication, or rather *ostentare*, to show as it were his
    inclina-|tion   1165
    And they thy glorie through my griefe will show: 1369
    *(sweete chuck) with some delightfull ostentation, or show,   1844
    *some show in the posterior of this day, to be rended by our   1852
    Haue not the grace to grace it with such show.   2245
    To haue one show worse then the Kings and his company.   2456
SHOWD = 1
    Quee. Who ere a was, a showd a mounting minde.   978
SHOWED *see* shewed
SHOWES = 2
    Then wish a Snow in Mayes new fangled showes: 115
    Their shallow showes, and Prologue vildly pende.   2228
SHOWNE = 2
    And feares by pale white showne: 406
    Dismaskt, their dammaske sweete commixture showne,   2219
SHRIMPE = 1
    And when he was a babe, a childe, a shrimpe,   2543
SHROUDE = 1
    Die when you will, a Smocke shalbe your shroude.   2418
SHROWDE = 1
    Kath. I and a shrowde vnhappie gallowes too.   1899
SHROWDED = 1
    I haue been closely shrowded in this bush,   1474
SHROWES = 1
    Quee. A Poxe of that iest, and I beshrow all Shrowes,   1934
SHUE = 1
    Well, I will loue, write, sigh, pray, shue, grone,   970
SHUT = 1
    Ar. Take away this villaine, shut him vp.   456
SHUTT = 1
    I wilbe thine: and till that instance shutt   2767
SHYNING = 1
    Haue no more profite of their shyning nights,   95

SHYRT = 2
    Clow. Ile do it in my shyrt. | *Duma.* Most resolute *Pompey.*   2654
    Brag. Gentlemen and Souldiers, pardon me, I will not | combat
    in my shyrt.   2659
SICCAMORE = 1
    Boy. Vnder the coole shade of a Siccamore,   1981
SICKE = 8
    To her decrepit, sicke, and bedred Father.   148
    Ros. Is the foole sicke. | *Ber.* Sicke at the hart.   681
    That the Louer sicke to death,   1444
    Sea sicke I thinke comming from *Muscouie.*   2325
    Of the olde rage: beare with me, I am sicke.   2350
    But seeke the weery beddes of people sicke.   2782
    Visite the speachlesse sicke, and still conuerse,   2812
SICKLY = 1
    Of him that makes it: then if sickly eares   2824
SICKNES = 1
    Quee. Goe sicknes as thou art.   2201
SIDE = 6*4
    Stand a side good bearer. *Boyet* you can carue,   1032
    *victorie: On whose side? the King: the captiue is inricht, on   1055
    *whose side? the Beggers. The catastrophe is a Nuptiall, on   1056
    *whose side? the Kinges: no, on both in one, or one in both.   1057
    Armatho ath toothen side, o a most daintie man,   1142
    And his Page atother side, that handfull of wit,   1146
    *againe a my side. I will not loue; if I do hang mee: I'fayth   1341
    He standes a side. The King entreth.   1353
    Enter Longauill. The King steps a side.   1376
    Brag. This side is *Hiems,* Winter.   2855
SIDES = 1
    Writ a both sides the leafe, margent and all,   1895
SIGH = 3*3
    *for a new deuisde cursie. I thinke scorne to sigh, mee thinks   368
    *with turning vp your eylids, sigh a note and sing a note
    som-|time   783
    By thy fauour sweete Welkin, I must sigh in thy face: 837
    *A verie Bedell to a humerous sigh, a Critick, nay a night-|watch
    Constable,   941
    And I to sigh for her, to watch for her,   966
    Well, I will loue, write, sigh, pray, shue, grone,   970
SIGHES = 4
    Th'annoynted soueraigne of sighes and groones: 948
    Saw sighes reeke from you, noted well your pashion.   1477
    Of sighes, of grones, of sorrow, and of teene: 1501
    Vntill his Incke were tempred with Loues sighes: 1698
SIGHT = 5
    Doth falsely blinde the eye-sight of his looke: 81
    To morrow you shall haue a sight of them.   663
    Did stumble with haste in his ey-sight to bee,   743
    Rosa. Come on then, weare the Fauours most in sight.   2028
    As precious ey-sight, and did value me   2383
SIGHTED = 1
    What peromptorie Eagle-sighted eye   1575
SIGNE = 2*1
    Armado. Boy, What signe is it when a man of great spi-|rite
    growes melancholy?   312
    Boy. A great signe sir that he will looke sadd.   314

SIGNE *cont.*
Folowing the signes, wood but the signe of shee.   2408
SIGNEOR = 3*1
 Boy. By a familier demonstration of the working, my | tough
signeor.   320
Arma. Why tough signeor? Why tough signeor?   322
 Boy. And I tough signeor, as an appertinent title to your   327
SIGNEOUR = 1
Const. Signeour *Arme Arme* commendes you: 199
SIGNES = 2
Folowing the signes, wood but the signe of shee.   2408
There stay vntill the twelue Celestiall Signes   2757
SIGNEUR = 1
Pag. Like the sequell I. Signeur *Costard* adew. *Exit.*   899
SIGNIFICANT = *1
*significant to the countrey Maide *Iaquenetta*: there is
remu-|neration,   896
SIGNIFIE = 1
Haste, signifie so much while we attende,   524
SIGNIOR = 1
This signior *Iunios* gyant dwarffe, dan *Cupid,*   946
SILENT = 1*1
*It is not for prisoners to be too silent in their wordes, and   466
No Woman may approch his silent Court: 515
SILKE = 1
Ber. O, why then threefarthing worth of Silke.   915
SILKEN = 1
Taffata phrases, silken tearmes precise,   2338
SILLIE = *1
Ar. By vertue thou inforcest laughter, thy sillie thought,   848
SILUER = 2
Nor shines the siluer Moone one halfe so bright,   1362
And Ladi-smockes all siluer white,   2862
SIMPATHISD = *1
Boy. A message well simpathisd, a Horse to be embassa-|doure
for an Asse.   819
SIMPLE = 1*3
Clo. By my soule a Swaine, a most simple Clowne.   1137
Nath. This is a gyft that I haue simple: simple, a foolish   1230
King. Farewel mad Wenches, you haue simple wits. *Exe.*   2181
SIMPLICITIE = 3*2
Clow. Such is the simplicitie of man to harken after the flesh   228
Holo. Twice sodd simplicitie, bis coctus, O thou monster   1172
The shape of Loues Tiburne, that hanges vp Simplicitie.   1386
A hudge translation of hipocrisie, | Vildly compyled, profound
simplicitie.   1941
To proue by Wit, worth in simplicitie.   1968
SIN = *1
*And sin to breake it: but pardon me, I am too sodaine bold,   601
SINCE = 5*3
*three ages since, but I thinke now tis not to be found: or if it   416
Long. And since her time are Colliers counted bright.   1616
Since all the power thereof it doth apply,   1967
Rosa. Since you are strangers, and come here by chance,   2120
Quee. Seuenth sweete adue, since you can cogg,   2140
*Linnen: since when, Ile be sworne he wore none, but a
dish-|cloute   2668

SINCE *cont.*

Yet since Loues argument was first on foote,	2705
From what it purposd, since to wayle friendes lost,	2707

SING = 4*1

Before the Birdes haue any cause to sing?	112
Ar. Sing Boy, My spirit growes heauie in loue.	426
Ar. I say sing. | *Boy.* Forbeare till this companie be past.	428
*with turning vp your eylids, sigh a note and sing a note som- | time	783
In honorable tearmes; nay he can sing	2252

SINGES = 5

That singes heauens prayse, with such an earthly tong.	1283
Mocks married men; for thus singes hee, | Cuckow.	2865
Mockes married men, for thus singes he, | Cuckow.	2874
Then nightly singes the staring Owle	2884
Then nightly singes the staring Owle,	2893

SINGING = *1

*through the throate, if you swallowed loue with sing- | ing	784

SINGLE = 1

Bold of your worthines, we single you,	519

SINGULED = *1

Brag. Arts-man preambulat, we will be singuled from the	1815

SINGULER = 1

Curat. A most singuler and choyce Epithat, | *Draw-out his Table-booke.*	1754

SINNE = 4

Tis deadlie sinne to keepe that oath my Lord,	600
Do not call it sinne in me,	1452
I that am honest, I that holde it sinne	1515
And euen that falshood in it selfe a sinne,	2733

SINNES = 1

Rosal. You must be purged to, your sinnes are rackt.	2778

SINNOWY = 1

The sinnowy vigour of the trauayler.	1658

SIR *l.*58 201 *209 *211 213 216 *220 223 279 *285 288 293 294 *295 *306 314 317 330 342 346 350 *358 388 390 394 *431 *451 458 460 692 700 *703 707 712 713 714 *822 825 830 *845 *846 847 866 *911 914 920 922 924 937 1028 *1133 *1159 1161 *1174 *1207 *1237 *1262 1264 *1294 *1302 1309 *1312 *1314 1316 *1329 1468 1532 1621 *1741 1775 *1821 *1825 *1827 *1829 *1850 *1851 *1863 1882 2156 2235 2392 2395 2415 2426 2429 2432 *2433 2434 *2436 *2439 2440 *2442 2445 *2451 2499 *2528 2550 2556 2558 2838 = 63*41

SIRRA *see also* surra = 2*1

Fer. I the best, for the worst. But sirra, What say you to this?	277
Arm. Sirra *Costard*, I will infranchise thee.	886
Brag. Chirra. | *Peda. Quari* Chirra, not Sirra?	1772

SIRS = 1

King. Hence sirs, away.	1560

SISTER = 1

Ros. Youle neare be friendes with him, a kild your sister.	1900

SIT = 4*1

Ferd. Well, sit you out: go home *Berowne*: adue.	119
*most grase, Birdes best peck, and Men sit downe to that nourishment	246
smile againe, and till then sit thee downe sorrow. *Exeunt.*	309
Like a demie God, here sit I in the skie,	1413

SIT *cont.*
    And Birdes sit brooding in the Snow,   2890
SITTING = *2
    *I was seene with her in the Manner house, sitting with her   217
    *Your Lion that holdes his Polax sitting on a close stoole,   2530
SITUATE = 1
    Maid. Thats hereby. | *Ar.* I know where it is situate.   439
SIXT = *1
    selfe to walke: the time When? about the sixt houre, When
    Beastes   245
SKIE = 1*1
    *of *Celo* the skie, the welken the heauen, & anon falleth like   1155
    Like a demie God, here sit I in the skie,   1413
SKILFULLY = *1
    Lad. Thou art an old Loue-monger, & speakest skilfully.   758
SKILL = 2
    If wounding then it was to shew my skill,   1003
    Heere stand I, Ladie dart thy skill at me,   2328
SKIPPING = 1
    All wanton as a childe, skipping and vaine.   2719
SLAUE = 3
    Boy. Come you transgressing slaue, away.   457
    Ber. O stay slaue, I must employ thee.   917
    Harke slaue, it is but this: 928
SLAUES = 1
    He throwes vppon the grosse worlds baser slaues   34
SLEEPE = 2
    And then to sleepe but three houres in the nyght,   46
    Not to see Ladyes, study, fast, not sleepe.   52
SLEEUE = 2
    This Gallant pins the Wenches on his sleeue.   2246
    I knew her by this Iewell on her sleeue.   2394
SLEIGHT = 1
    Some carry tale, some please-man, some sleight saine: 2402
SLENDER = 1
    And your waste Mistres were as slender as my wit,   1025
SLIPPER = 1
    Brag. I do adore thy sweete Graces Slipper.   2623
SLOW = 5
    for he is verie slow gated: but I go.   823
    Brag. The meaning prettie ingenius, is not Lead a mettal |
    heauie, dull, and slow?   826
    Brag. I say Lead is slow.   829
    Is that Lead slow which is fierd from a Gunne?   831
    Other slow Artes intirely keepe the braine: 1675
SMALL = 2*2
    Small haue continuall plodders euer wonne,   91
    (Clowne. Mee?) *that vnlettered small knowing soule,* (*Clow.*
    Mee?)   257
    *haue a loue of that colour, mee thinkes *Sampson* had small   392
    Boye. No, he is best indued in the small.   2597
SMALLER = 1
    Cutting a smaller haire then may be seene,   2174
SMALLEST = 1
    That violates the smallest branch herein.   25
SMELL = 1*1
    Clow. O marrie me to one Francis, I smell some *Lenuoy,*   887

SMELL   *cont.*
  Peda. Oh I smell false Latine, *dunghel* for *vnguem.*   1814
SMELLING = *3
  *smelling loue with your hat penthouse like ore the shop of   786
  Naso was the man. And why in deed *Naso*, but for smel-|ling   1288
  Be. Your nose smels no in his most tender smelling knight.   2518
SMELS = *1
  Be. Your nose smels no in his most tender smelling knight.   2518
SMILE = 2
  smile againe, and till then sit thee downe sorrow. *Exeunt.*   309
  To enforce the pained impotent to smile.   2815
SMOCKE = 1
  Die when you will, a Smocke shalbe your shroude.   2418
SMOCKES = 2
  And Ladi-smockes all siluer white,   2862
  And Maidens bleach their summer smockes: 2872
SMOKE = 1
  Brag. Sweete smoke of Rhetorike,   832
SMOOTHLY = *1
  *When it comes so smoothly off, so obscenly as it were, so fit.   1140
SMOT = 1
  As thy eye beames, when their fresh rayse haue smot.   1360
SMOTHFAST = 1
  Ile marke no wordes that smothfast wooers say,   2788
SMYLES = 2
  This is the floure that smyles on euery one.   2256
  That smyles, his cheeke in yeeres, and knowes the trick   2404
SMYLING = 1*1
  *smyling: O pardone me my starres, doth the incon-|siderate   850
  Forbid the smyling courtecie of Loue,   2703
SNAKE = *2
  *in minoritie: his enter and exit shalbe strangling a Snake;   1867
  *Snake; that is the way to make an offence gracious, though   1871
SNAP = *1
  *sweete tutch, a quicke venewe of wit, snip snap, quicke and   1796
SNATCH = 1
  It were a fault to snatch wordes from my tongue.   2309
SNAYLES = 1
  Then are the tender hornes of Cockled Snayles.   1689
SNEAPING = 1
  Ferd. Berowne is like an enuious sneaping Frost,   109
SNIP = *2
  *tune, but a snip and away: these are complementes, these   790
  *sweete tutch, a quicke venewe of wit, snip snap, quicke and   1796
SNOW = 2
  Then wish a Snow in Mayes new fangled showes: 115
  And Birdes sit brooding in the Snow,   2890
SNOWHITE = *1
  & most propostrous euent that draweth fro(m) my snowhite pen
  the   251
SNOW-WHITE = 1
  To the snow-white hand of the most bewtious Lady Rosaline.   1297
SNUFFE = 1
  Kath. Yole marre the light by taking it in snuffe: 1909
SNUFFT = *1
  *loue sometime through: nose as if you snufft vp loue by   785

SO *l.*12 38 64 72 83 87 117 153 157 166 170 191 *204 235 *236 237
*242 *247 *269 *275 290 302 *364 394 445 446 *475 *476 524 527
544 545 568 597 613 622 644 645 651 652 660 661 670 672 712 724
725 830 945 975 987 1005 *1024 *1058 *1059 *1111 *1140 *1185
*1211 *1237 *1254 *1258 *1284 *1290 *1338 1358 1362 1367 1383
1405 1430 1447 1451 1467 1487 1524 1525 1602 1624 1625 1632
1737 *1780 *1811 1855 *1864 *1869 *1884 *1902 1904 1912 1933
1948 1949 1957 1959 1965 2008 2018 2025 2026 2034 2047 2080
2086 2098 2124 2130 2137 *2150 2168 2175 2184 2229 2239 *2271
2281 2285 2291 2346 2359 2432 *2467 2484 *2507 2524 2576 2578
2594 2608 2678 2686 2696 2697 2708 2744 2745 2787 2797 2833
2852 = 113*36

SOCIETIE = 3*1

I beseech your societie.	1324
Nath. And thanke you to: for societie (saith the text) | is the happines of life.	1326
Thou makest the triumpherie, the corner cap of societie,	1385
That in loues griefe desirst societie:	1465

SODAINE = 1*2

*And sin to breake it: but pardon me, I am too sodaine bold,	601
*and sodaine breaking out of myrth (as it were) I haue	1847
The sodaine hand of death close vp mine eye.	2775

SODAINELIE = 2

And sodainelie resolue mee in my suite.	605
Nau. Madame I will, if sodainelie I may.	606

SODD = *1

Holo. Twice sodd simplicitie, bis coctus, O thou monster	1172

SOFT = 3

King. Soft, Whither away so fast?	1524
Loues feeling is more soft and sensible,	1688
Ile leaue it by degrees; soft, let vs see,	2351

SOFTLY = 1

Mar. Bleat softly then, the Butcher heares you crie.	2171

SOL = *1

*Who vnderstandeth thee not, loues thee not, *vt re sol la mi fa*:	1261

SOLACE = 1

We will with some strange pastime solace them:	1728

SOLD = *1

Clo. The Boy hath sold him a bargaine, a Goose, that's flat.	865

SOLE = 2*1

Ferd. Great Deputie the welkins Vizregent, and sole dominatur of	231
To parlee with the sole inheritoure	496
Sole Emperator and great generall | Of trotting Parrators (O my litle hart.)	951

SOLEMBE = 1

To checke their follie pashions solembe teares.	2010

SOLEMNIZED = 1

Betweene L.(ord) *Perigort* and the bewtious heire | Of *Iaques Fauconbridge* solemnized.	533

SOLICITER = 1

As our best mouing faire soliciter:	520

SOLOMON see Sallomon, Salomon

SOME = 36*15

Or studie where to meete some Mistris fine.	68
to a woman, for the forme in some forme.	221
Boy. The worlde was very guiltie of such a Ballet some	415
*example my digression by some mightie presedent. Boy,	420

SOME *cont.*

that I haue seene, some shall see.	463
Boy. What shall some see?	464
*manager is in loue; yea he loueth. Assist me some extempo-|rall	484
Prin. Some merrie mocking Lord belike, ist so?	544
A yeelding gainst some reason in my brest,	647
As Iewels in Christall for some Prince to buy.	747
**Ar.* Some enigma, some riddle, come, thy *Lenuoy* begin.	843
Some obscure presedence that hath tofore bin saine.	856
**Clow.* O marrie me to one Francis, I smell some *Lenuoy,*	887
some Goose in this.	888
Some men must loue my Ladie, and some Ione.	971
Some say a Sore, but not a sore, | till now made sore with shooting.	1217
Which is to mee some prayse, that I thy partes admire,	1278
Ber. I as some dayes, but then no Sunne must shine.	1426
King. What present hast thou there? | *Clow.* Some certaine treason.	1529
**King.* What, did these rent lines shew some loue of thine?	1568
Duma. I marie there, some flatterie for this euyll.	1635
Long. O some authoritie how to proceede,	1636
Some tricks, some quillets, how to cheate the diuell.	1637
Duma. Some salue for periurie. | *Ber.* O tis more then neede.	1638
Some enterteinment for them in their Tentes.	1724
We will with some strange pastime solace them:	1728
*let that passe. By the world I recount no fable, some certaine	1838
*(sweete chuck) with some delightfull ostentation, or show,	1844
*Sir *Holofernes,* as concerning some entertainement of time,	1851
*some show in the posterior of this day, to be rended by our	1852
Some thousand Verses of a faithfull Louer.	1940
I thought to close mine eyes some halfe an houre:	1982
That some plaine man recount their purposes.	2074
**Rosa.* The musique playes, vouchsafe some motion to it,	2117
**King.* Teach vs sweet Madame, for our rude transgression | Some faire excuse.	2364
Some carry tale, some please-man, some sleight saine:	2402
Some mumble newes, some trencher Knight, some Dick	2403
**Clow.* We wil turne it finely off sir, we wil take some care.	2451
**Bero.* We are shame proofe my Lord: & tis some policie	2455
*are Worthies a comming will speake their minde in some | other sort. *Exit Curat.*	2537
Keepe some state in thy exit, and vanish. Exit Boy.	2547
To some forlorne and naked Hermytage,	2755
Then if I haue much loue, Ile giue you some.	2790
Impose some seruice on me for thy Loue.	2801

SOMETHING = 2

Duma. In reason nothing. | *Bero.* Something then in rime.	107
This will I send, and something els more plaine.	1458

SOMETIME = *2

*loue sometime through: nose as if you snufft vp loue by	785
*please his Grace (by the worlde) sometime to leane vpon	1835

SOMETIMES = 1*1

**Boyet.* A woman sometimes, and you saw her in the light.	696
And out of question so it is sometimes:	1005

SOMMER = 3

Bero. Well, say I am, why should proude Sommer boast,	111
Blow like sweete Roses, in this sommer aire.	2215

SOMMER *cont.*

Figures pedanticall, these sommer flies,   2340
SOMTHING = *1
  Holo. I wil somthing affect the letter, for it argues facilitie.   1213
SOMTIME = *1
  *with turning vp your eylids, sigh a note and sing a note
  som-|time   783
SONG = 1
  The Song. | When Dasies pied, and Violets blew,   2859
SONGES = 1
  *The wordes of Mercurie, are harsh after the | songes of Apollo.   2897
SONGUE = 1
  Nor woo in rime like a blind harpers songue.   2337
SONNES = *2
  *for their Sonnes are well tuterd by you, and their   1238
  Nath. Me hercle, yf their Sonnes be ingenous, they shal   1241
SONNET = 3*1
  *God of Rime, for I am sure I shall turne Sonnet. Deuise   485
  Long. This same shall go. *He reades the Sonnet.*   1392
  Dumaine reades his Sonnet.   1437
  Did neuer Sonnet for her sake compile,   1471
SONNETS = *1
  *Well, she hath one a'my Sonnets already, the Clowne bore   1348
SONNETTING = 1
  Tush, none but Minstrels like of Sonnetting.   1495
SOONE = 1*1
  Rosa. Play Musique then: nay you must do it soone.   2110
  *honest man; looke you, and soone dasht. He is a marueylous   2534
SOONER = 1
  Prin. You will the sooner that I were awaie,   607
SOONEST = 1
  Ber. Diuels soonest tempt resembling spirites of light.   1606
SORE = 9
  Some say a Sore, but not a sore, | till now made sore with
  shooting.   1217
  The Dogges did yell, put ell to Sore, | then Sorell iumps from
  thicket: 1219
  Or Pricket-sore, or els Sorell, | the people fall a hooting.   1221
  If Sore be sore, then el to Sore, | makes fiftie sores o sorell: 1223
  Of one sore I an hundred make | by adding but one more l.   1225
SORELL = 3
  The Dogges did yell, put ell to Sore, | then Sorell iumps from
  thicket: 1219
  Or Pricket-sore, or els Sorell, | the people fall a hooting.   1221
  If Sore be sore, then el to Sore, | makes fiftie sores o sorell: 1223
SORES = 1
  If Sore be sore, then el to Sore, | makes fiftie sores o sorell: 1223
SORRIE = 1
  Marcad. I am sorrie Madame for the newes I bring   2675
SORROW = 3*1
  smile againe, and till then sit thee downe sorrow. *Exeunt.*   309
  *sorrow; for so they say the foole sayd, and so say I, and I the   1338
  Of sighes, of grones, of sorrow, and of teene: 1501
  Let not the cloude of Sorrow iustle it   2706
SORT = 1
  *are Worthies a comming will speake their minde in some | other
  sort. *Exit Curat.*   2537

SORTED = *1
  hight Costard, (*Clow*. O mee) *sorted and consorted contrary to*   259
SOUERAIGNE = 2
  A man of soueraigne peerelesse he is esteemd: 536
  Th'annoynted soueraigne of sighes and groones: 948
SOUERAIGNTIE = 2
  Boy. Do not curst wiues hold that selfe-soueraigntie   1011
  Of all complexions the culd soueraigntie,   1583
SOULDIER = 1*2
  *base for a Souldier to loue; so am I in loue with a base wench.   364
  *a Souldier, a man of trauayle, that hath seene the worlde: but   1841
  and I will right my selfe like a Souldier. *Exeunt Worthys*   2682
SOULDIERS = 1*1
  King. Saint *Cupid* then and Souldiers to the fielde.   1717
  Brag. Gentlemen and Souldiers, pardon me, I will not | combat
  in my shyrt.   2659
SOULE = 6*3
  *(*Clowne*. Mee?) *that vnlettered small knowing soule*, (*Clow*.
  Mee?)   257
  Arm. By my sweete soule, I meane, setting thee at libertie.   889
  But if thou striue (poore soule) what art thou then?   1072
  Clo. By my soule a Swaine, a most simple Clowne.   1137
  *put it to them. But *Vir sapis qui pauca loquitur*, a soule Femi-
  |nine saluteth vs.   1243
  sayes in his, What my soule verses.   1263
  All ignorant that soule, that sees thee without wonder.   1277
  Out of a new sad-soule, that you vouchsafe,   2689
  Mirth cannot moue a soule in agonie.   2818
SOULES = *1
  *Nauar, *my soules earthes God, and bodies fostring patrone:*   232
SOUND = 2*2
  A Louers eare will heare the lowest sound.   1686
  *And they wel mockt depart away with shame. *Sound Trom*.   2048
  Rosa. Helpe holde his browes, heele sound: why looke | you
  pale?   2323
  My loue to thee is sound, *sance* cracke or flaw.   2347
SOUNDES = *1
  Boy. The Trompet soundes, be maskt, the maskers come.   2049
SOUTH = 1
  By East, West, North, and South, I spred my conquering might: 2514
SOWED = 1
  Ber. Alone alone sowed Cockell, reapt no Corne,   1734
SOWER = *1
  *welcome the sower Cup of prosperitie, affliccio(n) may one day   308
SOWLA = 2
  Sowla, sowla. *Exeunt*. Shoot within.   1148
SOYLE = 3
  The onely soyle of his fayre vertues glose,   539
  If vertues glose will staine with any soyle,   540
  a Crab on the face of *Terra*, the soyle, the land, the earth.   1156
SPACE = 2
  And stay heere in your Court for three yeeres space.   56
  Three thousand times within this three yeeres space: 161
SPAINE = 2
  With a refined trauailer of Spaine,   174
  From tawnie Spaine lost in the worldes debate.   184

SPANIARD = *1
  *Boy. This *Armado* is a *Spaniard* that keepes here in court,   1079
SPANIARDS = *1
  *Spaniards Rapier: The first and second cause will not serue   480
SPARCLE = 1
  They sparcle still the right promethean fier,   1702
SPARE = 1
  It should none spare, that come within his power.   543
SPEACH = 3
  A better speach was neuer spoke before.   2002
  Nor to their pend speach render we no grace: 2039
  Enter Black-moores with musicke, the Boy with a | speach, and the
  rest of the Lordes disguysed.   2051
SPEACHES = 2
  King. Consture my speaches better, if you may.   2267
  O neuer will I trust to speaches pend,   2334
SPEACHLES = 1
  And would afforde my speachles vizard halfe.   2158
SPEACHLESSE = 1
  Visite the speachlesse sicke, and still conuerse,   2812
SPEAK = *1
  Bo. But to speak that in words, which his eie hath disclosd.   755
SPEAKE = 12*6
  The French kinges daughter with your selfe to speake: 145
  If I breake fayth, this word shall speake for me,   164
  *Now sir for the manner, It is the manner of a man to speake   220
  Boy. Speake you this in my praise Maister?   335
  His tongue all impacient to speake and not see,   742
  Clow. Thou hast no feeling of it *Moth*, I will speake that |
  (*Lenuoy.*   880
  When tongues speake sweetely, then they name her name,   931
  *and so foorth. Ah good olde *Mantuan,* I may speake   1258
  *such rackers of ortagriphie, as to speake dout fine, when he   1759
  Thus must thou speake, and thus thy body beare.   1992
  Yet feare not thou but speake audaciously.   1996
  If they do speake our language, tis our will   2073
  Quee. How blow? how blow? Speake to be vnderstood.   2216
  Rosa. Madame speake true: It is not so my Lord: 2291
  Bero. Speake for your selues, my wit is at an ende.   2363
  *and a feard to speake? Run away for shame *Ali-| sander.*   2532
  *are Worthies a comming will speake their minde in some | other
  sort. *Exit Curat.*   2537
  Quee. Speake braue *Hector*, we are much delighted.   2622
SPEAKERS = 1
  Boy. Why that contempt will kill the speakers hart,   2041
SPEAKES = 2*1
  Boy. He speakes the meer contrarie, crosses loue not him.   344
  And when Loue speakes, the voyce of all the Goddes,   1695
  Quee. A speakes not like a man of God his making.   2471
SPEAKEST = *1
  Lad. Thou art an old Loue-monger, & speakest skilfully.   758
SPEAKST = 1
  And thereupon thou speakst the fairest shoote.   986
SPECIAL = *1
  *special honours it pleaseth his greatnes to impart to *Armado*   1839
SPECIALL = 2
  Not by might mastred, but by speciall grace.   163

SPECIALL *cont.*
    For such a summe from speciall officers, | Of *Charles* his father.   658
SPECIALTIES = 1
    Where that and other specialties are bound: 662
SPEEDE = 2
    All causes to the purpose of his speede: 2699
    Your oth I will not trust, but goe with speede   2754
SPEEDES = 1
    Ber. Your wit's too hot, it speedes too fast, twill tire.   615
SPELD = 1
    is Ab speld backward with the horne on his head?   1786
SPEND = 2
    And spend his prodigall wittes in booteles rimes,   1954
    Bero. We number nothing that we spend for you,   2097
SPENDE = 3
    How will he scorne, how will he spende his wit?   1484
    Or grone for Ione? or spende a minutes time,   1520
    A tweluemonth shall you spende and neuer rest,   2781
SPENDING = 1
    In spending your Wit in the prayse of mine.   510
SPENT = 1
    I neuer spent an houres talke withall.   560
SPHINX = 1
    Subtil as *Sphinx*, as sweete and musicall,   1693
SPIED = 1
    Spied a blossome passing faire,   1440
SPIGHT = 1
    When spight of cormorant deuouring Time,   8
SPILL = 1
    As I for praise alone now seeke to spill   1009
SPIRIT = 2*2
    Arm. I am ill at reckning, it fitteth the spirit of a Tapster.   349
    Ar. Sing Boy, My spirit growes heauie in loue.   426
    *extrauagant spirit, full of formes, figures, shapes, obiectes,   1231
    nimble stiring spirit, she might a bin Grandam ere she died.   1903
SPIRITE = *1
    Armado. Boy, What signe is it when a man of great spi-|rite
    growes melancholy?   312
SPIRITED = *1
    did I see that low spirited Swaine, that base Minow of thy myrth,   255
SPIRITES = 4
    Ber. Diuels soonest tempt resembling spirites of light.   1606
    Why vniuersall plodding poysons vp | The nimble spirites in the
    arteries,   1655
    Pag. Out of your fauours heauenly spirites vouchsafe   2062
    The liberall opposition of our spirites,   2691
SPIRRIT = 2
    Rosal. Why thats the way to choake a gibing spirrit,   2819
    But if they will not, throw away that spirrit,   2828
SPIRRITS = 1
    Boyet. Now Maddame summon vp your dearest spirrits,   492
SPIT = *1
    *like a Rabbet on a spit, or your handes in your pocket like a   788
SPLEENE = 1*1
    *my spleene, the heauing of my lunges prouokes me to
    redi-|culous   849
    That in this spleene rediculous appeares,   2009

SPOKE = 3*2
    And though I haue for barbarisme spoke more   121
    Arm. I spoke it tender iuuenal, as a congruent apethaton   324
    A better speach was neuer spoke before.   2002
    But while tis spoke each turne away his face.   2040
    Que. You nickname vertue, vice you should haue spoke: 2275
SPOKEN = *1
    Peda. *Via* good-man *Dull*, thou hast spoken no worde all | this
    while.   1880
SPORT = 13*1
    Lon. *Costard* the swaine and he, shalbe our sport,   190
    A Phantasime a Monarcho, and one that makes sport | To the
    Prince and his Booke-mates.   1080
    Nat. Very reuerent sport truly, and done in the testimonie | of a
    good conscience.   1151
    Peda. Most *Dull*, honest *Dull*, to our sport: away. *Exeunt.*   1886
    Theres no such sport, as sport by sport orethrowne: 2044
    Theres no such sport by sport, as sport orethrowne: 2045
    Forestall our sport, to make vs thus vntrue?   2412
    That sport best pleases, that doth best know how: 2460
    Bero. A right description of our sport my Lord.   2465
    Might well haue made our sport a Comedie.   2837
SPRED = 1
    By East, West, North, and South, I spred my conquering might: 2514
SPRING = 2*2
    Ber. The Spring is neare when greene geese are a bree-|(ding.   103
    That bites the first borne infants of the Spring.   110
    From whence doth spring the true *Promethean* fire.   1654
    *This *Ver*, the Spring: The one maynteined by the Owle, | th'other
    by the Cuckow.   2856
SPRUCE = 1*1
    *& thrasonicall. He is too picked, to spruce, too affected,   1751
    Three pilde Hiberboles, spruce affection: 2339
SPUR = *1
    Kath. Tis long of you that spur me with such questions.   614
SPURD = 1
    Quee. Was that the king that spurd his horse so hard,   975
SQUIER = 1
    Do not you know my Ladies foote by'th squier?   2413
SQUIRILITIE = 1
    Nath. *Perge*, good M.(aister) *Holofernes perge*, so it shall please |
    you to abrogate squirilitie.   1211
STABLE = 1
    Boyet. O I am stable with laughter, Wher's her Grace?   1971
STAFFE = *1
    Nath. Let me heare a staffe, a stanze, a verse, *Lege domine.*   1265
STAIE = 1
    For youle proue periurde if you make me staie.   608
STAIED = 1
    +And staied the oddes by adding foure.   856 +9
STAINE = 1
    If vertues glose will staine with any soyle,   540
STAIRES = 1
    The staires as he treades on them kisse his feete.   2255
STAND = 9
    Our late edict shall strongly stand in force,   15
    That we must stand and play the murtherer in?   982

STAND *cont.*
A Stand where you may make the fairest shoote.	984
Stand a side good bearer. *Boyet* you can carue,	1032
Heere stand I, Ladie dart thy skill at me,	2328
That you stand forfait, being those that sue.	2360
And stand betweene her backe sir and the fier,	2415
Worthy, but I am to stand for him.	2449
Quee. Stand aside good *Pompey.*	2539

STANDARDS = 1
Berow. Aduaunce your standards, and vpon them Lords.	1718

STANDE = 1
Muster your Wits, stande in your owne defence,	1977

STANDES = 2*1
Standes in attainder of eternall shame.	168
*I am the King (for so standes the comparison) thou the Beg-|ger,	1058
He standes a side. The King entreth.	1353

STANDEST = 1
Gainst thee thou Lambe, that standest as his pray:	1069

STANDETH = *1
*seest. But to the place Where? It standeth North North-east & by	253

STANDS = *1
Boyet. Your Nose saies no, you are not: for it stands too | (right.	2516

STANZE = *1
Nath. Let me heare a staffe, a stanze, a verse, *Lege domine.*	1265

STAPLE = *1
*then the staple of his argument. I abhorre such phanatticall	1757

STARING = 2
Then nightly singes the staring Owle	2884
Then nightly singes the staring Owle,	2893

STARRE = 2
That giue a name to euery fixed Starre,	94
Shee (an attending Starre) scarce seene a light.	1580

STARRES = *2
*smyling: O pardone me my starres, doth the incon-|siderate	850
Bero. Thus pooure the Starres downe plagues for periurie.	2326

STARRS = 1
Vouchsafe bright Moone, and these thy Starrs to shine,	2104

STARUE = 1
When she did starue the generall world beside,	502

STATE = 4*1
*hand, a foote, a face, an eye: a gate, a state, a brow, a brest,	1522
Flat treason gainst the kingly state of youth.	1643
So perttaunt like would I ore'sway this state,	1957
Trim gallants, full of Courtship and of state.	2290
Keepe some state in thy exit, and vanish. Exit Boy.	2547

STATES = 1
Berow. Our states are forfait, seeke not to vndoo vs.	2358

STATUTE = 1
Ros. Well, better wits haue worne plaine statute Caps,	2202

STATUTES = 1
My fellow Schollers, and to keepe those statutes	21

STAY = 9*3
And stay heere in your Court for three yeeres space.	56
Bero. No my good Lord, I haue sworne to stay with you.	120
Ber. I cannot stay thankes-giuing. *Exit.*	690
Ber. O stay slaue, I must employ thee.	917

STAY *cont.*

*concerne much: stay not thy complement, I forgiue thy | dewtie,
adue.   1307

Long. By whom shall I send this (companie?) Stay.   1411

Clow. Walke aside the true folke, and let the traytors stay.   1561

So shall we stay mocking entended game,   2047

And so adue sweete *Iude.* Nay, Why dost thou stay?   2578

King. Madame Not so, I do beseech you stay.   2686

There stay vntill the twelue Celestiall Signes   2757

Long. Ile stay with patience, but the time is long.   2796

STAYED = 1

In *Russian* habite: heere they stayed an houre,   2295

STAYING = 1

Staying the oddes by adding foure.   862

STEEPE = 1

Against the steepe vp rising of the hill?   976

STEP = 1

Bero. Now step I foorth to whip hipocrisie.   1488

STEPS = 4

Enter Longauill. The King steps a side.   1376

Berow. Tell her we measure them by weerie steps. | *Boy.* She
heares her selfe.   2092

Rosa. How manie weerie steps,   2094

Berowne steps foorth.   2621

STILE = 1*1

Bero. Well sir, be it as the stile shall giue vs cause to clime | in
the merrines.   211

Boy. I am much deceiued, but I remember the stile.   1077

STILL = 19*4

Still and contemplatyue in lyuing art.   18

Lon. He weedes the corne, & still lets grow the weeding.   101

that shallow vassall (Clown. Still mee.) *which as I remember,*   258

For still her cheekes possesse the same, | Which natiue she doth
owe   409

*men. Adue Valoure, rust Rapier, be still Drum, for your   483

Whose edge hath power to cut whose will still wils,   542

By the hartes still rethoricke, disclosed with eyes.   733

+Were still at oddes being but three.   856 +3

+Were still at oddes, being but three.   856 +7

Were still at oddes, being but three.   860

Still a repairing: euer out of frame,   957

But being watcht, that it may still go right.   959

Maria. You still wrangle with her *Boyet*, and she strikes | at the
brow.   1104

My teares for glasses, and still make me weepe.   1371

Can you still dreame and poare and thereon looke.   1648

Still clyming trees in the *Hesperides.*   1692

They sparcle still the right promethean fier,   1702

Ros. Looke what you do, you do it still i'th darke.   1911

Ros. Great reason: for past care, is still past cure.   1915

That we may do it still without accompt.   2099

King. Yet still she is the Moone, and I the Man.   2116

Lets mocke them still as well knowne as disguysde: 2224

Visite the speachlesse sicke, and still conuerse,   2812

STIR = 1*1

Bero. Pompey is mooued more Ates more Atees stir them, | or
stir them on.   2644

STIRING = 1
nimble stiring spirit, she might a bin Grandam ere she died.   1903
STOLE = 1
I stole into a neighbour thicket by,   1986
STOLNE = 1
*Boy. They haue been at a great feast of Languages, and | stolne
the scraps.   1776
STOMACKE = 1
*Clo. Well sir I hope when I do it, I shall do it on a full |
stomacke.   451
STOMACKS = 1
Say, Can you fast? your stomacks are too young: 1644
STOOLE = *1
*Your Lion that holdes his Polax sitting on a close stoole,   2530
STOOPE = 1
Ber. Stoope I say, her shoulder is with child.   1424
STOORE = 1
Is of that nature, that to your hudge stoore,   2304
STOP = 1
Dum. Proceeded well, to stop all good proceeding.   100
STOPPS = 1
Ferd. These be the stopps that hinder studie quit,   75
STOPT = 1
When the suspitious head of theft is stopt.   1687
STRAIGHT = 2
No poynt (quoth I) my seruant, straight was mute.   2196
Bero. Loe, he is tilting straight. Peace, I haue don.   2423
STRAINES = 1
As Loue is full of vnbefitting straines,   2718
STRANGE = 2*2
*Iag. I sir from one mounsier Berowne, one of the strange |
Queenes Lordes.   1294
We will with some strange pastime solace them: 1728
*learned without opinion, and strange without heresie: I did   1744
Thou bidst me begge, this begging is not strange.   2109
STRANGER = *1
*of the stranger Queenes: which accidentally, or by the way   1304
STRANGERS = 1*1
Rosal. What would these strangers? | Know their mindes Boyet.   2071
*Rosa. Since you are strangers, and come here by chance,   2120
STRANGLE = 1
Thus did he strangle Serpents in his Manus,   2544
STRANGLING = *1
*in minoritie: his enter and exit shalbe strangling a Snake;   1867
STRAWES = 1
When Shepheards pipe on Oten Strawes,   2869
STRAYING = 1
Full of straying shapes, of habites and of formes: 2721
STREETE = 1
The streete should see as she walkt ouer head.   1630
STREETES = 1
Ber O if the streetes were paued with thine eyes,   1627
STRENGTH = *1
*and he had an excellent strength: Yet was Salomon so   476
STREWING = 1
Forerunne faire Loue, strewing her way with flowers.   1731

STRICKT = 2
  But there are other strickt obseruances: 40
  O mee, with what strickt patience haue I sat,   1502
STRICTEST = 1
  And to the strictest decrees Ile write my name.   126
STRIKE = 1
  That his owne hand may strike his honour downe,   24
STRIKES = *1
  *Maria. You still wrangle with her *Boyet*, and she strikes | at the
  brow.   1104
STRIUE = 2
  Onely for praise sake, when they striue to be | Lords ore their
  Lordes?   1012
  But if thou striue (poore soule) what art thou then?   1072
STRIUES = 1
  Where zeale striues to content, and the contentes   2461
STRONG = 1*1
  *Arm. O wel knit *Sampson*, strong ioynted *Sampson*; I do excel   379
  Mar. Follie in Fooles beares not so strong a note,   1965
STRONGLY = 2
  Our late edict shall strongly stand in force,   15
  Which each to other hath so strongly sworne.   302
STROOKEN = 1
  Bowes not his vassall head, and strooken blind.   1573
STRUNG = 1
  As bright *Appolos* Lute, strung with his haire.   1694
STUBBORNE = *1
  *Long. I feare these stubborne lines lacke power to moue. 1387
STUCKE = 2
  With two pitch balles stucke in her face for eyes.   963
  Long. Stucke with Cloues. | *Dum.* No clouen.   2604
STUDDIES = 1
  Berow. Studdies my Ladie? Mistres looke on me,   2798
STUDENT = 1
  Brag. Almost I had. | *Boy.* Negligent student, learne her by hart. 803
STUDENTES = 1
  3. *Lad.* An other of these Studentes at that time,   556
STUDIE = 15*3
  Or studie where to meete some Mistris fine.   68
  Studie to breake it, and not breake my troth.   71
  Studie knowes that which yet it doth not know,   73
  Ferd. These be the stopps that hinder studie quit,   75
  Studie me how to please the eye in deede,   85
  Studie is lyke the heauens glorious Sunne,   89
  So you to studie now it is too late,   117
  Ber. So Studie euermore is ouershot,   153
  While it doth studie to haue what it would,   154
  And so to studie three yeeres is but short.   191
  Ar. I haue promised to studie three yeeres with the duke. 345
  Arma. True. | *Boy.* Why sir is this such a peece of studie? Now
  heere is   357
  *put yeeres to the worde three, and studie three yeeres in two 359
  Till painefull studie shall outweare three yeeres,   514
  Studie his byas leaues, and makes his booke thine eyes. 1272
  And where that you haue vowd to studie (Lordes)   1646
  And studie too, the causer of your vow.   1661
  O we haue made a Vow to studie, Lordes,   1669

STUDIED = *1
  *three studied ere yele thrice wincke: and how easie it is to   358
STUDIES = 4
  Ferd. I, that is studies god-like recompence.   63
  If studies gaine be thus, and this be so,   72
  For interim to our studies shall relate,   182
  Haue found the ground of Studies excellence,   1650
STUDY = 7
  That is, to lyue and study heere three yeeres.   39
  Not to see Ladyes, study, fast, not sleepe.   52
  I onely swore to study with your grace,   55
  What is the ende of study, let me know?   59
  Bero. Com'on then, I will sweare to study so,   64
  As thus, to study where I well may dine,   66
  To fast, to study, and to see no woman: 1642
STUFFE = 1
  Duma. I neuer knew man holde vile stuffe so deare.   1625
STUMBLE = 2
  Did stumble with haste in his ey-sight to bee,   743
  Boyet. A light for Mounsier *Iudas*, it growes darke, he | may
  stumble.   2583
SUB = *1
  *Nath. Facile precor gellida, quando pecas omnia sub vmbra
  ru-| minat,*   1257
SUBDEWES = 1
  To any Lady that subdewes a Lord.   1015
SUBDUE = *1
  *not; his disgrace is to be called Boy, but his glorie is to sub-|due   482
SUBIECT = *1
  Ar. I will haue that subiect newly writ ore, that I may   419
SUBIECTES = 1
  Varying in subiectes as the eye doth roule,   2722
SUBMISSIUE = 1
  Submissiue fall his princely feete before,   1070
SUBSCRIBE = 2
  Your othes are past, and now subscribe your names: 23
  Subscribe to your deepe othes, and keepe it to.   27
SUBTIL = 1
  Subtil as *Sphinx*, as sweete and musicall,   1693
SUCH = 25*11
  *the tearme of three yeeres, he shall indure such publique   140
  Clow. Such is the simplicitie of man to harken after the flesh   228
  Arma. True. | *Boy.* Why sir is this such a peece of studie? Now
  heere is   357
  Boy. Most maculate thoughts Maister, are maskt vnder | such
  colours.   396
  Boy. The worlde was very guiltie of such a Ballet some   415
  Prin. Such short liued wits do wither as they grow.   546
  Deliuers in such apt and gracious wordes,   565
  With such bedecking ornaments of praise.   571
  Kath. Tis long of you that spur me with such questions.   614
  For such a summe from speciall officers, | Of *Charles* his father.   658
  Meane time receiue such welcome at my hand,   666
  His faces owne margent did coate such amazes,   750
  *sensible in the duller partes: and such barren plantes are   1179
  That singes heauens prayse, with such an earthly tong.   1283
  King. Come sir, you blush: as his, your case is such.   1468

SUCH *cont.*

Fayth infringed, which such zeale did sweare.	1483
A wife of such wood were felicitie.	1598
Her feete were much too daintie for such tread.	1628
Teaches such beautie as a womans eye:	1663
Such fierie Numbers as the prompting eyes,	1673
Such as the shortnesse of the time can shape,	1729
*then the staple of his argument. I abhorre such phanatticall	1757
*phantasims, such insociable and poynt deuise companions,	1758
*such rackers of ortagriphie, as to speake dout fine, when he	1759
*that the Curate and your sweete selfe, are good at such erup-|tions,	1846
*And so she died: had she bin Light like you, of such a mery	1902
Rosa. The blood of youth burnes not with such excesse,	1963
With such a zelous laughter so profund,	2008
Theres no such sport, as sport by sport orethrowne:	2044
Theres no such sport by sport, as sport orethrowne:	2045
King. Blessed are cloudes, to do as such cloudes do.	2103
Rosa. We can affoord no more at such a price.	2126
Haue not the grace to grace it with such show.	2245
I neuer swore this Lady such an oth.	2390
Cannot picke out fiue such, take each one in his vaine.	2488
If for my Loue (as there is no such cause)	2752

SUDDEN *see* sodaine

SUDDENLY *see* sodainelie

SUE *see also* shue = 2

What? I loue, I sue, I seeke a wife,	955
That you stand forfait, being those that sue.	2360

SUFFER = *2

Clo. I suffer for the trueth sir: for true it is, I was taken	306
*safe, and you must suffer him to take no delight, nor no pe-|nance,	432

SUFFICIT = 1

Pedant. Satis quid sufficit.	1740

SUFFISE = 2

Ferd. It shall suffise me; at which enteruiew,	664
If knowledge be the marke, to know thee shall suffise.	1275

SUGER = 1

Quee. Honie, and Milke, and Suger: there is three.	2136

SUGGESTED = 1

Suggested vs to make, therefore Ladies	2728

SUGGESTIONS = 1

Suggestions are to other as to me:	169

SUITE = 4

And sodainelie resolue mee in my suite.	605
Quee. Berowne did sweare him selfe out of all suite.	2194
The holy suite which faine it would conuince,	2704
What humble suite attendes thy answere there,	2800

SUMME = 4

summe of deus-ace amountes to.	354
Being but the one halfe of, of an intire summe,	626
Receiud that summe, yet there remaines vnpaide	629
For such a summe from speciall officers, | Of *Charles* his father.	658

SUMMER *see also* sommer = 1

And Maidens bleach their summer smockes:	2872

SUMMON = 1

Boyet. Now Maddame summon vp your dearest spirrits,	492

SUNNE = 7*1
Studie is lyke the heauens glorious Sunne, 89
King. So sweete a kisse the golden Sunne giues not, 1358
*Then thou faire Sunne, which on my earth doost shine, 1402
Ber. I as some dayes, but then no Sunne must shine. 1426
O tis the Sunne that maketh all thinges shine. 1595
In conflict that you get the Sunne of them. 1720
Page. Once to beholde with your Sunne beamed eyes, 2065
With your Sunne beamed eyes. 2066
SUNSHINE = 1
Vouchsafe to shew the sunshine of your face, 2100
SUPERFLUOUS = 1
Rosa. There, then, that Vizard, that superfluous case, 2316
SUPERSCRIPT = 1
Nath. I will ouerglaunce the superscript. 1296
SUPERUISE = 1
accent. Let me superuise the cangenet. 1285
SUPPE = 1
Bero. I, if a'haue no more mans blood in his belly then wil |
suppe a Flea. 2647
SUPPER = *1
which is called Supper: So much for the time When. Now for the 247
SURE = 2*2
Boy. Then I am sure you know how much the grosse 353
*God of Rime, for I am sure I shall turne Sonnet. Deuise 485
Ber. O nothing so sure, and thereby all forsworne. 1632
Mar. Dumaine is mine as sure as barke on tree. 2206
SURELY = 2
reason for it. He surely affected her for her wit. 393
Quee. None are so surely caught, when they are catcht, 1959
SURETIE = 1
A hundred thousand more, in suretie of the which, 630
SURMOUNTED = 1
Brag. This Hector *far surmounted* Hanniball. 2626
SURNAMD = 1
Clow. It is great sir, Pompey *surnamd the great.* 2499
SURNAMDE = 1
Clow. I Pompey *am,* Pompey *surnamde the bigge.* | *Duma.* The
great. 2497
SURPRISD = 1
Armed in argumentes, you'll be surprisd. 1976
SURRA = 1
These othes and lawes will proue an idle scorne. | Surra, Come
on. 304
SURRENDER = 1
A Maide of grace and complet maiestie, | About surrender vp of
Aquitaine, 146
SURUAYEST = *1
ebon coloured Incke, which here thou viewest, beholdest, suruayest,
or 252
SUSPITIOUS = 1
When the suspitious head of theft is stopt. 1687
SUTE = 2
Despight of sute, to see a Ladies face. 2021
For my great sute, so easely obtainde. 2697
SUTERS = 1
Like humble visage Suters his high will. 525

SWAINE = 3*6
> *Lon.* Costard the swaine and he, shalbe our sport,   190
> **did I see that low spirited Swaine, that base Minow of thy myrth,*   255
> **apprehended with the aforesayd Swaine, I keepe hir as a vessell of*   270
> *giue enlargement to the Swaine, bring him festinatly hither,   776
> **Brag.* Fetch hither the Swaine, he must carrie me a letter.   817
> I shoote thee at the Swaine.   834
> *Clo.* By my soule a Swaine, a most simple Clowne.   1137
> **Iudas Machabeus;* this Swaine (because of his great lim   1860
> *He presents *Hector* of *Troy,* the Swaine *Pompey* the great, the   2478

SWALLOWED = 1*1
> *through the throate, if you swallowed loue with sing-|ing   784
> Thou art easier swallowed then a flapdragon.   1781

SWAY = 1
> So perttaunt like would I ore'sway his state,   1957

SWEARE = 11*1
> *Bero.* Com'on then, I will sweare to study so,   64
> Sweare me to this, and I will nere say no.   74
> *Quee.* We will reade it, I sweare.   1038
> *To see him kisse his hand, & how most sweetly a wil sweare: 1144
> If Loue make me forsworne, how shall I sweare to loue?   1267
> Thou for whom *Ioue* would sweare,   1454
> Fayth infringed, which such zeale did sweare.   1483
> That I may sweare Beautie doth beautie lacke,   1600
> Consider what you first did sweare vnto: 1641
> *Quee.* Berowne did sweare him selfe out of all suite.   2194
> *Quee.* Not so my Lord, it is not so I sweare,   2285
> *Kath.* Yet sweare not, least ye be forsworne agen.   2792

SWEAT = 1
> *That oft in fielde with Targ and Shield did make my foe to sweat,*   2500

SWEEPERS = 1
> *Duma.* To looke like her are Chimnie-sweepers blake.   1615

SWEET = 1*5
> **Ar.* Sweet inuocation of a child, most pretty & pathetical.   401
> *Lon.* Nay my coller is ended. She is a most sweet Ladie.| *Exit*
> *Longauil.*   705
> **Be.* Shot by heauen, proceed sweet *Cupid,* thou hast thumpt   1355
> *let that passe; the very all of all is: but sweet hart, I do implore   1842
> **Berow.* White handed Mistres, one sweet word with thee.   2135
> **King.* Teach vs sweet Madame, for our rude transgression | Some
> faire excuse.   2364

SWEETE = 41*22
> *Bero.* Sweete Lord and why? | *Long.* To fright them hence with
> that dread penaltie.   136
> **more sweete vnderstanding a Woman: him, I (as my euer esteemed*   264
> **by thy sweete Graces Officer* Anthonie Dull, *a man of*   266
> **thy Lawes furie, and shall at the least of thy sweete notice, bring*   271
> **Arm.* Most sweete *Hercules:* more authoritie deare Boy,   373
> *name more; and sweete my childe let them be men of good |
> repute and carriage.   374
> So sweete and voluble is his discourse.   568
> ** Pri.* Sweete health and faire desires consort your grace.   675
> No Sheepe (sweete Lambe) vnlesse we feede on your lippes.   722
> **Brag.* Sweete Ayer, go tendernes of yeeres, take this Key,   775
> *Brag.* Sweete smoke of Rhetorike,   832
> By thy fauour sweete Welkin, I must sigh in thy face: 837
> **Arm.* By my sweete soule, I meane, setting thee at libertie.   889

SWEETE *cont.*
 Clow. My sweete ounce of mans flesh, my in-conie Iew: 901
 Clow. Gardon, O sweete gardon, better then remuneratio(n). 935
 *a leuenpence-farthing better: most sweete gardon. I will 936
 Here sweete, put vp this, twilbe thine annother day. 1091
 O my troth most sweete iestes, most inconie vulgar wit, 1139
 Which not to anger bent, is musique, and sweete fier. 1281
 *of progression, hath miscarried. Trip and goe my sweete, 1305
 *it, the Foole sent it, and the Lady hath it: sweete Clowne, 1349
 King. So sweete a kisse the golden Sunne giues not, 1358
 Sweete leaues shade follie. Who is he comes heere? 1375
 Long. In loue I hope, sweete fellowship in shame. 1381
 O sweete *Maria*, Empresse of my Loue, 1388
 Would let her out in Sawcers, sweete misprison. 1434
 Youth so apt to pluck a sweete. 1451
 Ber. Sweete Lords, sweete Louers, O let vs imbrace, 1562
 King. And *Aethiops* of their sweete complexion crake. 1617
 Subtil as *Sphinx*, as sweete and musicall, 1693
 *sweete tutch, a quicke venewe of wit, snip snap, quicke and 1796
 Brag. At your sweete pleasure, for the Mountaine. 1819
 Bra. Sir, it is the Kings most sweete pleasur & affection, 1821
 *well culd, chose, sweete, & apt I do assure you sir, I do assure. 1827
 *with my excrement, with my mustachie: but sweete hart 1837
 *(sweete chuck) with some delightfull ostentation, or show, 1844
 *that the Curate and your sweete selfe, are good at such
 erup-|tions, 1846
 Quee. Sweete hartes we shalbe rich ere we depart, 1888
 Holde take thou this my sweete, and giue mee thine, 2024
 Curtsie sweete hartes, and so the Measure endes. 2124
 Quee. Seuenth sweete adue, since you can cogg, 2140
 Ber. One word in secret. | *Quee*. Let it not be sweete. 2142
 Boye. Tapers they are with your sweete breaths puft out. 2185
 Blow like sweete Roses, in this sommer aire. 2215
 Dismaskt, their dammaske sweete commixture showne, 2219
 Mende him who can, the Ladies call him sweete. 2254
 King. A blister on his sweete tongue with my hart, 2260
 King. All haile sweete Madame, and faire time of day. 2265
 Bero. This iest is drie to me, gentle sweete, 2300
 sweete breath, as will vtter a brace of wordes. 2468
 Brag. That is al one my faire sweete honie monarch, 2472
 *And lay my Armes before the Leggs of this sweete Lasse of
 France. 2503
 And so adue sweete *Iude*. Nay, Why dost thou stay? 2578
 Brag. Sweete Lord *Longauill* raine thy tongue. 2613
 Brag. The sweete War-man is dead and rotten, 2617
 Sweete chucks beat not the bones of the buried: 2618
 *But I will forward with my deuice; sweete royaltie bestow | on
 me the sence of hearing. 2619
 Brag. *I do adore thy sweete Graces Slipper.* 2623
 Brag. Sweete bloodes, I both may and will. 2663
 Queen. I sweete my Lord, and so I take my leaue. 2833
 Brag. Sweete Maiestie vouchsafe me. 2842
 To holde the Plough for her sweete loue three yeere. 2847
SWEETEHART *see* sweet, sweete
SWEETEHARTES *see* sweete
SWEETELY = 1
 When tongues speake sweetely, then they name her name, 931

SWEETER = *1
    *sweeter Foole, sweetest Lady. By the worlde, I woulde not   1350
SWEETES = 1
    There's halfe a dosen sweetes.   2139
SWEETEST = *1
    *sweeter Foole, sweetest Lady. By the worlde, I woulde not   1350
SWEETLY = *2
    *To see him kisse his hand, & how most sweetly a wil sweare: 1144
    *sweetly varried like a scholler at the least: but sir I assure ye   1159
SWELL = 1
    Do but beholde the teares that swell in me,   1368
SWIFT = 3
    Brag. The way is but short, away. | *Boy.* As swift as Lead sir.   824
    Boy. You are too swift sir to say so.   830
    Courses as swift as thought in euery power,   1681
SWIFTER = *1
    *Fleeter then Arrowes, bullets wind thought swifter thinges.   2177
SWINE = 1
    for a Swine: tis prettie, it is well.   1253
SWOON *see* sound
SWORD = 2*2
    *If drawing my Sword against the humor of affection, would   365
    Mar. Dumaine was at my seruice, and his sword,   2195
    You leere vpon me, do you: ther's an eie | Woundes like a leaden
    sword.   2419
    *Ile flash, Ile do it by the Sword: I bepray you let me bor-|row
    my Armes againe.   2651
SWORE = 6
    I onely swore to study with your grace,   55
    Longa. You swore to that *Berowne*, and to the rest.   57
    Bero. By yea and nay sir, than I swore in iest.   58
    One rubbd his elbow thus, and fleerd, and swore,   2001
    Rosa. Madame, he swore that he did hold me deare,   2382
    I neuer swore this Lady such an oth.   2390
SWORNE = 11*2
    Haue sworne for three yeeres tearme, to liue with me: 20
    If you are armd to do, as sworne to do,   26
    So much deare Liedge, I haue already sworne,   38
    Or hauing sworne too hard a keeping oth,   70
    Bero. No my good Lord, I haue sworne to stay with you.   120
    Yet confident Ile keepe what I haue sworne,   123
    Which each to other hath so strongly sworne.   302
    Nau. Heare me deare Lady, I haue sworne an oth,   592
    I heare your grace hath sworne out Houskeeping: 599
    But alacke my hand is sworne,   1448
    Or keeping what is sworne, you will proue fooles,   1707
    But will you heare; the King is my Loue sworne.   2203
    *Linnen: since when, Ile be sworne he wore none, but a
    dish-|cloute   2668
SYCAMORE *see* Siccamore
SYMPATHISD *see* simpathisd
SYTHES = 1
    That honour which shall bate his sythes keene edge,   10
TABER = 1
    the Taber to the worthies, and let them dance the hey.   1885
TABLE = *1
    *the table with a Grace, I will on my priuiledge I haue with   1320

TABLES = 1
That when he playes at Tables chides the Dice   2251
TABLE-BOOKE = 1
  Curat. A most singuler and choyce Epithat, | *Draw-out his*
Table-booke.   1754
TAFFATA = 2
  Berow. Beauties no richer then rich Taffata.   2054
  Taffata phrases, silken tearmes precise,   2338
TAKE = 14*8
  *deliuer me from the reprobate thought of it, I would take   366
  *safe, and you must suffer him to take no delight, nor no
pe-|nance,   432
  Ar. Take away this villaine, shut him vp.   456
  Prin. It was well done of you to take him at his word.   718
  Brag. Sweete Ayer, go tendernes of yeeres, take this Key,   775
  take *salue* for *lenuoy*, and the word *lenuoy* for a *salue*?   851
  Heere (good my glasse) take this for telling trew: 993
  Holde take thou this my sweete, and giue mee thine,   2024
  So shall *Berowne* take me for *Rosaline.*   2025
  Weele not be nice, take handes, we will not daunce.   2121
  King. Why take we handes then? | *Rosa.* Onely to part friendes.   2122
  Mar. Say you so? Faire Lord, take that for your faire Lady   2150
  Take all and weane it, it may proue an Oxe.   2165
  Rosa. But that you take what doth to you belong,   2308
  You gaue me this: but take it sir againe.   2392
  Clow. We wil turne it finely off sir, we wil take some care.   2451
  Cannot picke out fiue such, take each one in his vaine.   2488
  Bero. Take away the Conquerour, take away *Alisander.*   2527
  Page. Maister, let me take you a button hole lower. Do   2656
  Queen. I sweete my Lord, and so I take my leaue.   2833
  Brag. I will kisse thy royall finger, and take leaue.   2845
TAKEN = 2*6
  The manner of it is, I was taken with the manner.   214
  *vppon the Forme, and taken following her into the Parke: 218
  Fer. It was proclaymed a yeeres imprisonment to be ta-|ken with
a Wench.   283
  Clo. I was taken with none sir, I was taken with a Demsel.   285
  Clo. If it were, I denie her Virginitie: I was taken with a | Maide.   291
  Clo. I suffer for the trueth sir: for true it is, I was taken   306
  To be ore-hard and taken napping so.   1467
TAKING = 1
  Kath. Yole marre the light by taking it in snuffe: 1909
TALE = 2
  Some carry tale, some please-man, some sleight saine: 2402
  Marcad. Euen so: my tale is tolde.   2678
TALENT = 2*1
  Nath. A rare talent.   1227
  Dull. If a talent be a claw, looke how he clawes him | with a
talent.   1228
TALES = 1
  That aged eares play treuant at his tales,   566
TALKE = 4*2
  Item, Yf any man be seene to talke with a woman within   139
  I neuer spent an houres talke withall.   560
  Arm. We will talke no more of this matter.   884
  Ma. Come come, you talke greasely, your lips grow fowle.   1131
  Ber. Ile proue her faire, or talke till doomse-day heere.   1623

TALKE *cont.*
With Visages displayde to talke and greete.   2036
TALKT = 1
And talkt apace: and in that houre (my Lord)   2296
TALLER = 1
Mari. The liker you, few taller are so young.   2797
TALLEST = 1*1
   Quee. The thickest, and the tallest.   1023
   *Clow. The thickest, and the tallest: it is so, trueth is trueth.   1024
TANQUAM = *1
   * Ped. Noui hominum tanquam te, His humour is loftie, his   1748
TAPERS = *1
   *Boye. Tapers they are with your sweete breaths puft out.   2185
TAPSTER = *1
   *Arm. I am ill at reckning, it fitteth the spirit of a Tapster.   349
TARG = 1
   That oft in fielde with Targ and Shield did make my foe to sweat,   2500
TASKE = 2
But now to taske the tasker, good *Boyet,*   511
With groning wretches: and your taske shall be,   2813
TASKER = 1
But now to taske the tasker, good *Boyet,*   511
TASKES = 1
O these are barraine taskes, too hard to keepe,   51
TASKT = 1
   Quee. And will they so? the Gallants shalbe taskt: 2018
TASTE = 1*1
   *set before vs, that we thankful should be: which we taste,   1180
Loues tongue proues daintie, *Bachus* grosse in taste,   1690
TAUGHT = *1
   *loue, and it hath taught me to rime, and to be mallicholie: 1345
TAWNIE = 1
From tawnie Spaine lost in the worldes debate.   184
TE *I.**1260 *1748 = *3
TEACH = 3*1
To teach a teacher ill beseemeth mee.   603
Rosa. Shall I teach you to know. | *Boy.* I my continent of beautie.   1094
Action and accent did they teach him there.   1991
   *King. Teach vs sweet Madame, for our rude transgression | Some
faire excuse.   2364
TEACHER = 1
To teach a teacher ill beseemeth mee.   603
TEACHES = 1*1
Teaches such beautie as a womans eye: 1663
   * Page. Yes yes, he teaches boyes the Horne-booke: What   1785
TEARE = 3
Thou shinst in euerie teare that I do weepe,   1365
These numbers will I teare, and write in prose.   1389
Kin. How now, What is in you? Why dost thou teare it?   1542
TEARES = 6
As doth thy face through teares of mine giue light: 1364
Do but beholde the teares that swell in me,   1368
My teares for glasses, and still make me weepe.   1371
Your eyes do make no couches in your teares.   1492
To checke their follie pashions solembe teares.   2010
My wofull selfe vp in a mourning house, | Rayning the teares of
lamentation,   2768

TEARME = 1*1
Haue sworne for three yeeres tearme, to liue with me:	20
*the tearme of three yeeres, he shall indure such publique	140

TEARMES = 2
In honorable tearmes; nay he can sing	2252
Taffata phrases, silken tearmes precise,	2338

TEENE = 1
Of sighes, of grones, of sorrow, and of teene:	1501

TEETH = 1
To shew his teeth as white as Whales bone,	2257

TEL = 1*1
Ar. But tel me, How was there a *Costard* broken in a shin?	877
Dul. You two are book-men, Can you tel me by your wit,	1189

TELL = 14*2
Ther's villanie abrod, this letter will tell you more.	200
wordes, the dauncing Horse will tell you.	360
Arm. Tell me precisely of what complexion? | *Boy.* Of the sea-water Greene sir.	387
Ar. I will tell thee wonders. | *Ma.* With that face.	442
I am lesse proude to heare you tell my worth,	508
Tell him, the Daughter of the King of France	521
Pag. I will tell you sencibly.	879
Ped. Sir tell not mee of the Father, I do feare colourable	1314
No thought can thinke, nor tongue of mortall tell.	1373
Where lies thy griefe, o tell me good *Dumaine?*	1508
O dismisse this audience, and I shall tell you more.	1556
King. Twere good yours did: for sir to tell you plaine,	1621
*deede too: but let that passe, for I must tell thee it will	1834
Brag. Shall I tell you a thing? | *Peda.* We attende.	1876
And manie miles: the Princesse bids you tell,	2090
Berow. Tell her we measure them by weerie steps. | *Boy.* She heares her selfe.	2092

TELLING = 2*1
Cost. It may be so: but if he say it is so, he is in telling true: | but so. | *Ferd.* Peace.	236
You are not ignorant all telling fame	512
Heere (good my glasse) take this for telling trew:	993

TEMPRED = 1
Vntill his Incke were tempred with Loues sighes:	1698

TEMPT = 1
Ber. Diuels soonest tempt resembling spirites of light.	1606

TEMPTED = 1*1
*There is no euill angel but Loue, yet was *Sampson* so temp-|ted,	475
Had he bin *Adam* he had tempted *Eue.*	2247

TENDER = 6*2
Arm. How canst thou part sadnes and melancholy, my | tender Iuuenall?	318
Boy. Why tender iuuenall? Why tender iuuenall?	323
Arm. I spoke it tender iuuenal, as a congruent apethaton	324
*apperteining to thy young dayes, which we may nominate | tender.	325
Make tender of to thy true worthines.	668
Then are the tender hornes of Cockled Snayles.	1689
Be. Your nose smels no in his most tender smelling knight.	2518

TENDERNES = *1
Brag. Sweete Ayer, go tendernes of yeeres, take this Key,	775

TENDRING = *1
*Who tendring their owne worth from where they were | (glast, 748
TENT = 1*1
Should be presented at our Tent to vs. 2230
*Boyet. Gone to her Tent. Please it your Maiestie com-|maunde 2236
TENTES = 1
Some enterteinment for them in their Tentes. 1724
TENTS = 1
Quee. Whip to our Tents as Roes runs ore land. Exeunt. 2232
TERME = 2
As not to see a woman in that terme, 41
You shall this tweluemonth terme from day to day, 2811
TERRA = 1
a Crab on the face of Terra, the soyle, the land, the earth. 1156
TERROR = 1
Now to our periurie, to add more terror, 2409
TESTIMONIE = *1
*Nat. Very reuerent sport truly, and done in the testimonie | of a
good conscience. 1151
TEXT = 2*1
*Nath. And thanke you to: for societie (saith the text) | is the
happines of life. 1326
Peda. And certes the text most infallibly concludes it. 1328
Kath. Faire as a text B in a Coppie booke. 1930
TH see also ath, atother, by'th, i'th, toothen = 7*1
Thendeuour of this present breath may buy: 9
Or vainely comes th'admired Princesse hither. 150
Th'annoynted soueraigne of sighes and groones: 948
Th'allusion holdes in the Exchange. 1199
*Holo. God comfort thy capacitie, I say th'allusion holdes | in the
Exchange. 1202
God amende vs, God amende, we are much out a th'way. 1409
O that I knew he were but in by th'weeke, 1951
*This Ver, the Spring: The one maynteined by the Owle, | th'other
by the Cuckow. 2856
THAN see also then = 1
Bero. By yea and nay sir, than I swore in iest. 58
THANKE = 6*2
*therfore I will say nothing: I thanke God I haue as little
pa-|tience 467
Cost. I thanke your worship, God be wy you. 916
Quee. I thanke my Beautie, I am faire that shoote, 985
*Nath. And thanke you to: for societie (saith the text) | is the
happines of life. 1326
Nay I haue Vearses too, I thanke Berowne, 1922
And Lord Berowne (I thanke him) is my deare. 2396
Quee. Prepare I say: I thanke you gracious Lords 2687
Duma. O shall I say, I thanke you gentle Wife? 2786
THANKES = 3
If your Ladishyp would say thankes Pompey, I had done. 2505
Lady. Great thankes great Pompey. 2506
Excuse me so comming too short of thankes, 2696
THANKES-GIUING = 1
Ber. I cannot stay thankes-giuing. Exit. 690
THANKFUL = *1
*set before vs, that we thankful should be: which we taste, 1180

THANKFULL = *1
*gyft is good in those whom it is acute, and I am thankfull | for
it.   1235
THAT *l*.5 10 13 22 24 25 39 41 57 *60 63 73 75 77 87 88 90 94 96
105 110 116 122 *128 135 137 167 171 173 176 181 239 *246 *250
*251 *255 *257 *258 *275 301 314 338 339 389 *392 *419 *421
*431 443 460 463 *473 497 518 *528 538 543 545 549 554 556 562
566 570 580 600 607 *614 618 628 629 634 637 652 662 684 692
*698 707 *715 *723 736 744 751 752 *755 *792 794 813 831 856
871 875 *880 882 919 *939 956 959 964 968 975 982 985 995 1004
1008 1010 1011 1015 *1020 1042 *1047 1069 *1074 *1079 1080
1089 1096 1098 *1108 *1111 *1121 1146 *1174 *1180 *1181 1188
1206 *1230 *1249 *1273 1276 1277 1278 1283 *1337 1361 1365
1368 1383 *1384 1386 1427 1430 1435 1444 1453 1459 1465 1482
1486 1491 1493 1515 *1521 1525 *1552 1571 1577 1586 1595 1600
1601 1602 1608 1613 1646 1647 1660 1670 1704 1708 1709 1720
1733 *1811 *1834 *1838 *1841 *1842 *1843 *1846 *1864 1868
*1871 1892 1896 1897 1933 1934 1950 1951 1956 1958 1980 1984
1988 1990 1999 2007 2009 2035 2041 *2055 2059 2067 2069 2074
2080 2084 2097 2099 2101 2129 2134 *2150 2238 2244 2249 2251
2256 2258 2261 2273 2296 2304 2308 2310 2313 2316 2317 2357
2360 2373 2382 2385 2404 2460 2462 2472 2500 2515 *2530 2542
2608 2610 2611 2612 *2636 2637 *2669 *2673 2689 2701 2727
2729 2732 2733 2763 2767 2788 2807 2820 2823 2824 2827 2828
2829 2843 *2849 = 224*61
THATS = 7*3
Boy. And thats great maruaile, louing a light Wench.   427
Maid. Thats hereby. | *Ar.* I know where it is situate.   439
He reputes me a Cannon, and the Bullet thats hee: 833
Clo. The Boy hath sold him a bargaine, a Goose, that's flat.   865
Let me see a fat *Lenuoy*, I thats a fat Goose.   868
*Remuneration, O that's the latine word for three-farthings: 903
*What was a month old at *Cains* birth, that's not fiue weeks | old
as yet?   1190
Kath. You waigh me not, O thats you care not for me.   1914
Rosal. Why thats the way to choake a gibing spirrit,   2819
Berow. That's too long for a Play.   2840
THE *see also* a'the, th' = 564*275
THEE *l*.127 *265 309 *380 438 442 444 676 834 838 *845 886 *889
*894 *895 917 1069 1083 *1108 *1111 *1259 *1261 1269 *1270
1275 1276 1277 1311 *1337 1366 *1384 1396 1398 1403 1449 1453
1489 1578 1624 *1779 *1831 *1832 *1834 1883 2023 *2135 2264
2332 2347 2386 2496 2572 2574 2649 2791 = 37*20
THEEFE = 1
A true man, or a theefe, that gallops so.   1525
THEFT = 1
When the suspitious head of theft is stopt.   1687
THEIR *l*.5 37 95 180 *466 738 744 *748 1013 *1238 *1241 *1242
*1331 1360 1617 1620 1677 1683 1724 1980 1989 2000 2010 2014
2033 2039 *2055 2057 2058 2059 2072 2074 2176 2190 2209 2218
2219 2222 2228 2229 2353 2463 2464 *2480 *2537 2742 2825
2872 = 42*10
THEIRS = 2
Quee. The effect of my intent is to crosse theirs: 2030
To make theirs ours, and ours none but our owne.   2046
THEM *l*.137 167 *374 390 503 663 749 *793 853 *1243 1718 1719
1720 1723 1724 1725 1728 *1791 1793 1859 1885 2020 2080 2086

THEM *cont.*
2092 2189 2224 2225 2255 2298 2342 *2447 2450 *2453 2575
*2644 2645 2737 2745 2852 = 33*7
THEMSELUES *see also* selues = *1
  Clow. O Lord sir, the parties themselues, the actors sir   2442
THEN *see also* than *l.*7 46 64 96 108 115 122 *250 309 *353 355 407
*424 *454 499 509 581 591 612 623 633 644 *762 766 835 872 875
*906 915 931 *935 *943 981 994 1000 1003 1004 *1043 *1044 1072
1100 1127 1129 1182 1220 1223 1370 *1402 1404 1426 1433 1581
1590 1624 1629 *1633 1639 1640 1666 1689 1699 1706 1717 1726
*1757 1781 2023 2028 2054 2088 *2108 2110 2122 2130 2133 2137
2169 2171 2174 *2177 2268 2270 2316 2371 2373 2407 2456 *2636
*2641 *2647 2740 2743 2764 2773 2776 2790 2791 2824 2826 2839
2864 2873 2884 2893 = 86*19
THERE *l.*40 42 45 50 172 173 *254 *413 *475 557 629 877 885 *896
930 *1185 1420 1493 1529 1635 1668 *1808 1991 2136 2316 2428
2483 *2533 *2536 2752 2757 2800 = 24*8
THEREBY = 1
  Ber. O nothing so sure, and thereby all forsworne.   1632
THEREFORE = 20*2
  Therefore braue Conquerours, for so you are,   12
  Therefore this Article is made in vaine,   149
  with Iaquenetta, and *Iaquenetta* is a trew girle, and therefore   307
  hard for Hercules Clubb, and therefore too much oddes for a   479
  Therefore to's seemeth it a needfull course,   516
  Therefore of all handes must we be forsworne.   1567
  And therefore is she borne to make blacke fayre.   1610
  And therefore redd that would auoyde disprayse,   1613
  And therefore finding barraine practizers,   1676
  King. And winn them too, therefore let vs deuise,   1723
  Therefore Ile darkly ende the argument.   1910
  Ros. In deede I waigh not you, and therefore light.   1913
  Quee. Therefore I do it, and I make no doubt,   2043
  Bero. Thou greeuest my gall. | *Quee.* Gall, bitter, | *Bero.*
  Therefore meete.   2144
  Therefore change Fauours, and when they repaire,   2214
  Quee. I will, and therefore keepe it. *Rosaline,*   2380
  Boyet. Therefore as he is, an Asse, let him go: 2577
  Formd by the eye, and therefore like the eye.   2720
  Suggested vs to make, therefore Ladies   2728
  Haue we not been, and therefore met your Loues,   2741
  Full of deare guiltines, and therefore this,   2751
  Therefore if you my fauour meane to get,   2780
THEREOF = 2*1
  Clowne. Sir the Contempts thereof are as touching me.   201
  *lewe thereof, impose on thee nothing but this: Beare this   895
  Since all the power thereof it doth apply,   1967
THEREON = 1
  Can you still dreame and poare and thereon looke.   1648
THERES = 3
  Theres no such sport, as sport by sport orethrowne: 2044
  Theres no such sport by sport, as sport orethrowne: 2045
  There's halfe a dosen sweetes.   2139
THERETO = 1
  Aboue this Worlde: adding thereto more ouer,   2384
THEREUPON = 1
  And thereupon thou speakst the fairest shoote.   986

THEREWITHALL = 1
And therewithall to winne me, yf you please,   2809
THERFORE = 2*2
  Arma. And therfore apt, because quicke.   334
  *therfore I will say nothing: I thanke God I haue as little
  pa-|tience   467
as an other man, & therfore I can be quiet. *Exit.*   468
  Long. It did moue him to passion, & therfore lets heare it.   1545
THERS = 4
  Ther's villanie abrod, this letter will tell you more.   200
  +Ther's the morrall: Now the *lenuoy.*   856 +4
This seald-vp counsaile. Ther's thy guerdon: goe.   934
You leere vpon me, do you: ther's an eie | Woundes like a leaden
sword.   2419
THESE *l.*33 36 51 53 75 93 304 556 *790 *792 *793 794 814 997
  1026 *1232 *1387 1389 1491 *1558 *1568 1706 1710 1721 1722
  1943 1947 2027 2071 2104 *2166 2184 2340 2355 2357 *2480
  *2481 2712 2727 2765 2774 2785 2836 = 33*11
THEY = 59*18
THEYLE = 1*1
  Vnto his seuerall Mistres: which they'le know   2016
  King. We were descried, theyle mock vs now dounright.   2318
THICKEST = 2*1
  Quee. The thickest, and the tallest.   1023
  Clow. The thickest, and the tallest: it is so, trueth is trueth. 1024
Are not you the chiefe woman? You are the thickest heere.   1027
THICKET = 2
The Dogges did yell, put ell to Sore, | then Sorell iumps from
thicket: 1219
I stole into a neighbour thicket by,   1986
THIN = 1
If frostes and fastes, hard lodging, and thin weedes,   2761
THINBELLIES = *1
  *your eyes, with your armes crost on your thinbellies doblet   787
THINE = 8*2
  *hir to tryall. Thine in all complements of deuoted and hartburning
  Thine in the dearest designe of industri,* | Don Adriana de   272
Armatho.   1066
Here sweete, put vp this, twilbe thine annother day.   1091
Studie his byas leaues, and makes his booke thine eyes.   1272
Did not the heauenly Rethorique of thine eye,   1393
  King. What, did these rent lines shew some loue of thine?   1568
Ber O if the streetes were paued with thine eyes,   1627
Holde take thou this my sweete, and giue mee thine,   2024
And by this Virgin palme now kissing thine,   2766
I wilbe thine: and till that instance shutt   2767
THING = 10*1
To know the thing I am forbid to know: 65
But like of each thing that in season growes.   116
It doth forget to do the thing it should: 155
And when it hath the thing it hunteth most,   156
  Ar. Why? sadnes is one & the selfe same thing deare imp.   315
Do one thing for me that I shall intreate.   919
For. No thing but faire is that which you inherrit.   995
Youle not be periurde, tis a hatefull thing: 1494
When shall you see mee write a thing in rime?   1519
Brag. Shall I tell you a thing? | *Peda.* We attende.   1876

THING *cont.*
O he hath drawen my picture in his letter. | *Quee.* Any thing like? 1926
THINGES = 6*1
To thinges of sale, a sellers prayse belonges: 1589
O tis the Sunne that maketh all thinges shine. 1595
*Fleeter then Arrowes, bullets wind thought swifter thinges. 2177
Your wits makes wise thinges foolish when we greete 2301
Wise thinges seeme foolish, and rich thinges but poore. 2305
When great thinges labouring perish in their byrth. 2464
THINGS = *1
Ber. Things hid & bard (you meane) from cammon sense. 62
THINKE = 9*3
When I was wont to thinke no harme all nyght, 48
*for a new deuisde cursie. I thinke scorne to sigh, mee thinks 368
*three ages since, but I thinke now tis not to be found: or if it 416
Pag. Do the wise thinke them other, is not *lenuoy* a *salue*? 853
Forr. I know not, but I thinke it was not he. 977
No thought can thinke, nor tongue of mortall tell. 1373
Quee. I thinke no lesse: Dost thou not wish in hart 1945
Will they not (thinke you) hange them selues to nyght? 2189
I dare not call them fooles; but this I thinke, 2298
Sea sicke I thinke comming from *Muscouie*. 2325
Clow. It pleased them to thinke me worthie of *Pompey* 2447
King. I thinke *Hector* was not so cleane timberd. 2594
THINKES = 1*1
*haue a loue of that colour, mee thinkes *Sampson* had small 392
Quee. A time me thinkes too short, 2748
THINKS = *1
*for a new deuisde cursie. I thinke scorne to sigh, mee thinks 368
THIRDE = 1
The thirde he caperd and cryed, All goes well. 2005
THIRSTIE = 1
When they are thirstie, fooles would faine haue drinke. 2299
THIS *1.*9 22 72 74 127 129 134 143 149 *151 158 161 164 181 194
198 200 226 261 *275 *277 288 293 294 335 *358 408 429 *433
456 530 535 *587 730 *775 795 *809 *869 884 888 *895 *904 907
921 927 928 934 945 946 993 1034 1036 *1074 *1079 1083 1091
*1230 *1254 1282 1292 *1302 *1306 *1312 *1339 *1342 1392 1395
1403 1407 1411 1458 1474 1535 1556 1631 *1633 1635 1652 1701
*1745 *1762 1823 *1852 *1853 *1859 *1860 *1878 1881 1893
*1905 1921 1937 1943 2009 2022 2024 2029 2070 2083 2085 2109
2125 2191 2210 2215 2240 2246 2248 2250 2256 2264 *2271 2298
2300 2306 *2314 2343 2359 *2374 2379 2384 2390 2392 2393 2394
2395 2411 2421 2469 2502 *2503 *2529 2541 2546 2562 2582 2592
2593 2598 2626 2740 2751 2753 2759 2763 2766 2771 2773 2808
2811 2855 *2856 = 119*36
THITHER = 3
Prin. I wilbe welcome then, Conduct me thither. 591
Ber. First from the Parke let vs conduct them thither, 1725
me any seruice to her thither, 2237
THOM = 1
And Thom beares Logges into the hall, 2881
THOROUGH = 1
To the court of his eye, peeping thorough desier. 739
THOSE *1.*21 96 216 *806 *1181 *1235 *1270 *1273 *1322 1359 2105
2352 2360 2727 2732 = 9*6

THOU *l.*252 *318 332 *340 *380 *449 453 460 *758 780 795 799
808 821 *848 *880 *890 918 923 925 933 986 *1020 1042 *1043
*1058 *1061 1068 1069 1072 1082 1085 *1090 *1097 1114 1115
*1172 1173 1282 *1355 1365 1367 1370 1372 1385 1398 1399
*1402 1454 1490 1529 1538 1540 1542 *1779 1781 1790 *1802
*1807 *1809 *1810 *1811 *1812 *1813 *1870 *1880 1945 1992
1995 1996 2022 2024 2107 2109 2144 2201 2263 2264 2425 2446
2553 2561 2576 2578 2630 2634 2635 *2673 2771 = 61*32

THOUGH = 12*2

The minde shall banquet, though the body pine,	29
And though I haue for barbarisme spoke more	121
Queene. Good L.(ord) *Boyet,* my beautie though but meane,	504
And shape to win grace though he had no wit.	552
Though so denide faire harbour in my house,	672
My lippes are no Common, though seuerall they be.	726
Though *Argus* were her eunuch and her garde.	965
A giuing hand, though fowle, shall haue faire praise.	998
Though to my selfe forsworne, to thee Ile faythfull proue.	1269
*Snake; that is the way to make an offence gracious, though	1871
And leape for ioy, though they are lame with blowes:	2213
A worlde of tormentes though I should endure,	2279
Duma. Though my mockes come home by me, I will | now be merrie.	2590
And though the mourning brow of progenie	2702

THOUGHT = 4*3

*deliuer me from the reprobate thought of it, I would take	366
Mee thought all his senses were lokt in his eye,	746
Ar. By vertue thou inforcest laughter, thy sillie thought,	848
No thought can thinke, nor tongue of mortall tell.	1373
Courses as swift as thought in euery power,	1681
I thought to close mine eyes some halfe an houre:	1982
*Fleeter then Arrowes, bullets wind thought swifter thinges.	2177

THOUGHTES = 1

Your owne good thoughtes excuse me, and farewell.	673

THOUGHTS = *2

Boy. Most maculate thoughts Maister, are maskt vnder | such colours.	396
*Those thoughts to me were Okes, to thee like Osiers bowed	1270

THOUSAND = 8

Three thousand times within this three yeeres space:	161
The payment of a hundred thousand Crownes,	625
A hundred thousand more, in suretie of the which,	630
A hundred thousand Crownes, and not demaunds	639
One paiment of a hundred thousand Crownes,	640
For he hath been fiue thousand yeere a Boy.	1898
I am comparde to twentie thousand fairs.	1925
Some thousand Verses of a faithfull Louer.	1940

THRASONICALL = *1

*& thrasonicall. He is too picked, to spruce, too affected,	1751

THRED = *1

Peda. He draweth out the thred of his verbositie, finer	1756

THREE = 36*13

You three, *Berowne, Dumaine,* and *Longauill,*	19
Haue sworne for three yeeres tearme, to liue with me:	20
Longauill. I am resolued, tis but a three yeeres fast:	28
That is, to lyue and study heere three yeeres.	39
And then to sleepe but three houres in the nyght,	46

THREE *cont.*

And stay heere in your Court for three yeeres space.	56
And bide the pennance of each three yeeres day.	124
*the tearme of three yeeres, he shall indure such publique	140
Three thousand times within this three yeeres space:	161
And so to studie three yeeres is but short.	191
Clow. In manner and forme folowing sir all those three.	216
Ar. I haue promised to studie three yeeres with the duke.	345
Boy. Which the base vulgar do call three.	356
*three studied ere yele thrice wincke: and how easie it is to	358
*put yeeres to the worde three, and studie three yeeres in two	359
Boy. Of all the foure, or the three, or the two, or one of	the foure.	385
*three ages since, but I thinke now tis not to be found: or if it	416
*but a' must fast three dayes a weeke: for this Damsell	433
Enter the Princesse of Fraunce, with three	*attending Ladies and three Lordes.*	490
Till painefull studie shall outweare three yeeres,	514
Boy. And out of hart Maister: all those three I will	proue.	806
Brag. I am all these three.	814
Boy. And three times as much more, and yet nothing	at all.	815
+Were still at oddes being but three.	856 +3
+Were still at oddes, being but three.	856 +7
Were still at oddes, being but three.	860
And among three to loue the worst of all,	961
*He came, one; see, two; ouercame, three. Who came? the	1050
*care a pin, if the other three were in. Heere comes one with	1351
All three of you, to be thus much ore'shot?	1497
But I a Beame do finde in each of three.	1499
King. What?	*Ber.* That you three fooles, lackt me foole, to make vp the	(messe.	1551
Brag. For the rest of the Worthies?	*Peda.* I will play three my selfe.	1873
Quee. Honie, and Milke, and Suger: there is three.	2136
Three pilde Hiberboles, spruce affection:	2339
Write *Lord haue mercie on vs*, on those three,	2352
Whether the three Worthis shall come in or no?	2427
Ber. What, are there but three?	*Clow.* No sir, but it is vara fine, For euerie one pursents three.	2428
	2430
Bero. And three times thrice is nine.	2431
we know: I hope sir three times thrice sir.	*Bero.* Is not nine.	2434
Bero. By Ioue, I all wayes tooke three threes for nine.	2438
Whose Clubb kilde Cerberus *that three headed* Canus,	2542
With three folde loue I wish you all these three.	2785
To holde the Plough for her sweete loue three yeere.	2847

THREEFARTHING = 1

Ber. O, why then threefarthing worth of Silke.	915

THREES = 1

Bero. By Ioue, I all wayes tooke three threes for nine.	2438

THREE-FARTHINGS = *2

*Remuneration, O that's the latine word for three-farthings:	903
*Three-farthings remuneration, What's the price of this yncle?	904

THRESHOLD = 1

Fell ouer the threshold, and broke my shin.	883

THRICE = 4*1

Boy. How many is one thrice tolde?	348
*three studied ere yele thrice wincke: and how easie it is to	358

THRICE *cont.*
   Page. Thrice worthie Gentleman.   1875
   Bero. And three times thrice is nine.   2431
   we know: I hope sir three times thrice sir. | *Bero.* Is not nine.   2434
THRIUE = *1
   *first shew thriue, these foure will change habites, and present |
   the other fiue.   2481
THROATE = *3
   *through the throate, if you swallowed loue with sing-|ing   784
   *in the world but lie, and lie in my throate. By heauen I doe 1344
   *Berow. To moue wilde laughter in the throate of death?   2816
THRONE = 1
   Nere to plucke thee from thy throne: 1449
THROUGH = 5*3
   *through the throate, if you swallowed loue with sing-|ing   784
   *loue sometime through: nose as if you snufft vp loue by   785
   Through the transparent bosome of the deepe,   1363
   As doth thy face through teares of mine giue light: 1364
   And they thy glorie through my griefe will show: 1369
   Through the Veluet, leaues the wind,   1442
   Thrust thy sharpe wit quite through my ignorance,   2330
   *seene the day of wrong through the litle hole of discretion, 2681
THROW = 2
   Abate throw at Nouum, and the whole world againe,   2487
   But if they will not, throw away that spirrit,   2828
THROWES = 1
   He throwes vppon the grosse worlds baser slaues   34
THRUST = 1
   Thrust thy sharpe wit quite through my ignorance,   2330
THUMBE = *1
   *that worthies thumbe, he is not so big as the end of his Club. 1864
THUME = 1
   Another with his fynger and his thume,   2003
THUMP = 1
   Boy. Thump then, and I flee.   835
THUMPT = *1
   *Be. Shot by heauen, proceed sweet *Cupid*, thou hast thumpt 1355
THUNDER = *1
   *Thy eie *Ioues* lightning beares, thy voyce his dreadful thu(n)der 1279
THUS = 20*5
   As thus, to study where I well may dine,   66
   If studies gaine be thus, and this be so,   72
   Before I came: Marrie thus much I haue learnt,   578
   *Clow. True, and I for a Plantan, thus came your argument | (in, 873
   Thus will I saue my Credite in the shoote,   1001
   *roabes, for tittles tytles, for thy selfe, mee. Thus expecting 1062
   Thus dost thou heare the nemean Lion roare,   1068
   Good hart, What grace hast thou thus to reproue   1490
   All three of you, to be thus much ore'shot?   1497
   Are we betrayed thus to thy ouer-view?   1513
   It is Religion to be thus forsworne.   1714
   *my poore shoulder, and with his royall finger thus dallie   1836
   Yf Fayrings come thus plentifully in.   1889
   Thus must thou speake, and thus thy body beare.   1992
   One rubbd his elbow thus, and fleerd, and swore,   2001
   Boy. They do, they do; and are appariled thus, | Like *Muscouites*,
   or *Russians*, as I gesse.   2012

THUS *cont.*

Not yet no daunce: thus change I like the Moone.	2111
Kin. Wil you not daunce? How come you thus estranged?	2112
Bero. Thus pooure the Starres downe plagues for periurie.	2326
Forestall our sport, to make vs thus vntrue?	2412
Thus did he strangle Serpents in his Manus,	2544
Thus purifies it selfe and turns to grace.	2734
Mocks married men; for thus singes hee, | Cuckow.	2865
Mockes married men, for thus singes he, | Cuckow.	2874

THY *l.**244 *248 *254 *255 *260 *263 *266 *271 *325 336 *449 668
676 688 837 *843 *848 *890 *894 934 *1031 *1044 *1059 *1060
*1061 *1062 *1063 1064 *1202 1278 *1279 *1307 1356 1360 1364
1369 1370 1378 1400 1446 1449 1457 1464 1508 1509 1512 1513
1596 1626 *1779 *1802 *1809 *1831 *1832 1972 1992 2104 2328
2330 2331 *2467 2547 *2588 2613 2623 2776 2800 2801
2845 = 40*37

THYSELFE *see also* selfe

Tl see te

TIBURNE = 1

The shape of Loues Tiburne, that hanges vp Simplicitie.	1386

TILL = 11

smile againe, and till then sit thee downe sorrow. *Exeunt.*	309
Ar. I say sing. | *Boy.* Forbeare till this companie be past.	428
Till painefull studie shall outweare three yeeres,	514
Kath. Not till it leaue the rider in the mire.	616
Clow. Till there be more matter in the shin.	885
Some say a Sore, but not a sore, | till now made sore with shooting.	1217
Ber. Ile proue her faire, or talke till doomse-day heere.	1623
Till this mad man shewed thee, and what art thou now?	2264
From morne till night out of his Pauilion.	2609
I wilbe thine: and till that instance shutt	2767
Duma. Ile serue thee true and faythfully till then.	2791

TILTING = 1

Bero. Loe, he is tilting straight. Peace, I haue don.	2423

TIMBERD = 1

King. I thinke *Hector* was not so cleane timberd.	2594

TIME *see also* tyme = 16*3

When spight of cormorant deuouring Time,	8
selfe to walke: the time When? about the sixt houre, When Beastes	245
which is called Supper: So much for the time When. Now for the olde time, which we may name tough. | *Arma.* Prettie and apt.	247 328
3. *Lad.* An other of these Studentes at that time,	556
Ber. What time a day? | *Kath.* The houre that fooles should aske.	617
Meane time receiue such welcome at my hand,	666
Or grone for Ione? or spende a minutes time,	1520
Long. And since her time are Colliers counted bright.	1616
Such as the shortnesse of the time can shape,	1729
King. Away, away, no time shalbe omitted,	1732
That will be time and may by vs befitted.	1733
Sir Holofernes, as concerning some entertainement of time,	1851
King. All haile sweete Madame, and faire time of day.	2265
King. The extreame partes of time extreamly formes,	2698
For your faire sakes, haue we neglected time.	2713
As bombast and as lyning to the time:	2739
Quee. A time me thinkes too short,	2748

TIME *cont.*
  Long. Ile stay with patience, but the time is long.   2796
TIMES = 4*1
  Three thousand times within this three yeeres space: 161
  Boy. And three times as much more, and yet nothing | at all.   815
  And wayte the season, and obserue the times,   1953
  Bero. And three times thrice is nine.   2431
  we know: I hope sir three times thrice sir. | *Bero.* Is not nine.   2434
TIMON see Tymon
TIRE = 1
  Ber. Your wit's too hot, it speedes too fast, twill tire.   615
TIRED see tyred
TIRES see tyres
TIS *1.*28 157 *416 600 *614 731 *1200 1253 1494 1595 1639 2040
  2073 2411 *2455 2484 *2507 2524 *2536 2633 = 14*6
TITLE = 2*1
  Boy. And I tough signeor, as an appertinent title to your   327
  To haue his title liue in *Aquitaine.*   641
  Dul. What is *dictima?* | *Nath.* A title to *Phebe,* to *Luna,* to the
  Moone.   1194
TITLES see tytles
TITTLES = *1
  *roabes, for tittles tytles, for thy selfe, mee. Thus expecting   1062
TO *see also* toothen = 359*100, 5*3
  Subscribe to your deepe othes, and keepe it to.   27
  Ber. It is so varried to, for it was proclaimed Virgin.   290
  Cl. Shes to hard for you at pricks, sir challeng her to bowle   1133
  Nath. And thanke you to: for societie (saith the text) | is the
  happines of life.   1326
  *& thrasonicall. He is too picked, to spruce, too affected,   1751
  to od as it were, too peregrinat as I may call it.   1752
  A can carue to, and lispe: Why this is hee   2248
  Rosal. You must be purged to, your sinnes are rackt.   2778
TOCHING = 1
  *woman when queene *Guinouer* of Brittaine was a litle wench | as
  toching the hit it.   1112
TODAY see day
TOFORE = 1
  Some obscure presedence that hath tofore bin saine.   856
TOGEATHER = 1*1
  *which put togeather, is in manner and forme following.   219
  The treason and you goe in peace away togeather.   1534
TOKENS = 2
  For the Lords tokens on you do I see.   2356
  Quee. No, they are free that gaue these tokens to vs.   2357
TOLDE = 5
  Boy. How many is one thrice tolde?   348
  Who gaue thee this letter? | *Clow.* I tolde you, my Lord.   1083
  The measure then of one is easlie tolde.   2088
  Tolde our intentes before: which once disclosd,   2406
  Marcad. Euen so: my tale is tolde.   2678
TOM see Thom
TOMBES = 1
  Liue registred vpon our brazen Tombes,   6
TOMORROW see morow, morrow
TONG = 1
  That singes heauens prayse, with such an earthly tong.   1283

TONGED = 1
Pay him the due of honie-tonged *Boyet*.   2259
TONGUE = 18*1
On who the musique of his owne vaine tongue   177
Boy. My fathers wit, and my mothers tongue assist me.   399
Which his fayre tongue (conceites expositer)   564
His tongue all impacient to speake and not see,   742
By adding a tongue which I know will not lie.   757
Well learned is that tongue, that well can thee commend.   1276
No thought can thinke, nor tongue of mortall tell.   1373
Loues tongue proues daintie, *Bachus* grosse in taste,   1690
*discourse peremptorie: his tongue fyled, his eye ambitious,   1749
Maria. What, was your vizard made without a tongue?   2154
Long. You haue a double tongue within your Maske,   2157
King. A blister on his sweete tongue with my hart,   2260
It were a fault to snatch wordes from my tongue.   2309
Nor to the motion of a Schoole-boyes tongue: 2335
Brag. Sweete Lord *Longauill* raine thy tongue.   2613
is heauie in my tongue. The King your father | *Quee*. Dead for
my life.   2676
A heauie hart beares not a humble tongue.   2695
Before I saw you: and the worldes large tongue   2803
Of him that heares it, neuer in the tongue   2823
TONGUES = 4*1
Not vttred by base sale of chapmens tongues: 507
*the tongues ende, canarie to it with your feete, humour it   782
When tongues speake sweetely, then they name her name,   931
Lend me the florish of all gentle tongues,   1587
Boyet. The tongues of mocking Wenches are as keene | As is the
Rasors edge inuisible: 2172
TONIGHT *see* nyght
TONGUE *see* tung
TOO *see also* to = 34*16
And make a darke nyght too of halfe the day: 49
O these are barraine taskes, too hard to keepe,   51
Or hauing sworne too hard a keeping oth,   70
Too much to know, is to know nought but fame: 97
So you to studie now it is too late,   117
I am in loue too. Who was *Sampsons* loue my deare Moth?   381
Boy. As I haue read sir, and the best of them too.   390
*It is not for prisoners to be too silent in their wordes, and   466
*seduced, and he had a very good wit. *Cupids* Butshaft is too   478
*hard for *Hercules* Clubb, and therefore too much oddes for a   479
Is a sharpe Wit matcht with too blunt a Will: 541
And much too little of that good I saw,   554
*not yet: the roofe of this Court is too high to be yours, and   587
welcome to the wide fieldes too base to be mine.   588
*And sin to breake it: but pardon me, I am too sodaine bold,   601
Ber. Your wit's too hot, it speedes too fast, twill tire.   615
Prin. You do the King my father too much wrong,   649
Boy. You are too hard for mee. *Exeunt omnes*.   768
*man after the olde painting, and keepe not too long in one   789
Boy. You are too swift sir to say so.   830
**Bo*. I feare too much rubbing: good night my good owle.   1135
*Sir I do inuite you too, you shall not say me nay: *pauca verba*.   1329
King. And mine too good Lord.   1429
Were Louers too, ill to example ill,   1461

TOO *cont.*

King. Too bitter is thy iest.	1512
She passes prayse, then prayse too short doth blot.	1590
Her feete were much too daintie for such tread.	1628
Say, Can you fast? your stomacks are too young:	1644
And studie too, the causer of your vow.	1661
King. And winn them too, therefore let vs deuise,	1723
*& thrasonicall. He is too picked, to spruce, too affected,	1751
to od as it were, too peregrinat as I may call it.	1752
*deede too: but let that passe, for I must tell thee it will	1834
Kath. I and a shrowde vnhappie gallowes too.	1899
But *Rosaline*, you haue a Fauour too?	1917
Nay I haue Vearses too, I thanke *Berowne*,	1922
The numbers true, and were the numbring too,	1923
The Letter is too long by halfe a mile.	1944
Rosa. My face is but a Moone, and clouded too.	2102
*Too too vaine, too too vaine: but we will put it (as they say)	2474
Boyet. Your Nose saies no, you are not: for it stands too │ (right.	2516
Long. His Legge is too bigge for *Hectors.* │ *Duman.* More Calfe	
certaine.	2595
Excuse me so comming too short of thankes,	2696
Quee. A time me thinkes too short,	2748
Berow. That's too long for a Play.	2840

TOOE = 1

The fourth turnd on the tooe, and downe he fell:	2006

TOOKE = 1*2

*I do loue, that Countrey girle that I tooke in the Parke	421
Ro. You tooke the moone at ful, but now shee's changed?	2114
Bero. By Ioue, I all wayes tooke three threes for nine.	2438

TOOT = 1

Ros. But shall we dance, if they desire vs toot?	2037

TOOTHEN = 1

Armatho ath toothen side, o a most daintie man,	1142

TOOTH-DRAWER = 1

Bero. I and worne in the cappe of a Tooth-drawer:	2571

TOP = 1

on the top of the Mountaine? │ *Peda.* Or *Mons* the hill.	1817

TORMENTES = 1

A worlde of tormentes though I should endure,	2279

TORNE = 1

Our louing lawfull, and our fayth not torne.	1634

TORTURE = 1

That same *Berowne* ile torture ere I go.	1950

TOS = 1

Therefore to's seemeth it a needfull course,	516

TOUCH = 2

And one day in a weeke to touch no foode:	43
Neuer durst Poet touch a pen to write,	1697

TOUCHING = 2

Clowne. Sir the Contempts thereof are as touching me.	201
*was a man when King *Pippen* of Fraunce was a litle boy, as │	
touching the hit it.	1109

TOUGH = 4*1

Boy. By a familier demonstration of the working, my │ tough	
signeor.	320
Arma. Why tough signeor? Why tough signeor?	322
Boy. And I tough signeor, as an appertinent title to your	327

TOUGH *cont.*
olde time, which we may name tough. | *Arma.* Prettie and apt. 328
TOWARD = 1
Toward that shade I might beholde addrest, 1984
TOWNES = 1
Tis won as townes with fire, so won so lost. 157
TOWNE-GATES = *1
*great carriage: for he carried the Towne-gates on his backe 377
TOY = *2
*Ber. A toy my Leedge, a toy: your grace needs not feare it. 1543
TOYES = 1
And *Crittick Tymon* laugh at idle toyes. 1507
TOYLE = 1*1
*They haue pitcht a Toyle, I am toyling in a pytch, pytch 1336
Scarce shew a haruest of their heauie toyle. 1677
TOYLING = *1
*They haue pitcht a Toyle, I am toyling in a pytch, pytch 1336
TO-WHO = 2
Tu-whit to-who. | A merrie note, 2885
Tu-whit to-who. | A merrie note, 2894
TRAINE = 2
And traine our intelects to vaine delight. 76
And in her traine there is a gentle Ladie: 930
TRANSFORMED = 2
Dumaine transformed, foure Woodcocks in a dysh. 1416
To see a King transformed to a Gnat. 1503
TRANSGRESSING = 1
Boy. Come you transgressing slaue, away. 457
TRANSGRESSION = *1
*King. Teach vs sweet Madame, for our rude transgression | Some
faire excuse. 2364
TRANSLATION = 1
A hudge translation of hipocrisie, | Vildly compyled, profound
simplicitie. 1941
TRANSPARENT = 1
Through the transparent bosome of the deepe, 1363
TRAUAILE = 1
Are numbred in the trauaile of one Mile? 2096
TRAUAILER = 1
With a refined trauailer of Spaine, 174
TRAUAILING = 1
And trauailing along this coast I heere am come by chaunce, 2502
TRAUAYLE = *1
*a Souldier, a man of trauayle, that hath seene the worlde: but 1841
TRAUAYLER = 1
The sinnowy vigour of the trauayler. 1658
TRAUEILER = *1
*of thee as the traueiler doth of *Venice, vemchie, vencha, que non* 1259
TRAYTORS = *1
*Clow. Walke aside the true folke, and let the traytors stay. 1561
TRAYTOUR = 1
Bero. A kissing traytour. How art thou proud *Iudas?* 2553
TREAD = 3*1
*doth tread. I shall be forsworne (which is a great argument 472
Her feete were much too daintie for such tread. 1628
To tread a Measure with you on this grasse. 2085
When Turtles tread and Rookes and Dawes, 2871

TREADE = 1
To treade a Measure with her on this grasse.   2083
TREADES = 1
The staires as he treades on them kisse his feete.   2255
TREASON = 5
  King. What present hast thou there? | *Clow.* Some certaine
  treason.   1529
  King. What makes treason heere? | *Clow.* Nay it makes nothing
  sir.   1531
  The treason and you goe in peace away togeather.   1534
  Our person misdoubts it: twas treason he said.   1536
  Flat treason gainst the kingly state of youth.   1643
TREASURE = 1
If so our Copper byes no better treasure.   1737
TREE = 3
  Mar. Dumaine is mine as sure as barke on tree.   2206
  The Cuckow then on euerie tree,   2864
  The Cuckow then on euerie tree,   2873
TREES = 1
Still clyming trees in the *Hesperides.*   1692
TREMBLES = 1
  Dum. Hector trembles.   2643
TRENCHER = 2
  Some mumble newes, some trencher Knight, some Dick   2403
  Holding a trencher, iesting merrilie?   2416
TREUANT = 1
That aged eares play treuant at his tales,   566
TREW = 1 *1
  *with *Iaquenetta,* and *Iaquenetta* is a trew girle, and therefore   307
  Heere (good my glasse) take this for telling trew: 993
TREYES = 1
  Ber. Nay then two treyes, an if you grow so nice,   2137
TRICK = 1
That smyles, his cheeke in yeeres, and knowes the trick   2404
TRICKE = 2
  Bero. Yet I haue a tricke,   2349
  I see the tricke ant: here was a consent,   2399
TRICKS = 1
Some tricks, some quillets, how to cheate the diuell.   1637
TRIM = 1
Trim gallants, full of Courtship and of state.   2290
TRIP = *1
  *of progression, hath miscarried. Trip and goe my sweete,   1305
TRIUMPH = 2
  Ayre would I might triumph so.   1447
  How will he triumph, leape, and laugh at it?   1485
TRIUMPHERIE = 1
Thou makest the triumpherie, the corner cap of societie,   1385
TRIUMPHING = 1
So ridest thou triumphing in my wo.   1367
TROM = *1
  *And they wel mockt depart away with shame. *Sound Trom.*   2048
TROMPET = *1
  Boy. The Trompet soundes, be maskt, the maskers come.   2049
TROTH = 6
  Studie to breake it, and not breake my troth.   71
  Clo. By my troth most plesant, how both did fit it.   1118

TROTH *cont.*

O my troth most sweete iestes, most inconie vulgar wit,	1139
You would for Parradise breake Fayth and troth,	1480
For vertues office neuer breakes mens troth.	2276
King. What meane you Madame: by my life my troth,	2388

TROTTING = 1

Sole Emperator and great generall | Of trotting Parrators (O my litle hart.)	951

TROW = 1

And trow you what he calde me? | *Quee.* Qualme perhaps.	2198

TROY = 1*1

*He presents *Hector* of *Troy*, the Swaine *Pompey* the great, the *Queen.* Was not that *Hector*? | *Duma.* The worthie Knight of	2478
Troy.	2843

TROYAN = 1*1

King. Hector was but a *Troyan* in respect of this.	2592
Clow. Faith vnlesse you play the honest *Troyan*, the poore	2631

TRUE = 13*12

Cost. It may be so: but if he say it is so, he is in telling true: | but so. | *Ferd.* Peace.	236
Clo. I suffer for the trueth sir: for true it is, I was taken	306
Arma. True. | *Boy.* Why sir is this such a peece of studie? Now heere is	357
*of falsehood) if I loue. And how can that be true loue, which	473
Make tender of to thy true worthines.	668
Clow. True, and I for a Plantan, thus came your argument | (in,	873
Clown. True, true, and now you wilbe my purgation, | and let me loose.	892
*true that thou art beautious, trueth it selfe that	1042
Dul. Tis true in deede, the Collusion holdes in the Ex- | (change.	1200
A true man, or a theefe, that gallops so.	1525
Bero. True true, we are fower: will these turtles be gon?	1558
Clow. Walke aside the true folke, and let the traytors stay.	1561
As true we are as flesh and blood can be,	1563
From whence doth spring the true *Promethean* fire.	1654
home, it reioiceth my intellect, true wit.	1797
The numbers true, and were the numbring too,	1923
Out | *Boy.* True, out in deede.	2060
Rosa. Madame speake true: It is not so my Lord:	2291
Rosa. It is not so, for how can this be true,	2359
Boy. Most true, tis right: you were so *Alisander*.	2524
Boy. True, and it was inioyned him in *Rome* for want of	2667
By being once falce, for euer to be true	2731
Duma. Ile serue thee true and faythfully till then.	2791

TRUELOUES = 1

That shall expresse my trueloues fasting paine.	1459

TRUELY = *1

Curat.Nath. Truely M.(aister) *Holofernes*, the epythithes are	1158

TRUER = *1

*truer then trueth it selfe: haue comiseration on thy	1044

TRUETH = 5*5

To seeke the lyght of trueth, while trueth the whyle	80
Clo. I suffer for the trueth sir: for true it is, I was taken	306
Was there with him, if I haue heard a trueth.	557
Clow. The thickest, and the tallest: it is so, trueth is trueth.	1024
*true that thou art beautious, trueth it selfe that	1042
*truer then trueth it selfe: haue comiseration on thy	1044

TRUETH *cont.*
  King. How Madame? *Russians?* | *Quee.* I in trueth My Lord.   2288
  Brag. The naked trueth of it is, I haue no Shirt.   2665
TRULY = *1
  Nat. Very reuerent sport truly, and done in the testimonie | of a
  good conscience.   1151
TRUST = 2
  O neuer will I trust to speaches pend,   2334
  Your oth I will not trust, but goe with speede   2754
TRYALL = 1*1
  hir to tryall. Thine in all complements of deuoted and hartburning   272
  But that it beare this tryall, and last Loue,   2763
TUMBLE = 1
  With that they all did tumble on the ground,   2007
TUMBLERS = 1
  And weare his coloures like a Tumblers hoope.   954
TUNE = 2*2
  were, it would neither serue for the writing, nor the tune.   417
  Boy. No my complet Maister, but to Iigge off a tune at   781
  *tune, but a snip and away: these are complementes, these   790
  And profound *Sallomon* to tune a Iigge.   1505
TUNG = 1
  Ber. Lets see the penaltie. On payne of loosing her tung.   132
TURND = 1*1
  The fourth turnd on the tooe, and downe he fell: 2006
  Page. A holy parcell of the fayrest dames that euer turnd their |
  backes to mortall viewes.   2055
TURNDE = 2
  As Wit turnde Foole, follie in Wisedome hatcht: 1960
  Page. That euer turnde their eyes to mortall viewes.   2059
TURNE = 6*3
  Fer. This Maide will not serue your turne sir.   293
  Clo. This Maide will serue my turne sir.   294
  *my turne: *Passado* he respects not, the *Duella* he regards   481
  *God of Rime, for I am sure I shall turne Sonnet. Deuise   485
  O, but for my Loue, day would turne to night,   1582
  But while tis spoke each turne away his face.   2040
  The Ladyes turne their backes to him.   2057
  Duman. Let vs confesse and turne it to a iest.   2320
  Clow. We wil turne it finely off sir, we wil take some care.   2451
TURNES = 2
  The other turnes to a mirth-moouing iest,   563
  Her fauour turnes the fashion of the dayes,   1611
TURNING = 1*1
  *with turning vp your eylids, sigh a note and sing a note
  som- | time   783
  Turning mortall for thy loue.   1457
TURNS = 1
  Thus purifies it selfe and turns to grace.   2734
TURPH = *1
  *in a turph of Earth, Fier enough for a Flint, Pearle enough   1252
TURTLES = 1*1
  Bero. True true, we are fower: will these turtles be gon?   1558
  When Turtles tread and Rookes and Dawes,   2871
TUSH = 1
  Tush, none but Minstrels like of Sonnetting.   1495

TUTCH = *1
    *sweete tutch, a quicke venewe of wit, snip snap, quicke and   1796
TUTERD = *1
    *for their Sonnes are well tuterd by you, and their   1238
TUTORS = 1
    Of beautis tutors haue inritcht you with: 1674
TU-WHIT = 2
    Tu-whit to-who. | A merrie note,   2885
    Tu-whit to-who. | A merrie note,   2894
TWAINE = 2
    Quee. Did he not send you twaine? | *Kath.* Yes Madame: and
    moreouer,   1938
    Berow. Neither of either: I remit both twaine.   2398
TWAS = 4*1
    Dul. Twas not a *haud credo*, twas a Pricket.   1162
    Dul. I said the Deare was not a *haud credo*, twas a Pricket.   1170
    that, twas a Pricket that the Princesse kild.   1206
    Our person misdoubts it: twas treason he said.   1536
TWELUE = 1
    There stay vntill the twelue Celestiall Signes   2757
TWELUEMONTH = 5*1
    A tweluemonth shall you spende and neuer rest,   2781
    Kath. Not so my Lord, a tweluemonth and a day,   2787
    You shall this tweluemonth terme from day to day,   2811
    Berow. A tweluemonth? well; befall what will befall,   2831
    Ile iest a tweluemonth in an Hospitall.   2832
    King. Come sir, it wants a tweluemonth an'aday, | And then twill
    ende.   2838
TWELUEMONTHS = 1
    Longauill. What saies *Maria*? | *Mari.* At the tweluemonths ende,   2793
TWENTIE = 2
    I am comparde to twentie thousand fairs.   1925
    Quee. Twentie adieus my frozen Muskouits.   2183
TWERE = 1
    King. Twere good yours did: for sir to tell you plaine,   1621
TWICE = 2*1
    Holo. Twice sodd simplicitie, bis coctus, O thou monster   1172
    You chide at him, offending twice as much.   1469
    Twice to your Visore, and halfe once to you.   2131
TWIL = *1
    Curat. Laus deo, bene intelligo. | *Peda. Bome boon for boon*
    prescian, a litle scratcht, twil serue.   1766
TWILBE = 1
    Here sweete, put vp this, twilbe thine annother day.   1091
TWILL = 2
    Ber. Your wit's too hot, it speedes too fast, twill tire.   615
    King. Come sir, it wants a tweluemonth an'aday, | And then twill
    ende.   2838
TWO = 6*8
    Arm. It doth amount to one more then two.   355
    *put yeeres to the worde three, and studie three yeeres in two   359
    Boy. Of all the foure, or the three, or the two, or one of | the
    foure.   385
    Lady Ka. Two hot Sheepes marie. | *Bo.* And wherefore not
    Shipps?   720
    With two pitch balles stucke in her face for eyes.   963
    *He came, one; see, two; ouercame, three. Who came? the   1050

TWO *cont.*

*Dul. You two are book-men, Can you tel me by your wit,	1189
*would not loue her; yes for her two eyes. Well, I do nothing	1343
*Ber. I could put thee in comfort, not by two that I know,	1384
Pag. The Sheepe, the other two concludes it o u.	1794
And change you Fauours two, so shall your Loues	2026
Ber. Nay then two treyes, an if you grow so nice,	2137
*Clow. Fellow *Hector*, she is gone; she is two months on | her way.	2628
*that the two Learned men haue compiled, in prayse of the	2849

TYBURNE *see* Tiburne
TYME = 1

Duma. How followes that? | *Ber.* Fit in his place and tyme.	105

TYMON = 1

And *Crittick Tymon* laugh at idle toyes.	1507

TYRANTS = 1

And plant in Tyrants milde humilitie.	1700

TYRED = *1

*the Ape his keeper, the tyred Horse his rider: But *Damosella*	1291

TYRES = 1

As motion and long during action tyres	1657

TYTLES = *1

*roabes, for tittles tytles, for thy selfe, mee. Thus expecting	1062

U = 1

Pag. The Sheepe, the other two concludes it o u.	1794

VAINE = 8*5

And traine our intelects to vaine delight.	76
Bero. Why? all delightes are vaine, but that most vaine	77
Therefore this Article is made in vaine,	149
On who the musique of his owne vaine tongue	177
*What vaine? What Wethercock? Did you euer heare better?	1075
*For as it would ill become me to be vaine, indiscreet, or a | (foole,	1183
*his gate maiesticall, and his generall behauiour vaine, redicu-|lous,	1750
Rosa. O vaine peticioner, begg a greater matter,	2106
*Too too vaine, too too vaine: but we will put it (as they say)	2474
Cannot picke out fiue such, take each one in his vaine.	2488
All wanton as a childe, skipping and vaine.	2719

VAINELY = 1

Or vainely comes th'admired Princesse hither.	150

VALOUR = 1

Most rude melancholie, Valour giues thee place.	838

VALOURE = 1*1

*men. Adue Valoure, rust Rapier, be still Drum, for your	483
For Valoure, is not Loue a *Hercules*?	1691

VALUE = 1

As precious ey-sight, and did value me	2383

VALUED = 1

Although not valued to the monies worth.	632

VANE *see* vaine
VANISH = 1

Keepe some state in thy exit, and vanish. Exit Boy.	2547

VAPOURE = 1

Vowes are but breath, and breath a vapoure is.	1401

VAPOUR-VOW = 1

Exhalst this vapour-vow in thee it is:	1403

VARA = 1

Ber. What, are there but three? | *Clow.* No sir, but it is vara fine,   2428

VARIED = 1

To euery varied obiect in his glaunce: 2723

VARLING = 1

Are Angels varling cloudes, or Roses blowne.   2220

VARNISH = 1*1

Arma. I confesse both, they are both the varnish of a com-|pleat
man.   351

Beautie doth varnish Age, as if new borne,   1593

VARRIE = 1

Ber. Once more Ile marke how Loue can varrie Wit.   1436

VARRIED = 1*1

Ber. It is so varried to, for it was proclaimed Virgin.   290

*sweetly varried like a scholler at the least: but sir I assure ye   1159

VARYING = 1

Varying in subiectes as the eye doth roule,   2722

VASSALL = 1*2

that shallow vassall (Clown. Still mee.) which as I remember,   258

*heroicall Vassall. The magnanimous and most illustrate   1045

Bowes not his vassall head, and strooken blind.   1573

VEALE = *2

Mar. Veale quoth the Dutch-man: is not veale a Calfe?   2159

VEARSES = 1

Nay I haue Vearses too, I thanke *Berowne,*   1922

VEDE *see* vnde

VEINE = 1

Bero. This is the lyuer veine, which makes flesh a deitie.   1407

VELUET = 2

A whitly wanton, with a veluet brow,   962

Through the Veluet, leaues the wind,   1442

VEMCHIE = *1

*of thee as the traueiler doth of *Venice, vemchie, vencha, que non*   1259

VENCHA = *1

*of thee as the traueiler doth of *Venice, vemchie, vencha, que non*   1259

VENETIA *see vemchie, vencha*

VENEWE = *1

*sweete tutch, a quicke venewe of wit, snip snap, quicke and   1796

VENI = *1

Veni, vidi, vici: Which to annothanize in the vulgar, O base   1048

VENICE = *1

*of thee as the traueiler doth of *Venice, vemchie, vencha, que non*   1259

VENIT = 1

Curat. Vides ne quis venit? | *Peda. Video, et gaudio.*   1770

VENTRICLE = *1

*the ventricle of Memorie, nourisht in the wombe of prima-|ter,   1233

VENUS = *1

Lad. 3. Then was *Venus* like her mother, for her father is | but
grim.   762

VENUTO = *1

bien venuto, where I will proue those Verses to be very
vn-|learned,   1322

VER = 1*1

*This *Ver,* the Spring: The one maynteined by the Owle, | th'other
by the Cuckow.   2856

B. Ver begin.   2858

VERBA = *1
*Sir I do inuite you too, you shall not say me nay: *pauca verba.*　1329
VERBOSITIE = *1
Peda. He draweth out the thred of his verbositie, finer　1756
VERIE = 1*4
Arm. I do affect the verie ground (which is base) where her　470
for he is verie slow gated: but I go.　823
*A verie Bedell to a humerous sigh, a Critick, nay a night-|watch
Constable,　941
Holo. Sir you haue done this in the feare of God verie
reli-|giously:　1312
*haue it to buy Ginger bread: Holde, there is the verie　1808
VERSE = *1
Nath. Let me heare a staffe, a stanze, a verse, *Lege domine.*　1265
VERSES = 2*2
sayes in his, What my soule verses.　1263
*coloures. But to returne to the Verses, Did they please you | sir
Nathaniel?　1315
bien venuto, where I will proue those Verses to be very
vn-|learned,　1322
Some thousand Verses of a faithfull Louer.　1940
VERTUE = 3*2
Of all that Vertue loue, for Vertue loued.　549
Ar. By vertue thou inforcest laughter, thy sillie thought,　848
The vertue of your eie must breake my oth.　2274
Que. You nickname vertue, vice you should haue spoke:　2275
VERTUES = 3
The onely soyle of his fayre vertues glose,　539
If vertues glose will staine with any soyle,　540
For vertues office neuer breakes mens troth.　2276
VERTUOUS = 1
*Who are the Votaries my louing Lordes, that are vowfel-|lowes
with this vertuous Duke?　528
VERY *see also* vara = 3*8
Boy. The worlde was very guiltie of such a Ballet some　415
*seduced, and he had a very good wit. *Cupids* Butshaft is too　478
Bo. If my obseruation (which very seldome lyes　732
Nat. Very reuerent sport truly, and done in the testimonie | of a
good conscience.　1151
*Daughters profite very greatly vnder you: you are a good |
member of the common wealth.　1239
Holo. I sir, and very learned.　1264
bien venuto, where I will proue those Verses to be very
vn-|learned,　1322
*I do assure ye very good friende: for what is inwarde　1830
*let that passe; the very all of all is: but sweet hart, I do implore　1842
*good neighbour fayth, and a very good Bowler: but for　2535
And often at his very loose decides　2700
VESSELL = *2
Ferd. For Iaquenetta (*so is the weaker vessell called*) which I　269
*apprehended with the aforesayd Swaine, I keepe hir as a vessell of　270
VIA = 1*2
*as it were *in via,* in way of explication *facere*: as it were　1164
Peda. Via good-man *Dull,* thou hast spoken no worde all | this
while.　1880
Cried *via* we will doo't come what wil come.　2004

275

VICE = *1
    Que. You nickname vertue, vice you should haue spoke: 2275
VICI = *1
    Veni, vidi, vici: Which to annothanize in the vulgar, O base   1048
VICTORIE = *1
    *victorie: On whose side? the King: the captiue is inricht, on   1055
VIDELISET = *1
    *and obscure vulgar; *videliset*, He came, see, and ouercame: 1049
VIDEO = 1
    Curat. Vides ne quis venit? | Peda. Video, et gaudio.   1770
VIDES = 1
    Curat. Vides ne quis venit? | Peda. Video, et gaudio.   1770
VIDI = *1
    Veni, vidi, vici: Which to annothanize in the vulgar, O base   1048
VIEW = 1
    Are we betrayed thus to thy ouer-view?   1513
VIEWES = 2
    *Page. A holy parcell of the fayrest dames that euer turnd their |
    backes to mortall viewes.*   2055
    Page. That euer turnde their eyes to mortall viewes.   2059
VIEWEST = *1
    ebon coloured Incke, which here thou viewest, beholdest, suruayest,
    or   252
VIGOUR = 1
    The sinnowy vigour of the trauayler.   1658
VILDLY = 2
    A hudge translation of hipocrisie, | Vildly compyled, profound
    simplicitie.   1941
    Their shallow showes, and Prologue vildly pende.   2228
VILE = 2
    Duma. I neuer knew man holde vile stuffe so deare.   1625
    Duma. O vile, then as she goes what vpward lyes?   1629
VILLAINE = 3*1
    Ar. Villaine, thou shalt fast for thy offences ere thou be |
    pardoned.   449
    Ar. Take away this villaine, shut him vp.   456
    Ber. Why villaine, thou must know first.   925
    Berow. Their eyes villaine, their eyes.   2058
VILLANIE = 1
    Ther's villanie abrod, this letter will tell you more.   200
VIOLATES = 1
    That violates the smallest branch herein.   25
VIOLETS = 1
    The Song. | When Dasies pied, and Violets blew,   2859
VIR = *1
    *put it to them. But *Vir sapis qui pauca loquitur*, a soule Femi-
    |nine saluteth vs.   1243
VIRGIN = 4
    Clo. This was no Damsel neither sir, she was a Virgin.   288
    Ber. It is so varried to, for it was proclaimed Virgin.   290
    virgin, Was this directed to you?   1292
    And by this Virgin palme now kissing thine,   2766
VIRGINITIE = *1
    Clo. If it were, I denie her Virginitie: I was taken with a | Maide.   291
VIRTUE *see also* vertue
VIRTUES *see also* vertues

VIRTUOUS *see* vertuous
VISAGE = 1
  Like humble visage Suters his high will. 525
VISAGES = 1
  With Visages displayde to talke and greete. 2036
VISIT = 1
  Ar. I will visit thee at the Lodge. 438
VISITATION = 2
  Berow. Nothing but peace, and gentle visitation. 2077
  Rosa. What would they, say they? | *Boy.* Nothing but peace, and
  gentle visitation. 2078
VISITE = 4
  To morow shall we visite you againe. 674
  Quee. But what, but what, come they to visite vs? 2011
  King. We came to visite you, and purpose now, 2269
  Visite the speachlesse sicke, and still conuerse, 2812
VISITED = 1
  These Lordes are visited, you are not free, 2355
VISORE = 1
  Twice to your Visore, and halfe once to you. 2131
VIZARD = 4*1
  Maria. What, was your vizard made without a tongue? 2154
  And would afforde my speachles vizard halfe. 2158
  *Ber. Where, when, what Vizard? why demaund you this? 2314
  Rosa. There, then, that Vizard, that superfluous case, 2316
  Nor neuer come in vizard to my friend, 2336
VIZARDS = 2
  Or euer but in vizards shew their faces. 2190
  Ros. Which of the Vizards was it that you wore? 2313
VIZGERENT = *1
  *Ferd. Great Deputie the welkins Vizgerent, and sole dominatur of 231
VMBRA = *1
  *Nath. Facile precor gellida, quando pecas omnia sub vmbra
  ru-|minat, 1257
VMPIER = 1
  Haue chose as vmpier of their mutenie. 180
VNBEFITTING = 1
  As Loue is full of vnbefitting straines, 2718
VNBOOSOME = 1
  Their seuerall counsailes they vnboosome shall, 2033
VNCASING = *1
  *you not see, Pompey is vncasing for the Combat: What 2657
VNCONFIRMED = *1
  *vntrained, or rather vnlettered, or ratherest vnconfirmed
  fa-|shion, 1167
VNDE = *1
  *te vnde, que non te perreche. Olde *Mantuan,* olde *Mantuan,* 1260
VNDER = 3*5
  *Boy. Most maculate thoughts Maister, are maskt vnder | such
  colours. 396
  *Daughters profite very greatly vnder you: you are a good |
  member of the common wealth. 1239
  *Vnder pardon sir, What are the contentes? or rather as Hor-|race 1262
  him with thy Birdbolt vnder the left papp: in fayth secrets. 1356
  Boy. Vnder the coole shade of a Siccamore, 1981
  Clow. Not so sir, vnder correction sir, I hope it is not so. 2432

VNDER   *cont.*
Clow. Vnder correction sir we know where-vntill it doth |
   amount.   2436
Kin. The Ship is vnder sayle, and heere she coms amaine.   2489
VNDERSTAND = 2
   Quee. I vnderstand you not, my griefes are double.   2710
   And by these badges vnderstand the King,   2712
VNDERSTANDETH = *1
*Who vnderstandeth thee not, loues thee not, *vt re sol la mi fa*:   1261
VNDERSTANDING = *2
*more sweete vnderstanding a Woman: him, I (as my euer esteemed   264
*or pageant, or antique, or fierworke: Now vnderstanding   1845
VNDERSTOOD = 1
   Quee. How blow? how blow? Speake to be vnderstood.   2216
VNDERSTOODE = 1
   Dull. Nor vnderstoode none neither sir.   1882
VNDERTAKE = *1
*the parentes of the foresaid childe or pupill, vndertake your   1321
VNDESERUING = 1
   My Ladie (to the maner of the dayes) | In curtesie giues
   vndeseruing praise.   2292
VNDOO = 1
   Berow. Our states are forfait, seeke not to vndoo vs.   2358
VNDRESSED = *1
*after his vndressed, vnpolished, vneducated, vnpruned,   1166
VNEDUCATED = *1
*after his vndressed, vnpolished, vneducated, vnpruned,   1166
VNGUEM = 1
   Peda. Oh I smell false Latine, *dunghel* for *vnguem*.   1814
VNHAPPIE = 1
   Kath. I and a shrowde vnhappie gallowes too.   1899
VNIUERSALL = 1
   Why vniuersall plodding poysons vp | The nimble spirites in the
   arteries,   1655
VNLEARNED = *1
bien venuto, where I will proue those Verses to be very
   vn-|learned,   1322
VNLESSE = 1*1
   No Sheepe (sweete Lambe) vnlesse we feede on your lippes.   722
Clow. Faith vnlesse you play the honest *Troyan*, the poore   2631
VNLETTERED = *2
(Clowne. Mee?) *that vnlettered small knowing soule, (Clow.*
   Mee?)   257
*vntrained, or rather vnlettered, or ratherest vnconfirmed
   fa-|shion,   1167
VNLIKE = 1
   Bo. Not vnlike sir, that may be.   707
VNLOCKE = 1
   Clymbe ore the house to vnlocke the little gate.   118
VNMEETE = 1
   Vow alacke for youth vnmeete,   1450
VNPAIDE = 1
   Receiud that summe, yet there remaines vnpaide   629
VNPEELED = 1
   To let you enter his vnpeeled house.   582

VNPLEASING = 2
  Cuckow, Cuckow: O word of feare, | Vnpleasing to a married
  eare.   2867
  Vnpleasing to a married eare.   2877
VNPOLISHED = *1
  *after his vndressed, vnpolished, vneducated, vnpruned,   1166
VNPRUNED = *1
  *after his vndressed, vnpolished, vneducated, vnpruned,   1166
VNSALLIED = 1
  Now by my maiden honour yet as pure, | As the vnsallied Lilly I
  protest,   2277
VNSATISFIED = 1
  But that one halfe which is vnsatisfied,   634
VNSEEMING = 1
  In so vnseeming to confesse receit,   651
VNSEENE = 2
  All vnseene, can passage finde: 1443
  Vnseene, vnuisited, much to our shame.   2284
VNTILL = 4*2
  [:] *Pag.* Vntill the Goose came out of doore,   856 +8
  Arm. Vntill tne Goose came out of doore,   861
  Vntill his Incke were tempred with Loues sighes: 1698
  Clow. Vnder correction sir we know where-vntill it doth |
  amount.   2436
  *will shew wher-vntill it doth amount: for mine owne part, I   2443
  There stay vntill the twelue Celestiall Signes   2757
VNTO = 4
  All liberall reason I will yeelde vnto.   665
  of the partie written to the person written vnto.   1299
  Consider what you first did sweare vnto: 1641
  Vnto his seuerall Mistres: which they'le know   2016
VNTRAINED = *1
  *vntrained, or rather vnlettered, or ratherest vnconfirmed
  fa-|shion,   1167
VNTRUE = 1
  Forestall our sport, to make vs thus vntrue?   2412
VNUISITED = 1
  Vnseene, vnuisited, much to our shame.   2284
VNUM = *1
  *about your Infamie *vnu(m) cita* a gigge of a Cuckolds horne.   1805
VOCATUR = *1
  **vocatur* nebour; neigh abreuiated ne: this is abhominable,   1762
VOLABLE = 1
  Brag. A most acute Iuuenall, volable and free of grace,   836
VOLUBLE = 1
  So sweete and voluble is his discourse.   568
VOLUMES = *1
  *Wit, write Pen, for I am for whole volumes in folio. *Exit.*   486
VOTARIE = 1
  I am a Votarie; I haue vowde to *Iaquenetta*   2846
VOTARIES = *2
  *Who are the Votaries my louing Lordes, that are vowfel-|lowes
  with this vertuous Duke?   528
  Ped. Sir *Holofernes,* this *Berowne* is one of the Votaries   1302
VOUCHSAFE = 9*3
  Vouchsafe to read the purpose of my comming,   604
  Pag. Out of your fauours heauenly spirites vouchsafe   2062

VOUCHSAFE *cont.*

Vouchsafe to shew the sunshine of your face,	2100
Vouchsafe bright Moone, and these thy Starrs to shine,	2104
*King. Then in our measure, do but vouchsafe one change,	2108
*Rosa. The musique playes, vouchsafe some motion to it,	2117
Our eares vouchsafe it. | King. But your legges should do it.	2118
*Duman. Will you vouchsafe with me to change a word? | Maria.	
Name it.	2147
King. That she vouchsafe me audience for one word.	2238
To leade you to our Court, vouchsafe it then.	2270
Out of a new sad-soule, that you vouchsafe,	2689
Brag. Sweete Maiestie vouchsafe me.	2842

VOW = 8*1

Doth noyse abroad *Nauar* hath made a Vow,	513
My Vow was earthly, thou a heauenly Loue.	1399
Exhalst this vapour-vow in thee it is:	1403
Vow alacke for youth vnmeete,	1450
To breake the vow I am ingaged in.	1516
And studie too, the causer of your vow.	1661
O we haue made a Vow to studie, Lordes,	1669
And in that Vow we haue forsworne our Bookes:	1670
*Quee. This Feelde shall holde me, and so hold your vow:	2271

VOWD = 1

And where that you haue vowd to studie (Lordes)	1646

VOWDE = 1

I am a Votarie; I haue vowde to *Iaquenetta*	2846

VOWED = 2

Ah neuer fayth could hold, yf not to beautie vowed.	1268
Of heauenly Othes vowed with integritie.	2282

VOWELS = *1

*Pag. The last of the fiue Vowels if You repeate them, | or the fift if I.	1791

VOWES = 2

Vowes for thee broke deserue not punishment.	1396
Vowes are but breath, and breath a vapoure is.	1401

VOWFELLOWES = *1

*Who are the Votaries my louing Lordes, that are vowfel-|lowes with this vertuous Duke?	528

VOYCE = 1*1

*Thy eie *Ioues* lightning beares, thy voyce his dreadful thu(n)der	1279
And when Loue speakes, the voyce of all the Goddes,	1695

VP *see also* seald-vp = 18*3

A Maide of grace and complet maiestie, | About surrender vp of *Aquitaine,*	146
Ar. Take away this villaine, shut him vp.	456
Clo. Let me not be pent vp sir, I will fast being loose.	458
Boyet. Now Maddame summon vp your dearest spirrits,	492
We will giue vp our right in *Aquitaine,*	635
And if you proue it, Ile repay it backe, | Or yeelde vp *Aquitaine.*	654
*with turning vp your eylids, sigh a note and sing a note som-|time	783
*loue sometime through: nose as if you snufft vp loue by	785
This seald-vp counsaile. Ther's thy guerdon: goe.	934
Against the steepe vp rising of the hill?	976
Breake vp this Capon. | Boyet I am bound to serue.	1034
Here sweete, put vp this, twilbe thine annother day.	1091
The shape of Loues Tiburne, that hanges vp Simplicitie.	1386

VP *cont.*
  *King. What? | **Ber.* That you three fooles, lackt me foole, to
make vp the | (messe.   1551
  Why vniuersall plodding poysons vp | The nimble spirites in the
arteries,   1655
  As would be crambd vp in a sheete of paper   1894
  How manie inches doth fill vp one mile?   2091
  Berow. This fellow peckes vp Wit as Pidgions Pease,   2240
  My wofull selfe vp in a mourning house, | Rayning the teares of
lamentation,   2768
  To flatter vp these powers of mine with rest,   2774
  The sodaine hand of death close vp mine eye.   2775
VPHOLD = 1
  Most honourablie doth vphold his word,   2387
VPON = 12*7
  Liue registred vpon our brazen Tombes,   6
  As paynefully to poare vpon a Booke,   79
  **ground Which? which I meane I walkt vpon, it is ycliped Thy
Park.*   248
  *Boy. A man, if I liue (and this) by, in, and without, vpon the   809
  *Boy. Marrie sir, you must send the Asse vpon the Horse,   822
  Forr. Heereby vpon the edge of yonder Coppice,   983
  *King Cophetua set eie vpon the pernicious and indubitate   1046
  *Rosa. Shall I come vpon thee with an olde saying, that   1108
  *and deliuered vpon the mellowing of occasion: But the   1234
  To those fresh morning dropps vpon the Rose,   1359
  Dares looke vpon the heauen of her brow,   1576
  Berow. Aduaunce your standards, and vpon them Lords.   1718
  *please his Grace (by the worlde) sometime to leane vpon   1835
  Vpon the next occasion that we meete,   2035
  (Those cloudes remooued) vpon our waterie eyne.   2105
  King. Vpon mine honour no.   2376
  Much vpon this tis: and might not you   2411
  And laugh vpon the apple of her eie?   2414
  You leere vpon me, do you: ther's an eie | Woundes like a leaden
sword.   2419
VPPON = 2*2
  He throwes vppon the grosse worlds baser slaues   34
  By fixing it vppon a fayrer eye,   86
  *vppon the Forme, and taken following her into the Parke: 218
  *Clo. Nay nothing M.(aster) *Moth,* but what they looke vppon.   465
VPRIGHT = 1
  Duma. As vpright as the Ceder.   1423
VPRISING *see* rising
VPSHOOT = 1
  Clo. Then will she get the vpshoot by cleauing the is in.   1129
VPWARD = 1
  Duma. O vile, then as she goes what vpward lyes?   1629
VS *see also* let's, to's *l.*7 11 160 *206 *211 631 *1180 *1181 1245
  1409 1562 1712 1723 1725 1733 *1831 1980 2011 2037 2225 2230
  2287 2297 *2318 2320 2351 2352 2357 2358 *2364 2412 *2433
  *2453 2715 2717 2725 2728 2732 2747 = 30*9
VSE = 2
  And I will vse him for my Minstrelsie.   187
  You haue in that forsworne the vse of eyes: 1660
VSED = 1
  This ciuill warre of wittes were much better vsed   730

VSHERING *see* hushering
VSURPING = 1
    It mournes, that painting vsurping haire   1608
VT = *1
    *Who vnderstandeth thee not, loues thee not, *vt re sol la mi fa*:   1261
VTTER = 1
    sweete breath, as will vtter a brace of wordes.   2468
VTTERS = 1
    And vtters it againe when God dooth please.   2241
VTTRED = 1
    Not vttred by base sale of chapmens tongues: 507
VULGAR = 2*2
    Boy. Which the base vulgar do call three.   356
    Veni, vidi, vici: Which to annothanize in the vulgar, O base   1048
    *and obscure vulgar; *videliset*, He came, see, and ouercame: 1049
    O my troth most sweete iestes, most inconie vulgar wit,   1139
WAGG = 1
    Making the bolde wagg by their prayses bolder.   2000
WAIGH = 2
    Ros. In deede I waigh not you, and therefore light.   1913
    Kath. You waigh me not, O thats you care not for me.   1914
WAISTE *see* wast, waste
WAITE = 1
    Nor neuer more in Russian habite waite.   2333
WAKES = 1
    At Wakes and Wassels, meetings, markets, Faires.   2243
WALDE = *1
    *A Ladie walde about with Diamondes: Looke you, what I | haue
    from the louing King.   1890
WALKE = 2*2
    Then those that walke and wot not what they are.   96
    selfe to walke: the time When? about the sixt houre, When
    Beastes   245
    To see him walke before a Lady, and to beare her Fann.   1143
    Clow. Walke aside the true folke, and let the traytors stay.   1561
WALKT = 1*1
    ground Which? which I meane I walkt vpon, it is ycliped Thy
    Park.   248
    The streete should see as she walkt ouer head.   1630
WALL = 1
    Winter. | When Isacles hang by the wall,   2878
WANT = 1*2
    *want no instruction: If their Daughters be capable, I will   1242
    Where nothing wantes, that want it selfe doth seeke.   1586
    Boy. True, and it was inioyned him in *Rome* for want of   2667
WANTES = 1
    Where nothing wantes, that want it selfe doth seeke.   1586
WANTON = 4
    A whitly wanton, with a veluet brow,   962
    Ber. O Rimes are gardes on wanton *Cupids* hose, | Disfigure not
    his Shop.   1390
    Playing in the wanton aire: 1441
    All wanton as a childe, skipping and vaine.   2719
WANTONS = 1
    As grauities reuolt to wantons be.   1964

WANTS = 1
King. Come sir, it wants a tweluemonth an'aday, | And then twill
ende.   2838
WARBLE = *1
*Bra. Warble child, make passionate my sense of hearing. | *Boy.*
Concolinel.   772
WARD = *1
*for the best ward of mine honour, is rewarding | my dependants.
Moth, follow.   897
WARE = *1
*Ros. Ware pensalls, How? Let me not die your debtor,   1931
WARELY = 1
The King and his companions warely,   1985
WARES = 1
He is Witts Pedler, and retales his wares: 2242
WARRANT = 1
Hath Wisedomes warrant, and the helpe of Schoole,   1961
WARRE = 2
That warre agaynst your owne affections,   13
This ciuill warre of wittes were much better vsed   730
WARRES = 1
Disbursed by my father in his warres.   627
WART = *1
*heauens were so pleased, that thou wart but my Ba-|stard;   1811
WAR-MAN = 1
Brag. The sweete War-man is dead and rotten,   2617
WAS *see also* twas = 49*28
WASHT = 2
For feare their colours should be washt away.   1620
Ile finde a fayrer face not washt to day.   1622
WASSELS = 1
At Wakes and Wassels, meetings, markets, Faires.   2243
WAST = 1
a wast, a legge, a limme.   1523
WASTE = 2
And your waste Mistres were as slender as my wit,   1025
One a these Maides girdles for your waste should be fit.   1026
WATCH = 2
And neuer going a right, being a Watch: 958
And I to sigh for her, to watch for her,   966
WATCHT = 1
But being watcht, that it may still go right.   959
WATER = 3
* Fer. Sir I will pronounce your sentence: You shall fast a | weeke
with Branne and Water.   295
Arm. Tell me precisely of what complexion? | *Boy.* Of the sea-
water Greene sir.   387
Thou now requests but Mooneshine in the water.   2107
WATERIE = 1
(Those cloudes remooued) vpon our waterie eyne.   2105
WAUE = *1
*Brag. Now by the sault waue of the meditaranium, a   1795
WAX = 1
Rosa. That was the way to make his god-head Wax: 1897
WAXE = 1
Breake the necke of the Waxe, and euery one giue eare.   1039

WAY = 9*3
> *Boy.* What then, do you see? | *Lad.* I, our way to be gone.   766
> *Brag.* The way is but short, away. | *Boy.* As swift as Lead sir.   824
> *as it were *in via*, in way of explication *facere*: as it were   1164
> *of the stranger Queenes: which accidentally, or by the way   1304
> God amende vs, God amende, we are much out a th'way.   1409
> Forerunne faire Loue, strewing her way with flowers.   1731
> *Snake; that is the way to make an offence gracious, though   1871
> *Rosa.* That was the way to make his god-head Wax: 1897
> That kist his hand, a way in courtisie.   2249
> *Clow.* Fellow *Hector*, she is gone; she is two months on | her
> way.   2628
> *Rosal.* Why thats the way to choake a gibing spirrit,   2819
> *King.* No Madame, we will bring you on your way.   2834

WAYES = 2
> *Bero.* By Ioue, I all wayes tooke three threes for nine.   2438
> When Blood is nipt, and wayes be full,   2883

WAYLE = 1
> From what it purposd, since to wayle friendes lost,   2707

WAYTE = 1
> And wayte the season, and obserue the times,   1953

WAYWARD = 1
> This wimpled whyning purblind wayward Boy,   945

WE = 82*16

WEAKER = *1
> *Ferd. For* Iaquenetta (*so is the weaker vessell called*) *which I*   269

WEALTH = 4
> To loue, to wealth, to pompe, I pine and die,   35
> *Boyet.* Here comes a member of the common wealth.   1017
> *Daughters profite very greatly vnder you: you are a good |
> member of the common wealth.   1239
> For all the wealth that euer I did see,   1486

WEANE = 1
> Take all and weane it, it may proue an Oxe.   2165

WEARE = 4
> And weare his coloures like a Tumblers hoope.   954
> Holde *Rosaline*, this Fauour thou shalt weare,   2022
> *Rosa.* Come on then, weare the Fauours most in sight.   2028
> *Quee.* Pardon me sir, this Iewell did she weare,   2395

WEARES = *1
> *of *Iaquenettaes*, and that a weares next his hart for a | Fauour.   2669

WEARING = 1
> *Berow.* Why he comes in like a periure, wearing papers.   1380

WEART = 1
> *Bero.* And thou weart a Lyon, we would do so.   2576

WEATHER = 2
> *Ar.* And so farewell. | *Ma.* Faire weather after you.   446
> Many can brooke the weather, that loue not the winde.   1188

WED = 1
> That he would wed me, or els die my Louer.   2385

WEDDED = 1
> *Ber.* Is she wedded or no? | *Boy.* To her will sir, or so.   711

WEE *l.*2407 = 1

WEEDE = 1
> To weede this wormewood from your fructfull braine,   2808

WEEDES = 1*1
> *Lon.* He weedes the corne, & still lets grow the weeding.   101

WEEDES *cont.*
If frostes and fastes, hard lodging, and thin weedes,   2761
WEEDING = *1
 Lon. He weedes the corne, & still lets grow the weeding.   101
WEEKE = 3*1
And one day in a weeke to touch no foode: 43
 Fer. Sir I will pronounce your sentence: You shall fast a | weeke
with Branne and Water.   295
*but a' must fast three dayes a weeke: for this Damsell   433
O that I knew he were but in by th'weeke,   1951
WEEKS = 1*1
*What was a month old at *Cains* birth, that's not fiue weeks | old
as yet?   1190
And rought not to fiue-weeks when he came to fiuescore.   1198
WEELE = 1
Weele not be nice, take handes, we will not daunce.   2121
WEEPE = 2
Thou shinst in euerie teare that I do weepe,   1365
My teares for glasses, and still make me weepe.   1371
WEEPING = 1
The King was weeping ripe for a good word.   2193
WEERIE = 3
 Berow. Tell her we measure them by weerie steps. | *Boy.* She
heares her selfe.   2092
 Rosa. How manie weerie steps,   2094
Of manie weerie miles you haue ore gone,   2095
WEERY = 1
But seeke the weery beddes of people sicke.   2782
WEIGH *see* waigh
WEIGHT = 1
Matchles *Nauar*, the plea of no lesse weight,   498
WEL = 1*3
 Arm. O wel knit *Sampson*, strong ioynted *Sampson*; I do excel   379
 Dum. A gallant Lady *Mounsir*, fare you wel. *Exit.*   694
 Mar. A marke marueilous wel shot, for they both did hit.   1119
*And they wel mockt depart away with shame. *Sound Trom.*   2048
WELCOME = 8*3
*welcome the sower Cup of prosperitie, affliccio(n) may one day   308
 Nauar. Faire Princesse, Welcome to the court of *Nauar.*   585
 Prin. Faire I giue you backe againe, and welcome I haue   586
welcome to the wide fieldes too base to be mine.   588
 Nau. You shalbe welcome Madame to my Court.   590
 Prin. I wilbe welcome then, Conduct me thither.   591
Meane time receiue such welcome at my hand,   666
 Ber. O you are welcome sir, adew.   713
 Boy. Farewell to me sir, and welcome to you. *Exit Bero.*   714
 Ber. Welcome pure wit, thou partst a faire fray.   2425
 Quee. Welcome *Marcade*, but that thou interrupptest our |
merriment.   2673
WELKEN = *1
*of *Celo* the skie, the welken the heauen, & anon falleth like   1155
WELKIN = 1
By thy fauour sweete Welkin, I must sigh in thy face: 837
WELKINS = *1
 Ferd. Great Deputie the welkins Vizgerent, and sole dominatur of   231
WELL = 43*16
Which I hope well is not enrolled there.   42

WELL *cont.*

Which I hope well is not enrolled there.	50
As thus, to study where I well may dine,	66
Ferd. How well hees read to reason against reading.	99
Dum. Proceeded well, to stop all good proceeding.	100
Bero. Well, say I am, why should proude Sommer boast,	111
Ferd. Well, sit you out: go home *Berowne*: adue.	119
Fer. How well this yeelding rescewes thee from shame.	127
For well you know here comes in Embassaie,	144
*Bero. Well sir, be it as the stile shall giue vs cause to clime | in the merrines.	211
*Ber. This is not so well as I looked for, but the best that | euer I heard.	275
Fer. Well, it was proclaimed Damsel.	287
Ar. Define, define, well educated infant.	398
with the rational hinde *Costard*: she deserues well.	422
**I must keepe her at the Parke, she is alowde for the Day | womand. Fare you well.	434
*Clo. Well sir I hope when I do it, I shall do it on a full | stomacke.	451
*Clo. Well, if euer I do see the merry dayes of desolation	462
Well fitted in artes, glorious in armes:	537
Nothing becoms him ill that he would well.	538
*2. Lad. The young *Dumaine*, a well accomplisht youth,	548
And go well satisfied to France againe.	648
Prin. It was well done of you to take him at his word.	718
*Boy. A message well simpathisd, a Horse to be embassa-|doure for an Asse.	819
To sell a bargaine well is as cunning as fast and loose:	867
Ber. O my good knaue *Costard*, exceedingly well met.	910
Clow. Well, I will do it sir: Fare you well.	922
Well, I will loue, write, sigh, pray, shue, grone,	970
Well Lords, to day we shall haue our dispatch,	979
And shooting well, is then accounted ill:	1000
Rosa. Well then I am the shooter. | *Boy.* And who is your Deare?	1100
**for their Sonnes are well tuterd by you, and their	1238
for a Swine: tis prettie, it is well.	1253
Well learned is that tongue, that well can thee commend.	1276
Nath. Marueilous well for the pen.	1317
**that defiles; defile, a foule worde: Well, set thee downe	1337
**foole: Well proued wit. By the Lord this Loue is as madd	1339
**as Aiax, it kills Sheepe, it kills mee, I a Sheepe well prooued	1340
**would not loue her; yes for her two eyes. Well, I do nothing	1343
**Well, she hath one a'my Sonnets already, the Clowne bore	1348
Ber. An amber colour Rauen was well noted.	1422
Saw sighes reeke from you, noted well your pashion.	1477
And beauties crest becomes the heauens well.	1605
Brag. Men of peace well incontred. | *Ped.* Most millitarie sir salutation.	1774
**well culd, chose, sweete, & apt I do assure you sir, I do assure.	1827
**you may cry, Well done *Hercules*, now thou crusshest the	1870
Quee. Well bandied both, a set of Wit well played.	1916
That well by hart hath cond his embassage	1990
The thirde he caperd and cryed, All goes well.	2005
Methegline, Wort, and Malmsey; well runne dice:	2138
Ros. Well, better wits haue worne plaine statute Caps,	2202
Lets mocke them still as well knowne as disguysde:	2224

WELL   *cont.*
    Quee. And were you well aduisde? | *King.* I was faire Madame.   2369
    *Ber. Well said old mocker, I must needes be friendes with |
    (thee.   2495
    Bero. Well folowed, *Iudas* was hanged on an Elder.   2559
    *Berow. A tweluemonth? well; befall what will befall,   2831
    Might well haue made our sport a Comedie.   2837
WEL-LIKING = 1
    Rosa. Wel-liking Wits they haue grosse grosse, fat fat.   2187
WENCH = 7*3
    with, o with, but with this I passion to say wherewith: | *Clo.* With a
    Wench.   261
    Clo. Sir I confesse the Wench.   279
    *Fer. It was proclaymed a yeeres imprisonment to be ta-|ken with
    a Wench.   283
    *base for a Souldier to loue; so am I in loue with a base wench.   364
    Boy. And thats great maruaile, louing a light Wench.   427
    Enter *Clowne, Constable,* and *Wench.*   430
    *woman when queene *Guinouer* of Brittaine was a litle wench | as
    toching the hit it.   1112
    Kath. So do not you, for you are a light Wench.   1912
    And to begin Wench, so God helpe me law,   2346
    *wench is cast away: shee's quicke, the childe bragges in her |
    bellie already: tis yours.   2632
WENCHES = 5*2
    Boy. Do you heare my mad Wenches? | *Lad.* No.   764
    *are humours, these betraie nice wenches that would be be-|traied   792
    Light Wenches may proue plagues to men forsworne,   1736
    Arme Wenches arme, incounters mounted are,   1974
    Boyet. The tongues of mocking Wenches are as keene | As is the
    Rasors edge inuisible: 2172
    *King. Farewel mad Wenches, you haue simple wits. *Exe.*   2181
    This Gallant pins the Wenches on his sleeue.   2246
WERE *l.**291 417 460 577 597 607 645 *698 730 746 *748 856 +3
    856 +7 860 965 1025 *1140 *1164 *1165 *1176 *1185 *1270 *1351
    1455 1461 1479 *1548 1566 1598 1627 1628 1698 1706 1752 *1811
    *1847 1920 1921 1923 1924 1933 1946 1951 2068 2192 2225 2227
    2294 2309 *2318 2367 2369 2371 *2439 2524 = 41*16
WERT *see also* wart *l.**890 2263 = 1*1
WEST = 1*1
    *East from the West corner of thy curious knotted garden; There   254
    By East, West, North, and South, I spred my conquering might: 2514
WETHERCOCK = *1
    *What vaine? What Wethercock? Did you euer heare better?   1075
WHALES = 1
    To shew his teeth as white as Whales bone,   2257
WHAT *l.*59 96 123 *151 154 194 215 *277 *312 338 *370 384 387
    464 *465 574 596 617 692 *695 735 766 808 821 913 923 955 *988
    *1053 *1061 1072 *1074 *1075 *1190 1194 *1262 1263 1377 1405
    1482 1490 1500 1502 1529 1531 1542 *1551 *1568 1575 1578 1629
    1631 1641 1707 *1785 1800 *1812 *1830 *1890 1911 1918 1935
    1979 1987 2004 2011 2029 2071 2075 2076 2078 *2127 2154 2198
    2221 2225 2227 2263 2264 2308 *2314 2372 2381 2388 2397 2428
    *2433 2556 2562 2630 *2657 2664 2707 2717 2777 2783 2793 2800
    *2831 = 81*26
WHATS = 4*2
    To whom he sendes, and whats his Embassie.   494

WHATS cont.

    Bero. Whats her name in the capp? | *Boy. Katherin* by good happ.   709
    *Three-farthings remuneration, What's the price of this yncle?   904
    Quee. Whats your will sir? Whats your will?   1028
    **Ros.* Whats your darke meaning mouce, of this light word?   1905
WHEN *l.*8 48 67 69 *103 156 *245 *312 *451 502 920 924 931 1007
    1012 *1109 *1112 *1140 *1196 1198 1360 1482 1519 *1521 1649
    1666 1671 1687 1695 *1759 *1760 1959 1966 1983 2214 2241 2251
    2299 2301 *2314 2371 *2374 2379 2405 2418 2464 *2512 *2522
    2543 2618 +1 *2668 2789 2860 2869 2871 2879 2883 2888 2892 =
    43*16, *2
    **selfe to walke: the time When? about the sixt houre, When*
    Beastes   245
    **which is called Supper: So much for the time When. Now for the*   247
WHENCE = 1
    From whence doth spring the true *Promethean* fire.   1654
WHERE *l.*66 68 83 *250 440 *470 598 662 *748 981 984 992 *1273
    *1319 *1322 1463 1508 1509 1510 1538 1540 1585 1586 1599 1646
    1662 1665 *1857 2263 *2314 2461 = 23*8, *2
    **Then for the place Where? where I meane, I did incounter that*
    ob- | *seene*   250
    **seest. But to the place Where? It standeth North North-east & by*   253
WHEREFORE = 2
    Boy. Little prettie, because little: wherefore apt.   333
    Lady Ka. Two hot Sheepes marie. | *Bo.* And wherefore not
    Shipps?   720
WHEREWITH = 1
    with, o with, but with this I passion to say wherewith: | *Clo.* With a
    Wench.   261
WHERE-VNTILL = *1
    **Clow.* Vnder correction sir we know where-vntill it doth |
    amount.   2436
WHERS = 2
    Boyet. O I am stable with laughter, Wher's her Grace?   1971
    King. Faire sir, God saue you: Wher's the Princesse?   2235
WHER-VNTILL = *1
    *will shew wher-vntill it doth amount: for mine owne part, I   2443
WHETHER = 1
    Whether the three Worthis shall come in or no?   2427
WHICH *l.*10 42 45 50 *60 73 78 193 *219 *247 *248 *252 *258 *260
    *269 302 *325 328 356 410 *470 *471 *472 *473 564 630 634 642
    652 664 732 736 *755 757 831 960 995 *1018 1022 *1048 1087
    *1180 1248 1278 1281 *1304 *1402 1407 1483 *1763 *1798 1823
    2016 2017 2273 2313 2406 2462 2701 2704 2724 2806 2810 2821 =
    44*22, *1
    **ground Which? which I meane I walkt vpon, it is ycliped Thy*
    Park.   248
WHILE = 7
    To seeke the lyght of trueth, while trueth the whyle   80
    While it doth studie to haue what it would,   154
    Haste, signifie so much while we attende,   524
    * *Peda. Via* good-man *Dull,* thou hast spoken no worde all | this
    while.   1880
    But while tis spoke each turne away his face.   2040
    While greasie Ione doth keele the pot.   2887
    While greasie Ione doth keele the pot.   2896

WHIP = 2*3
  *Ber. O and I forsoth in loue, I that haue been loues whip?   939
  Bero. Now step I foorth to whip hipocrisie.   1488
  *Peda. Thou disputes like an Infant: goe whip thy Gigg.   1802
  *Pag. Lende me your Horne to make one, and I will whip   1804
  Quee. Whip to our Tents as Roes runs ore land. *Exeunt.*   2232
WHIPPING = 1
  To see great *Hercules* whipping a Gigge,   1504
WHIPT = *2
  *Boy. To be whipt: and yet a better loue then my maister.   424
  *Clow. Then shall *Hector* be whipt for *Iaquenetta* that is   2636
WHIRLES = 1
  And Iustice alwayes whirles in equall measure: 1735
WHISPER = 2
  What did you whisper in your Ladies eare?   2372
  What did the *Russian* whisper in your eare?   2381
WHIT = 2
  Tu-whit to-who. | A merrie note,   2885
  Tu-whit to-who. | A merrie note,   2894
WHITE = 9*3
  Arm. My loue is most immaculate white and red.   395
  Boy. Yf she be made of white and red,   403
  And feares by pale white showne: 406
  *A dangerous rime maister against the reason of white & red.   411
  *Longauill. I beseech you a word, What is she in the white?   695
  And to her white hand see thou do commend   933
  To the snow-white hand of the most bewtious Lady Rosaline.   1297
  *Berow. White handed Mistres, one sweet word with thee.   2135
  To shew his teeth as white as Whales bone,   2257
  By this white Gloue (how white the hand God knowes)   2343
  And Ladi-smockes all siluer white,   2862
WHITHER = 1
  King. Soft, Whither away so fast?   1524
WHITLY = 1
  A whitly wanton, with a veluet brow,   962
WHO *l*.87 134 177 381 493 *528 547 *748 978. *1050 *1054 1083
  1093 1101 *1154 *1261 1375 *1570 1599 1716 *1746 1918
  2254 = 16*8
WHOERE *see* who
WHOLE = 1*1
  *Wit, write Pen, for I am for whole volumes in folio. *Exit.*   486
  Abate throw at Nouum, and the whole world againe,   2487
WHOLLY = 1
  And shape his seruice wholly to my deuice,   1955
WHOLSOME *see* holsome
WHOM *l*.179 494 727 *943 *1053 1085 *1235 1394 1411 1454
  1711 = 8*3
WHORESON = *1
  *Berow. Ah you whoreson loggerhead, you were borne to | do me
  shame.   1548
WHOSE = 6*3
  Whose edge hath power to cut whose will still wils,   542
  Lon. Pray you sir, Whose daughter?   700
  *victorie: On whose side? the King: the captiue is inricht, on   1055
  *whose side? the Beggers. The catastrophe is a Nuptiall, on   1056
  *whose side? the Kinges: no, on both in one, or one in both.   1057
  Loue, whose Month is euer May: 1439

WHOSE *cont.*
   Whose Clubb kilde Cerberus *that three headed* Canus,   2542
   Whose influence is begot of that loose grace,   2820
WHY *l.**60 77 111 113 136 *151 *315 322 323 *358 595 738 *905
  *906 915 925 *1051 1096 *1288 1380 1433 1542 1566 1655 2041
  2080 2122 2155 2248 *2314 *2321 *2323 2470 2578 2819 = 26*12
WHYLE = 1
   To seeke the lyght of trueth, while trueth the whyle   80
WHYNING = 1
   This wimpled whyning purblind wayward Boy,   945
WIDE = 2
   welcome to the wide fieldes too base to be mine.   588
   Mar. Wide a'the bow hand, yfaith your hand is out.   1124
WIFE = 4
   What? I loue, I sue, I seeke a wife,   955
   A wife of such wood were felicitie.   1598
   Kath. A wife? a beard, faire health, and honestie,   2784
   Duma. O shall I say, I thanke you gentle Wife?   2786
WIGHT = 1
   Bero. Armado is a most illustrious wight,   188
WIL *l.**1144 *1213 2004 *2112 *2374 *2451 *2647 = 1*7
WILBE = 3*2
   Prin. I wilbe welcome then, Conduct me thither.   591
   *Clown. True, true, and now you wilbe my purgation, | and let me
   loose.   892
   Quee. See see, my beautie wilbe sau'd by merrit.   996
   *will be geuen to *Aiax.* He wilbe the ninth Worthie: a
   Con-|querour,   2531
   I wilbe thine: and till that instance shutt   2767
WILDE = *1
   *Berow. To moue wilde laughter in the throate of death?   2816
WILL *see also* he'le, Ile, they'le, twilbe, twill, weele, yele, yole,
  youle, you'll *l.*64 74 90 160 171 187 200 226 293 294 *295 304 314
  337 360 *363 404 *419 438 442 458 *467 *480 540 606 607 623
  633 635 665 677 686 729 757 *779 *806 856 +1 856 +5 *857 879
  *880 884 886 902 907 922 *926 *936 964 968 970 980 1001 1038
  *1061 1071 1129 *1207 *1242 1296 *1298 *1320 *1322 *1331
  *1341 *1342 1369 1370 1389 1397 1432 1458 1482 1484 1485
  *1521 *1558 1564 1624 1685 1686 1707 1728 1733 1793 *1804
  *1815 *1834 *1857 1868 1874 *1878 1883 *1884 1988 2004 2015
  2018 2019 2023 2038 2041 2067 2121 *2147 2168 2189 2203 2208
  2210 2211 2212 2239 2258 2268 2332 2334 2361 2380 2397 2418
  *2443 *2453 2468 *2474 *2481 *2529 *2531 *2537 2560 *2590
  *2619 2646 *2650 2658 *2659 2663 2682 2685 2753 2754 2806
  2826 2827 2828 *2831 2834 2845 *2848 2852 = 111*42, 11
   Like humble visage Suters his high will.   525
   Is a sharpe Wit matcht with too blunt a Will: 541
   Whose edge hath power to cut whose will still wils,   542
   Nau. Not for the worlde faire Madame, by my will.   594
   Prin. Why, will shall breake it will, and nothing els.   595
   Ber. Is she wedded or no? | *Boy.* To her will sir, or so.   711
   Quee. Whats your will sir? Whats your will?   1028
   If they do speake our language, tis our will   2073
   We are againe forsworne in will and error.   2410
WILLING = 3
   Then you much willing to be counted wise,   509
   Prince. All pride is willing pride, and yours is so: 527

WILLING *cont.*
  Boy. I was as willing to grapple as he was to boord. 719
WILLINGLY = 1
  Boy. Proud of imployment, willingly I go. *Exit Boy.* 526
WILS = 1
  Whose edge hath power to cut whose will still wils, 542
WILT *l.*808 918 = 2
WIMPLED = 1
  This wimpled whyning purblind wayward Boy, 945
WIN = 2*1
  And shape to win grace though he had no wit. 552
  Boy. Maister, will you win your loue with a french braule? 779
  As thou wilt win my fauour, good my knaue, 918
WINCKE = 1*1
  And not be seene to wincke of all the day. 47
  *three studied ere yele thrice wincke: and how easie it is to 358
WIND = 1*1
  Through the Veluet, leaues the wind, 1442
  *Fleeter then Arrowes, bullets wind thought swifter thinges. 2177
WINDE = 2
  Many can brooke the weather, that loue not the winde. 1188
  When all aloude the winde doth blow, 2888
WINDOW = 1
  Beholde the window of my hart, mine eye: 2799
WINGES = 1
  Seemeth their conference, their conceites haue winges, 2176
WINN = 2
  To loose an oth, to winn a Parradise? 1406
  King. And winn them too, therefore let vs deuise, 1723
WINNE = 1
  And therewithall to winne me, yf you please, 2809
WINTER = 2
  Brag. This side is *Hiems,* Winter. 2855
  Winter. | When Isacles hang by the wall, 2878
WINTERS = 1
  A witherd Hermite fiue score winters worne, 1591
WIPE = 1
  Would from my forehead wipe a periurde note: 1462
WISE = 10
  Ma. Lord how wise you are. 441
  Then you much willing to be counted wise, 509
  Prin. Were my Lord so, his ignoraunce were wise, 597
  Pag. Do the wise thinke them other, is not *lenuoy* a *salue?* 853
  If by mee broke, What foole is not so wise, 1405
  Quee. We are wise girles to mocke our Louers so. 1948
  As foolrie in the Wise, when Wit doth dote: 1966
  Your wits makes wise thinges foolish when we greete 2301
  Wise thinges seeme foolish, and rich thinges but poore. 2305
  Rosa. This proues you wise and rich: for in my eie. 2306
WISEDOME = 2
  As Wit turnde Foole, follie in Wisedome hatcht: 1960
  In your rich wisedome to excuse, or hide, 2690
WISEDOMES = 2
  For Wisedomes sake, a worde that all men loue: 1708
  Hath Wisedomes warrant, and the helpe of Schoole, 1961
WISH *see also* wysh = 9*1
  Then wish a Snow in Mayes new fangled showes: 115

WISH *cont.*
  Na. Thy owne wish wish I thee in euery place. *Exit.*   676
  Duma. O that I had my wish? | *Long.* And I had mine.   1427
  Wish himselfe the heauens breath.   1445
  Quee. I thinke no lesse: Dost thou not wish in hart   1945
  Quee. Then wish me better, I will giue you leaue.   2268
  And I will wish thee neuer more to daunce,   2332
  *to *Fortuna delaguar,* I wish you the peace of mind most royall |
  cupplement. *Exit.*   2475
  With three folde loue I wish you all these three.   2785
WIT = 25*7
  reason for it. He surely affected her for her wit.   393
  Boy. It was so sir, for she had a greene wit.   394
  Boy. My fathers wit, and my mothers tongue assist me.   399
  *seduced, and he had a very good wit. *Cupids* Butshaft is too   478
  *Wit, write Pen, for I am for whole volumes in folio. *Exit.*   486
  In spending your Wit in the prayse of mine.   510
  Is a sharpe Wit matcht with too blunt a Will: 541
  For he hath wit to make an ill shape good,   551
  And shape to win grace though he had no wit.   552
  His eye begets occasion for his wit,   561
  And your waste Mistres were as slender as my wit,   1025
  O my troth most sweete iestes, most inconie vulgar wit,   1139
  And his Page atother side, that handfull of wit,   1146
  **Dul.* You two are book-men, Can you tel me by your wit,   1189
  *neither sauouring of Poetrie, wit, nor inuention.   1323
  *foole: Well proued wit. By the Lord this Loue is as madd   1339
  Ber. Once more Ile marke how Loue can varrie Wit.   1436
  How will he scorne, how will he spende his wit?   1484
  *sweete tutch, a quicke venewe of wit, snip snap, quicke and   1796
  home, it reioiceth my intellect, true wit.   1797
  *purse of wit, thou Pidgin-egge of discretion. O and the   1810
  Quee. Well bandied both, a set of Wit well played.   1916
  As Wit turnde Foole, follie in Wisedome hatcht: 1960
  As foolrie in the Wise, when Wit doth dote: 1966
  To proue by Wit, worth in simplicitie.   1968
  Quee. O pouertie in wit, Kingly poore flout.   2188
  Berow. This fellow peckes vp Wit as Pidgions Pease,   2240
  Thrust thy sharpe wit quite through my ignorance,   2330
  Bero. Speake for your selues, my wit is at an ende.   2363
  Ber. Welcome pure wit, thou partst a faire fray.   2425
  That lie within the mercie of your wit: 2807
  With all the fierce endeuour of your wit,   2814
WITH *see also* wy = 120*44
WITHALL = 5
  I neuer spent an houres talke withall.   560
  Which we much rather had depart withall,   642
  acquainted you withall, to the ende to craue your assistance.   1848
  To Loues mistooke, and so be mockt withall.   2034
  And I will haue you, and that fault withall.   2827
WITHDRAW = 1
  Boyet. Ladies, withdraw: the gallants are at hand,   2231
WITHER = 1
  Prin. Such short liued wits do wither as they grow.   546
WITHERD = 1
  A witherd Hermite fiue score winters worne,   1591

WITHIN = 8*2

*Ber. Item, That no woman shall come within a myle of	128
*Item, Yf any man be seene to talke with a woman within	139
Three thousand times within this three yeeres space:	161
It should none spare, that come within his power.	543
Within the limit of becomming mirth,	559
You may not come (faire Princesse) within my gates,	669
I Costard running out, that was safely within,	882
Sowla, sowla. Exeunt. Shoot within.	1148
Long. You haue a double tongue within your Maske,	2157
That lie within the mercie of your wit:	2807

WITHOUT = 8*7

As honor (without breach of honor) may,	667
But here without you shalbe so receiude,	670
*without these, and make them men of note: do you	793
*Boy. A man, if I liue (and this) by, in, and without, vpon the	809
All ignorant that soule, that sees thee without wonder.	1277
Without the beautie of a womans face?	1651
*haue been sharpe & sententious: pleasant without scurillitie,	1742
*wittie without affection, audatious without impudencie,	1743
*learned without opinion, and strange without heresie: I did	1744
That we may do it still without accompt.	2099
Maria. What, was your vizard made without a tongue?	2154
To make a world-without-end bargaine in:	2749
Without the which I am not to be won:	2810

WITNESSE = 1

My Fauour were as great, be witnesse this,	1921

WITNESSETH = *1

*for so witnesseth thy lowlines. Shall I commande thy	1059

WITS = 9*1

Make rich the ribbes, but bancrout quite the wits.	31
Prin. Such short liued wits do wither as they grow.	546
Ber. Your wit's too hot, it speedes too fast, twill tire.	615
And Wits owne grace to grace a learned Foole.	1962
Muster your Wits, stande in your owne defence,	1977
*King. Farewel mad Wenches, you haue simple wits. Exe.	2181
Are these the breede of Wits so wondered at?	2184
Rosa. Wel-liking Wits they haue grosse grosse, fat fat.	2187
Ros. Well, better wits haue worne plaine statute Caps,	2202
Your wits makes wise thinges foolish when we greete	2301

WITTES = 2

This ciuill warre of wittes were much better vsed	730
And spend his prodigall wittes in booteles rimes,	1954

WITTIE = *1

*wittie without affection, audatious without impudencie,	1743

WITTS = 2

Prin. Good witts will be iangling, but gentles agree,	729
He is Witts Pedler, and retales his wares:	2242

WIT-OLD = *1

*Page. Offerd by a childe to an old man: which is wit-old.	1798

WIUES = 1

Boy. Do not curst wiues hold that selfe-soueraigntie	1011

WO = 1

So ridest thou triumphing in my wo.	1367

WOE = 3

O short liu'd pride. Not faire? alacke for woe | For. Yes Madam faire.	989

WOE *cont.*
   Shall we resolue to woe these gyrles of Fraunce?   1722
   If they returne in their owne shapes to woe?   2222
WOFULL = 1
   My wofull selfe vp in a mourning house, | Rayning the teares of
   lamentation,   2768
WOMAN = 8*5
   As not to see a woman in that terme,   41
   Ber. Item, That no woman shall come within a myle of   128
   Item, Yf any man be seene to talke with a woman within   139
   to a woman, for the forme in some forme.   221
   more sweete vnderstanding a Woman: him, I (as my euer esteemed   264
   Boy. A Woman, Maister. | *Arm.* Of what complexion?   383
   No Woman may approch his silent Court: 515
   Boyet. A woman sometimes, and you saw her in the light.   696
   A woman that is like a Iermane Cloake,   956
   Are not you the chiefe woman? You are the thickest heere.   1027
   *woman when queene *Guinouer* of Brittaine was a litle wench | as
   toching the hit it.   1112
   A Woman I forswore, but I will proue,   1397
   To fast, to study, and to see no woman: 1642
WOMAND = 1
   *I must keepe her at the Parke, she is alowde for the Day |
   womand. Fare you well.   434
WOMANS = 3
   Without the beautie of a womans face?   1651
   Now for not looking on a womans face,   1659
   Teaches such beautie as a womans eye: 1663
WOMBE = *1
   *the ventricle of Memorie, nourisht in the wombe of prima-|ter,   1233
WOMEN = 2
   Then fooles you were, these women to forsweare: 1706
   Or for Mens sake, the authour of these Women: 1710
WOMENS = 3
   From womens eyes this doctrine I deriue,   1652
   From womens eyes this doctrine I deriue.   1701
   Or Womens sake, by whom we Men are Men.   1711
WON = 3
   Tis won as townes with fire, so won so lost.   157
   Without the which I am not to be won: 2810
WONDER = 3*1
   Nauar shall be the wonder of the worlde.   16
   Pag. A wonder Maister, Heers a *Costard* broken in a shin.   841
   All ignorant that soule, that sees thee without wonder.   1277
   And wonder what they were, and to what ende   2227
WONDERED = 1
   Are these the breede of Wits so wondered at?   2184
WONDERS = 1
   Ar. I will tell thee wonders. | *Ma.* With that face.   442
WONNE = 1
   Small haue continuall plodders euer wonne,   91
WONT = 1
   When I was wont to thinke no harme all nyght,   48
WOO = 2
   Woo contrarie, deceyued by these remoues.   2027
   Nor woo in rime like a blind harpers songue.   2337

WOOD = 2
A wife of such wood were felicitie.   1598
Folowing the signes, wood but the signe of shee.   2408
WOODCOCKS = 1
Dumaine transformed, foure Woodcocks in a dysh.   1416
WOOE *see* woe
WOOED *see* wood
WOOERS = 1
Ile marke no wordes that smothfast wooers say,   2788
WOOING = 2
Hencefoorth my wooing minde shalbe exprest   2344
Berow. Our wooing doth not ende like an olde Play: 2835
WOOLWARD = 1
I goe Woolward for pennance.   2666
WOONDER = 1
Duma. By heauen the woonder in a mortall eye.   1419
WORD = 18*6
If I breake fayth, this word shall speake for me,   164
Dum. Sir, I pray you a word, What Ladie is that same?   692
Longauill. I beseech you a word, What is she in the white?   695
Not a word with him but a iest.   716
Boy. And euery iest but a word.   717
Prin. It was well done of you to take him at his word.   718
take *salue* for *lenuoy,* and the word *lenuoy* for a *salue*?   851
*Remuneration, O that's the latine word for three-farthings: 903
I will neuer buy and sell out of this word.   907
Ber. Amen, so I had mine: Is not that a good word?   1430
Berow. Is Ebonie like her? O word deuine!   1597
Ros. Whats your darke meaning mouce, of this light word?   1905
Berow. White handed Mistres, one sweet word with thee.   2135
Ber. One word in secret. | *Quee.* Let it not be sweete.   2142
Duman. Will you vouchsafe with me to change a word? | *Maria.*
Name it.   2147
Long. Let's part the word? | *Mar.* No, Ile not be your halfe: 2163
Long. One word in priuate with you ere I die.   2170
Rosa. Not one word more my Maides, break off, break off.   2178
The King was weeping ripe for a good word.   2193
King. That she vouchsafe me audience for one word.   2238
They did not blesse vs with one happie word.   2297
Most honourablie doth vphold his word,   2387
Cuckow, Cuckow: O word of feare, | Vnpleasing to a married
eare.   2867
Cuckow, cuckow: O word of feare,   2876
WORDE = 5*5
Cost. Not a worde of *Costart* yet. | *Ferd. So it is*   234
*put yeeres to the worde three, and studie three yeeres in two   359
Princ. We arrest your worde.   656
Quee. Thou fellow, a worde.   1082
*that defiles; defile, a foule worde: Well, set thee downe   1337
For Wisedomes sake, a worde that all men loue: 1708
Or for Loues sake, a worde that loues all men.   1709
*I maruaile thy M.(aister) hath not eaten thee for a worde, for
thou   1779
*congruent, and measurable for the after noone: the worde is   1826
Peda. Via good-man *Dull,* thou hast spoken no worde all | this
while.   1880

WORDES = 9*3
In high borne wordes the worth of many a Knight:	183
A man of fier new wordes, Fashions owne knight.	189
Clow. Be to me, and euerie man that dares not fight. | *Ferd.* No	
wordes.	239
wordes, the dauncing Horse will tell you.	360
*It is not for prisoners to be too silent in their wordes, and	466
Deliuers in such apt and gracious wordes,	565
Faire payment for foule wordes, is more then dew.	994
Clow. O they haue lyud long on the almsbasket of wordes.	1778
It were a fault to snatch wordes from my tongue.	2309
sweete breath, as will vtter a brace of wordes.	2468
Ile marke no wordes that smothfast wooers say,	2788
*The wordes of Mercurie, are harsh after the | songes of Apollo.	2897

WORDS = 1*2
Bero. How low so euer the matter, I hope in God for high |	
(words.	204
Bo. But to speak that in words, which his eie hath disclosd.	755
Bero. Honest plaine words, best pearce the eare of griefe,	2711

WORE = 1*1
Ros. Which of the Vizards was it that you wore?	2313
*Linnen: since when, Ile be sworne he wore none, but a	
dish-|cloute	2668

WORKING = 1*1
Boy. By a familier demonstration of the working, my | tough	
signeor.	320
We bend to that, the working of the hart.	1008

WORLD = 5*4
When she did starue the generall world beside,	502
*in the world but lie, and lie in my throate. By heauen I doe	1344
Gainst whom the world cannot holde argument,	1394
Clow. And I had but one peny in the world thou shouldst	1807
*let that passe. By the world I recount no fable, some certaine	1838
King. That more then all the world, I did respect her.	2373
Abate throw at Nouum, and the whole world againe,	2487
Curat. *When in the world I liud, I was the worldes commander:*	2512
Remote from all the pleasurs of the world:	2756

WORLDE = 6*5
Nauar shall be the wonder of the worlde.	16
Boy. The worlde was very guiltie of such a Ballet some	415
Nau. Not for the worlde faire Madame, by my will.	594
*sweeter Foole, sweetest Lady. By the worlde, I woulde not	1350
For where is any Authour in the worlde,	1662
That shew, containe, and nourish all the worlde.	1704
*please his Grace (by the worlde) sometime to leane vpon	1835
*a Souldier, a man of trauayle, that hath seene the worlde: but	1841
A worlde of tormentes though I should endure,	2279
Aboue this Worlde: adding thereto more ouer,	2384
Cura. *When in the worlde I liued, I was the worldes commander.*	2522

WORLDES = 6*2
And the hudge armie of the worldes desires.	14
The grosser manner of these worldes delyghts:	33
A man in all the worldes new fashion planted,	175
From tawnie Spaine lost in the worldes debate.	184
Your selfe, helde precious in the worldes esteeme,	495
Curat. *When in the world I liud, I was the worldes commander:*	2512
Cura. *When in the worlde I lieued, I was the worldes commander.*	2522

WORLDES *cont.*
Before I saw you: and the worldes large tongue   2803
WORLDS = 1
He throwes vppon the grosse worlds baser slaues   34
WORLD-WITHOUT-END = 1
To make a world-without-end bargaine in: 2749
WORMES = 1
These Wormes for louing, that art most in loue?   1491
WORMEWOOD = 1
To weede this wormewood from your fructfull braine,   2808
WORNE = 3
A witherd Hermite fiue score winters worne,   1591
Ros. Well, better wits haue worne plaine statute Caps,   2202
Bero. I and worne in the cappe of a Tooth-drawer: 2571
WORSE = 3
Ros. They are worse fooles to purchase mocking so.   1949
That hid the worse, and shewed the better face.   2317
To haue one show worse then the Kings and his company.   2456
WORSHIP = 2*1
Cost. I thanke your worship, God be wy you.   916
Clow. I will come to your worship to morrow morning.   926
That we (like sauages) may worship it.   2101
WORST = 2*1
Fer. I the best, for the worst. But sirra, What say you to this?   277
Nay to be periurde, which is worst of all: 960
And among three to loue the worst of all,   961
WORT = 1
Methegline, Wort, and Malmsey; well runne dice: 2138
WORTH = 6*2
In high borne wordes the worth of many a Knight: 183
I am lesse proude to heare you tell my worth,   508
Although not valued to the monies worth.   632
*Who tendring their owne worth from where they were | (glast,   748
Sir, your penny-worth is good, and your Goose be fat.   866
Ber. O, why then threefarthing worth of Silke.   915
To proue by Wit, worth in simplicitie.   1968
Clo. Tis not so much worth: but I hope I was perfect. I | made a
litle fault in great.   2507
WORTHIE = 3*3
Curat. Where will you finde men worthie enough to pre-|sent
them?   1857
Page. Thrice worthie Gentleman.   1875
Clow. It pleased them to thinke me worthie of *Pompey*   2447
Bero. My hat to a halfe-pennie, *Pompey* prooues the best |
Worthie.   2509
*will be geuen to *Aiax.* He wilbe the ninth Worthie: a
Con-|querour,   2531
Queen. Was not that *Hector?* | *Duma.* The worthie Knight of
Troy.   2843
WORTHIES = 8*4
Where seuerall worthies make one dignitie,   1585
Peda. Sir, you shall present before her the Nine Worthies,   1850
none so fit as to present the nine Worthies.   1855
*that worthies thumbe, he is not so big as the end of his Club.   1864
Brag. For the rest of the Worthies? | *Peda.* I will play three my
selfe.   1873
the Taber to the worthies, and let them dance the hey.   1885

LOVE'S LABOUR'S LOST

WORTHIES *cont.*
  Bero. Art thou one of the Worthies? 2446
  King. Heere is like to be a good presence of Worthies: 2477
  *Iudas Machabeus: And if these foure Worthies in their 2480
  *are Worthies a comming will speake their minde in some | other
  sort. *Exit Curat.* 2537
  Duma. Roome for the incensed Worthies. 2653
  Ber. Worthies away, the Scaene begins to cloude. 2679
WORTHINES = 3
  Bold of your worthines, we single you, 519
  Is my report to his great worthines. 555
  Make tender of to thy true worthines. 668
WORTHIS = 1
  Whether the three Worthis shall come in or no? 2427
WORTHY = 2
  Worthy, but I am to stand for him. 2449
  Was guyltie of it.) Farewell worthy Lord: 2694
WORTHYS = 1
  and I will right my selfe like a Souldier. *Exeunt Worthys* 2682
WOT = 1
  Then those that walke and wot not what they are. 96
WOULD *l.*154 *196 227 *365 *366 417 538 *678 680 684 *792 920
  1002 *1183 *1273 *1343 1431 1434 1447 1454 1460 1462 1480
  1481 1487 1582 1613 1649 1671 1699 *1763 *1843 1894 1919 1947
  1952 1957 1994 2071 2075 2076 2078 2158 2280 2299 2385 2426
  2505 2576 2608 2704 2773 = 42*10
WOULDE *l.**863 *1350 = *2
WOULDEST *l.**1812 = *1
WOULDST *l.*194 = 1
WOUNDES = 1
  You leere vpon me, do you: ther's an eie | Woundes like a leaden
  sword. 2419
WOUNDING = 3
  Not wounding, pittie would not let me doote. 1002
  If wounding then it was to shew my skill, 1003
  Full of comparisons and wounding floutes: 2805
WRANGLE = *1
  *Maria. You still wrangle with her *Boyet*, and she strikes | at the
  brow. 1104
WREATHED = 1
  Nor neuer lay his wreathed armes athwart 1472
WRETCHED = 1
  And wretched fooles secrets heedfully ore ey. 1414
WRETCHES = 1
  With groning wretches: and your taske shall be, 2813
WRIT = 3*1
  *Ar. I will haue that subiect newly writ ore, that I may 419
  It is writ to *Iaquenetta.* 1037
  Dum. Once more Ile reade the Ode that I haue writ. 1435
  Writ a both sides the leafe, margent and all, 1895
WRITE = 7*1
  And to the strictest decrees Ile write my name. 126
  So to the Lawes at large I write my name, 166
  *Wit, write Pen, for I am for whole volumes in folio. *Exit.* 486
  Well, I will loue, write, sigh, pray, shue, grone, 970
  These numbers will I teare, and write in prose. 1389
  When shall you see mee write a thing in rime? 1519

WRITE *cont.*
Neuer durst Poet touch a pen to write,   1697
Write *Lord haue mercie on vs*, on those three,   2352
WRITING = 2
were, it would neither serue for the writing, nor the tune.   417
Dum. It is *Berownes* writing, and heere is his name.   1547
WRITTEN = 2
of the partie written to the person written vnto.   1299
WRONG = 4*1
A man of complements whom right and wrong   179
Prin. You do the King my father too much wrong,   649
And wrong the reputation of your name,   650
Celestiall as thou art, Oh pardon loue this wrong,   1282
*seene the day of wrong through the litle hole of discretion,   2681
WY = 1
Cost. I thanke your worship, God be wy you.   916
WYSH = 1
More Sacks to the myll. O heauens I haue my wysh,   1415
YARDE = 1
Dum. He may not by the yarde.   2625
YCLIPED *see also* ecliped = *1
*ground Which? which I meane I walkt vpon, it is ycliped Thy
Park.   248
YDOLATARIE = 1
A greene Goose, a Goddesse, pure pure ydolatarie.   1408
YE *l.*1159 *1830 2792 = 1*2
YEA = 2*1
Bero. By yea and nay sir, than I swore in iest.   58
*manager is in loue; yea he loueth. Assist me some extempo-|rall   484
A man so breathed, that certaine he would fight; yea,   2608
YEAS = 1
In russet yeas, and honest kersie noes.   2345
YEELDE = 3
And if you proue it, Ile repay it backe, | Or yeelde vp *Aquitaine.*   654
All liberall reason I will yeelde vnto.   665
I would not yeelde to be your houses guest: 2280
YEELDING = 3
Fer. How well this yeelding rescewes thee from shame.   127
From reasons yeelding, your faire selfe should make   646
A yeelding gainst some reason in my brest,   647
YEERE = 4
hang me by the necke, if horns that yeere miscarrie. | Finely put
on.   1098
For he hath been fiue thousand yeere a Boy.   1898
Then at the expiration of the yeere,   2764
To holde the Plough for her sweete loue three yeere.   2847
YEERES = 9*6
Haue sworne for three yeeres tearme, to liue with me: 20
Longauill. I am resolued, tis but a three yeeres fast: 28
That is, to lyue and study heere three yeeres.   39
And stay heere in your Court for three yeeres space.   56
And bide the pennance of each three yeeres day.   124
*the tearme of three yeeres, he shall indure such publique   140
Three thousand times within this three yeeres space: 161
And so to studie three yeeres is but short.   191
Fer. It was proclaymed a yeeres imprisonment to be ta-|ken with
a Wench.   283

YEERES *cont.*

  *Ar. I haue promised to studie three yeeres with the duke.   345
  *put yeeres to the worde three, and studie three yeeres in two   359
  Till painefull studie shall outweare three yeeres,   514
  *Brag. Sweete Ayer, go tendernes of yeeres, take this Key,   775
  That smyles, his cheeke in yeeres, and knowes the trick   2404
YELE = *1
  *three studied ere yele thrice wincke: and how easie it is to   358
YELL = 1
  The Dogges did yell, put ell to Sore, | then Sorell iumps from
  thicket: 1219
YELLOW = 1
  And Cuckow-budds of yellow hew: 2861
YES = 4*3
  O short liu'd pride. Not faire? alacke for woe | *For.* Yes Madam
  faire.   989
  *would not loue her; yes for her two eyes. Well, I do nothing   1343
  *Page. Yes yes, he teaches boyes the Horne-booke: What   1785
  Quee. Nothing but this: yes as much loue in Rime,   1893
  Quee. Did he not send you twaine? | *Kath.* Yes Madame: and
  moreouer,   1938
  Kath. Yes in good faith.   2200
YET = 12*6
  Studie knowes that which yet it doth not know,   73
  Yet confident Ile keepe what I haue sworne,   123
  Cost. Not a worde of *Costart* yet. | *Ferd.* So it is   234
  *Boy. To be whipt: and yet a better loue then my maister.   424
  *There is no euill angel but Loue, yet was *Sampson* so temp-|ted,   475
  *and he had an excellent strength: Yet was *Salomon* so   476
  *not yet: the roofe of this Court is too high to be yours, and   587
  Receiud that summe, yet there remaines vnpaide   629
  *Boy. And three times as much more, and yet nothing | at all.   815
  *Holo. Most barbarous intimation: yet a kind of insinua-|tion,   1163
  *What was a month old at *Cains* birth, that's not fiue weeks | old
  as yet?   1190
  Yet feare not thou but speake audaciously.   1996
  Not yet no daunce: thus change I like the Moone.   2111
  King. Yet still she is the Moone, and I the Man.   2116
  Now by my maiden honour yet as pure, | As the vnsallied Lilly I
  protest,   2277
  Bero. Yet I haue a tricke,   2349
  Yet since Loues argument was first on foote,   2705
  Kath. Yet sweare not, least ye be forsworne agen.   2792
YF *l.*54 *139 403 *1241 1268 1533 1889 2809 = 6*2
YFAITH = 1
  Mar. Wide a'the bow hand, yfaith your hand is out.   1124
YIELDE *see* yeelde
YIELDING *see* yeelding
YNCLE = *1
  *Three-farthings remuneration, What's the price of this yncle?   904
YOLE = 1
  Kath. Yole marre the light by taking it in snuffe: 1909
YONDER = 1
  Forr. Heereby vpon the edge of yonder Coppice,   983
YOU = 248*92, *1
  *Pag. The last of the fiue Vowels if You repeate them, | or the fift
  if I.   1791

YOULE = 4
For youle proue periurde if you make me staie.   608
Youle not be periurde, tis a hatefull thing: 1494
Ros. Youle neare be friendes with him, a kild your sister.   1900
Rosa. Good Madame, if by me youle be aduisde,   2223
YOULL = 1
Armed in argumentes, you'll be surprisd.   1976
YOUNG = 3*2
*apperteining to thy young dayes, which we may nominate |
tender.   325
*2. *Lad.* The young *Dumaine*, a well accomplisht youth,   548
Young blood doth not obay an olde decree.   1565
Say, Can you fast? your stomacks are too young: 1644
Mari. The liker you, few taller are so young.   2797
YOUNGER = 1
And younger hearinges are quite rauished.   567
YOUR *l.*13 23 27 53 55 56 84 143 145 293 *295 299 *327 *454 *483
492 493 495 505 510 519 575 596 599 615 619 624 633 646 650 656
661 671 673 *675 686 702 722 737 740 *779 *782 *783 *786 *787
*788 *800 801 *810 *811 *857 866 *873 916 *926 1025 1026 1028
1078 1101 *1102 1124 1127 *1131 *1189 1301 1309 *1321 1324
1433 1468 1476 1477 1481 1492 1498 1535 *1543 1619 1644 1661
1718 *1741 *1804 *1805 1819 *1846 1848 *1859 1900 *1905 1908
*1931 1933 1975 1977 1978 2026 2029 2062 2065 2066 2070 2100
2119 *2127 2128 2131 *2150 2154 2156 2157 2164 *2166 2169
*2185 *2236 *2271 2274 2280 2301 2303 2304 *2321 2354 2363
2372 *2377 2381 2397 2418 *2439 2505 *2516 *2518 2526 *2530
2658 2676 2684 2688 2690 2693 2713 2714 2725 2735 2736 2741
2747 2750 2754 2760 2762 2778 2807 2808 2813 2814 2826 2830
2834 = 128*45
YOURS = 8*1
Prince. All pride is willing pride, and yours is so: 527
*not yet: the roofe of this Court is too high to be yours, and   587
Ber. Now God saue thy life. | *Ros.* And yours from long liuing.   688
King. Twere good yours did: for sir to tell you plaine,   1621
And if my face were but as faire as yours,   1920
Ber. O, I am yours and all that I possesse. | *Rosa.* All the foole
mine.   2310
*wench is cast away: shee's quicke, the childe bragges in her |
bellie already: tis yours.   2632
Our loue being yours, the errour that Loue makes   2729
Is likewise yours: we to our selues proue false,   2730
YOURSELFE *see* selfe
YOURSELUES *see* selues
YOUTH = 4*2
*2. *Lad.* The young *Dumaine*, a well accomplisht youth,   548
Vow alacke for youth vnmeete,   1450
Youth so apt to pluck a sweete.   1451
Flat treason gainst the kingly state of youth.   1643
*barbarous. Do you not educate youth at the Charg-house   1816
Rosa. The blood of youth burnes not with such excesse,   1963
ZANY *see* saine
ZEALE = 4
Fayth infringed, which such zeale did sweare.   1483
King. What zeale, what furie, hath inspirde thee now?   1578
Where zeale striues to content, and the contentes   2461
Dies in the zeale of that which it presentes: 2462

ZELOUS = 1
   With such a zelous laughter so profund,   2008
ZENELOPHON = *1
   *Begger *Zenelophon*: and he it was that might rightly say,   1047
  &l.*62 *101 *251 *253 *297 *315 *401 *411 *413 468 583 *758
  *1144 *1155 *1545 *1742 *1751 *1821 *1827 2152 *2455 = 3*18
1 = 1
2 = *2
3 = 1*1